Eighth Edition

Behavior Management

A Practical Approach for Educators

James E. Walker
Southern Illinois University

Thomas M. Shea
Southern Illinois University—Edwardsville, Emeritus

Anne M. Bauer
University of Cincinnati

PEARSON

Merrill
Prentice Hall

Upper Saddle River, New Jersey
Columbus, Ohio

Library of Congress Cataloging-in-Publication Data
Walker, James Edwin
  Behavior management: a practical approach for educators/James E. Walker, Thomas
M. Shea., Anne M. Bauer.—8th ed.
    p. cm.
  Includes bibliographical references and index.
  ISBN 0-13-110549-3 (pbk.)
    1. Teaching. 2. Individualized instruction. 3. Problem children—Education—United
States. I. Shea, Thomas M. II. Bauer, Anne M. III. Title.
LB1027.W29 2004
371.102'4—dc21

                                                                    2002033788

Vice President and Executive Publisher: Jeffery W. Johnston
Acquisitions Editor: Allyson P. Sharp
Editorial Assistant: Penny Burleson
Production Editor: Sheryl Glicker Langner
Production Coordination: Emily Hatteberg, Carlisle Publishers Services
Design Coordinator: Diane C. Lorenzo
Photo Coordinator: Sandy Schaefer
Cover Designer: Keith Van Norman
Cover art: Corbis
Production Manager: Laura Messerly
Director of Marketing: Ann Castel Davis
Marketing Manager: Amy June
Marketing Services Coordinator: Tyra Poole

This book was set in Garamond Light by Carlisle Communications, Ltd. It was printed
and bound by R.R. Donnelley & Sons Company. The cover was printed by Phoenix
Color Corp.

Photo Credits: Anne Vega/Merrill, p. 2; Tom Watson/Merrill, p. 28; Scott
Cunningham/Merrill, p. 56, 80, 318; Anthony Magnacca/Merrill, p. 122; KS
Studios/Merrill, p. 164; Dan Floss/Merrill, p. 200; Barbara Schwartz/Merrill,
p. 240; Todd Yarrington/Merrill, p. 284.

Pearson Education Ltd.
Pearson Education Singapore Pte. Ltd.
Pearson Education Canada, Ltd.
Pearson Education—Japan

Pearson Education Australia Pty. Limited
Pearson Education North Asia Ltd.
Pearson Educación de Mexico, S.A. de C. V.
Pearson Education Malaysia Pte. Ltd.

10 9 8 7 6 5 4 3 2 1
ISBN: 0-13-110549-3

To

Gwenn, Jamell, Jabrina, and Andrew

and

Kevin, Jane, and Emma and Michael and Bill

and

Riley, Demian, Tarie, CJ, Sarah, and Mick

PREFACE

This eighth edition of *Behavior Management: A Practical Approach for Educators* has been revised to improve its usability and readability. Revisions are based on developments in the field of behavior management reported in the literature since the original manuscript was written 27 years ago and on feedback from many professionals, students, and reviewers.

During the past three decades, the proliferation of behavior management philosophies, techniques, and instructional methodologies has increased the complexity of the educator's responsibilities and functions. New information is being published almost daily on the various perspectives of human behavior, including the behavioral, psychodynamic, biophysical, and environmental points of view that are discussed in this text.

Revisions in the text are, in large part, a result of direct and indirect feedback from many undergraduate and graduate students of education, from general and special education teachers participating in in-service programs, from professional colleagues, and from reviewers who have studied previous editions.

The text is written to provide a practical guide to experienced teachers, teachers-in-preparation, parents, and paraprofessionals for applying behavior management techniques both in general and special educational settings and in the home. It is designed to help teachers working in self-contained classes and resource programs, teachers engaging in itinerant and consultative services, and preschool, elementary, and secondary school teachers having responsibility for a diverse population of students. The text may be used for preservice and in-service courses and as a self-study guide. It has also been found to be of significant help to parents and parent educators.

Chapter 1 includes a definition of behavior management and a discussion of the ethical application of behavior management interventions, including the principles of normalization, fairness, and respect; the federal laws governing services for persons, especially children, with disabilities; and techniques for the individualization of instruction and related services. The chapter contains information on the most current revisions of federal laws governing the education of learners with disabilities.

Chapter 2 is devoted to models for understanding human behavior—including the psychodynamic, biophysical, environmental, and behavioral—and teacher effectiveness guidelines. The chapter uses an integrative ecological framework to coordinate the extant perspectives into a manageable assessment-intervention model of human behavior.

Chapter 3 focuses on the principles of behavior modification, the consequences of behavior, and schedules of reinforcement. Each of the five principles is discussed and exemplified. The consequences of behavior include positive reinforcement, extinction, negative reinforcement, and punishment. The chapter concludes with a discussion of fixed and variable ratio and interval schedules of reinforcement.

Chapter 4 reviews the steps in the behavior change process. It discusses selecting behaviors to be changed, collecting and recording preintervention or baseline data, identifying reinforcers, implementing interventions, collecting and recording intervention data, and evaluating the effects of the behavior change process. The chapter includes several methods for selecting potentially effective reinforcers, including preference scales and lists, child parent and teacher interviews, and direct observation. A chapter supplement includes an extensive list of potential reinforcers for use in school.

Chapter 5 presents, in detail, methods for increasing behavior. These include positive reinforcement, shaping, contingency contracting, token economy, and modeling. A supplement containing sample contract forms follows the chapter.

Chapter 6 is an extensive discussion of methods for decreasing behavior, including differential reinforcement, extinction, reprimands, loss of privileges, time-out, punishment, and desensitization. This chapter includes a discussion of the use of aversives in the educational setting. The discussion of time-out includes an overview of the various forms of time-out as well as several variables that may be considered before time-out is implemented, such as characteristics of the child, consistency of application, time-out area, duration of time-out, and evaluation of effectiveness.

Chapter 7 focuses on intervention techniques derived from psychodynamic theory. They include counseling techniques, the expressive media, and behavior influence interventions. The counseling techniques include life-space interviewing, reality therapy, and classroom conferences. Behavior influence techniques are suggested for circumstances in which the teacher or parent wishes immediate relief from or prevention of misbehavior. The expressive media offered as indirect management interventions include free play, puppetry, music, drama, art, bibliotherapy, and others. The chapter concludes with a discussion of the social skills curriculum.

In Chapter 8 attention shifts to the environmental and biophysical interventions. The environmental interventions include group composition and process, discussion groups, class meetings, the antecedents of effective management (organizing for instruction), milieu therapy, and the levels system. The environmental interventions include discussion of expulsion, suspension, and in-school suspension. The biophysical interventions include diet and medication. Consideration is given to central nervous system stimulants, antianxiety and antipsychotic medication, and anticonvulsants and antihistamines. The chapter concludes with a detailed discussion of the role of the educator in biophysical interventions. Educators are stated to have responsibilities in the areas of referral, collaboration with, and reporting of observations to physicians and other health professionals and modifying classroom structure and curriculum content in response to changes in student behavior as a consequence of medication. The educator is responsible for safeguarding and administering medication in the school.

Chapter 9 discusses parent education and home-school collaboration, including the need for home-school collaboration, the reactions of parents to the problems and needs of their children, and home-school collaboration strategies, including the passport and daily report card. The chapter presents a program for educating parents in effective behavior management techniques.

Chapter 10 concludes with a focus on current issues and concerns in behavior management. The authors discuss the integrative perspective and behavior management and educational issues that impact the implementation of behavior management strategies, such as inclusion, prereferral interventions, positive behavior support, homework strategies, and aggression and resistance in school. The impact of ethical, cultural, and linguistic diversity on behavior management is discussed. The chapter concludes with a discussion of a continuum of behavior management interventions from the most to the least intrusive and behavior management as prevention.

As aids to readers, objectives and key words and phrases are presented at the beginning of each chapter, and skill-building projects are presented at the end of each chapter. The eighth edition includes a glossary, sample worksheets and forms, and name and subject indices. An instructor's manual with a test bank of true-false, multiple-choice, and short-answer questions supports the information of the text.

As in all editions of this text, every effort has been made to write in nontechnical language for maximum readability by a broad audience of professionals, paraprofessionals, college students, and parents. The writing style was chosen in an effort to avoid the unnecessary technical jargon that causes so much of the professional literature to lose its significance and impact on a broad audience of readers. The reader will find the chapter references and lists of journals and texts in the instructor's manual to be excellent beginning points in a review of the technical literature.

The primary purpose of this text is the ethical, effective, and efficient management of behavior and learning problems for children and youth as they learn to explore, manipulate, and ultimately control their world for personal satisfaction and benefit and for the betterment of society.

The authors of the first seven editions of *Behavior Management* (T. M. Shea and J. E. Walker) wish to express our thanks and appreciation to Dr. Anne M. Bauer, who is joining us as an author of this eighth edition. Anne offers us, and the reader, another perspective on behavior management in contemporary society. Welcome aboard!

Acknowledgments

We thank the reviewers of this and of all previous editions for their time and constructive suggestions. The reviewers for this edition were Michael Kallam, Pittsburgh State University; James Krouse, Clarion University; Louis Lanunziata, North Carolina University at Wilmington; George Scarlett, Tufts University; and Marshall Zumberg, Wayne State University.

We also would like to acknowledge the assistance and support of our many colleagues, friends, and students who have been exposed to and have responded to the materials in this text in its various editions since 1976. We have profited greatly from all their comments and suggestions.

DISCOVER THE COMPANION WEBSITE ACCOMPANYING THIS BOOK

The Prentice Hall Companion Website: A Virtual Learning Environment

Technology is a constantly growing and changing aspect of our field that is creating a need for content and resources. To address this emerging need, Prentice Hall has developed an online learning environment for students and professors alike—Companion Websites—to support our textbooks.

In creating a Companion Website, our goal is to build on and enhance what the textbook already offers. For this reason, the content for each user-friendly website is organized by topic and provides the professor and student with a variety of meaningful resources. Common features of a Companion Website include:

For the Professor—

Every companion Website integrates **Syllabus Manager**™, an online syllabus creation and management utility.

- **Syllabus Manager**™ provides you, the instructor, with an easy, step-by-step process to create and revise syllabi, with direct links into Companion Website and other online content without having to learn HTML.
- Students may logon to your syllabus during any study session. All they need to know is the web address for the Companion Website and the password you've assigned to your syllabus.
- After you have created a syllabus using **Syllabus Manager**™, students may enter the syllabus for their course section from any point in the Companion Website.
- Clicking on a date, the student is shown the list of activities for the assignment. The activities for each assignment are linked directly to actual content, saving time for students.
- Adding assignments consists of clicking on the desired due date, then filling in the details of the assignment—name of the assignement, instructions, and whether or not it is a one-time or repeating assignment.

- In addition, links to other activities can be created easily. If the activity is online, a URL can be entered in the space provided, and it will be linked automatically in the final syllabus.

- Your completed syllabus is hosted on our servers, allowing convenient updates from any computer on the Internet. Changes you make to your syllabus are immediately available to your students at their next logon.

For the Student—

- **Overview** and **General Information**—General information about the topic and how it will be covered in the website.

- **Web Links**—A variety of websites related to topic areas.

- **Content Methods and Strategies**—Resources that help to put theories into practice in the special education classroom.

- **Reflective Questions** and **Case-Based Activities**—Put concepts into action, participate in activities, examine strategies, and more.

- **National and State Laws**—An online guide to how federal and state laws affect your special education classroom.

- **Behavior Management**—An online guide to help you manage behaviors in the special education classroom.

- **Message Board**—Virtual bulletin board to post and respond to questions and comments from a national audience.

To take advantage of these and other resources, please visit the *Behavior Management: A Preactical Approach for Educators,* Eighth Edition, Companion Website at

www.prenhall.com/walker

BRIEF CONTENTS

CONTENTS

4　Steps in the Behavior Change Process　　80

5　Methods of Increasing Behavior　　122

6　Methods of Decreasing Behavior　　164

1

An Introduction to Behavior Management

♦ CHAPTER OBJECTIVES

After completing this chapter, you will be able to do the following:

1. Define behavior management and explain its purposes.

2. Discuss ethical issues with regard to the use of behavior management interventions.

3. Describe various perspectives of the ethics of behavior management.

4. Discuss ethical and professional guidelines for the application of behavior management interventions.

5. Explain the principles of normalization, fairness, and respect.

6. Explain selected laws governing education and services for persons with disabilities.

7. Describe procedures for the individualization of the education of learners with disabilities.

◆ ◆ ◆

Ms. Romero watches as Suzanne, wiping her eyes with a tissue from the decorative dispenser on the corner of the teacher's desk, slowly leaves the fourth-grade classroom. It has been a long, trying day for both teacher and student.

As the little Swiss clock on her desk chimes four o'clock, Ms. Romero leans back in her chair to ponder her dilemma. She feels exhausted. At this moment, she hates teaching. She hates reprimanding and scolding children, especially Suzanne, who tries so very hard to sit still and pay attention yet whose mind seems to wander constantly and who never remembers the correct book for the lesson. It seems as if she has had the same conversation with Suzanne and some of the other students a dozen or more times since school began last month.

The students are too active to settle down to enjoy language arts. Ms. Romero tries to find books they would be interested in. She has tried writing names on the board. She has tried calling parents. She has taken away free time. The students never change. The state proficiency tests are in March, with teacher and principal evaluation linked to student performance on the test. How is she going to make them learn?

Ms. Romero knows that her current efforts are not only ineffective; they also don't match what she wants for her students. She wants them to love to read. She wants them to feel valued in her classroom. Yet she feels as if she is just putting in time. She is exhausted and can't even remember driving home after school. She is grouchy and short tempered with her husband and children.

Perhaps there are more effective methods Ms. Romero could apply in an effort to help Suzanne and the others attend to their lessons.

Larry sits in the gym bleachers, anxiously waiting for Mr. Veritas to finish organizing the volleyball game. The whole class, except Larry, is choosing sides and preparing to begin the game.

Larry wishes he could be part of the activity, but he can't. He's afraid to let the others know that he's a poor player. He doesn't know exactly why he's a poor player, but every time a group game is organized, he must refuse to participate. He says, "No, I won't," "I can't," "I don't feel good," or "That's a dumb game."

Larry knows Mr. Veritas is unhappy with him but also very concerned about him. But Larry just can't play those games. He thinks it's really too bad that Mr. Veritas doesn't like him because Mr. Veritas is a nice guy and would be an interesting friend.

Mr. Veritas quickly organizes the teams, and the volleyball game begins. He believes that he must hurry and talk to Larry.

"Poor kid," Mr. Veritas thinks, "he's really OK, but he just won't play team games. Perhaps he refuses because of his weight problem. No, others in the class are as rotund as Larry, and they play team sports. Perhaps Larry is afraid he's not a good enough player. I'll talk to him again and see what I can do to help."

Perhaps there are effective methods for helping Larry increase his participation in team activities.

Ms. Komfort hums a little tune to herself as she cruises along Interstate 55 out of Memphis. What a marvelous day! What a great year it has been at John F. Kennedy Elementary School with her 25 first graders!

> For the first time in her teaching career, Ms. Komfort has interested, responsive, and enthusiastic children in her class. If the past 4 months of the school year are as good as the first 5 months, she will remain in teaching forever.
> "Sure hope it continues," she thinks.
> *Perhaps there are techniques to help Ms. Komfort maintain her children's enthusiasm for learning throughout the year.*

Teachers wish to teach; it is what they are prepared to do and the purpose for which they are employed and assigned to a school, a classroom, and a group of children for approximately 180 days each school year. Frequently, teachers are frustrated in efforts to attain their goals because of the behavioral and achievement problems of the individual children for whom they are responsible.

As a result of the theoretical, experimental, and pragmatic efforts of many scholars and practitioners, teachers have been made increasingly aware of a number of variables that must be considered if effective and efficient transactions are to be established between teachers and children. Teachers have become keenly aware of the following:

1. Every child is a unique individual, *similar* to all other children in many respects yet *different* from all other children.

2. No single set of therapeutic or remedial procedures is effective under *all conditions* with *all children*. We must remain open minded and give thoughtful consideration to many theoretical and methodological points of view if we are to effectively aid children.

3. No matter how well designed and executed classroom-centered intervention processes may be, their effectiveness will be limited unless they relate to the individual child's needs and desires (Brown & Bauer, 1994).

Educators have also become aware that the child's cognitive, affective, and psychomotor learning domains are inextricably interwoven. We understand that the child acts and reacts as a whole being. We recognize that a remedial intervention in the cognitive domain may influence the child's affective behavior, that intervention in the psychomotor domain will in all probability affect the child's cognitive and affective learning, and so on.

♦ **Examples**

Todd, a 6-year-old first grader, was diagnosed by a psychiatrist as having "attention deficit disorder with hyperactivity and impulsivity." According to his teacher, Todd was disruptive in the classroom, constantly running about, hitting children, tearing paper, and so on.

Todd's psychiatrist prescribed medication to help manage the disruptive behavior. The medication has been effective in modifying Todd's behavior. He has begun to identify his letters and numbers, he has learned to use scissors for cutting-and-pasting activities, and his behavior has improved in the classroom, especially during group activities. Todd has been heard to say, "See how good I am" and "I'm a big boy now."

It is evident that changes in Todd's behavior have influenced his cognitive skills (learning his letters and numbers) and his affective behavior (in group activities). In addition, his self-concept appears to have improved.

Scott, an 11-year-old fifth grader with a learning disability, had experienced difficulty in throwing and catching a ball and in running bases.

Scott is now enrolled in a program that includes physical therapy and adapted physical education. As a result of these interventions, he has developed skills in throwing, catching, and running.

Scott's teacher has noted that as Scott is increasing his competency in the psychomotor area, he is also improving cognitively (in such activities as reading and writing) and socially (his group behavior and peer relationships have improved).

Again, it is evident that changes in one learning domain influence the individual's competency in the other areas of learning.

Maryellen, a 13-year-old ninth grader, was identified by a school psychologist as a "slow learner."

Maryellen had experienced difficulty in academic subjects throughout her school years. Although she could learn and did learn the basic skills, she required more time and instruction than her classmates. As a consequence of her academic difficulties, Maryellen usually received Ds and Fs on report cards. Over the years she developed an "I don't care" attitude toward schoolwork and school. This attitude caused her to be frequently reprimanded and punished by her teachers.

On entering high school, Maryellen was placed in a remedial program. In this special program, academic work was designed to be responsive to Maryellen's rate and level of learning. Evaluations were based on individual performance.

Presently, Maryellen's teacher reports she is a happy, highly motivated slow learner.

It is evident that changes in Maryellen's academic program influenced her affective behavior.

This text is written primarily from the point of view of learning theory and behaviorism. However, the authors recognize that behaviorism is but one of the conceptual frameworks available to the practitioner for use in efforts to understand and change behavior. *Behavior modification is not a panacea that can effectively solve all problems of all children.*

Other conceptual frameworks (biophysical, psychodynamic, and environmental) have made and continue to make significant contributions to our knowledge of the behavior of children. The reader is encouraged not to cast aside these other points of view—not to become an exclusivist.

Behavior management processes and interventions based on social learning and behavior modification theories are presented in Chapters 3 through 6. Processes and interventions based on psychodynamic theory are presented in Chapter 7. And processes and interventions derived from environmental and biophysical theory are presented in Chapter 8.

The present chapter is devoted to a definition of behavior management, guidelines for the ethical application of behavior management interventions, selected public laws affecting services for persons with disabilities, and procedures for the individualization of the education of learners with disabilities.

DEFINITION OF BEHAVIOR MANAGEMENT

The majority of school staff meeting and discussion time and many hours of parents' home time is devoted to considerations of behavior management. The same few—but important—questions are asked repeatedly:

- How can this child's behavior be changed?
- How can this group behavior be changed?
- Should I punish this behavior?
- Should I discuss this behavior with the individual?
- Should I ignore this behavior?
- Will this intervention work?
- Is it ethical to use this intervention technique?
- Will it harm or help the child?

Hour after hour of teacher and parent time is devoted to discussions of these and similar questions and concerns about the management of children's behavior in the classroom, school, and home.

In this text, *behavior management interventions* are defined as all those actions (and conscious inactions) teachers and parents engage in to enhance the probability that children, individually and in groups, will develop effective behaviors that are personally fulfilling, productive, and socially acceptable (Shea & Bauer, 1987).

Behavior management is a complex problem that cannot be approached from a simplistic point of view. It is a teacher function that must be studied, planned, and objectively used and evaluated, with equal emphasis given to all relevant variables: the individual or group whose behavior is being studied, the behavior under consideration, the setting in which the behavior occurs, the individual applying the intervention, and the purpose of the intervention. A specific technique that is an effective intervention for one specific behavior of one specific child in a particular setting may be ineffective under another set of circumstances when applied by a different individual to change a different behavior. More specifically, behavior management must be individualized.

According to Jones (1993), we live and function in an increasingly complex society and, as teachers, are confronted with increasing amounts of student disruptive behavior. School personnel must demonstrate leadership, creativity, and patience as they develop more effective methods for preventing and responding to inappropriate student behaviors. Jones suggests that school personnel will be more effective when responding to disruptive behavior if "discipline" or "student management" is seen as an opportunity to teach students alternative ways to meet their needs within the school setting.

Jones encourages school personnel to respond to five questions in their efforts to evaluate classroom and schoolwide student management plans:

- Does the plan treat students with dignity?
- Do the responses of school personnel to inappropriate student behavior include an educational component; that is, does it teach the student new skills?
- Does the plan require and support an environmental analysis?
- Is the response to rule violation clear to everyone?
- Is there a sequential response to rule violation; that is, the response to the first violation of a rule is "consequence a," the response to the second violation of the same rule is "consequence b," and so on?

Smith and Rivera (1993) defined discipline as "order among pupils so learning can take place without competition from unproductive factors. It is a system of rules for conduct and a mechanism for ensuring that conduct codes are followed" (p. 2). The principles on which classroom order is established are as follows (Smith & Rivera, 1995):

- Develop a positive climate.
- Establish the basis for a positive learning environment.
- Apply prevention techniques.
- Institute collaborative relationships with parents and other professionals for both disciplinary concerns and for developing a positive climate.
- Ensure that the intervention matches the problem.
- Evaluate learner progress.

Self-discipline, the goal of all behavior management, is the process of attaining control over one's personal behavior in a variety of circumstances in association with many individuals and groups. Self-discipline is discussed in detail in Chapter 2.

ETHICS OF BEHAVIOR MANAGEMENT

The Question of Ethics

Both empirical and nonexperimental inquiry has led to the development of the principles of learning and their resultant interventions for the management of human behavior. It is difficult to refute the findings of experimental studies: The principles of learning or behavior modification presented in Chapter 3 are in operation, and the results of controlled research studies are, in the main, positive.

However, practitioners cannot sweep aside the ethical issues created by the application of these principles to the processes of human learning. The principles of learning have caused confusion, concern, and in some cases anxiety among those individuals holding more traditional views of human behavior.

In the application of behavior management interventions, the following questions are considered:

- Who shall decide who will be the manager of behavior?
- Who shall decide whose behavior is to be managed?
- How can behavior managers be controlled?
- What type of interventions shall be applied?
- Who will determine the interventions to be legitimized?
- To what ends will interventions be applied?

These questions have vast implications for our future (as individuals and as members of the human species) and for the future of society. They must be considered and responded to by the behavior management practitioner.

When these questions are applied to the education of children, they have profound implications for educational practice. The queries are rephrased here to emphasize these implications, which are not only philosophical issues but also pragmatic issues of immediate importance to educators:

- What is a child?
- Is a child free to make choices?
- Should a child be free to make choices?
- Does a child act in accordance with specific principles of behavior that are observable, measurable, and repetitive?
- Can a child's behavior be changed by external forces?
- Can an educator modify a child's behavior?
- Can another child or a parent change a child's behavior?
- Who shall determine whose and which behaviors are to be changed?
- Which interventions shall be applied in the classroom and school to change children's behavior?
- Who will legitimize and monitor the interventions being used to change the behavior of children?
- To what ends will the interventions be applied?

That people can and do exert control over the behavior of others would not be denied by the majority of researchers and practitioners, both behaviorists and traditionalists.

The central issue, then, appears to focus on the relative influences of our nature and environment on behavior. The behaviorist emphasizes the importance of the external environment in the determination of behavior and maintains that the influence of the environment is systematic, constant, and the prime determinant of behavior. This systematic, constant influence is observable and measurable. As a result, actions can be explained by means of the principles of behavior modification (or learning as discussed in Chapters 3 through 6). The principles are derived by applying the scientific methods of discovery to the modification of human behavior.

Few would deny that, in general, the majority of persons respond in a predictable, conventional manner under specified conditions. For example, if they go to a sports event, they cheer; to a funeral, they cry or sigh; to a college class, they sit passively, praying for the end; and so on.

In addition to the issues of whether and how human beings can be controlled, professionals in psychology, the social sciences, and education have focused attention on the issue of the *means* of control. Many professionals suggest that the overt controls applied to human behavior by means of behavior modification interventions are unacceptable and can lead to unethical practices. These individuals fail to recognize or acknowledge that other, more traditional forms of interventions, such as those reviewed in Chapters 7 and 8 (psychodynamic, environmental, and biophysical), may exert equally potent, although less obvious, control over human behavior. For example, traditional nondirective and directive psychotherapeutic interventions, such as client-centered counseling, individual and group psychotherapy, and psychoanalysis, have as their objective to change the child's behavior or to encourage the child to change his or her behavior with the therapist's assistance. The nondirective therapist and the permissive teacher influence the child's behavior, and this influence limits the child's freedom of choice. Such limiting (or controlling), rather than being denied, should be recognized, evaluated, and monitored for the child's benefit.

The reader is urged to devote time to systematic exploration of his or her responses to the questions in this section.

Ethical Perspective

The ethics of behavior management can be approached from several points of view: political, legal, professional, and research. An extensive discussion of each is not feasible in this text; thus, the reader is urged to continue the study of the ethics of behavior management using the chapter references.

From a political perspective, the current quest for excellence in the schools has become standardized, with each state required to develop standards and to assess student proficiency. In this effort, children and youth whose behavior continues to challenge the system are rarely treasured. They do not enhance the school's "pass rate" on proficiency tests. It is at this point in development of education that educators find themselves discussing the ethics of behavior management. Behavior problem students, unequally valued to their complying, achieving peers, bring teachers who are accountable for student achievement to the point of using behavior management methods and strategies that would not be applied with the more highly valued students and during less stressful and competitive times.

From a legal perspective, it must be recognized that proactive decisions are seldom found. It appears to be the nature of the courts and the legislatures to react to the misuse or potential misuse of various interventions rather than to actively set standards. It also appears that decisions and laws are concerned primarily with normal students and confined to corporal punishment, suspension, and expulsion. Few decisions and laws focus on the use of *aversives* in general. The legal aspects of expulsion, suspension, and in-school suspension are discussed in Chapter 8. Corporal punishment is discussed in Chapter 6.

Summarizing and defining the implications of research in behavior management must be approached with great caution. In general, however, there is little definitive empirical research; much of the published research is about severely handicapped populations. Evans and Meyer (1985) reported that theoretical and review articles questioning the use of aversives generally conclude that (a) aversive procedures are associated with short-term improvement, (b) little long-term improvement and generalization data are reported, and (c) in comparison to information on the effects of aversives, relatively little research is available regarding outcomes associated with alternative nonaversive procedures.

There has been considerable activity among professional, parent, and citizen organizations with regard to the use of aversive and other behavior management interventions. Few position statements discuss the use of any and all behavior management procedures regardless of the theories from which they are derived. Most statements are concerned with the use of behavioral strategies.

From an ethical perspective, it is generally agreed that the principles underlying behavior management interventions can provide practitioners with the means to an end, but the principles cannot decide the end of intervention: That decision depends on the practitioner's values (Turnbull et al., 1986). *Ethics* are defined as the rules that guide moral (right, good, or correct) behavior (Tymchuk, 1976). According to Sexton (1987), there are two general schools of ethics: formalism and utilitarianism. *Formalism* suggests that all individuals are born with rights and needs that are superordinate to the interests of society. From this point of view, behavior management interventions that intrude on an individual's rights are unethical. *Utilitarianism* suggests that the interests of society precede the interests of the individual. Individuals' rights are given by society, and individuals are valued for their actual or potential contributions to (or the degree of burden they place on) society. From this perspective, the use of aversive management is deemed acceptable if it facilitates the movement of the individual from the position of "burden on society" to "contributing member." In a review of the literature, considerable support for both of these positions can be found (Singer & Irvin, 1987; Skiba & Deno, 1991).

Scheuermann and Evans (1997) discuss the use of controversial interventions and ethical practice in the education of learners with emotional and behavioral disorders. They are concerned that unproven interventions lacking a research base are being applied with learners by practitioners in the effort to improve learner performance. The authors reinforce the position of Hippocrates that the practitioner's first and most important concern in the education and treatment of learners is to "do no harm." In their discussion of the work of Silver (1986) and Simpson (1995), the authors define controversial interventions as those lacking research findings to support their effectiveness yet promising extraordinary success. They suggest that "any treatment, program, strategy, or technique that is unsupported by objective data produced through systematic manipulation of variables and repeated inquiries by independent evaluators" (p. 20) is controversial.

Scheuermann and Evans present several characteristics of controversial interventions and recommend that practitioners apply these when selecting intervention for application with learners. Controversial treatments do the following:

- Offer immediate or near immediate positive results
- Suggest cures for the disability
- Offer easy application without extensive preparation or education
- Present marketing strategies that appeal to the emotions
- State that faith in the treatment is necessary for success
- Require exclusive use of the treatment
- Contradict generally accepted treatment strategies
- Cannot be evaluated using accepted research methods
- Rely on testimonials to substantiate effectiveness
- Are promoted and implemented by "experts" working outside their field of expertise.

In their article, Scheuermann and Evans present suggestions offered by Green (1996) for avoiding the selection of unproven interventions for application with learners with behavior problems:

1. Be skeptical: If it sounds too good to be true, it usually is.
2. Question the promoters of the intervention about how it works and how they know that it works.
3. Ask to see the research results or other evidence of its effectiveness.
4. Obtain and read the research and, if concerned, ask an expert to interpret the research.
5. Proceed with care. Go slowly. Question why the application must be applied exclusively and do not eliminate presently effective interventions.
6. Ask, Is this intervention "reasonable"?

The Council for Exceptional Children (1997) updated and published their Code of Ethics and Standards of Practice with regard to serving persons with disabilities. The standards for behavior management state, "Special education professionals participate with other professionals and with parents in an interdisciplinary effort in the management of behavior. Professionals:

1. Apply only those disciplinary methods and behavioral procedures which they have been instructed to use and which do not undermine the dignity of the individual or the basic human rights of persons with exceptionalities, such as corporal punishment.
2. Clearly specify the goals and objectives for behavior management practices in the person's with exceptionalities Individualized Education Program.

3. Conform to policies, statutes, and rules established by state/provincial and local agencies relating to the judicious application of disciplinary methods and behavioral procedures.

4. Take adequate measures to discourage, prevent, and intervene when a colleague's behavior is perceived as being detrimental to exceptional students.

5. Refrain from aversive techniques unless repeated trials of other methods have failed and only after consultation with parents and appropriate agency officials."

The Rights of Children

In his seminal work, Allen (1969) proposed three principles to guide individuals in the helping professions in their actions toward clients (children and adults) with disabilities. These principles serve as the foundation of all behavior management decisions made by teachers of both general and special education students.

They are (a) the principle of normalization, (b) the principle of fairness, and (c) the principle of respect for the dignity and worth of the individual.

Principle of Normalization. The *principle of normalization* is to let the person with a disability or who varies from his or her peers obtain an existence as close to the normal as is possible (Farrell, 1995; Wolfenberger, 1972).

When applying this principle, the practitioner must use as a point of reference the child's real environment (including the behavior of the children and adults within it) as well as the ideal environment. This principle demands understanding the similarities and differences among various groups in society. The practitioner must base decisions on knowledge of the individual child's growth and development, needs, desires, strengths, and disabilities.

Before implementing an intervention, the practitioner must respond to the following question: Will the implementation of this specific intervention facilitate the child's movement toward the normally anticipated and observed behavior in this setting, or will it simply eliminate the child (and the behavior) as an inconvenience or annoyance to others in the environment, such as the child's teacher, peers, administrator, and parents?

Many children attend programs for learners with disabilities simply because they are different; that is, they are African American, Hispanic, Asian American, or Native American or slow learners, nonreaders, poor, and so on. These children may be segregated primarily because they are an annoyance or inconvenience to others; they challenge the system (Shea & Bauer, 1994). In this "special placement," their opportunity to obtain "an existence as normal as possible" is inhibited or restricted, if not totally frustrated.

Principle of Fairness. The *principle of fairness* is fundamental fairness—due process of law—which requires that in decision making affecting one's life, liberty, or vital interests, the elements of due process will be observed, including the right to notice, to a fair hearing, to representation by counsel, to present evidence, and to appeal an adverse decision (Allen, 1969).

Although this principle is phrased in legal terminology, it can be simply stated: Is the intervention selected to change this child's behavior fair to the child as an individual?

At times interventions are arbitrarily applied on the whim of a practitioner without concrete evidence that the child is, in fact, exhibiting the target behavior. Frequently interventions are applied that only serve to prohibit the child from finding *any* success in school. For example, a child who had difficulty learning French grammar is prohibited from going to recess, playing on the school athletic teams, and so on. This child may be capable of meeting success only in these prohibited activities. As do all humans, the child has a need for success. Interventions such as these are unfair.

Unfairness is evidenced when a practitioner refuses to apply an intervention that is obviously needed if the child is to function in school. For example, we are confronted with practitioners who will not use tangible rewards simply because they do not "believe in them." Yet the child whom they are attempting to help is found to respond only to tangible rewards.

Other examples of unfairness might include the following:

- Refusal to try to modify a child's behavior systematically
- Arbitrary placement of a child in a special therapy or instructional program without first attempting classroom interventions
- Unwillingness of teachers to provide needed services or request consultation because they believe that seeking help is a sign of incompetence

If the principle of fairness is to be implemented, we must begin all decisions from the point of view of the child's welfare: What does this child need?

Principle of Respect. The *principle of respect* is one's right to be treated as a human being and not as an animal or a statistic (Allen, 1969).

In actions toward children, are practitioners demonstrating respect for them as human beings? All interventions must be judged against this question. When the intervention is evaluated from this point of view, many common "therapeutic" practices are found to violate the principle of respect. The following are examples:

- Physical punishment (spankings, slaps, and paddlings)
- Psychological punishment (sarcasm, embarrassment, and name-calling)
- Deprivation (prohibiting a child normal opportunities for success, food, water, or typical school activities)
- Segregation (arbitrary special class placement)
- Isolation (inconsistent, long-term use of time-out)
- Medication (capricious use of symptom-control medications)
- Extrahuman punishment (use of restraints and electric shockers)

All these interventions have been used and remain in use today. Generally, they are applied by individuals who justify the use of any means to attain their end. All these interventions have been justified by some as the "only way" to accomplish an objective. These techniques are used (and justified) frequently simply because they are convenient, efficient, and seemingly effective.

It cannot be denied that a beaten child will obey, that an electric cattle prod will get a child to pay attention, and that segregation and isolation will reduce conflict. However, practitioners must establish limits on the interventions that can be applied with children. They must judge these interventions in the light of this third principle; that is, could or do the interventions inflict damage on the individual child or relegate the child to a less-than-human classification?

It is absolutely necessary that all behavior management practitioners develop an ethical system that incorporates the principles of normalization, fairness, and respect for the dignity and the worth of the child. This value system must avoid the pitfall of justifying "any means to attain a desired end."

Any intervention can be misused and abused if the person using it lacks an ethical system of personal and professional values. Practitioners must never forget that knowledge is power and that with power comes the responsibility to apply that power for the benefit of all persons.

PUBLIC LAW AND PERSONS WITH DISABILITIES

In this section, federal legislation that has and will continue to have a significant impact on the lives of persons with disabilities is discussed. These laws include the *Individuals with Disabilities Education Act* (IDEA 97) and its antecedents, the Americans with Disabilities Act of 1990, and Section 504 of the Rehabilitation Act of 1973.

IDEA 97

The Education for All Handicapped Children Act of 1975, Public Law 94-142, mandated a free appropriate public education for all children with disabilities. This first law included a legal definition of special education, the specific categories of disabilities, and the related services to be provided to persons with disabilities and their families. The law required the following:

1. Each individual with an identified disability who needs special education and related services is to have an *individualized education program (IEP)* written in response to his or her individual needs.

2. Parents were to participate in the child's assessment, the IEP development process, the approval of the IEP and the educational placement, and the evaluation of the IEP.

3. The general and special education teachers were to be participating members of the IEP decision-making team.

4. Children with disabilities were to be placed for services in the least restrictive environment necessary to meet their unique educational needs.

Subsequent laws pertaining to the education of children with disabilities further evolved during the l980s and 1990s. *Public Law 99-457,* the Education of the Handicapped Act Amendments of 1986, included provisions for states to initiate major program developments so that by 1991 a comprehensive national early intervention system would be in place throughout the nation.

Public Law 99-457 extended the rights and protections of Public Law 94-142, beginning in the 1991 school year, to children 3 to 5 years of age. State grant programs for infants and toddlers (birth to 2 years of age) were included in the law. Parents are to be significantly involved in their child's service program through a written *individualized family service plan* (IFSP). The law mandates the IFSP rather than the IEP in an effort to emphasize the importance of the family and its essential nature to the development and education of young children as the focus of service. The plan is developed by a multidisciplinary team and the parents (Trohanis, 1986).

In IDEA, Public Law 101-476, several shortcomings in general and special education services for persons with disabilities were addressed. The language or label to be assigned to children to be served under special education law was changed from "handicapped children" to "children with disabilities." "Autism" and "traumatic brain injury" were added to the categories of children with disabilities. The definition of "related services" was expanded to include "rehabilitation counseling" and "social work services."

In IDEA, *transition services* were added and defined as a coordinated set of activities for a student, designed with specific outcomes in mind. These services are to promote the student's movement from school to postschool activities, including postsecondary education, vocational training, integrated employment (including supported employment), continuing and adult education, adult services, independent living arrangements, and community participation. Transition activities are to be based on individual needs and responsive to individual preferences and interests. Activities may include instruction, community experience, the development of employment and other postschool adult living objectives, functional vocational evaluation, and, when necessary and appropriate, the acquisition of daily living skills.

Public Law 101-476 added two provisions to the IEP mandate: (a) a statement of needed transition services and (b) the requirement that the educational agency reconvene the IEP team to identify alternative strategies to meet student transition objectives when a participating agency, other than the educational agency, fails to provide agreed-on services. A statement of needed transition services, or *transition plan,* is a plan written for learners with disabilities who are 16 years of age (or younger when appropriate) that includes interagency responsibilities or linkages. It is written before the student leaves school.

In 1997, after 2 years of negotiation, Congress reauthorized IDEA. Most of the delay in reauthorization was due to concern with special education students who are violent and extremely disruptive to the educational process. In addition, Congress viewed the reauthorization process as an opportunity to strengthen and improve IDEA by "strengthening the role of parents; ensuring access to general education curriculum and reforms; focusing on teaching and learning while reducing unnecessary paperwork requirements; assisting education agencies in addressing the costs of improving special education and related services to children with disabilities; giving increased attention to racial, ethnic, and linguistic diversity to prevent inappropriate identification and mislabeling; ensuring that schools are safe and conducive to learning; and encouraging parents and educators to work out their differences using nonadversarial means" (Senate Report, quoted in Yell & Schriner, 1997, p. 5).

According to Yell and Shriner (1997), IDEA 97 is a restructuring of previous legislation with regard to the education of learners with disabilities. IDEA 97 focused attention on the general provisions of the law (definitions, findings, and purposes), assistance for education of all children with disabilities (local and state eligibility criteria, special education services, evaluations, IEP requirements, placement, and procedural safeguards), infants and toddlers with disabilities (programs and services), and national activities to improve education of children with disabilities (discretionary programs, state grants, personnel preparation, research, technical assistance, and dissemination of information and technology).

The IEP remains the heart of the provision of services to learners with disabilities. In IDEA 97, Congress made several changes with regard to the development of the IEP. The team is required by law to consider a specific set of topics and to make statements in the document related to these considerations. An IEP must contain information regarding the following (Warger, 1999):

- Present level of learner performance, including a statement of how the disability affects the student's involvement and progress in the general education curriculum
- Measurable annuals goals, including benchmarks or short-term objectives
- Educational needs resulting from the learner's disability
- All needed services and supports, including special education, related services, and program modifications and supports for school personnel
- Extent of nonparticipation with learners without identified disabilities
- Progress reporting
- Modification needed for participation in statewide or districtwide assessment or, if it is determined that the learner cannot participate, why the assessment is inappropriate for the learner and how the learner will be assessed
- Transition needs for learners age 14 and older

In addition, the IEP team must consider the strengths of the learner, the parents' concerns for enhancing the learner's education, and the results of initial evaluation or more recent evaluation of the learner. Finally, if there are special factors (device or service) that are related to the learner's access to a free, appropriate public education, the team must consider these and include a statement to that effect in the IEP. Special factors might include, among others, learner's behavior, language and Braille needs, other communication needs, and assistive technology devices.

Of particular importance to the topic of this text are provisions of IDEA 97 with regard to learner behavior. If the learner's behavior interferes with his or her learning or the learning of others, the IEP team must consider the interventions needed to address the behavior, including positive interventions and supports (Yell & Shriner,

1997). It must be stated in the IEP that inappropriate behavior is being addressed programmatically and not just punitively. In the effort to determine whether the learner's behavior is a concern, the team should address the following questions (Warger, 1999):

- Does the student need to learn and/or use new behaviors, skills, and/or strategies?
- Does the student demonstrate behaviors that are unsafe and/or that significantly interfere with the learning environment?
- Does the student's current presenting behavior require a behavior intervention plan?
- Is the student routinely removed from the general education classroom because of inappropriate behavior?
- Is the learner's behavior related to or a manifestation of a disability?

If the answer is yes to any of these questions, the team will need to ascertain a present level of education performance in the affected area. Using that information, the team will then develop annual goals and short-term objectives or benchmarks and state these needs, goals, and objectives on the IEP.

Public Law 101–336

Federal legislation was enacted that has had a significant impact on the lives of Americans with disabilities and the values and beliefs by which persons with disabilities are judged and interacted with in our society. The *Americans with Disabilities Act* (ADA), *Public Law 101–336,* was passed by Congress and signed by President George Bush on July 26, 1990. The ADA is patterned after Section 504 of the Rehabilitation Act of 1973, which has effectively guaranteed the civil rights of persons with disabilities for the past two decades.

Among the provisions of the ADA are a modification of the definition of a person with a disability, requirements in transportation and telecommunications, employment and public accommodations, and protection for persons with acquired immunodeficiency syndrome (AIDS), human immunodeficiency virus (HIV), and drug and alcohol problems. In the ADA, a person with disabilities is broadly defined as someone who has a physical or mental impairment that substantially limits that person in some major life activity, has a record of such impairment, or is regarded as having such an impairment. The definition includes three categories of persons with disabilities: (a) persons with actual physical or mental impairments (e.g., learning disabilities or hearing impairments), (b) persons who are discriminated against as a consequence of their past experience with a disability (e.g., a record of impairment, previous medical disabilities, or mental illness), and (c) persons who are not actually impaired but are regarded as impaired as a result of disfigurement.

The ADA mandates that public and private intercity and rail transportation be accessible. Paratransit services for persons with disabilities are required, unless such services would cause undue financial burden. Rural and small communities must make a "good-faith" effort to comply with transportation requirements. Private transit providers must make their buses accessible, and all new rail transit vehicles must be built to be accessible. Key rail stations must be accessible with exemptions in extraordinary cases (Amtrak stations must be accessible by 2010).

The ADA requires all common telecommunications carriers to provide intrastate and interstate relay services for telephone calls made by users of telecommunication devices for the deaf (TDDs) and users of voice telephones. The relay system requires that an intermediary be available 24 hours a day, 7 days a week, to transmit messages to and from persons with or without a TDD.

The ADA includes antidiscrimination protection for persons with AIDS and HIV. It also includes employment mandates that apply to all employers with 15 or more employees. Employers cannot refuse to employ a person because of a disability if the person is qualified to perform the job. And the employer is required to make reasonable accommodations in the workplace for a person with a disability, unless such accommodations would impose undue hardship on the employer.

The ADA prohibits public accommodations from discriminating against persons with disabilities. Public accommodations are defined as businesses or services that are used every day by all persons (e.g., department stores and restaurants). Public accommodations are prohibited from both excluding and not serving persons with disabilities. New buildings must be accessible when constructed. Changes in existing buildings are required only if such changes are "readily achievable." Public accommodations in buildings being renovated must be made accessible. The auxiliary goods and services available within public accommodations must be made accessible to persons with disabilities by such means as Braille signs, large-print signs, and tape recordings.

Section 504 of the Rehabilitation Act of 1973

Students do not need to be enrolled in special education to receive related services under the mandate of *Section 504* of the Rehabilitation Act of 1973 (Public Law 93-112). Section 504 suggests that a learners education may be composed of general and/or special education and should include the aids and services needed to provide a free, appropriate public education planned to respond to the individual student's needs (NICHCY, 1991).

INDIVIDUALIZED PROGRAMS

A key provision of Public Law 94-142 and its subsequent revisions is the IEP to be written for each child who is declared eligible for special education services, whether service is provided in a general or a special educational setting. The IEP is developed in response to each child's educational needs. The IEP is

> a written document for each child with a disability, developed in any meeting by a representative of the local educational agency or an intermediate educational unit who shall be qualified to provide, or supervise the provision of, specially designed instruction to

meet the unique needs of the child with a disability, the teacher, the parents or guardian of such child, and, whenever appropriate, the child. (Public Law 94-142, Section 4)

As noted in the previous section, the law specifically requires the participation of the parent or guardian, the general and special education teachers, and, when appropriate, the child in the IEP development process. The child with disabilities is to be integrated into the general education program for education activities unless such a placement is detrimental to the child's overall educational progress. A sample IEP is presented in Figure 1.1 (adapted from Shea & Bauer, 1994).

Public Law 101–476 mandates that a plan for "transition services" be included in the IEP for learners with disabilities who are 14 years of age. A sample individualized transition plan (ITP) is presented in Figure 1.2 (Shea & Bauer, 1994).

Finally, Public Law 99–457 mandates that an individualized family service plan (IFSP) be developed for all children who are under its protection. The IFSP is similar to the IEP but emphasizes the importance of the family to the child's education and related services program. A sample IFSP is presented in Figure 1.3 (Shea & Bauer, 1994).

A correlation can be made between the IEP process and the steps in the behavior change process (described in detail in Chapter 4). Briefly, the behavior change process requires the following steps:

(a) Collect baseline data (IEP assessment)

(b) Select objectives for the behavior change program (IEP short-term instructional objectives)

(c) Design and implement a specific behavior change intervention or strategy (IEP instructional or educational program)

(d) Collect intervention data to evaluate the effectiveness of the behavior change intervention (IEP evaluation)

♦ SUMMARY

Chapter 1 opens with a discussion of the individuality of children and the resultant need to individualize behavior management. Behavior management interventions are defined as all those actions (and conscious inactions) teachers and parents engage in to enhance the probability that children, individually and in groups, will develop effective behaviors that are personally fulfilling, productive, and socially acceptable. Attention is focused on the ethics of behavior management. An effort is made to differentiate between the formalism and utilitarianism perspectives of ethics. The use of aversive interventions and corporal punishment is reviewed, and some guidelines for application are offered.

The rights of children and the principles of normalization, fairness, and respect are discussed and exemplified. Selected public laws impacting on the education of children and youth with disabilities and Americans with disabilities are discussed. The chapter concludes with an overview of the procedures of the individualized education program, the individualized transition plan, and the individualized family service plan and their relationship to the steps in the behavior change process.

Cosmopolitan School District
INDIVIDUAL EDUCATION PROGRAM

Name _Georgia Barca_   Date of Birth _7/24/92_

School _P.S.47_   Date of IEP Conference _8/27/04_

Address _589 Smytha_   Date of Initial Placement _9/15/04_

Summary of Present Levels of Performance	
Strengths	Weaknesses
Excellent student in reading, spelling, math, and language arts.	Exhibits problem behaviors in both small- and large-group activities. Impulsive, distractible

Annual Goals	Description/Amount of Time in Regular Education Program	Special Concerns	Committee Signature/Position
Interact appropriately with others in class and on playground in large- and small-group activities	100% in regular 6th grade	Work with support teacher and parents	Mort Walker (teacher) Michael Bebe (director) Mary Lou Herzog (parent) Elosie Johnson (consultant)

Recommendations for Specific Procedures, Techniques, Materials	Objective Evaluation Criteria for Annual Goals
1. parent-teacher home-school daily report card and token economy 2. buddy system on playground	1. daily charting and graphing 2. home-school notebook 3. weekly conference call with parent
Placement Recommendation Regular 6th grade in neighborhood school	

White copy: Referring School
Yellow copy: Special Education Office
Blue copy: Parents

Figure 1.1
Sample IEP

Name   _G. Barca_

Short-Term Objectives	Education and/or Support Services	Responsible Person(s)	Amount of Time	Beginning and Ending Date	Review Date
G. will interact appropriately in social studies team	Token economy	Teacher/Student	Full period	9/15/04	10/6/04
G. will interact appropriately during "opening" activities	Token economy	Teacher	15 minutes	9/15/04	10/6/04
G. will play cooperatively during morning recess	Observation time-out	Teacher/ Playground Supervisor	20 minutes	9/22/04	10/6/04

Figure 1.1
Continued

Cosmopolitan School District
INDIVIDUAL TRANSITION PLAN

Name   Jane Henderson   DOB   2/27/86   Sex   F   Grade   11

School   James Jones Attendance Ctr

Address   Boyle Ave. City

Initiation Date   1/16/04   Review Date   3/16/04

Placement at time of ITP: James Jones—11th grade—

Conference Participants

Name	Role/Function	Signature
Dolores J. Hea	Parent/Guardian	
Michael T. Hea	Parent/Guardian	
G. L. Honig	Representative of Special District	
Ken Bums	Teacher	
Jane Henderson	Student	

Goals of Transition Plan

I. Community Living Goals: N/A

Objectives	Activities	Responsibility
Will remain living at home for duration of this ITP		

II. Employment Goals: Full-time employment at Pasta House

Objectives	Activities	Responsibility
Complete training	Attend 4 sessions	Jane and Father
Arrange transportation	Obtain Bi State Schedule	Jane and Teacher
Purchase uniforms	Go to Sears	Jane and Mother

III. Education Goals:

Objectives	Activities	Responsibility
Complete training	1. Attend sessions	Jane
	2. Read/study trainee manual	Jane/teacher/P.H. rep
	3. Follow trainer instructions on the job	Trainer

Comments: Will have 3 weeks to learn to be waitress.

Figure 1.2
Sample ITP

Cosmopolitan School District
INDIVIDUAL FAMILY SERVICE PLAN

Date completed   5/12/04 _____   Date Evaluated   4/15/04 _____

Dates Reviewed _____   _____   _____

Name   Seebreeze, Sara _____   DOB   6/12/99   Sex   F

Home Address   97853 Highway of Kings _____

Telephone (Home)   997-4341 _____   (Work)   874-7616 (Ext. 17) Mother _____

Parent(s)/Guardian(s)   Robert and Carol Hartwell _____

Individualized Family Service Plan Team

Name	Role/Function	Signature
Carol Hartwell	Parent/Guardian	
Robert Hartwell	Parent/Guardian	
Charlotte H. Hoge	Case Manager	
Robert Jason	MSW	
Debra Jolly	Sp/Lang	

Services (Frequency, Intensity, and Duration)

Immediate, daily, 3 hrs, preschool

Signatures of Parent(s) or Guardian(s)

I/we have participated in the development of this Individualized Family Service Plan for our child and our family. I/we understand this IFSP, give our permission for its implementation, and will cooperate in its implementation.

_____   (signature)   5/12/04   (date)
_____   (signature)   May 12, 2004   (date)

Figure 1.3
Sample IFSP

Individualized Family Service Plan (continued)

Assessment Instruments and Procedures

REEL

Observation in preschool/hom

Sample language

Health and Medical Information

Bilateral severe hearing impairment

Developmental Levels

Motor skills—OK - Eye contact—OK

Can localize sound with aids

Does not sign

Child's Strengths

Very social, curious and interested, explores freely. Makes great effort to communicate

Child's Needs

Speech training, signing as needed, more socialization

Family's Strengths

Strong and willing family

Family's Needs

Training in signing and speech

Help in obtaining information and planning future

OUTCOMES

Objectives	Strategies	Duration	Responsible Person(s)
Verbal communication skills	Discussion play	3 months	Teacher/Sp/Lang
Socialization	Reg preschool	3 months	Case Manager
Signing	Formal training and generalizations into preschool and home	3 months	Case Manager, teacher, parent, sp/Lang.

Figure 1.3
Continued

◆ PROJECTS

1. Conduct a class discussion on the definition of behavior management interventions given in the text.

2. Using the current professional literature, locate three definitions of behavior management. Compare and contrast the definitions with one another and with the definition in the text.

3. Conduct a class discussion on the definition of ethics and differentiate between the formalism and utilitarianism perspectives of ethics.

4. Discuss and exemplify the principle of normalization, fairness, and respect and relate these principles to the standards of the Council for Exceptional Children for the ethical application of behavior management interventions.

5. Invite to class for a presentation or conduct an interview with a special education administrator on the impact of federal law on the education of children and youth with disabilities.

6. Discuss the relationships between the IEP, the ITP, and the IFSP and the steps in the behavior change process.

◆ REFERENCES

Allen, R. C. (1969). *Legal rights of the disabled and disadvantaged* (GPO 1969-0-360-797). Washington, DC: U.S. Department of Health, Education, and Welfare and National Citizens Conference on Rehabilitation of the Disabled and Disadvantaged.

Brown, M. S., & Bauer, A. M. (1994). Acting out or acting together? Social community formation and behavior management. *Beyond Behavior, 5*(3), 15–18.

Council for Exceptional Children. (1997a). CEC Code of Ethics and Standards for Practice. Available: *www.cec.sped.org/ps.code.html.*

Evans, I. M., & Meyer, L. H. (1985). *An educative approach to behavior problems: A practical decision model for intervention with severely handicapped learners.* Baltimore: Paul H. Brookes.

Farrell, P. (1995). The impact of normalization on policy and provision for people with learning difficulties. *Issues in Special Education and Rehabilitation, 10*(1), 47–54.

Green, G. (1996). Evaluating claims about treatments for autism. In C. Maurice, G. Green, & S. Luce (Eds.), *Behavioral interventions for young children with autism* (pp. 15–28). Austin, TX: PRO-ED.

Jones, V. (1993). Assessing your classroom and school-wide student management plan. *Beyond Behavior, 4*(3), 9–12.

National Information Center for Children and Youth with Disability (NICHCY). (1991). The education of children and youth with special needs: What do the laws say? *NICHCY News Digest, 1*(1), 1–15.

Scheuermann, B. & Evans, W. (1997). Hippocrates was right: Do no harm: Ethics in the selection of intervention. *Beyond Behavior, 8*(3), 18–22.

Sexton, J. D. (1987). Involuntary euthanasia: Withholding treatment from infants with severe handicaps. In M. Rotatori, M. Banbury, & R. Foxx (Eds.), *Issues in special education* (pp. 13–22). Mountain View, CA: Mayfield.

Shea, T. M., & Bauer, A. M. (1987). *Teaching children and youth with behavior disorders* (2nd ed.). Upper Saddle River, NJ: Prentice Hall.

Shea, T. M., & Bauer, A. M. (1994). *Learners with disabilities: A social systems perspective of special education.* Madison, WI: Brown & Benchmark.

Silver, L. (1986). Controversial approaches to treating learning disabilities and attention deficit disorder. *American Journal of Diseases of Childhood, 140,* 1045–1052.

Singer, G. S., & Irvin, L. K. (1987). Human rights review of intrusive behavioral treatments for students with severe handicaps. *Exceptional Children, 54,* 46–52.

Simpson, R. (1995). Children and youth with autism in an age of reform: A perspective on current issues. *Behavioral Disorders, 21*(1), 7–20.

Skiba, R. J., & Deno, S. L. (1991). Terminology and behavior reduction: The case against "punishment." *Exceptional Children, 57*(4), 298–313.

Smith, D. D., & Rivera, D. P. (1993). *Effective discipline.* Austin, TX: PRO-ED.

Smith, D. D., & Rivera, D. P. (1995). Discipline in special education and general education settings. *Focus on Exceptional Children, 27*(5), 1–14.

Trohanis, P. (1986). *A brief introduction to PL 99–457: A new national agenda for young special needs children.* Chapel Hill: University of North Carolina Press.

Turnbull, H. R., III, Guess, D., Backus, L. H., Barber, P. A., Feidler, C. R., Helmstetter, E., & Summers, J. A. (1986). A model for analyzing the moral aspects of special education and behavioral interventions: The moral aspects of aversive procedures. In Dokecki & R. Zaner (Eds.), *Ethics of dealing with persons with severe handicaps: Toward a research agenda* (pp. 167–210). Baltimore: Paul H. Brookes.

Tymchuk, A. J. (1976). A perspective on the ethics of mental retardation. *Mental Retardation, 14,* 14–47.

Warger, C. (1999). *New IDEA '97 requirements: Factors to consider in developing an IEP* (ERIC Digest E578). Reston, VA: ERIC Clearinghouse on Disabilities and Gifted Education. (ERIC Document Reproduction Service No. ED 434 434)

Wolfenberger, W. (1972). *The principles of normalization in human services.* Toronto: National Institute on Mental Health.

Yell, M. L., & Shriner, J. G. (1997). The IDEA Amendments of 1997: Implications for special and general education teachers, administrators, and teacher trainers. *Focus on Exceptional Children, 30*(1), 1–19.

2

Models of Human Behavior and Teacher Effectiveness Guidelines

◆ KEY TERMS

Behavioral psychology
Behavioral theory
Biophysical theory
Comprehensive intervention
Ecology
Environment
Integrative framework
Keystone behavior
Psychodynamic model
Psychoeducational approach
Sociology

◆ CHAPTER OBJECTIVES

After completing this chapter, you will be able to do the following:

1. Discuss the relationships between ideas, actions, and outcomes (i.e., theories, interventions, and results).

2. Characterize the basic principles and components of the four traditional models of the etiology of human behavior (psychodynamic, biophysical, environmental, and behavioral).

3. Describe the integrative framework and discuss its implications for analyzing behavior management problems and selecting, implementing, and evaluating interventions.

4. Recognize the value of keystone behaviors and comprehensive interventions.

5. Identify and discuss the teacher effectiveness.

◆ ◆ ◆

A group of four college students studying to be teachers and their instructor, Professor Garfunkel, were observing a class of children with behavior problems. The subject of their observation was the behavior of 6-year-old John, who had recently been enrolled in the class.

The group observed John's behavior for 10 minutes and then closed the curtains of the observation window to discuss and evaluate their observations. After a brief discussion, they reached consensus on the behavior they observed:

- John entered the classroom, slammed the door, took off his coat and hat, and dropped them to the floor.
- John ran to the toy box, picked up a truck, ran it over the top of a desk and a bookcase, and threw it on the floor.
- John picked up a doll that was near the toy box, banged it several times on the floor, and threw it at the teacher's assistant.
- John ran around the room three times. While running, he bumped into two children.
- John stopped near the sand table and twirled around on his toes, with his hands fully extended above his head, six or seven times before running to the sink.
- John stopped in front of the sink and turned on both faucets. He looked into the sink and remained in this position for the final 4 minutes of the observation period.

After the students reached agreement on the behaviors that John exhibited in the classroom during the 10-minute observation period, Dr. Garfunkel asked each student to discuss what they thought to be the reason for John's behavior. The following summaries by James, Charlotte, Melissa, and Richard, respectively, are inferences about John's behavior:

> John behaves as he does because he has not learned to act appropriately in the classroom setting. He has evidently been rewarded for similar behavior in the past by the teacher or assistant. The teacher reinforced his behavior during our observation by attempting to stop him.

(James is enrolled in experimental psychology and behavior modification courses this semester.)

> John is obviously hyperactive as a result of brain damage. He should be administered appropriate symptom-control medication.

(Charlotte is an ex–premed student who transferred into special education this semester.)

> John behaves the way he does because he is emotionally driven. The behavior is his way of expressing hostility and frustration. This behavior is beneficial for John, and he should be encouraged to continue expressing himself.

(Melissa is enrolled in courses in neo-Freudian theory and practice this semester.)

> John behaves as he does because of the classroom environment. It is noisy, confusing, and cluttered and lacks organization. He is only imitating what he sees

others doing in the classroom. John needs an uncluttered, orderly, structured classroom environment.

(Richard is an ex–sociology major who recently transferred to special education.)

Each student interpreted John's behavior from a perspective that evolved from their personal formal and informal learning and experience (Shea & Bauer, 1987). The perspectives articulated by the four students represent only a few of the many perspectives on human behavior available in the literature.

The various theories of psychology—the study of human behavior—applied in the education of children and youth with behavior problems are based in part on the theorist's perspective of the principles underlying human conduct and thought.

In the field of psychology, there are several perspectives on human behavior (e.g., psychodynamic, behavioral, and humanistic). In an effort to analyze, organize, and synthesize the perspectives of human behavior applicable to the management of the behavior of children and youth, Rhodes and Paul (1978), in a classic analysis, suggested the following points of view: psychodynamic, biophysical, behavioral, and environmental (sociological and ecological). These perspectives are discussed in the first section of this chapter. The second section is devoted to a discussion of several important teacher effectiveness guidelines.

MODELS OF HUMAN BEHAVIOR

What makes us behave as we do toward self, others, and the environment? How can we change our behavior and the behavior of others from inappropriate to appropriate? From unacceptable to acceptable? From destructive to constructive?

Four of the responses theoreticians have made and continue to make to these questions are the psychodynamic, biophysical, environmental, and behavioral explanations of human behavior. Argyris and Schon (1992) call the perspective from which we analyze and attempt to understand behavior our "theory-of-action," philosophy, or "espoused beliefs." They are those beliefs that guide our actions in our work with children. The vignettes of the four teacher-trainees that introduced the chapter are an example of the influence an individual's perspective of the etiology of human behavior may have on the inferences one makes about the behavior and how one responds to behavior. In this section, these theoretical models are related to the behavior of children.

Ideas, Actions, and Outcomes

"What we believe about the behavior of students affects how we respond and act toward them" (Wood, 1978, p. 119). In an intervention, ideas, actions, and outcomes are tied together and greatly affect each other. Ideas, in and of themselves, are inert unless active energy is added to their influence. Active energy, by itself, is meaningless and chaotic unless it is directed. In an intervention, the conceptual framework or theory directs and channels action by providing an analysis of the nature of the problem that dictates the intervention and by suggesting the outcome or result toward which the intervention is directed. According to Fink (1988), it is often presumed that teachers' "espoused beliefs" govern their actual behavior. However, we frequently find that considerable variance exists between behavior and philosophy. Training and experience can decrease this discrepancy.

"One form of intervention, carried out within two different conceptual frameworks, can have radically different meanings and lead to radically different experiences and outcomes for the participants" (Rhodes & Tracy, 1972, pp. 23–24).

Educators' perceptions of children and the behavior children exhibit, if Rhodes and Tracy are correct, are in large part determinants of the behavior management interventions selected and imposed. For example, the teacher who perceives the child as determined primarily by the environment approaches the problems of behavior management from a radically different point of view from the teacher who perceives a child as controlled primarily by intrapsychic or biophysical factors. The teacher who perceives the child as controlled by the environment may change the location of the child's seat, develop additional rules for movement and behavior, or reorganize the lesson format or teaching strategy. The teacher who views the child as controlled by intrapsychic factors may encourage the child to express his or her feelings and emotions or may encourage the expression of feelings through art or music. The teacher who sees biophysical factors as significant in the child's behavior may provide the child with a highly structured learning environment that includes repeated drill and practice of lessons or may refer the child to the appropriate medical personnel for treatment.

Figure 2.1
Conceptual frameworks of children's behavior

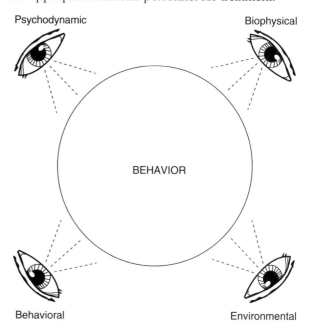

Each of the models of human behavior presented in the following section is an explanation of behavior; each has led to the development of an educational strategy or methodology for application with children having behavior problems. Figure 2.1 depicts the relationship of the various theories or conceptual frameworks to the behavior of children. More specifically, conceptual models are ways of looking at behavior.

Psychodynamic

As used in this text, the *psychodynamic model* refers to a group of theoretical constructs that have evolved from the original theoretical formulations of Freud (1989). These formulations have in common a belief in the existence of a dynamic intrapsychic life. Proponents of this model vary in their views on the following: the impact of the environment on the individual's intrapsychic life, the basic instinctive forces energizing psychic life, and the functions of the components of the personality. The effects of nonintrapsychic variables, such as the environment and heredity, have been discussed by Adler and Jung (Munroe, 1955), Erikson (1963), and many others.

Psychodynamic theorists see the causes of human behavior as being within the individual. Behavior is determined by a dynamic intrapsychic life. The relationship between the individual and behavior problems from the psychodynamic perspective is depicted in Figure 2.2.

Freud perceived the personality as being composed of three interrelating components: the id, the superego, and the ego:

> The id is the lusty infant who wants immediate gratification. Physical pleasure is what the id is after, and it will use the libido (sexual energy) to get what it wants. The id's typical remark in the personality dialogue is, "Gimmie, I want it. Now!" Because of its animalistic antisocial nature, the rest of the personality and society have kept the id mostly unconscious. It still influences us, but unconsciously....
>
> The superego is the conscience. Should and shame are the staples of its vocabulary, and its favorite line is, "You should be ashamed of yourself!" While the id is predominantly unconscious, the superego is partly conscious and partly unconscious. The unconscious part contains the remonstrations and rules we were taught. "Don't do that. Don't play with ... Nasty! Nice people don't ..." The superego is judgmental.

Figure 2.2
Etiology of behavior from the psychodynamic perspective

Source. Roberts (1975)

Between the id and the superego lives the hero and executive of the Freudian personality structure, the ego. Not only is he caught between the id and the superego and forced to moderate their conflicting pressures, he also is the one who is mostly aware of outside social reality. Thus, his line to the others is, "Now, let's be realistic about this...." The ego generally straddles the conscious and the unconscious. In a healthy personality he is the manager and can call the shots without being overpowered by the id or the superego. Each of three parts has a genius all of its own. The ego's armamentarium includes his "ego defenses." Sublimination, for example, is the redirection of socially unacceptable impulses into acceptable channels: Don't play in the toilet, dear. Why don't you go out and play in the sandbox? A large part of our work as teachers is to provide socially acceptable outlets for otherwise destructive desires. (Roberts, 1975, p. 7)

From the psychodynamic perspective, personality development occurs as the child moves through a series of psychosexual steps that must be completed in order for the individual to avoid later problems. The first stage is the *oral* stage, in which the individual's first contact with the environment occurs, relationships are initiated, and a basic attitude of trust or mistrust is developed. The *anal* stage follows, centering on elimination and conformity to demands for control. At the end of this stage, the individual either accomplishes autonomy or experiences shame and doubt. The third stage is *phallic,* in which the child becomes increasingly interested in the feelings of pleasure associated with the genitals. At this time, the individual must develop his or her personality and self-identification. The next stage of psychosexual development, *latency,* usually occurs during the elementary school years. During this period the individual channels energy into learning. Finally, during adolescence, the *genital* stage occurs, in which the individual's previous identities are consolidated.

Efforts to apply psychodynamic theories to educational processes have led teachers to develop the psychodynamic-interpersonal educational, or psychoeducational, strategy. This strategy is

concerned with the psychic origin and meaning of maladaptive behavior, as well as the child's interpersonal relationships with others, particularly the teacher. This orientation, shared by most psychotherapists, is consistent with the high priority given by them to understanding psychological causal factors and the development of a positive, trusting relationship between adult and child in formal education training. (Hewett, 1968, p. 9)

Significant contributions to this educational strategy have been made by Long, Morse, and Newman (1980); Morse (1985); Nichols (1984); and others. Although diversification exists among these theorists and practitioners, the primary objectives and methodologies to be applied in the educational setting remain relatively constant:

A primary goal is to understand why the child is behaving as he is in school. This goal may be achieved by some through interpretation of behavior in a psychodynamic context, using psychoanalytic concepts. Others may view the child more in relationship to his total environment and be concerned with understanding why he lacks adaptive capacities for dealing with the stresses and demands associated with learning and adjustment in school. For the teacher, a major goal is the communication of acceptance to the child and the establishment of a secure and meaningful relationship. Formal educational goals are of secondary importance. (Hewett, 1968, pp. 17–18)

In the classroom, emphasis is placed on (a) developing a mentally healthy atmosphere, (b) accepting the child and the pathological conditions without reservation, and (c) encouraging and assisting the child in learning, beginning at a level and under circumstances in which the child can perform successfully. Assuming the role of educational therapist, the teacher accepts the child, tolerating and interpreting the child's behavior. The *psychoeducational approach* is a general term that is representative of a theory, method, or viewpoint on the education of troubled children. As a generic term, it includes a variety of psychological and educational approaches to helping such children and youth (Fink, 1988; Nichols, 1984).

Psychodynamic theories no longer dominate educational programs as they did in the 1950s and 1960s. However, this theoretical perspective remains a dominant force in contemporary society in such forms as popular literature, child care books, movies, novels, television shows, and casual conversations. In Chapter 7, several intervention strategies associated with the psychodynamic model are reviewed in detail.

Biophysical

The *biophysical theory* of the etiology of learning and behavior problems of children places emphasis on organic origins of human behavior. The proponents of this conceptual model postulate a relationship between physical defects, malfunctions, and illnesses and the individual's behavior. This relationship is depicted in Figure 2.3.

Schroeder and Schroeder (1982) discussed the two primary subgroups of biophysical theories: deficit and developmental. The deficit subgroup includes theories related to genetics, temperament, neuropsychopharmacology, nutrition, and neurologic dysfunction. Developmental theories include neurological organization, perceptual motor learning, physiological readiness, sensory integration, and development. Several interventions evolving from these subgroups of biophysical theory are discussed in Chapter 8.

Though not the dominant theory of causation in the education of children, the biophysical model does have proponents among professionals and parents of children with serious emotional and behavioral disturbances, autism, learning disabilities, and developmental disabilities. The practitioner who is influenced by the

Figure 2.3
Etiology of behavior from the
biophysical perspective

**Organic
Problem
within**

biophysical model is concerned primarily with changing or compensating for the individual's malfunctioning organic mechanisms or processes that are causing the inappropriate behavior. Organic defects may be a consequence of either heredity or environment (trauma). Environmental effects may occur before, during, or after birth.

Biophysical disabilities can be classified into four groups (National Foundation–March of Dimes, 1975):

1. *Structural defects.*   One or more parts of the body are defective in size or shape (e.g., neural tube defect, clubfoot, and cleft palate).

2. *Functional defects.*   One or more parts of the body are malfunctioning (e.g., blindness and deafness).

3. *Inborn errors of metabolism.*   The body is unable to convert certain chemicals to other chemicals needed for normal body functioning (e.g., phenylketonuria and Tay-Sachs disease).

4. *Blood diseases.*   The blood is unable to conduct its normal functions (e.g., sickle-cell disease and hemophilia).

Several curative and preventive medical interventions have been developed to mitigate or modify the effects of biophysical defects. Among these interventions are prenatal and postnatal health care, proper nutrition and diet, general and specific physical examinations, symptom-control medications, and genetic counseling. These interventions are presented in detail in Chapter 8.

Among the proponents of biophysical theories as they apply to the education of children and youth are those evolved from Cruickshank, Bentzen, Ratzenburg, and Tannhauser (1961) and Fernald (1988). An excellent summary of this theoretical perspective as it applies in the educational setting to children and youth with behavioral problems is provided by Hewett (1968):

> The primary goal of the sensory-neurological strategy is to discover the child's sensory and neurologically based deficit, often through extensive observation and diagnostic testing. Once these deficits are uncovered, the child is viewed as a learner who must be trained to accurately perceive and comprehend stimuli and to demonstrate motor efficiency before he is given complex learning tasks. (p. 24)

In the educational setting, the teacher who is influenced by the biophysical model will emphasize order and routine in the classroom and daily schedule, frequent repetition of learning tasks, the sequential presentation and learning of tasks, and a reduction of extraneous environmental stimuli.

Environmental

The impact of the *environment* on human behavior is a dominant theme in contemporary society. Many decisions made by governments, corporate groups, and individuals are made with a conscious awareness of the relationship between people and the environment. Environmental impact studies are standard, accepted components of all proposals to construct highways, airports, dams, lakes, industrial complexes, high-rise buildings, and so on. Both professionals and laypersons are increasingly concerned with any environmental changes that may affect human behavior, such as those concerning recreation areas, water pollution, waste disposal, and nuclear power. Many are concerned with the effects of environmental changes on issues such as employment, human services, and neighborhood composition.

Sociology traditionally is the study of the development, structure, interaction, and behavior of organized groups of humans. Sociology is composed of a number of subgroups focusing on specific areas of this social science, such as social psychology, small-group study, or educational sociology.

In an educational setting, sociology focuses on the formal and informal composition of and interactions among groups. It is concerned with groups that affect an organization both within and outside the organization. Applied to the education of children, sociology is the study of social forces that in some manner affect individuals and groups.

Ecology is the study of the interrelationships between an organism and its environment. As it applies to education, ecology is the study of the reciprocal relationship between the child or group and others (individuals, groups, and objects) in the environment.

Sociology and ecology as etiological models of human behavior are depicted in Figure 2.4.

The environmental theorists maintain that isolating a child's behavior from the environment in which it occurs denies the phenomenal nature of that behavior (Rhodes & Paul, 1978). *Environmental* theorists assume instead that "the child is an inseparable part of a small social system, an ecological unit, made up of the child, his family, his school, his neighborhood, and community" (Hobbs, 1966, p. 1108). Reactions of others in the child's ecosystem influence the way the child acts (Algozzine, 1980). This perspective emphasizes the learner's behavior as a result of a specific collective in a specific setting or environment or place at a specific time in history (Rhodes & Paul, 1978).

Figure 2.4
Etiology of behavior from the
sociological and ecological
perspectives

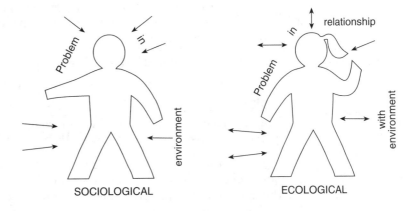

An environmental theory of importance to educators is the *deviance perspective:*

> The deviance perspective focuses on mental illness as the breaking of social rules. In particular, mental illness is related to implicit rules governing ordinary social interaction. From a deviance perspective, two important questions arise. (1) What are the social forces promoting conformity or rule-breaking? (2) What relationships exist between those enforcing the rules and those breaking the rules? (Des Jarlais, 1972, p. 263)

In an effort to respond to these questions, theorists have generated several models to account for deviant behavior. Among them are the following:

- *Social disorganization.* The theory of social disorganization was developed from the findings of a series of urban studies. Among the researchers associated with this school of thought were Hawley (1950) and Park and Burgess (1925). This perspective attempts to measure and characterize the differences between communities considered organized or "natural" and communities considered disorganized. Characteristics of the organized community, in opposition to those of the disorganized community, include low crime and delinquency rates, stable family units, a low rate of mental illness, and so on. The sources of such characteristics of the community (both organized and disorganized) are assumed to be related to such variables as the availability of employment, education, religious services, and recreational facilities. The disorganized community lacks appropriate services.

- *Labeling theory.* The labeling of children who deviate from the norms and rules of the school and community has long been a concern of educators. Many fear the effects of the label and its implications for the child's behavior and educators' expectations of the child (Algozzine, Mercer, & Countermine, 1977).

  The theory of labeling emphasizes that one does not become a deviant by breaking rules. One must be labeled a deviant before the social expectations defining the particular form of deviance are activated. Once an individual is officially labeled a deviant, this person assumes the role expectations of that particular form of deviance in order to conform to the expectations of society.

This theoretical perspective is closely related to Parsons's (1964) concept of the sick role. He proposed four societal expectations that encourage individuals labeled "sick" to assume this role:

1. Sick persons are relieved of their normal role obligations.

2. Because they are sick, they are not morally responsible for their condition.

3. Sick persons must express their desire to return to normal functioning.

4. Sick persons must seek technically competent help from appropriate caretakers (psychiatrists, psychologists, social workers, and teachers).

A variety of interventions has evolved out of environmental theories. Some of these interventions are reviewed in detail in Chapter 8.

The application of the environmental model in educational programs for children is characterized by (a) an awareness of the impact of the environment on the group and individual and the monitoring and manipulation of the environment for the benefit of the individual and group and (b) an awareness of the dynamic reciprocal interrelationship that exists between the group and individual and the environment and the monitoring and manipulation of this relationship for the benefit of the individual and group.

In summary, the environmental framework is based on several assumptions about behavior, the environment, and the interactions between an individual and environment (Swap, Prieto, & Harth, 1982). These assumptions are as follows:

1. The child is not disturbed. Disturbance is a consequence of either the environment's effect on the child or the interactions between the child and the environment.

2. Environmental interventions, to be effective, must in some manner alter the ecological system in which the child functions. The implementation of environmental interventions is based on an assessment of the child, the specific environment in which the child is functioning, and the interactions between these two elements. Although the interventions may focus on one or more of these factors, it impacts all of them.

3. Environmental interventions are eclectic. It will be apparent in the discussion in Chapter 8 that environmental interventions are chosen from many theoretical perspectives. Interventions are selected and applied as needed within the environmental framework.

4. Interventions in an ecological system may have unanticipated consequences. Because of the complexity of the child, the environment, and the relationship between the two elements, it is difficult to predict with certitude the specific effects an intervention may have on the relationship's many variables. Thus, frequent and careful evaluation of the impact of interventions is essential.

5. Each interaction between child and setting is unique. This assumption recognizes the uniqueness of each child, the environment in which he or she is functioning, and the reciprocal relationship between child and environment.

Behavioral

Behavioral psychology is the predominant educational psychology taught in colleges and universities today.

The statement "what you do is influenced by what follows what you do" (Sarason, Glaser, & Fargo, 1972, p. 10) is an excellent summary of the essence of the *behavioral theory,* specifically in reference to behavior modification. Behavior modification is the primary focus of Chapters 3 through 6. A brief overview of this model is presented here to facilitate the reader's efforts to compare and contrast it with the three previously presented models of human behavior.

The behavior modifier is concerned primarily with what behavior an individual exhibits and what intervention can be designed and imposed to change this observable behavior. For the behavior modification practitioner, *behavior* is defined as all human

Figure 2.5
Etiology of behavior from the
behavior modification
perspective

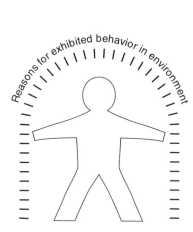

acts that are observable and measurable, excluding biochemical and physiological processes. The behavioral theorists and practitioners see the causes of human behavior as existing outside the individual in the immediate environment. Thus, the individual's behavior is determined primarily by external forces. The relationship between the individual and his or her behavior as perceived by the behaviorist is depicted in Figure 2.5.

Those adhering to the behavior modification model assume that all human behavior (adaptive and maladaptive) is the consequence of the lawful application of the principles of reinforcement.

According to Roberts (1975), the principles of reinforcement are as follows:

1. Reinforcement always follows the exhibition of the behavior.
2. The behavior should be reinforced as soon as possible after it occurs.
3. The reinforcement must be appropriate for the individual or group being reinforced. A reinforcer is effective only if the individual or group being reinforced perceives the reinforcer as rewarding or punishing.
4. Many small rewards, presented frequently, are more effective than a few big ones.

The principles of reinforcement are presented in depth in Chapter 3. These rules are an indication of the behavior modifier's belief that human behavior is controlled by the individual's impinging environmental stimuli. The individual's behavior is changed by manipulation of environmental stimuli.

Behavioral theory, including behavior modification techniques and their applications to individual and group behavior problems, has its roots in the writings and research of Bandura (1969), Skinner (1971), and Wolpe (1961), among others. Although there have been and continue to be debates among theorists relative to various constructs and interventions within this theoretical model, practitioners have successfully applied its principles to a variety of human problems. Among the problem behaviors that have been modified as a consequence of the application of behavior modification interventions are the symptoms of psychoses, autism, neuroses, marital conflicts, specific learning problems, motivational problems, and speech problems. Researchers and practitioners have successfully modified tantrums, verbal and physical aggression, interpersonal interaction patterns, eating habits, mutism, and so on. Various behavior modification interventions in the school have been successfully implemented with children with disabilities. The goal of behavior modification interventions in the classroom with children with behavioral disorders (and, indeed, with all individuals) is best summarized by Hewett (1968):

> The basic goal for the behavior modifier is the identification of maladaptive behaviors which interfere with learning and assisting the child in developing more adaptive behavior. Every child is considered a candidate for learning something regardless of his degree of psychopathology and other problems. This "something" may only represent a starting point (e.g., chair sitting) and be but a small part of the eventual "something" the teacher hopes to accomplish (e.g., reading), but care will be taken to insure its mastery before more complex goals are introduced. The child's behavior is viewed in the broadest possible context without rigid adherence to a priority ranking of behavioral goals on the basis of inferences regarding emotional conflicts or brain dysfunctions. (p. 34)

There are a variety of behavior modification interventions that may be applied to change behavior. These interventions are presented in detail with practical examples in Chapters 5 and 6.

The procedures for applying behavior modification in the educational setting require the teacher to (a) observe and clarify the behavior to be changed; (b) select and present potent reinforces at the appropriate time; (c) design and impose, with consistency, an intervention technique based on the principles of reinforcement; and (d) monitor and evaluate the effectiveness of the intervention. The steps in the behavior change process are presented in detail in Chapter 4.

INTEGRATIVE FRAMEWORK

As we have learned in the previous sections, the behavior of children is a complex, dynamic phenomenon that may be perceived from various points of view. As the following examples show, the perceptions of parents, teachers, and others involved with children with behavior problems can have an enormous effect on assessment and intervention.

♦ *Examples*

John was born on December 23, 1993, in Central City Regional Hospital. He was a premature child with Down syndrome. When John was born, Martha, his mother, was alone in the delivery room, with the exception of the nurses and doctor. She was glad that the long, tiring pregnancy was over. Martha was only 16 years old, and the pregnancy had been very difficult.

Martha had never heard the phrase "Down syndrome"; she had no idea what the doctor was talking about when she was informed of John's problem. Martha only knew that John was not "right," and because she wanted a perfect baby, this made her unhappy. Her friends all had perfect babies.

Martha had no one to turn to during this crisis except the staff at the community shelter for single and indigent mothers, where she had been living for the past 5 months. John's father's parents refused to let their son even talk to Martha. He was still in high school and could not help with the baby. Martha's parents put her out of the house when they discovered that she was pregnant. Her only contact with family was through Aunt Jean, who came to visit her at the shelter. Aunt Jean had troubles of her own and with her kids and couldn't help Martha very much.

Martha hoped the school would let her return so she could graduate with her friends. The principal said the school board was thinking about opening a nursery in the high school. But now that John was "different," she wondered, if they did open one, whether they would accept him.

The social worker at the shelter said she would help Martha get on welfare, get food stamps, and find a studio apartment in the city. The social worker said there were some areas of the city where cheap housing was available for people on welfare. Martha knew she couldn't return to her job at the fast-food restaurant. She wouldn't make enough money to support herself and John.

Paul was born on December 23, 1993, in West Suburban Medical Center. He was a full-term child with Down syndrome. When Paul was born, his father, George, was with his mother, Mary, in the delivery room, as were several nurses and doctors. As a result of tests given during the early stages of pregnancy, the parents were aware that Paul was to be born with Down syndrome.

This was Mary's third pregnancy; it was for the most part unexceptional, and the delivery was routine. Mary was 28 years of age. Her two other children, a boy and girl, were in elementary school and doing well in academics and in cocurricular and community activities. The children enjoyed school, taking after their parents, who were both college graduates and professionals.

Mary and George had read a great deal about Down syndrome during the past few months and hoped that Paul would be born without medical complications. Though they were not overjoyed to be the parents of a child with potentially serious disabilities, they felt prepared and equal to the challenge. Both sets of grandparents were aware of the problems that Paul might present and volunteered to help when Mary and baby returned home from the hospital. This was important because George, the manager of a department in a computer firm, could not take many days off from work. Mary was going to remain home with the baby for 6 weeks before returning to her job as a special education teacher.

The local chapter of Down Syndrome Association was in telephone contact with the family while mother and baby were in the hospital. The association recommended a visit with the parents of a child with Down syndrome. Mary and George accepted the offer. The medical center made arrangements for Mary and George to be interviewed by a home visitor who specialized in developmental disabilities. This professional arranged to visit the parents in their home and enroll Paul in an infant stimulation program.

Children's behavior can be perceived from a psychodynamic, biophysical, behavioral, or environmental point of view. The very complexity and diversity of the theoretical perspectives and children's behavior preclude simple assessment and intervention. However, through the application of an *integrative framework*, it may be possible to coordinate the extant perspectives into a manageable assessment-intervention model (Shea & Bauer, 1987).

From an ecological perspective, rather than being seen as rooted within the child or in the environment exclusively, behavior is seen as a result of the interaction between the child, the child's idiosyncratic behaviors, and the unique environments in which the child functions (Forness, 1981). Ecological practitioners would suggest that traditional practitioners are missing educationally and socially relevant variables because of their limiting single-theory perspective.

Before discussing the integrative framework, it is necessary to become familiar with a few specialized terms:

1. *Ecology* is the interrelationship of humans with the environment and involves reciprocal association (Thomas & Marshall, 1977). According to Scott (1980), ecology is all the surroundings of behavior. From this point of view, it is assumed that the child is an inseparable part of an ecological unit, which is composed of the child, the classroom, the school, the neighborhood, and the community.

2. *Development* is defined as the continual adaptation of the child and the environment to each other. It is seen as progressive accommodation that takes place throughout the life span between growing individuals and their changing environments. It is based on "the person's evolving conception of the ecological environment and his relationship to it, as well as the person's growing capacity to discover, sustain, and alter its properties" (Bronfenbrenner, 1979, p. 9).

3. *Behavior* is the expression of the dynamic relationships between the individual and the environment (Marmor & Pumpian-Mindlin, 1950). Behavior occurs in a setting that includes specific time, place, and object props as well as the individual's previously established pattern of behavior (Scott, 1980). To understand behavior, it is necessary to examine the systems of interaction surrounding the behavior; assessment is not restricted to a single setting. In addition, according to Bronfenbrenner (1977), examination must take into account those aspects of the environment beyond the immediate situation in which the individual is functioning and that impact on the behavior.

4. *Congruence* is the match, or goodness of fit, between the individual and the environment. Thurman (1977) suggests that the individual whom we judge to be normal is functioning in an ecology that is congruent: The individual's behavior is in harmony with the norms of the environment. When there is a lack of congruence, the individual is viewed as either deviant or incompetent.

The integrated framework presented here includes several interrelated contexts that may impinge on an individual. These contexts, which affect the individual's development and behavior, are the *ontogenic system,* the *microsystem,* the *mesosystem,* the *exosystem,* and the *macrosystem* (Belsky, 1980; Bronfenbrenner, 1979). These systems, or contexts, have recently been referred to by Shea and Bauer (1987) as (a) the learner (ontogenic system), (b) interpersonal relationships (microsystem), (c) relationships

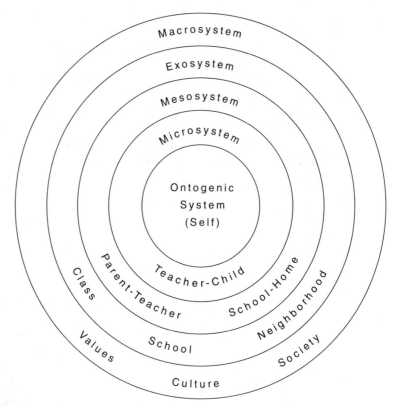

Figure 2.6
The five systems of the integrative framework

Source. Shea and Bauer (1987)

between settings (mesosystem), (d) group interactions (exosystem), and (e) society (macrosystem). The relationship of the five systems is depicted in Figure 2.6.

The ontogenic system includes the child's personality, skills, abilities, and competencies. Each student exhibits intraindividual factors for working the environment. Among the many factors included in this system are the child's intelligence, coping skills, and academic skills.

The microsystem includes the interrelationships within the immediate setting in which the individual is functioning, such as the teacher-child and child-child relationships in the classroom. It must be remembered that both teacher and child are actors and reactors in the classroom environment.

The mesosystem is the interrelationships between the settings in which the child is actually functioning at a particular point in time. It is a system of microsystems. The mesosystem may include relationships among school, home, church, and community.

The exosystem is the larger social system in which the microsystem and mesosystem are embedded. It includes both formal and informal social structures, such as law enforcement, recreational, political, and economic systems. Though a child may not actively participate in these systems or be directly influenced by them, they do influence the child's microsystem and mesosystem and thus, indirectly, the child.

The final system—the macrosystem—includes the overriding cultural beliefs and values as well as the general perceptions of the social institutions common to a particular culture in which the child is functioning. The beliefs, values, and attitudes of the macrosystem directly and indirectly influence the child's behavior. Areas of the macrosystem that may impact the child include society's perceptions of education, teachers, special education, children, children with disabilities, and so on.

As can be seen, the ontogenic system is related most closely with psychodynamic and biophysical conceptual frameworks. Interventions of an ontogenic nature are discussed in Chapters 7 and 8 under the heading biophysical interventions. The microsystem is closely related to the behavioral perspective and is discussed in Chapters 3 through 6. Interventions related directly and indirectly to the mesosystem are discussed in Chapter 8 under the heading environmental interventions and in Chapters 9 and 10.

Comprehensive Interventions and Keystone Behaviors

One recent shift in thinking about students who present challenging behaviors is that of *comprehensive interventions*. Comprehensive interventions take on two goals concurrently. First, they are aimed at producing rapid, lasting, and generalized reduction in challenging behaviors. Second, they are designed to increase the student's success at home, at school, or in the community at the same time (Horner & Carr, 1997). Comprehensive interventions are based on assessments that identify what factors can predict and maintain a problem behavior. In addition, several different interventions may be used at the same time, such as changing instruction, classroom structure, and the consequences of behavior. Comprehensive interventions are ways of acting; they are applied throughout the day.

The focus of comprehensive interventions is *keystone behaviors*. Keystone behaviors are those that have the potential to make the greatest positive effect on a student's behavior (Evans & Meyer, 1985). For example, a keystone behavior for a preschool child may be turn taking. If the child is able to wait, engage in a conversation without interrupting, or play a game alternating turns, he or she will be more successful. In the early grades, initiating and maintaining individual effort is a keystone behavior. Being able to begin an assigned task and take it through completion may have a significant impact on the student's learning and interactions. In upper grades, being able to take notes is a keystone skill that cuts across classes and settings. By identifying keystone behaviors, you are more likely to increase the student's potential for success.

TEACHER EFFECTIVENESS GUIDELINES

Teachers have a significant impact on their students' learning. In their analysis of the cumulative and residual effects of teachers on student achievement, Sanders and Rivers (1996) found that the effects of teachers on student achievement are both additive and cumulative with little potential for students to "catch up" with their peers. In addition, when teacher effectiveness increases, the lower-achieving students are the first to benefit. In their study utilizing the teacher evaluation model in Tennessee, Wright, Horn, and Sanders (1997) demonstrated that the most significant factor affecting student academic gain is teacher effectiveness. Unfortunately, the residual effects of ineffective teachers were still measurable 2 years later.

In a discussion of effective teaching of students with behavior problems, Webber, Anderson, and Otey (1991) proposed a dozen mind-sets to make the teaching-learning process more effective and less stressful for both teacher and students. Webber and associates state that it is essential for teachers to believe that all problems have solutions and that a single problem may have many solutions. Effective teachers are realistic in their perception of the problems they and their students confront. They teach from a realistic perspective and remain optimistic toward self, students, and the tasks that they confront. Teachers perceive students with a sensitivity that allows them to understand student behavior.

Effective teachers carefully monitor student progress. They recognize small changes in student learning and behavior and respond appropriately. They see conflict and crisis as manageable and as significant opportunities for learning.

In addition, effective teachers demonstrate to students that they truly care about them and their well-being. They do not demand or expect positive reinforcement from their students. They care about students and demonstrate that they care. Effective teachers are flexible and willing to consider and implement new techniques for instruction and management. They are willing to "risk" to help their students, to take chances, and to move into uncharted territory. They recognize that mistakes will be made by both teacher and learners and that mistakes should be seen as learning opportunities. They understand that academics are essential to the learning and success of their students and that the more involved students are in academic tasks, the less opportunity there is for inappropriate behavior.

According to Webber and associates, teachers of students with behavior problems must recognize that at times they may be psychologically hurt by their students. They must be prepared to suffer some pain in their interactions with students. The discomfort students with behavior problems inflict on others is frequently symptomatic of their personal emotional difficulties rather than a personal attack. Teachers should plan to accommodate such personal discomfort and to prevent it from becoming overwhelming.

Teachers must be careful not to become enmeshed in what Webber and associates refer to as "junk thoughts." They must think straight and eliminate irrational thoughts from their work with students. Finally, life in the classroom is often funny (i.e., humorous). Effective teachers understand that a sense of humor is essential to survival in the classroom.

According to McEwan (2001) and the Educational Research Service Bulletin (2001), there are 10 characteristics of an effective teacher. These are grouped into three categories: personal, teaching, and intellectual. The personal traits include the following:

- Dedication to teaching and facilitating learning and growth
- Caring for students, parents, colleagues, and personal well-being (effective teachers empathize with students, respect them, and treat them fairly)
- Exhibiting the capacity for leadership among students, parents, and colleagues

Teaching traits include the following:

- The capacity to organize and manage a classroom, behavior, and time
- Enthusiasm for teaching in the presentation of lessons to students
- The ability to motivate students
- Superior instruction

Intellectual traits include the following:

- An enjoyment of learning (reading, studying, and exploring)
- Being "in tune" with contemporary society and the cultures and subcultures in which teachers function
- Good mental health, leading to a rich and varied intellectual life

Lovitt (cited in ERIC Digest No. 3407, 1990) offers the following guidelines for managing inappropriate behavior in the classroom.

- Evaluate the environment and circumstances that maintain appropriate student behaviors
- Maintain data to determine whether the intervention is effective; compare data taken before the intervention was implemented with data taken after the intervention was implemented
- Consider various interventions for possible implementation; combinations of interventions or approaches are often more effective than a single intervention
- Teach the students new behaviors and ignore inappropriate behaviors unless they interfere with the individual's or group's learning

The following teacher effectiveness guidelines and discussion were derived from the works cited previously and the work of Tisdale (1985) and Shea and Bauer (1987). They are presented here primarily to stimulate thought and discussion.

Model and Leader

Outside the family, the teacher is in all probability the most important element in the child's environment. No other variable in the school appears to have a greater potential impact on a student than the interpersonal relationship developed between teacher and child.

Educational programs can be operated successfully under extremely adverse conditions (without adequate facilities, materials, equipment, funds, personnel, transportation, and so on). However, no program has ever been successfully operated without teachers who can and do relate positively and productively with children.

Personal Traits

Authentic teachers must be authentic people—real people. There are several personal traits that effective teachers appear to have in common:

- *Self-insight*. They know why they wish to work with children. They have an understanding of why they engage in the activities that make up their lifestyle.
- *Self-acceptance, self-appraisal, and realistic self-confidence*. They accept themselves as they are but seek to improve themselves. They are realistically confident in themselves and their capability to be effective but are not so overconfident of their abilities as to be considered naive.
- *Love and acceptance of children*. They love and are able to demonstrate their love for children. They understand that love and compliance are not identical. Sometimes love is demonstrated through discipline. They accept children as worthwhile human beings even though they must at times reject a child's behavior. They are capable of accepting, without reservation, individuals who are different from themselves—whether these individuals are short or tall, male or female, black, white, brown, red, or yellow, rotund or slim, deformed or normal, intelligent or retarded, or conforming, deviant, or radical.
- *An understanding of the behavior of children*. They not only understand human behavior at a cognitive level but are also able to empathize with children who manifest deviancy.
- *Curiosity and willingness to learn*. Like children, they are curious about their environment and enthusiastically explore it.
- *Patience with self and others*. They realize that they are imperfect and that they make mistakes. They also recognize this quality in others. They realize that learning is a slow, complex process for many individuals.
- *Flexibility*. They are flexible. They know when to change a lesson, intervention, or activity for the benefit of the students and when to change in order to attain a broader objective.
- *Humor*. They have a well-developed sense of humor. Mistakes, accidents, and humorous happenings occur in the classroom daily. Teachers who cannot laugh will certainly cry. They are capable of laughing at themselves and with their students. They never laugh at their students.

Teachers become models for the children they instruct. For better or worse, children will probably model at least some of their behavior after a teacher. It is of questionable value for children to have teachers who lack the capacity to understand and accept themselves and their students.

Knowledge and Skills

In addition to the personal traits just presented, effective teachers need specific knowledge and skills to successfully work with children. Following are the work-related characteristics of such individuals:

1. They establish routines in the daily lives of those in the classroom group.

2. They establish and enforce behavioral limits. They accomplish this difficult task without personal emotional involvement.

3. They do not permit emotionally charged situations to get out of control. They intrude themselves into conflicts and cause them to end with fairness to all involved.

4. They are consistent. All children are confused by teachers who condone a specific deviant behavior one day but do not condone the same deviation the next day.

5. They personally investigate an incident before acting rather than taking action on the basis of second- or third-person information and rumors. They confer with all children and adults involved in the incident prior to initiating action.

6. They ignore certain behaviors. Many unacceptable behaviors manifested by children are normal, age-appropriate behaviors. Others are simply not of sufficient potential impact to require a response by the teacher. Effective teachers are selective in responding to and ignoring behaviors.

7. They communicate verbally and nonverbally with their students. They talk *with* students, not *to* them. They learn that many of the concepts they considered to be universal knowledge are mysteries to many students. They are tuned in to the language and action of contemporary children and youth.

8. They learn to avoid personal confrontations with students when it is therapeutically appropriate. However, they confront an individual or group when necessary for the benefit of that person or group.

9. They learn to change activities and lessons for therapeutic purposes. They are not so personally committed to their lesson or subject that they fail to recognize student disinterest, dislike, and resistance.

10. They work both independently and as team members by communicating with colleagues and supervisors.

11. They make a direct appeal to students when the students' actions are confusing and discomforting to them personally. Frequently, a direct appeal to a child's basic humanness and common sense will solve behavior problems as quickly and as effectively as sophisticated behavior management interventions.

12. They provide each child under their supervision with security. Effective teachers communicate to students that they will be provided needed security from physical and psychological harm while under teacher supervision.

The beginning teacher seldom arrives in the classroom with fully developed behavior management skills in addition to instructional competence in all the needed subject matter areas. These skills are developed through experience and with the assistance of colleagues and supervisors.

Self-Discipline

Self-discipline is the desired result of all behavior management interventions presented in this text. Self-discipline, or the process of attaining control over one's personal behavior in a variety of circumstances in association with a variety of individuals and groups, is not an instantaneous process. Self-control is developed by human beings over many years and includes a number of developmental phases. During the process of attaining self-control, children naturally progress and regress as they and their environment change. A child may appear perfectly self-controlled one day and not the following day. Progress—maturing and growing—is often measured in slowly increasing lengths of time between occurrences of unacceptable behavior exhibited by the child.

The word *discipline* is derived from *disciple,* or follower of a master's teaching. This concept contains the idea of something learned from a teacher whose example the learner personally desires to model or imitate. The best discipline is derived from the respect and understanding of one human being for another. Discipline should be cooperative and voluntary, not simply imposed from above by an authority figure. Harsh, punitive, and negative disciplinary techniques are avoided in home, classroom, and school. The majority of children, especially those with behavior problems, have a poor or distorted self-image as a result of repeated failure and negative discipline. Many of these children have psychologically isolated themselves from the effects of negative discipline. Benign and positive interventions leading ultimately to self-discipline are suggested to teachers of both regular and special classes.

Time

All children, at one time or another during their school years, exhibit some behavior problems. This simple fact is all too frequently overlooked by teachers.

It is not unusual to have a teacher become extremely frustrated with a child because the child's deviant behavior does not respond to intervention immediately. This same frustration among teachers is also exhibited relative to academic training. Perhaps we are too impatient and too easily frustrated as a result of living most of our adult lives in a society conditioned to instant change, instant solutions to problems, and minimal frustration. The teacher must be patient and adjust to slow, time-consuming progress. Miracles and instant "cures" are few in number and difficult to observe when they do occur.

Children learn certain habitual ways of acting and reacting in their environment. These coping skills are developed over a span of years. Although unacceptable to others, they have been and continue to be more or less successful for the child. The child cannot and should not be forced to relinquish these coping mechanisms or survival behaviors immediately and begin using new, more acceptable and productive ways of coping.

To change deviant behavior requires time and energy. Teachers must be patient and focus on the child's progress rather than on the desired end product.

Objectives and Goals

Although teachers develop long-term goals for the children with whom they work, such goals are generally not a daily concern. Long-term goals are divided into a series of properly sequenced short-term objectives. These objectives provide structure for the daily, weekly, and monthly program of lessons and activities. The long-term goals provide the needed direction for the overall program for the individual child.

An important objective for each child enrolled in school should be to have a pleasant and positive experience. The program must be enjoyable and rewarding for the child, or it will not meet the normal childhood needs of seeking out and exploring the new, the different, the unknown, and the exciting.

Although the teacher has many academic remedial objectives for a particular child, these remedial tasks cannot be so demanding of the child's time and energy that school becomes drudgery. School must be a positive experience, offering the child a variety of opportunities to learn new skills and to participate in new activities of a nonacademic as well as an academic nature.

Empathy

Children with behavior difficulties do not need their teacher's sympathy. Ill-founded sympathy distorts the problems the teacher is attempting to help the child overcome. It places the teacher in an emotional situation that prohibits objective analysis of the child's behavior. A teacher who becomes too emotionally involved in a child's problem frequently functions in a biased, nonhelpful way. Such a teacher reacts to the child and others concerned with the child's welfare on a subjective rather than an objective level.

Although relationships based on sympathy are to be avoided in the educational setting, those based on empathy are necessary and should be encouraged. The teacher must be able to understand how the child feels and must be able to perceive the child's world from the child's point of view. This capacity is frequently referred to as "taking the position of the other."

The capacity to empathize permits the teacher to provide the child with direction, guidance, and support when such assistance is needed.

Expectations

Many years ago, we might have been told by our grandparents or parents, "As the twig is bent, so grows the tree." Some professionals ignore this simple truth. However, researchers have confirmed what our grandparents took for granted: Our expectations for children have a significant effect on their performance (Rubin & Balow, 1971).

This self-fulfilling prophecy means that, to a significant extent, if we believe a child is and will continue to be an incompetent, the probability is increased that the child will function as an incompetent. If we believe and communicate to a child that he or she will not learn to read, behave, compute, socialize, speak, and so on, the probability is significantly increased that the child will not accomplish these tasks.

Conversely, if we believe and communicate to a child that he or she will learn to be-have, read, play, socialize, and speak, the probability is increased that the child will respond to our expectations and learn these tasks.

As educators, we must maintain high but realistic expectations for students. Classrooms should be environments developed around a "can-do" attitude. Children must be told repeatedly throughout each day, "You can do it." "You know and I know you can do it." "You did it!" "Great!" "Super!" "Beautiful!"

Obviously, such a can-do attitude is meaningless and perhaps harmful unless the program is designed to ensure that the child receives the needed social-emotional support and skill training required to complete a task and fulfill our expectations.

Freedom and Independence

As a general policy, students should be encouraged to grow and learn as much as pos-sible without teacher assistance. Within realistic limits, anything that children can do for themselves, they should do. The instructor's function is to facilitate, not to dominate, the child's activity program. The teacher is available to instruct, demonstrate, assist, counsel, and offer encouragement. All young people need freedom to explore, inves-tigate, and implement new behaviors without adult interference if they are to grow. Of-ten, they will succeed in their efforts; occasionally, they will fail and require assistance.

Although constant failure is not recommended, occasional failure is a part of every person's life. The teacher cannot and should not shelter children from all fail-ure; at times they should be allowed to confront the logical consequences—success and failure—of their actions. It is the teacher's function to help the children learn to cope appropriately with both success and failure.

Complete freedom for many children becomes counterproductive. A child at-tends school to learn productive skills and behaviors. The teacher is responsible for planning the curriculum for or, preferably, in cooperation with the child. To do oth-erwise would be irresponsible and a disservice to the child. Behavior management and curriculum are partners: One is of little value without the other.

Democracy without structure, discipline, or predictability becomes anarchy. Children are learners; they are not adults skilled in the principles and practices of democracy. They must be encouraged to learn and apply democratic principles in the classroom and school under teacher supervision if they are to live by these prin-ciples as adults.

♦ SUMMARY

This chapter is designed to provide the reader with the theoretical foundations and teaching perspectives needed to enhance understanding of the practices and proce-dures applied in behavior management and presented in Chapters 3 through 8.

The relationship between four models of human behavior and behavior man-agement interventions evolving from these models is discussed. The four models are the psychodynamic, biophysical, environmental, and behavioral. The psychoeducational perspective, as part of the psychodynamic model, is reviewed in some detail. It is suggested that each of the models contributes to our understanding of human behavior and, therefore, should be familiar to teachers and parents. To increase understanding of the relationships between behavior and the models, an integrative framework is presented to facilitate the organization of the significant amount of data presented about each of the models.

The second part of the chapter focuses attention on several important teacher effectiveness guidelines. The effective or authentic teacher is discussed as a model and leader of students. The personal traits and the knowledge and skills needed by effective teachers are reviewed. Other important guidelines, including self-discipline, time, goals and objectives, empathy, expectations, and freedom and independence, are discussed.

In Chapters 3 through 6, the reader's attention is turned to processes and procedures associated with the behavioral model. Chapters 3 and 4 present the principles of reinforcement and the steps in the behavior change process, respectively. Chapters 5 and 6 present several behavior modification techniques applied to change behavior.

◆ PROJECTS

1. Using the professional literature, research and write a five- or six-page paper on one of the models of human behavior discussed in this chapter.

2. Using the professional literature, research and write a five- or six-page paper contrasting two of the models of human behavior discussed in this chapter.

3. Survey several teachers in your community and determine the personal traits and knowledge and skills they believe essential to functioning as an effective teacher of students with behavior problems.

4. Discuss the following topics in class: "Empathy, not sympathy," "Change takes time," and "Oh! Yes! I expect you to do it and I know you can."

◆ REFERENCES

Algozzine, B. (1980). The disturbing child: A matter of opinion. *Behavioral Disorders, 5*(2), 112–115.

Algozzine, B., Mercer, D. C., & Countermine, T. (1977). The effects of labels on behavior and teacher expectations. *Exceptional Children, 44*(2), 131–132.

Argyris, C., & Schon, D. A. (1992). *Theory in practice: Increasing professional effectiveness.* San Francisco: Jossey-Bass.

Bandura, A. (1969). *Principles of behavior modification.* New York: Holt, Rinehart & Winston.

Belsky, J. (1980). Child maltreatment: An ecological integration. *American Psychologist, 53,* 320–335.

Bronfenbrenner, U. (1977). Toward an experimental ecology of human development. *American Psychologist, 32,* 513–531.

Bronfenbrenner, U. (1979). *The ecology of human development.* Cambridge, MA: Harvard University Press.

Cruickshank, W., Bentzen, F., Ratzenburg, F., & Tannhauser, M. (1961). *A teaching methodology for brain-injured and hyperactive children.* Syracuse, NY: Syracuse University Press.

Des Jarlais, D. C. (1972). Mental illness of social deviance. In W. C. Rhodes & M. L. Tracy (Eds.), *A study of child variance: Vol. 1. Conceptual project in emotional disturbance* (pp. 259–322). Ann Arbor: University of Michigan Press.

Educational Research Service Bulletin. (2001). *Highly Effective Teachers, 29*(4), 1–2.

ERIC Digest No. 3407. (1990). *Managing inappropriate behavior in the classroom.* Reston, VA: ERIC Clearinghouse on Handicapped and Gifted Children. (ERIC Document Reproduction Service No. ED 371 506)

Erikson, E. H. (1963). *Childhood and society.* New York: W. W. Norton.

Evans, I. M., & Meyer, L. H. (1985). *An educative approach to behavior problems: A practical decision model for interventions with severely handicapped learners.* Baltimore: Paul H. Brookes.

Fernald, G. (1988). *Remedial techniques in basic school subjects.* New York: McGraw-Hill.

Fink, A. H. (1988). The psychoeducational philosophy: Programming implications for students with behavioral disorders. *Behavior in Our Schools, 2*(2), 8–13.

Forness, S. R. (1981). Concepts of learning and behavior disorders: Implications for research and practice. *Exceptional Children, 48,* 56–64.

Freud, S. (1989). *An outline of psychoanalysis* (Rev. ed.). New York: W. W. Norton.

Hawley, A. (1950). *Human ecology: A theory of community structure.* New York: Ronald Press.

Hewett, F. M. (1968). *The emotionally disturbed child in the classroom: A developmental strategy for educating children with maladaptive behavior.* Boston: Allyn & Bacon.

Hobbs, N. (1966). Helping disturbed children: Psychological and ecological strategies. *American Psychologist, 21*(12), 1105–1115.

Horner, R. H., & Carr, E. G. (1997). Behavioral support for students with severe disabilities: Functional assessment and comprehensive intervention. *Journal of Special Education, 31,* 84–104.

Long, N. J., Morse, W. C., & Newman, R. G. (1980). *Conflict in the classroom* (4th ed.). Belmont, CA: Wadsworth.

Marmor, J., & Pumpian-Mindlin, E. (1950). Toward an integrative conception of mental disorders. *Journal of Nervous and Mental Disease, 3,* 19–29.

McEwan, E. K. (2001). *Ten traits of highly effective teachers: How to hire, coach, and mentor successful teachers.* Thousand Oaks, CA: Corwin.

Morse, W. C. (1985). *The education and treatment of socioemotionally impaired children and youth.* Syracuse, NY: Syracuse University Press.

Munroe, R. L. (1955). *Schools of psychoanalytic thought: An exposition, critique, and attempt at integration.* New York: Holt, Rinehart & Winston.

National Foundation–March of Dimes. (1975). *Birth defects: The tragedy and the hope.* White Plains, NY: Author.

Nichols, P. (1984). Down the up staircase: The teacher as therapist. In J. Grosenick, S. Huntze, E. McGinnis, & C. Smith (Eds.), *Social/affective intervention in behavioral disorders* (pp. 43–66). Des Moines: State of Iowa Department of Public Instruction.

Park, R. E., & Burgess, E. W. (1925). *The city.* Chicago: University of Chicago Press.

Parsons, T. (1964). *The social system.* New York: Free Press.

Rhodes, W. C., & Paul, J. L. (1978). *Emotionally disturbed and deviant children: New views and approaches.* Upper Saddle River, NJ: Prentice Hall.

Rhodes, W. C., & Tracy, M. L. (Eds.). (1972). *A study of child variance: Vol. 2. Interventions.* Ann Arbor: University of Michigan Press.

Roberts, T. B. (1975). *Four psychologies applied to education: Freudian-behavioral-humanistic-transpersonal.* Cambridge, MA: Schenkman Publishing.

Rubin, R., & Balow, B. (1971). Learning and behavior disorders: A longitudinal study. *Exceptional Children, 38,* 293–298.

Sanders, W. L., & Rivers, J. C. (1996). *Cumulative and residual effects of teachers on future student academic achievement* (Research Progress Report). Knoxville: University of Tennessee Value-Added Research and Assessment Center.

Sarason, I. G., Glaser, E. M., & Fargo, G. A. (1972). *Reinforcing productive classroom behavior.* New York: Behavioral Publications.

Schroeder, S. R., & Schroeder, C. (1982). Organic factors. In J. L. Paul and B. Epanchin (Eds.), *Emotional disturbance in children* (pp. 152–183). Columbus, OH: Merrill.

Scott, M. (1980). Ecological theory and methods for research in special education. *Journal of Special Education, 4,* 279–294.

Shea, T. M., & Bauer, A. M. (1987). *Teaching children and youth with behavior disorders* (2nd ed.). Upper Saddle River, NJ: Prentice Hall.

Shea, T. M., & Bauer, A. M. (1997). *An introduction to special education: A social systems perspective* (2nd ed.). Madison, WI: Brown & Benchmark.

Skinner, B. F. (1971). *Beyond freedom and dignity.* New York: Alfred A. Knopf.

Swap, S. M., Prieto, A. G., & Harth, R. (1982). Ecological perspective of the emotionally disturbed child. In R. L. McDowell, G. W. Adamson, & F. H. Wood (Eds.), *Teaching emotionally disturbed children* (pp. 70–98). Boston: Little, Brown.

Thomas, E. D., & Marshall, M. J. (1977). Clinical evaluation and coordination of services: An ecological model. *Exceptional Children, 44,* 16–22.

Thurman, S. K. (1977). Congruence of behavioral ecologies: A model for special education programming. *Journal of Special Education, 11,* 329–333.

Tisdale, P. C. (1985). The teacher's ten commandments. *The Directive Teacher, 7*(1), 6–8.

Webber, J., Anderson, T., & Otey, L. (1991). Teacher mindsets for surviving in 80 classrooms. *Intervention in School and Clinic, 26*(5), 288–292.

Wolpe, J. (1961). The systematic desensitization treatment of neuroses. *Journal of Nervous and Mental Disease, 132,* 189–203.

Wood, F. H. (1978). Punishment and special educators: Some concluding comments. In F. H. Wood & K. C. Lakin (Eds.), *Punishment and aversive stimulation in special education: Legal, theoretical and practical issues in their use with emotionally disturbed children and youth* (pp. 119–122). Minneapolis: University of Minnesota Press.

Wright, S. P., Horn, S. P., & Sanders, W. L. (1997). Teacher and classroom context effects on student achievement: Implications for teacher evaluation. *Journal of Personnel Evaluation in Education, 11*(1), 57–67.

3

Principles of Behavior Modification

Consequences
Continuous schedule
Differential reinforcement
Discrimination
Extinction
Fixed interval schedule
Fixed ratio schedule
Generalization
Negative reinforcement
Positive reinforcement
Principles of reinforcement
Punishment
Reinforcers
Schedule of reinforcement
Target behavior
Variable interval schedule
Variable ratio schedule

After completing this chapter, you will be able to do the following:

1. Discuss and exemplify the principles of reinforcement.

2. Identify and illustrate the consequences of behavior.

3. Understand and characterize the concepts of generalization and discrimination.

4. Describe and give examples of the most common schedules of reinforcement.

◆ ◆ ◆

Mr. Rodrigues has completed his first semester as principal of San Jose Mission High School. It has been a challenging semester for the new principal, but something is not going right among the faculty and staff. The morale of the office staff is low, teachers are not motivated, students are going through the motion of learning, and the community acts as if it doesn't know the school exists. Mr. Rodrigues wonders how he might create a more positive, exciting educational atmosphere. Conversations among staff and teachers suggest that Mr. Rodrigues is an administrator who believes that if a person is being paid for a job, that should be ample reward. The teachers and staff think their efforts are not appreciated. The students appear to reflect the attitudes of the staff and teachers.

Maybe if Mr. Rodrigues were taught something about the basic principles of reinforcement, his relations with his staff, students, and the community would improve.

Linda has about had it with her husband, Bob, and football. Saturday football, Sunday football, Monday night football, Tuesday night football from Canada, Wednesday night college football highlights, Thursday night pro football highlights, and Friday night football forecasts are more than she can take. In the prime of her life, she has lost Bob to over-sized giants who wear funny uniforms with team names like Lions, Falcons, Raiders, Bears, Fighting Irish, Trojans, and Pioneers, some of which stand in front of television cameras and wave, "Hi, Mom."

Linda has attended workshops for football widows. She has gone so far as to have the name and number of Bob's favorite player printed on a very "naughty" nightgown and dance seductively in front of the television, only to be told, "Linda, would you please move; I can't see the game."

Is it possible that Linda could change Bob's behavior? Perhaps if Linda knew something about the basic principles of reinforcement, she could become the football player in Bob's life.

Most persons go through life unaware of the many factors in their lives and the influences these factors have on the way they behave. They appear unaware of the fact that as "normal" human beings they tend to be attracted to those experiences that are pleasurable and avoid those that are not pleasurable. Most persons receive pleasure from smiles, positive comments, a pat on the back, an excellent grade in a course, and a bonus in their paychecks. They avoid situations where physical or mental pain is inflicted, and they avoid associating with persons they don't like to be around.

"What you do is influenced by what follows what you do" (Sarason, Glaser, & Fargo, 1972). According to Downing, Moran, Myles, and Ormsbee (1991), "Individual behavior is influenced by what occurs immediately before (antecedent) and after (consequent) the action or response" (p. 86). The consequences and probable consequences of behavior, more than any other factor, determine the behavior that an individual exhibits (Shea & Bauer, 1987). In the field of behavior modification, the consequences of behavior are called *reinforcers*. These reinforcers may increase or decrease behavior (Morris, 1985).

Reinforces can be classified in a number of ways. Basically, they are classified as tangible or primary reinforcers (food, drinks, and tokens) and social or secondary reinforcers (praise, smiles, and other signs of approval).

For example, why does a child attend school? What reinforces school-attending behavior? A child may go to school because of the following:

1. It is warmer in the school than in the home.
2. The people at school give the child more attention than the people at home or in the neighborhood.
3. The child plans after-school activities with friends during the morning recess.
4. The child eats the hot meal provided each noon by the school.

It can be understood, then, that a child may attend school for both tangible (heat and food) and social (attention and friends) reinforcers.

Reinforcers may be positive (rewarding, pleasure giving) or negative (aversive, punishing). Tangible and social reinforcers may be positive reinforcers, that is, desirable consequences for which behavior is exhibited. Or they may be negative, that is, undesirable consequences for which behavior is inhibited.

A child who considers school aversive might exhibit inappropriate behavior in an attempt to avoid school. If the child were successful in this attempt, the inappropriate behavior would increase; thus, school-attending behavior would decrease. For example, two situations that would result in an increase in school-avoiding behavior are the following:

1. The child is allowed to remain at home during the school day because he or she complains of being ill.
2. The child is allowed to remain at home because a homework assignment is not completed.

If the child were not allowed to avoid school by exhibiting these behaviors, they would probably decrease.

Punishment would also be effective in getting a child to attend school. Among the punishments that could be employed are (a) a reprimand from the child's parent; (b) loss of allowance or the use of a bike; and (c) loss of privileges, such as watching television or attending the movies.

The consequences of behavior, then, are the determinants of behavior. Human beings tend to repeat behaviors that are, in their perception, rewarded or praised. They tend not to repeat behaviors that are, in their perception, punished.

In the remainder of this chapter, the basic principles of reinforcement are presented and exemplified. These principles can be systematically applied by the teacher in the classroom and by the parents in the home.

The effective and efficient application of behavior modification techniques involves more than the simple memorization and application of the principles of reinforcement. For effective implementation, it is necessary that the teacher or parent be intuitive, creative, and empathetic.

PRINCIPLES OF REINFORCEMENT

The *principles of reinforcement* are a set of rules to be applied in the behavior change process. The successful behavior modifier relies heavily on these principles when planning and implementing a behavior change program.

Principle 1: Reinforcement Is Dependent on the Exhibition of the Target Behavior

If we are attempting, via planned intervention, to change a specific behavior (i.e., a *target behavior*) in an individual, we must reinforce *only* the behavior we are planning to change and only after that behavior is exhibited. In planning and implementing an intervention, we must *take caution to ensure that nontarget behaviors are not reinforced unwittingly*.

♦ *Examples*

Ms. Jones was attempting to increase Bill's in-seat behavior in her classroom. It had been ascertained through systematic observation that Bill received attention from her for out-of-seat behavior. When Bill was out of his seat, Ms. Jones proceeded to yell or otherwise reprimand him. Although Bill was receiving negative attention (in Ms. Jones's perception), his attempts to receive attention—positive or negative—were apparently being met in this situation. Bill's inappropriate behavior (being out of his seat) kept increasing as Ms. Jones's behavior (yelling or scolding) kept increasing.

Ms. Long was faced with a problem similar to that of Ms. Jones—Jerry's in-seat behavior. She was reported to have said that she had to dust Jerry's chair every morning because he never used it.

At first she applied Ms. Jones's technique, that is, yelling. Then she planned a behavior modification intervention. She would totally ignore Jerry's out-of-seat behavior. She would in *no* way reinforce this particular inappropriate behavior. However, whenever Jerry's overactive bottom hit his assigned seat, she would immediately reward him. She would praise him in front of the whole class, if necessary, and pat his shoulder.

As a result of this intervention, not only did Jerry learn to sit in his seat, but Ms. Long discovered she liked him.

In the second example, the approach was effective in bringing about the desired behavior. In the first example, however, Ms. Jones is still yelling, and Bill is still high on all the attention he is receiving.

In conclusion, Principle 1 suggests that if we desire to modify a specific behavior, we must reinforce *only* that behavior and *only* after it is exhibited.

Principle 2: The Target Behavior Is to Be Reinforced Immediately After It Is Exhibited

The importance of presenting the reinforcer immediately after the target behavior is exhibited cannot be overstressed. This principle is especially true during the initial stages of the behavior change process, when we are attempting to establish a new behavior. Inappropriate and nonfunctional behaviors occur from time to time in every individual's behavioral repertoire. If reinforcers are delayed in a planned intervention program, nontarget behaviors (rather than the target behavior) may be accidentally or unwittingly reinforced, thus increasing the probability that a nontarget behavior will be exhibited in the future.

◆ *Example*

Mr. Riley was attempting to increase the number of math problems Pat completed during the period. He planned to reward Pat immediately after he completed each assigned group of problems. The number of problems in each group would be increased on a weekly basis if Pat responded to the intervention as predicted.

Mr. Riley was very inconsistent in the presentation of the reinforcer (tokens). As a result, Pat spent considerable time waiting at his desk and waving his hand frantically to gain his teacher's attention.

After a few weeks, it was found that the intervention program was ineffective in increasing the number of completed problems. However, Pat now sat at his desk for much longer periods of time with a bored expression.

Mr. Riley became aware of Pat's behavior and of his personal inconsistency. He began to reinforce Pat immediately after Pat had completed each group of problems. Within a short time, Pat was completing his problems and had doubled his production.

When attempting to establish a new behavior or increase the frequency of an existing behavior, we must reinforce that behavior as soon as it occurs.

Principle 3: During the Initial Stages of the Behavior Change Process, the Target Behavior Is Reinforced Each Time It Is Exhibited

If newly acquired behavior is to be sustained at the appropriate frequency rate, the reinforcer must be administered each time the behavior is exhibited. Frequently beginning behavior modifiers reinforce new but not yet habituated behaviors with such inconsistency and so infrequently that the child becomes confused, and the target behavior does not become an established part of the child's behavioral repertoire.

♦   *Examples*

Ms. Traber worked several months with Matt, rewarding approximations of a desired behavior (in this case, a complete sentence). Finally, after 6 months, Matt said a complete sentence: "I want a candy." Matt was immediately rewarded with a candy, and for the next several weeks he consumed many candies; he was given many opportunities to receive the reward. In addition, during this phase of the behavior change process, Matt increased his variety of complete sentences to include "I want a glass of milk," "I want some juice," "I want some soda," "I want a puzzle," and the like.

Russell never requested any materials or assistance in the junior high school classroom without whining, screaming, or both. He would yell, "I want my paper" or "Give me some help." Mr. Hicks had taken about as much of this behavior as he could tolerate. He decided to ignore all whining and screaming from Russell. Russell's initial reaction to being ignored dramatically increased his inappropriate behavior, but Mr. Hicks stuck to the plan.

After 2 weeks of mutual frustration, Russell raised his hand one day during social studies. He politely requested Mr. Hicks's assistance. He immediately received the assistance, verbal praise, and a pat on the back. Mr. Hicks was very pleased with Russell (and himself). A mutual admiration society developed and continued.

Mr. Hicks then focused his attention on the problem of another student in the class. As a result, Mr. Hicks became an inconsistent reinforcer, and Russell began whining and screaming anew.

Mr. Hicks forgot that Russell's inappropriate behavior had been learned over 12 or 13 years and could not be changed overnight and after only a few successes.

A newly acquired, unconditioned, or not fully habituated behavior cannot be sustained if it is not reinforced each time it occurs. Consistent reinforcement during the *initial* stages of the behavior change process is essential.

Principle 4: When the Target Behavior Reaches a Satisfactory Level, It Is Reinforced Intermittently

Although this principle may appear to be a contradiction of Principle 3, it is not. The behavior modifier must be consistent in the application of inconsistent (intermittent) reinforcement *after* the target behavior is established at a satisfactory level. This practice appears to be the way in which a newly acquired behavior can be firmly established and become self-sustaining.

Once a target behavior has been established at a satisfactory level, the presentation of the reinforcer is changed from continuous to intermittent. This change in the reinforcer presentation increases the probability that the behavior will be maintained at a satisfactory level. It appears that if the student whose behavior is being changed does not know exactly when the reinforcer will be given but does know reinforcement will occur, the target behavior will continue to be exhibited at a satisfactory level.

◆ *Examples*

Ms. Williams wished to increase Phil's frequency of voluntary responses during current event discussions. In this situation, poker chips were used as a reinforcer. The chips could be saved and cashed in at the end of the discussion period for a tangible reward from the class store.

Initially, Ms. Williams reinforced Phil each time he volunteered a response during the discussion. After several weeks, Phil's frequency of responses was at a satisfactory level; that is, it was equal or nearly equal to the average frequency of responses of the other members of the discussion groups. At this point in the behavior modification process, Ms. Williams changed from giving continuous to intermittent reinforcement.

With intermittent reinforcement, Phil's behavior remained at a high level. Phil became aware that he would be rewarded when he responded, but not every time. It also became evident to Ms. Williams that Phil was enjoying his participation in the class discussions.

Mr. Jones and Ms. Walker had similar problems in their classroom groups. In Mr. Jones's room, Jared would not participate in class discussions. In Ms. Walker's room, Herman presented the same problem.

Mr. Jones wished to increase the frequency of Jared's responses during group discussions. He introduced an intervention similar to the one used by Ms. Williams in the previous example. However, once Jared had attained an acceptable level of performance, Mr. Jones discontinued all reinforcement. Because of the lack of reinforcement, Jared's newly acquired behavior decreased.

Ms. Walker also initiated an intervention program to increase Herman's level of participation. Ms. Walker kept Herman on the continuous reinforcement schedule until he became bored with the tokens and the tangible rewards he could purchase with them. Like Mr. Jones's program, Ms. Walker's was ineffective. Herman's participation decreased to its original level. He remained an infrequent participant in group discussions.

The reinforcement schedules most commonly applied in behavior modification intervention are discussed later in this chapter.

Principle 5: If Tangible Reinforcers Are Applied, Social Reinforcers Are Always Applied with Them

All reinforcement, even during the initial phases of the behavior change process, must include the presentation of social and tangible reinforcers simultaneously if a tangible reinforcer is used. The purpose of the behavior change process is to help the student perform the target behavior not for a tangible reward but for the satisfaction of personal achievement. As discussed in the previous chapter, the goal of all behavior management is self-control or self-discipline.

If tangible reinforcers, such as tokens, chips, candy, stars, smiling faces, or checks, are presented, they must always be accompanied by a social reward, such as a smile, a pat on the back, praise, or a wink. In this way, the child associates the social reinforcer with the tangible reinforcer. As the behavior change process progresses, the tangible reinforcer is extinguished (phased out), and the target behavior is maintained by social reinforcers alone. If the change process is effective, behavior is maintained by self-satisfaction, occasional unplanned social reinforcers, and delayed tangible rewards.

◆ *Examples*

When Ms. Williams was initially attempting to increase Phil's discussion group participation (see example in previous section), she provided Phil with verbal praise and a token each time he exhibited the desired behavior. However, when Phil was placed on an intermittent schedule, Ms. Williams continued to provide consistent social reinforcement but only occasional token reinforcement. During the final phase of the behavior change process, Phil was provided only intermittent social reinforcement to maintain the desired behavior.

Mr. Whiteface wanted to modify George's hand-raising behavior. A grape was given to George every time he raised his hand. The reward was delivered by a dispenser affixed to George's desk. When George raised his hand, Mr. Whiteface would push a button to activate the dispenser and release a grape.

In this way, Mr. Whiteface rewarded George consistently. In addition, he gave George social reinforcers for the new behavior. He would say, "That was very good, George"; "I like the way you are raising your hand, George"; or "Fine," "Great," "Good."

After 6 months on the program, George functioned with intermittent social reinforcement only. The dispensing of grapes had been terminated, and George's hand-raising behavior remained at a high rate.

Practitioners are cautioned to apply this important principle when using reinforcers: *Always apply tangible and social reinforcers simultaneously if tangible reinforcers are used.*

Potentially effective reinforcers, both tangible and social, are discussed in Chapter 4.

CONSEQUENCES OF BEHAVIOR

Behavioral *consequences* (results) have a direct influence on the behavior a child exhibits. Behavior can be modified, that is, increased, initiated, or extinguished, by systematic manipulation of its consequences. The possible consequences of human behavior are classified as positive reinforcement, extinction, negative reinforcement, and punishment.

In Table 3.1 are several examples of (a) classification of the consequence, (b) appropriate and inappropriate behavior, (c) the consequence of that behavior (not necessarily a planned intervention), and (d) the probable effect of the consequence on the behavior in the future. The reader is encouraged to study Table 3.1 carefully.

Table 3.1
Behavior: Consequence, probable effect, and classification

Classification	Original Behavior Exhibited	Consequence	Probable Effect on the Original Behavior in the Future
Positive reinforcement	Jane cleans her room	Jane's parents praise her	Jane will continue to clean her room
Positive reinforcement	Shirley brushes her teeth after meals	Shirley receives a nickel each time	Shirley will continue to brush her teeth after meals
Extinction	Jim washes his father's car	Jim's car-washing behavior is ignored	Jim will stop washing his father's car
Positive reinforcement	Alton works quietly at his seat	The teacher praises and rewards Alton	Alton will continue to work quietly at his seat
Punishment	Gwenn sits on the arm of the chair	Gwenn is reprimanded each time she sits on the arm of the chair	Gwenn will not sit on the arm of the chair
Negative reinforcement	Bob complains that older boys consistently beat him up, and he refuses to attend school	Bob's parents allow him to remain at home because of his complaints	Bob will continue to miss school
Punishment	Elmer puts Elsie's pigtails in the paint box	The teacher takes away Elmer's recess	Elmer will not put Elsie's pigtails in the paint box
Extinction	Shirley scolds Joe	Joe ignores Shirley's scolding	Shirley will stop scolding Joe
Negative reinforcement	Jason complains of headaches when it is time to do homework	Jason is allowed to go to bed without doing his homework	Jason will have headaches whenever there is homework to do

Positive Reinforcement

Positive reinforcement is the presentation of a desirable reinforcer after a behavior has been exhibited. The reinforcer, or consequences of behavior, tends to increase or sustain the frequency or duration with which the behavior is exhibited in the future (Alberto & Troutman, 1990). Everyone receives positive reinforcement throughout each day. The process of positive reinforcement involves increasing the probability of a behavior recurring by reinforcing it with a reinforcer that is appropriate and meaningful to the individual (Downing et al., 1991). A reinforcer is reinforcing only if it is perceived as reinforcing by the individual.

♦ *Examples*

Kevin has received a superior report card and is praised by his parents and brother. As a result of the positive reinforcer (praise), the probability of Kevin's continuing to study hard and receive superior report cards in the future is increased. If Kevin's report card were ignored or severely criticized because of a single poor grade, the probability of his continuing his efforts and receiving superior report cards in the future would be decreased.

Ms. Pompey has identified stars as positive reinforcers with her classroom group. She puts a star on Cynthia's paper because Cynthia has successfully completed her homework assignment. Cynthia enjoys receiving stars. By placing a star on Cynthia's paper, Ms. Pompey knows she is increasing the probability of Cynthia's completing her homework assignments in the future.

Extinction

Extinction is the removal of a reinforcer that is sustaining or increasing a behavior (Alberto & Troutman, 1990). Extinction is an effective method for decreasing undesirable behaviors exhibited by individuals (Downing et al., 1991). Unplanned and unsystematically applied extinction techniques have been naturally applied throughout history. For example, parents tend to *ignore* many unacceptable behaviors exhibited by children, such as roughhousing, arguing, and showing reluctance to go to bed, in the hope that these behaviors will decrease in frequency. The ineffectiveness of ignoring as an unplanned intervention is frequently a result of the inconsistency of its application rather than its inadequacy as a behavior change technique. We insist that there be no roughhousing or arguing and that the child be in bed at the designated time one day but do not insist on these rules the next day. The inconsistency on our part, as a teacher or parent, tends to confuse children and reinforce the unacceptable behavior.

Extinction involves the removal or withdrawal of the reinforcer responsible for maintaining behavior. In the classroom setting, the target behavior will be extinguished once the reinforcer has been withdrawn for a sufficient period of time.

♦ *Examples*

John, a ninth grader, was always making funny sounds with his mouth in Mrs. Rawlin's class. These activities got him a lot of attention not only from his peers but also from Mrs. Rawlin. She usually stopped the class and told John how immature he was behaving for his age and that he was making a fool of himself. The class responded with laughter. John laughed the loudest. After several meetings with the school counselor about John's classroom behavior, Mrs. Rawlin agreed to implement another approach.

The next time John made a funny sound, Mrs. Rawlin told the class to ignore him and that those students who did would be rewarded with free time. John continued to make sounds for a few days, but because of the lack of attention from peers and teacher, the behavior began to change. Over the course of 7 school days, John's behavior was extinguished, and Mrs. Rawlin was able to conduct her class without disruptions. John is now receiving attention from his peers and Mrs. Rawlin for appropriate behavior.

Eight-year-old Robin was constantly tattling on every child who committed the slightest transgression within his purview. Robin's teacher, Ms. Fye, was reinforcing Robin's behavior by responding and attending to him when he tattled on others. Finally, she planned an intervention program employing extinction to decrease Robin's behavior. She would ignore all his tattling.

Each time Robin approached her to tattle on a classmate, Ms. Fye did one of the following:

1. Intervened before Robin had an opportunity to tattle and focused his attention on another topic (picture, book, and so on)

2. Turned her back on him and attended to another child who was performing appropriately

3. Turned her back on him and walked away without any sign of recognition

During the initial phase of the behavior change process. Robin's tattling increased for a brief period. As the program continued, the behavior decreased and was extinguished (Figure 3.1).

During the extinction process, there are two behavior response phases. During the initial phase, immediately after the reinforcer sustaining the behavior has been removed, the target behavior usually increases or decreases dramatically. During the second phase, the target behavior changes systematically.

The response during the initial phase is a natural, human one that occurs when an individual is suddenly confronted with a situation in which established methods of gaining goals become nonfunctional. It is natural to become confused under such conditions and continue to try the previously effective method of attaining a goal.

It is during this initial phase that beginning practitioners frequently throw up their hands in frustration and abandon a project. However, if they persist, the behavior will in all probability extinguish.

Figure 3.1
Frequency of Robin's tattling behavior a week before the removal of the reinforcer and 2 weeks afterward

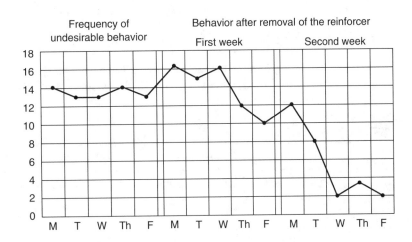

Robin's rate of tattling before and during the extinction process is presented in Figure 3.1. The reader should note that Robin's tattling behavior increased on the first 3 days of extinction, then decreased dramatically during the next 7 days.

The teacher or parent should be patient and consistent; the behavior will change.

Negative Reinforcement

Negative reinforcement is the removal of an already operating aversive stimulus (negative reinforcer). As a consequence of the removal of the aversive stimulus, the target behavior is strengthened. Several examples of this process are presented in this section and in Tables 3.1 (p. 65) and 3.2.

Axelrod (1983) has described the technique of negative reinforcement in the classroom setting as "an operation in which a student performs a behavior and the teacher removes something the student dislikes" (p. 8). Downing et al. (1991) concur with this assertion.

As stated earlier, negative reinforcement is the removal of an aversive stimulus in an effort to change the frequency of a behavior. In contrast, punishment is the addition of an aversive stimulus or the subtraction (taking away) of a pleasurable item or activity in an effort to change the frequency of a behavior.

Axelrod provides two excellent examples of negative reinforcement.

♦ Example

A group of students are working very diligently at their desks *after* the teacher has stated that they will not be required to do homework assignments that evening if their classroom assignments are completed during the allotted time during the school day.

In this example, the homework assignment, which was already given by the teacher, is the aversive stimulus (most students perceive homework as aversive). It is removed, and as a result the students' in-classroom work is increased.

♦ Example

Jimmy is in the process of twisting Tommy's arm. This situation is causing Tommy considerable pain. Jimmy says, "Say 'Uncle Dudley-Do-Good,' and I'll let you go." Tommy, in

Table 3.2
Effects of consequences

	Positive Reinforcer	**Aversive Stimulus**
Add	Positive reinforcement (behavior increases)	Punishment (behavior decreases)
Remove	Extinction (behavior decreases)	Negative reinforcement (behavior increases or decreases)

agony, screams, "Uncle Dudley-Do-Good." Jimmy, with a smile on his innocent face, releases Tommy's arm, and the pain ends.

In this example, arm twisting, which was already giving Tommy pain (and Jimmy pleasure), is the aversive stimulus. It is removed, and as a result Tommy's comfort level is increased.

The following example is provided to offer additional clarification of negative reinforcement.

♦ *Example*

Mr. and Mrs. Reynolds have a 2-year-old daughter, Alice, who wakes up crying (aversive stimulus) in the middle of the night. She wants to sleep with Mommy and Daddy. In an effort to get their sleep and stop Alice from crying, the parents permit her to sleep with them (thus removing the aversive stimulus of crying). By allowing Alice to sleep in their bed, the parents are increasing both their and Alice's sleeping behavior.

However, the parents' method of stopping Alice's crying (allowing Alice to sleep with them) actually reinforces the frequency of the crying.

Cipani (1995) suggests that there is empirical research that links inappropriate behaviors during instructional tasks with factors *other* than teacher attention. Research has found that inappropriate behavior may be maintained because of its effect on the lesson or assignment.

♦ *Example*

Mrs. McGinnis has given Marylou a spelling assignment. Marylou has a reading problem. For her, the assignment is very aversive. She hates spelling. She has tried over and over to learn her spelling words, without success. Immediately after being given the assignment, Marylou becomes restless and goes off task. She begins to tap her pencil on the desk, hum loudly, and tap her foot.

Mrs. McGinnis becomes distracted by Marylou's inappropriate behavior and reprimands her. Marylou answers the teacher back and as a consequence is sent to the back of the classroom to sit in the "think about your behavior" chair. She leaves her spelling on her desk.

In this example, spelling is an aversive or a negative reinforcer for Marylou. It is interfering with her exhibition of appropriate classroom behavior.

Cipani suggests three questions that teachers should ask to diagnose whether negative reinforcement is a factor in maintaining inappropriate behavior:

- Does the inappropriate behavior serve to stop instruction or the completion of an assignment?
- Does the learner have the skill and ability to complete the assignment task?

- Does the frequency of inappropriate behavior increase when specific instructional conditions are present?

Finally, Cipani suggests that to remediate behavior problems caused by negative reinforcement, the teacher either (a) provide the student with a strong incentive to engage in the aversive task or (b) develop the student's level of competency in the task to a point at which it becomes less aversive.

Punishment

Punishment, a group of behavioral reduction procedures, appears to be the most frequently used of the behavior change techniques. The behavior reduction procedures include, from the least to the most intrusive and restrictive, differential reinforcement, extinction, verbal aversives, response cost, time-out, overcorrection, and physical aversives (Kerr & Nelson, 1989). Each of these procedures is presented in detail in Chapter 6.

Although it is frequently used with children, punishment is perhaps the least effective of the behavior modification interventions discussed in this text. Those using punishment have been reinforced by its immediate result; however, it has been determined that the long-term effects of punishment are limited. McDaniel (1980) points out that punishment tends to *suppress* the undesirable behavior rather than extinguish it. This suppression is of short duration, and frequently the behavior recurs in the absence of the punisher.

Punishment is viewed by the behavior modification practitioner as two distinct operations. Punishment is accomplished by the *addition* of an aversive stimulus to the environment. Examples of this operation are paddling, electric shock, additional homework, and the like. Punishment may also be seen as the *subtraction* (taking away) of a pleasurable item or activity. Examples of this operation include loss of extracurricular activities, recess, and the like. Punishment is not to be confused with extinction (see earlier section).

♦ Examples

Anita, one of Mr. Cooper's fifth-grade pupils, constantly talks in class. She disturbs her classmates when she should be completing her assignments. To stop Anita's inappropriate behavior, Mr. Cooper scolds her and has her stand in the corner of the classroom with a dunce cap on her head.

These techniques are very effective while Mr. Cooper is in the room. However, when Mr. Cooper leaves the classroom for whatever reason, the long-term ineffectiveness of punishment becomes apparent. On these occasions, Anita goes around the room yelling and screaming, to the glee of her classmates.

Joe is in Mr. Dee's junior high school class for the socially maladjusted. Joe enjoys using four-letter words. In addition, he takes great pleasure in the expression on Mr. Dee's face when he tosses a few well-chosen words at him. Mr. Dee believed he could eliminate this behavior via the 3-P method, that is, a punishing paddle on the posterior. He designed the following intervention, which he explained to Joe:

"Each time you swear in my presence, you will assume the hands-on-ankles position and receive four swats."

Mr. Dee's intervention has had the following results:

1. Joe's language has improved in Mr. Dee's presence but not in his absence (according to a burnt-eared substitute).
2. Mr. Dee has a very tired arm.
3. Joe continues to use his vocabulary on Mr. Dee to gain attention, especially when there are visitors in the classroom.
4. Others in the class encourage Joe to curse so that they can enjoy the circus.

It can be stated that *some punishments will remove some unacceptable behaviors* (Shea, Bauer, & Lynch, 1989). It has been found, however, that when a punished behavior recurs, it usually does so at a rate higher than before the punishment was originally imposed. Another concern associated with punishment is its potential and actual effect on the physical and emotional health of the child. In some cases, punishment may cause emotional problems. The fact that the punished child identifies the punishment with the punisher rather than with the inappropriate behavior should be of great concern to teachers and parents who, as previously discussed, are models for children. Children who are punished or abused often punish or abuse their children. The results of punishment do not appear sufficient to justify its use as a behavior change agent.

Effects of Consequences

A thorough understanding of the relationships among the four basic consequences of behavior is a primary requisite for the effective application of behavior modification principles and techniques.

In general, positive reinforcement *increases* the target behavior; punishment and extinction *decrease* the target behavior. Negative reinforcement may *increase or decrease* behavior, depending on the particular target behavior (see Table 3.2).

Generalization

Generalization, or the transfer of learning, is the process by which a behavior reinforced in the presence of one stimulus will be exhibited in the presence of another stimulus (Morris, 1985). The generalization process is an important element of learning. If the process of generalization did not occur, each response would have to be learned in every specific situation … "transfer of behavior does not occur automatically, but needs to be planned and programmed as part of the training process" (Vaughn, Bos, & Lund, 1986, p. 176).

According to Landrum and Lloyd (1992), when modifying the behavior of children and youth who have emotional and behavioral disorders, practitioners should keep in mind that

> interventions that produce lasting change that can be observed in other settings, at different times, with other trainers, and in the absence of the programmed stimuli under which the desired responses were initially emitted are preferable to interventions that do not provide such changes. (p. 594)

Ideally, the transfer of training will occur across four dimensions: time, setting, responses, and individuals (Wahler, Berland, & Coe, 1979).

♦ *Examples*

A young child learns the name of an animal (dog). He calls a specific dog "dog" and will soon generalize the name "dog" to all four-legged animals within the classification. He will at times label other four-legged animals, such as cats, cows, and crawling brothers and sisters, with the name "dog."

A toddler is reinforced for calling her father "Daddy." She will generalize and call all male figures "Daddy" at an early stage of her development. She may call the mailman, milkman, and others "Daddy." This may result in considerable stress between husband and wife.

If we wish to function successfully in the environment, we must apply the concepts learned in one situation to many and varied situations. For example, as young children we learn honesty, respect for authority, and the basic principles of computation. It is hoped that each year we can generalize this learning to the completion of our income tax returns.

Baer (1981) and Stokes and Baer (1977) make several suggestions for teaching students to generalize. They suggest that natural contingencies facilitate the learning of generalization. Natural contingencies are those that commonly occur in the environment as a consequence of a behavior. In addition, training more exemplars may help students to generalize. Reinforcing generalization and self-reports of the target behavior assist in generalization. It is important to remember that just because a student behaves in a desired way in one situation does not mean that generalization of that behavior to other settings has occurred. At least initially, generalization should be programmed.

Vaughn et al. (1986) recommend several practical strategies for teachers wishing to help their students develop generalization skills. The recommended strategies include the following:

1. Varying the amount, power, and type of reinforcers applied to students, such as fading reinforcers, changing from tangible to social reinforcers, or using the same reinforcers in different settings.

2. Varying the instructions given to students, such as using alternative and parallel directions, rewording directions, and using photographs and pictures.

3. Varying the medium and the media of the instructional materials used by students to complete tasks. In the written medium, this could mean varying things such as paper size and color, writing instruments, and inks. The teacher may use other instructional media, such as films or computers.

4. Varying the response modes students use to complete tasks, such as changing from written to oral responses or using a variety of test question formats.

5. Varying the stimulus provided to students, such as changing the size, color, and shape of illustrations or using concrete objects.

6. Varying the instructional setting, such as changing the work location or changing from individual to small group study.

7. Varying instructors, such as using aides, peers, or parents.

Vaughn et al. (1986) recommend that teachers carefully plan, monitor, and evaluate the effects of generalization instruction on students.

Discrimination

Discrimination is another important learned behavior. Through discrimination, we learn that we act one way in one situation and another way in a different situation (Axelrod, 1983). If it were not for the process of discrimination, we would generalize behaviors to a variety of situations in which they would be inappropriate.

♦ *Example*

We behave differently in church than we do at a cocktail party (most of us) and differently in class than we do at a football game (although some classes are stimulating and some football games boring). Our behaviors in these situations are reinforced by the rewards we receive.

Discrimination is the result of *differential reinforcement*. Reinforcing a behavior in the presence of one stimulus and not reinforcing it in the presence of another stimulus is differential reinforcement. (Differential reinforcement is discussed in detail in Chapter 6.)

♦ *Example*

Teaching a young child to discriminate between the words *cat* and *rat* may be accomplished by listening and reacting to the child's responses. The child is reinforced for the appropriate response only. In this way, the child discriminates between the words *rat* and *cat* when they are presented in the future.

SCHEDULES OF REINFORCEMENT

A *schedule of reinforcement* is the pattern with which the reinforcer is presented in response to the exhibition of the target behavior (Rusch, Rose, & Greenwood, 1988). The schedule of reinforcement that is applied has a significant effect on the behavior change process. The most common types of reinforcement schedules are continuous, fixed ratio, variable ratio, fixed interval, and variable interval.

Continuous Schedules

The *continuous schedule* of reinforcement requires the presentation of the reinforcer immediately after each occurrence of the target behavior (Cooper, Heron, & Heward, 1987). The continuous schedule is most often applied during the initial stage of a behavior change program (Downing, 1990). Frequently, its use will change the behavior rapidly in the desired direction. It is not recommended for long-term use, however, because individuals tend to satiate on this schedule, and initial behavior change gains may be lost. In addition, it presents a very unrealistic and artificial procedure for classroom application.

♦ *Examples*

Ms. Bantle wished to increase Deanna's hand-raising behavior during history. To do this, she decided, at least initially, to reinforce Deanna each time she raised her hand. Application of this continuous schedule rapidly increased the target behavior to an acceptable level.

Mr. McCloud was disturbed by Bobby's out-of-seat behavior. He planned an intervention to increase Bobby's in-seat behavior. During the initial intervention, he reinforced Bobby's in-seat behavior each time it occurred. This continuous schedule quickly increased Bobby's in-seat behavior.

Fixed and Variable Schedules

The primary distinctions among fixed and variable (intermittent) ratio and interval schedules are related to the timing and frequency with which the reinforcer is presented. The ratio schedules, fixed and variable, focus on the *completion of specific tasks* before the reinforcer is presented to the child. Reinforcer presentation on the interval schedules, fixed and variable, depends on the exhibition of specific behaviors for *definite periods of time* (Downing, 1990).

Table 3.3 summarizes the schedules discussed in the following sections.

Fixed Ratio Schedules.   When a *fixed ratio schedule* is applied, the reinforcer is presented after a specific number of appropriate responses are emitted by the child.

Table 3.3
Relationships among the common reinforcement schedules

	Ratio	Interval
Fixed	Child completes 20 problems to receive 10 minutes of free time	Child is rewarded for remaining in seat for 5 minutes
Variable	Teacher rewards child, on an average, every third time child raises hand	Teacher gives child individual attention, on an average, every 15 minutes in response to acceptable behavior during the time period

♦ *Examples*

Every time John answers 15 social studies questions correctly, he is given 10 minutes to read a comic book. John's reward (comic book reading) is based on his successful completion of a fixed number (15) of social studies questions.

Every time Sheila reads five brief passages in her reading workbook with 80% accuracy, she is allowed to listen to her favorite record album for 5 minutes. In this case, Sheila is on a fixed ratio schedule.

The fixed ratio schedule usually results in a high rate of response. Consequently, it is most effectively and appropriately applied during the beginning phase of the behavior change process.

Variable Ratio Schedules. The *variable ratio schedule* is designed to sustain the level of response to reinforcement once the acceptable level of behavior has been attained by means of a continuous or fixed ratio schedule. When the variable ratio schedule is applied, the ratio of the reinforcer presentation varies around a response mean or average. This variability is instrumental in sustaining the appropriate level of response.

♦ *Examples*

Mr. Davis has Kerry raising his hand and participating in class discussions. He accomplished this via a fixed ratio schedule. He now wishes to change to a variable ratio schedule. Kerry is placed on a variable ratio schedule of 5 (the reinforcer is presented around a response mean of 5). Kerry may be reinforced the seventh time he raises his hand, the sixth time, the third, the fourth, or the fifth. If this schedule (7, 6, 3, 4, and 5) is averaged, the response mean or variable ratio is 5. The fact that Kerry does not know when Mr. David will call on him to respond (but does know that he will be called on) maintains his hand-raising behavior at a high level.

Slot machines (in our experience) operate on a variable ratio schedule. The gambler puts quarters in the slot and is occasionally reinforced with small rewards. This occasional reinforcement keeps the person playing until he or she is broke, but the loser always has the hope that the next pull of the arm will result in the super jackpot.

Inexperienced practitioners are cautioned not to change from a continuous or fixed ratio to a variable ratio schedule too early in the behavior change process. The desired behavior must be adequately established on a fixed ratio schedule before it can be changed to a variable ratio schedule. Many behavior change programs have failed as a result of the practitioner's impatience in making this transition.

Fixed Interval Schedules.   On the *fixed interval schedule,* a specified period of time must elapse before the reinforcer is presented. The reinforcer is presented immediately *after the first response after* the specified time has elapsed. The following examples should clarify this seeming confusion.

♦ *Examples*

Debbie does not remain in her seat during language lessons. Mr. Quick has decided to reinforce Debbie on a fixed interval schedule of 10. Thus, every time Debbie remains in her seat for 10 minutes during language lessons, she is rewarded.

Most people work on a fixed interval (1 week, 2 weeks, or 1 month) pay schedule. They receive their paychecks after the pay period has elapsed.

With fixed interval schedules, the longer the time interval between reinforcements, the lower will be the level of performance. This would suggest that initially during an intervention, reinforcers should be presented at frequent intervals.

Variable Interval Schedules.   The *variable interval schedule* is similar to the variable ratio schedule. However, the presentation of the reinforcer is based on a behavioral response mean or average. The individual whose behavior is being modified is not aware of when reinforcement will occur. However, the individual does know that he or she will be reinforced for exhibiting a certain behavior.

♦ *Example*

Mr. Quick has decided to place Debbie on a variable interval schedule of 10. On this schedule, Debbie will continue to be reinforced for in-seat behavior. She may be reinforced the first time after only 9 minutes of appropriate behavior, the second time after 4 minutes, the third time after 9 minutes, the fourth time after 15 minutes, and the fifth time after 13 minutes. This is a reinforcement schedule of 9, 4, 9, 15, and 13. It is based on a variable interval with a mean or average of 10 minutes.

Again, the behavior modifier should be cautious when changing from fixed ratio or fixed interval to variable ratio or variable interval schedules. If this is done too early or too late in the behavior change process, the newly acquired behavior may be extinguished.

The specific schedule to be applied varies with the behavior being changed. For example, if the concern is to keep an individual in his or her seat for a period of time, an interval schedule would be the most appropriate. However, if the behavior is related to the completion of specific numbers or kinds of tasks, a ratio schedule should be applied. The selection and application of the appropriate schedule is part of the art of behavior modification. Knowing when and how to apply a specific schedule of reinforcement becomes less confusing with experience.

♦ SUMMARY

The basic principles of reinforcement are presented in this chapter, followed by a discussion of the concepts of positive and negative reinforcement, extinction, and punishment. An understanding of these operations and their effects on behavior is essential. To use the previously mentioned operations, the reader must understand how they are different as well as how they are interrelated.

The concepts of generalization and discrimination are discussed. Generalization increases the probability that a behavior reinforced in the presence of one stimulus will be exhibited in the presence of another stimulus. Discrimination is the process by which we learn to behave differently in different situations.

A discussion of the schedules of reinforcement is also presented. A schedule of reinforcement is the pattern with which the reinforcers are presented in response to the exhibition of a behavior. The most common types of schedules are continuous, fixed ratio, fixed interval, variable ratio, and variable interval. It is essential that the practitioner of behavior modification have a thorough knowledge of these schedules.

♦ PROJECTS

1. Explain the five basic principles of reinforcement.
2. Give examples of how positive reinforcement, extinction, negative reinforcement, and punishment can be used to change the behavior of children.
3. List several factors involved in the use of punishment as a behavior change technique.
4. Describe two examples for each of the following: continuous, fixed ratio, fixed interval, variable ratio, and variable interval schedules of reinforcement as applied in the classroom or home setting.
5. Compare the concepts of generalization and discrimination.

♦ REFERENCES

Alberto, P. A., & Troutman, A. C. (1990). *Applied behavior analysis for teachers* (3rd ed.). Upper Saddle River, NJ: Merrill/Prentice Hall.

Axelrod, S. (1983). *Behavior modification for the classroom teacher.* New York: McGraw-Hill.

Baer, D. M. (1981). *How to plan for generalization.* Austin, TX: PRO-ED.

Cipani, E. O. (1995). Be aware of negative reinforcement. *Teaching Exceptional Children, 27*(4), 36–40.

Cooper, J. O., Heron, T. E., & Heward, W. L. (1987). *Applied behavior analysis.* Columbus, OH: Merrill.

Downing, J. A. (1990). Contingency contracts: A step-by-step format. *Intervention in School and Clinic, 26*(2), 111–113.

Downing, J. A., Moran, M. R., Myles, B. S., & Ormsbee, C. K. (1991). Using reinforcement in the classroom. *Intervention in School and Clinic, 27*(2), 85–90.

Kerr, M. M., & Nelson, C. M. (1989). *Strategies for managing problem behaviors in the classroom* (2nd ed.). Upper Saddle River, NJ: Merrill/Prentice Hall.

Landrum, T. J., & Lloyd, J. W. (1992). Generalization in social behavior research with children and youth who have emotional or behavioral disorders. *Behavior Modification, 16*(4), 593–616.

McDaniel, T. (1980). Corporal punishment and teacher liability: Questions teachers ask. *The Clearing House, 54*(1), 10–13.

Morris, R. J. (1985). *Behavior modification with exceptional children: Principles and practices.* Glenview, IL: Scott, Foresman.

Rusch, F. R., Rose, T., & Greenwood, C. R. (1988). *Introduction to behavior analysis in special education.* Upper Saddle River, NJ: Prentice Hall.

Sarason, I. G., Glaser, E. M., & Fargo, G. A. (1972). *Reinforcing productive classroom behavior: A teacher's guide to behavior modification.* New York: Behavioral Publications.

Shea, T. M., & Bauer, A. M. (1987). *Teaching children and youth with behavior disorders.* Upper Saddle River, NJ: Prentice Hall.

Shea, T. M., Bauer, A. M., & Lynch, E. M. (1989, September). *Changing behavior: Ethical issues regarding behavior management and the control of students with behavioral disorders.* Paper presented at the CEC/CCBD conference, "Find the answer for a decade ahead," Charlotte, NC.

Stokes, T. F., & Baer, D. M. (1977). An implicit technology of generalization. *Journal of Applied Behavior Analysis, 10*(2), 349–367.

Vaughn, S., Bos, C. S., & Lund, K. A. (1986). But they can do it in my room: Strategies for promoting generalization. *Teaching Exceptional Children, 18*(3), 176–180.

Wahler, R. G., Berland, R. M., & Coe, T. D. (1979). Generalization processes in child behavior change. In B. B. Lahey & A. E. Kazdin (Eds.), *Advances in clinical child psychology* (Vol. 2, pp. 36–71). New York: Plenum.

Steps in the Behavior Change Process

◆ KEY TERMS

Abscissa points
Baseline data
Counting behavior
Fading
Functional behavioral assessment
Graphing (charting) behavior
Instructional objectives
Interobserver reliability
Intervention data
Measurability
Observability
Ordinate points
Phasing out
Preference list
Preference scales
Prompting
Time sampling

◆ CHAPTER OBJECTIVES

After completing this chapter, you will be able to do the following:

1. Characterize the steps in the behavior change process, including

   (a) selecting target behaviors,

   (b) collecting and recording baseline data,

   (c) identifying reinforcers,

   (d) implementing interventions and collecting and recording intervention data, and

   (e) evaluating the effects of intervention.

2. Describe and exemplify the observer reliability process.

3. Define various forms of prompting.

4. Design classroom reinforcement area.

◆ ◆ ◆

George, a junior high student at the John T. Belfast School, appears to be having problems in school. Mrs. Chung, a social studies teacher, notices that George does not participate in class discussions, associate with other students, or take part in cocurricular activities. Mrs. Chung wishes there were some way she could help George become involved with his peers. She feels guilty about George's isolation and believes that she has in some manner let him down. The one thing Mrs. Chung has noticed about George is that he likes to draw.

One day, out of frustration, Mrs. Chung refers George for placement in a special class. However, the school psychologist's report reveals that George has an IQ of 144 with no signs of learning disabilities. Next she decides to show some of George's drawings to the school art teacher, Mr. Bonetti, who is impressed by the creative quality of George's efforts. He shows the drawings to an art professor at the university. He agrees that the drawings are the work of a genius.

Perhaps if Mrs. Chung could learn the steps in the behavior change process, George, her young genius, would become more involved with other students.

Mrs. Anderson teaches algebra and geometry at Thomas Edison High School. She enjoys teaching and is a conscientious instructor. Her students respect her, she is admired by her colleagues, and the principal refers to her as "my perfect teacher." Mrs. Anderson has been presented the "Outstanding Teacher of the Year" award twice by the school board. She was voted "Teacher of the Year" by the state education association. However, Mrs. Anderson has a serious problem. It is not at school but at home.

Mrs. Anderson is a single parent. She is head of a household that includes three teenagers, ages 13, 15, and 17. Her children take little responsibility for caring for themselves or the house. After Mrs. Anderson has taught school, attended faculty meetings, corrected papers, called parents, changed her bulletin board, prepared monthly reports, and planned for the next day, she goes home to her other job. At home she must prepare meals, wash and iron, clean the house, do the yard work, take out the garbage, wash and fuel the car, shop for food and clothing, care for the dog, and finally care for three teenagers.

Perhaps if Mrs. Anderson could learn the steps in the behavior change process, she could change her home situation.

In this chapter, the specific steps and procedures applied during the behavior change process are discussed and exemplified in detail. Teachers and parents should follow these steps closely: (a) select a target behavior, (b) collect and record baseline data, (c) identify reinforcers, (d) implement intervention and collect and record intervention data, and (e) evaluate the effects of intervention. The chapter also includes a discussion of observer reliability, prompting, and design of the classroom reinforcement area.

SELECTING A TARGET BEHAVIOR

The initial step in the behavior change process is the identification of the target behavior. The target behavior is the behavior to be changed or modified. A target behavior may be an existing behavior that the teacher or parent desires to increase or decrease or a nonoccurring behavior, that is, a behavior that is not observable in the individual's behavioral repertoire but one to be developed.

In most classroom situations, it is not difficult for the teacher to identify a variety of behaviors needing change (target behaviors). The teacher may recognize the following:

1. Percy does not communicate verbally.
2. Jake should increase his reading skills.
3. Mary should stop yelling in the classroom.
4. Joseph needs to learn to listen to instructions before he begins an assignment.
5. Shauna should improve her table manners in the lunchroom.

All these are potential target behaviors that the teacher could identify in the classroom.

It should be remembered that whenever an individual or a group is singled out for observation and study for the purpose of initiating a behavior change program, it is inevitable that several individual and group target behaviors will be identified. All children and adults manifest behaviors that are unacceptable to some other individuals or groups of individuals under certain conditions.

Decisions leading to the selection of a behavior for modification should be governed by the following considerations, among others:

- Type of behavior
- Frequency of the behavior
- Duration of the behavior
- Intensity of the behavior
- Overall number of behaviors needing modification

It is generally recommended that the beginning behavior modifier not attempt to change more than one individual or group behavior at a time. Implementing several behavior change programs simultaneously frequently results in inefficiency, and otherwise useful interventions prove ineffective. Individual and group behaviors needing modification should be ranked in priority (Morris, 1985). The teacher then systematically works through the priority list from the most important to the least important of the potential target behaviors. The importance of a specific behavior should be determined on the basis of its effect on the child's functioning. Schopler, Reichler, and Lansing (1980) suggest the following order of priorities be applied to changing the behaviors of children with developmental disabilities:

1. Problems that risk the child's life
2. Problems that risk the child's continuing to live with the family

3. Problems that limit the child's participation in special education

4. Problems that limit the child's adaptation to the community outside home and school

---

♦ *Example*

Ilion manifests a variety of unacceptable behaviors. Among the behaviors of greatest concern to his teacher, Mr. Wise, are (a) withdrawal from group activities, (b) unacceptable eating habits, (c) inability to communicate with his classmates and Mr. Wise via speech, and (d) unsatisfactory gross motor skills.

Mr. Wise recognizes that a program cannot be initiated to modify all of Ilion's potential target behaviors at a single time. Because of the nature of the behaviors, the proposed interventions could be in conflict with one another. Mr. Wise must respond to the following question: Is it more important for Ilion, at this time, to participate in the luncheon discussion [behaviors 1 and 3 would be targets], or is it more important to improve his gross motor skills and eating habits [behaviors 2 and 4 would be targets]?

In response to this question, Mr. Wise develops the following priority list for Ilion's program:

- First priority: Increase participation in group activities
- Second priority: Increase verbalization with others
- Third priority: Increase gross motor skills
- Fourth priority: Increase acceptance of a variety of foods

Priorities vary with individual student needs and the setting in which the behavior change intervention is applied. However, the objective of all behavior change is to benefit the student (Alberto & Troutman, 1990) or, as stated previously, self-discipline or self-control.

Cooper, Heron, and Heward (1987) suggest these nine factors that should be considered when establishing target behavior priorities:

1. Determine whether the behavior is of danger to the individual or others.

2. Determine whether the frequency of the behavior or, in the case of a new behavior, the opportunities to use the behavior warrant intervention.

3. Determine the duration of the problem or, in the case of a new behavior, how long the individual's need for the new behavior has existed.

4. Determine whether the behavior will produce a higher level of reinforcement for the individual than other behaviors under consideration. Generally, behaviors that produce a high level of reinforcement take priority over behaviors that produce a low level of reinforcement.

5. Determine the impact of the behavior on the individual's skill development and independence.

6. Determine whether learning the behavior will reduce the negative attention that the individual receives.

7. Determine whether learning the behavior will increase reinforcement for others in the individual's environment.

8. Determine the difficulty (time and energy) to be expended to change the behavior.

9. Determine the cost involved in changing the behavior.

With an increase in experience and skill in the behavior change process, the teacher or parent may wish to program more than one individual or group target behavior simultaneously. However, the beginning practitioner should refrain from multiple programming.

When selecting a target behavior, the practitioner must consider the frequency of the behavior. Some behaviors occur so infrequently that they do not necessitate or respond to a formal behavior modification intervention. Of course, the reverse is also true; some behaviors occur so frequently that they obviously require a behavior change program.

♦ *Example*

Ms. Lochman was very concerned about Martin, a member of her class. Six-year-old Martin appeared to be constantly out of his assigned seat. When out of his chair, he would grab other children's work, work tools, and lunches. Using a time-sampling technique, Ms. Lochman collected baseline data on Martin's out-of-seat behavior for 1 hour a day for 5 days. She found that during these observation periods, Martin was out of his seat 17 times an hour on an average. (Time sampling is discussed later in this chapter.)

This behavior was so frequent and so obtrusive that it usually brought all productive classroom activity to a halt until Ms. Lochman could control Martin and return him to his seat.

Teachers and parents are confronted daily with behaviors that are responsive to behavior change intervention. Such behaviors include lack of attention to tasks, incomplete assignments, fighting, not cleaning their room, tardiness to and from school, excessive television watching, neglecting music or dance practice, and independent reading, to name a few.

♦ *Example*

Ms. Derry, like many of her peers, does not approve of chewing gum in school. Johnny, a member of her classroom group, was seen chewing gum on the second day of school this year. Ms. Derry grabbed him, removed the gum from his mouth, and stuck it on his nose, where it stayed for the remainder of the day. Ms. Derry then proceeded to make plans for a formal behavior change program. After several hours of planning, she was satisfied with her elaborate scheme for gathering baseline data and applying the chosen intervention. Unfortunately (or fortunately), Johnny never chewed gum in school again (that she observed).

There are many behaviors like Johnny's that appear so infrequently that they do not require a formal behavior change program. Examples of such behaviors are the following:

- George's annual 2-minute tantrum
- Barbara's occasional reading reversal
- Don's infrequent falling out of his seat
- Judy's bimonthly bus-missing behavior

If a proposed target behavior is both obtrusive and occurs frequently, the teacher should next consider the duration of the behavior.

♦ *Examples*

For several weeks, Gerald was very nervous in school. His teacher, Ms. Farley, noted that he was frequently out of his seat, irritable, and ready to burst into tears. She had never seen Gerald in this condition. She attempted to discuss the situation with him but was rebuffed.

Ms. Farley decided to establish a formal behavior modification program to decrease the behaviors. However, before initiating the program, she discussed the situation with Gerald's mother. During the conversation, Gerald's mother indicated that she had observed similar behavior at home and was attempting to help Gerald regain his old composure. She thought the behavior was the result of the recent death of Gerald's grandfather. Gerald and his grandfather had been pals; they had always been together in the evenings. The death left a great void in Gerald's daily life. Gerald's mother said that her husband was rescheduling his evening activities so that he and Gerald could spend more time together.

Ms. Farley decided to hold the intervention program in abeyance for another few weeks. Within a short time, Gerald was his normal self. The program was never implemented.

Mr. Parker is Maryann's kindergarten teacher. He thoroughly enjoys his work with Maryann and her 16 classmates. The kindergarten is an interesting and exciting learning place for the children.

During the first few weeks of the school year, Mr. Parker observed that Maryann, although involved in the classroom activities, seldom if ever spoke to him, the paraprofessional, or her classmates. He decided to collect some baseline data on the frequency of Maryann's verbal behavior. In cooperation with the kindergarten paraprofessional, an observation schedule was set up to obtain some objective data. Using a time-sampling technique, they observed Maryann's behavior on an average of 1 hour a day for 10 days. Data indicated that Maryann spoke only four times a day, on an average, while in school. She directed all her verbalizations to one classmate.

Although Mr. Parker was very concerned about the behavior, he did not implement a behavior change program at this time. He had worked with kindergarten children in the past who were shy and quiet and did not begin to interact verbally in the classroom until just before Christmas vacation.

The paraprofessional continued to collect data 1 day each week until mid-December. No change was noted in Maryann's behavior.

Mr. Parker concluded that the behavior had endured too long and that a behavior change program was needed to help Maryann. He conferred with the school's language therapist, who evaluated Maryann. He also discussed the problem with Maryann's mother, who agreed to participate in a home-school behavior change program. The intervention was implemented immediately after the Christmas holidays.

The teacher or parent must also consider the intensity of the behavior. Some behaviors, although unacceptable, are relatively mild and unobtrusive. They do not generally interfere with the classroom process or the individual child's overall functioning. Of course, other behaviors, although infrequent, are so intense that they are extremely obtrusive. Not only do they adversely affect the individual's overall functioning, but they also interfere with the classroom program and group process. Such behaviors must be modified.

♦ *Examples*

Ricky, identified as having emotional/behavioral disorders, is 7 years old and included in first grade with supports. Ricky has temper tantrums that are totally unpredictable, frequent, and analogous to all the Fourth of July fireworks in all the towns of the United States igniting simultaneously. These tantrums involve lying on the floor with feet and arms flying and verbalizations that are interesting but disturbing combinations of four-letter words. The tantrums last up to 45 minutes, averaging about 25 minutes.

These tantrums destroy the classroom program, frighten the other children, and interfere with Ricky's overall functioning. The behavior must be changed.

Keith is 13 years old and in the seventh grade. Occasionally, he manifests some behaviors, normal for his age-group, that are bothersome, such as know-it-all behavior, big-shotism, and negativism. These behaviors are of minimal intensity. They are manifested by a wise remark at the termination of a conversation, his saying "No, I won't" before beginning the directed task, and the like. The behaviors are generally ignored by others and have little effect on either the classroom process or Keith's overall functioning.

The final characteristic to be considered in the selection of a target behavior is the type of behavior. Some behavior that is disturbing to some adults and children is really quite normal from a child development point of view. In fact, a child who did not manifest such behavior might be considered abnormal.

♦ *Examples*

Paul is a sixth grader and a straight-A student. When he is asked whether he likes school, his teacher, or the like, he says, "No, I hate it."

As most teachers realize, Paul's behavior is quite normal for a sixth-grade boy. It is within normal limits and of a kind that does not necessitate a formal intervention program.

Russell is 12 years old and in a junior high school special class. He has an uncontrolled temper and frequently tells his teacher to "go to Hades" or "drop dead" (among other things). Russell gets into occasional fights with his classmates. These fights are extremely vicious. On two occasions, he has inflicted injury on his opponent.

Russell's behavior is of a type that cannot simply be ignored. An intervention must be implemented for both his benefit and the safety of his peers.

After these variables (type, frequency, duration, intensity, and number) have been considered and a target behavior selected, the teacher must decide the direction of the behavior change process. A behavior may increase or decrease as a consequence of an intervention. Table 4.1 presents the behavior change directions and examples of each.

Behavior change programs, then, are implemented to increase acceptable behaviors or decrease unacceptable behaviors. Teachers can easily select behaviors they wish to increase or decrease. In most instances, the practitioner takes the child's manifestation of acceptable behaviors for granted and does not systematically reward such behaviors. More effort should be made to prevent unacceptable behaviors from developing via the systematic rewarding and maintenance of existing acceptable behaviors.

Two other important characteristics of the target behavior are *observability* and *measurability* (Rusch, Rose, & Greenwood, 1988). The behavior must be readily observable in the environment in which it occurs. In addition, the behavior must be quantifiable.

Table 4.1
Behavior change directions

Direction	Example
Increase	Group participation
	In-seat behavior
	Interaction with peers
	Typing skills
	Reading rate
	Number skills
	Study skills
Decrease	Verbal outbursts
	Inattentiveness
	Use of four-letter words
	Food intake
	Smoking
	Talking during study period
	Spelling errors

♦ *Examples*

Ernest, in Ms. Moral's words, is "an unhappy child." Ms. Moral would like to decrease his unhappiness (and increase his happiness). However, when she attempted to observe and quantify Ernest's unhappiness, she abandoned the behavior change program before the baseline data were collected.

Brian seldom participated in organized group activities on the playground. Mr. Spencer wished to increase his level of activity. He recorded Brian's group participation rate on the playground during morning recess. Mr. Spencer easily established Brian's baseline of activity; he could thus directly observe and quantify the frequency and duration of Brian's participation in group activities.

Roy is in Mr. Watson's fourth-grade class. He has perfect school attendance during the first 7 months of the school year. Mr. Watson would like to have Roy maintain his present level of attendance for the remaining 2 months of the school year. Roy is the only student in his class with a perfect attendance record. Mr. Watson and the class praise Roy for his attendance. If Mr. Watson and Roy's classmates have anything to do with it, Roy's perfect attendance will be maintained.

Statements describing the target behavior, the precise intervention, and the criteria for success or acceptability of performance should be written or otherwise communicated in objective and specific terminology. These statements are often referred to as *instructional objectives*. The following objectives are written so that the target behavior and the result of the intervention can be observed, quantified, and evaluated:

- Decrease the number of times Jack interrupts during social studies class
- Increase the number of pages Emma reads during each 15-minute study period
- Decrease the number of times Marion yells during the first hour of the morning
- Increase the number of times Ken uses the reference books located on the science table
- Decrease the amount of time Sharon puts her thumb in her mouth during the school day
- Increase Benji's skill in recognizing and naming the letters of the alphabet during language development class

Program objectives should be written as instructional objectives, whether the target behavior is in the cognitive, affective, or psychomotor learning domain. The instructional objective in its written form should respond to the following guidelines:

1. What is the child or group of children whose behavior is being modified expected to do or not to do?

    (a) Use action verbs to denote the behavior change process

    (b) List the specific resources and materials to be used by the child during the behavior change process

      (c) Indicate specifically the desired interaction between the child and the environment, including persons and objects

2. What is the level of performance (in terms of accuracy, duration, and skill) expected of the child?

3. What percentage of time or what percentage of occurrences of the desired behavior is the child expected to perform at the criterion level?

4. How will the anticipated changes in behavior be measured for evaluative purposes? What instrumentation is needed for the evaluation?

5. How long will the proposed intervention program be in force before its effectiveness is evaluated?

Further information on the writing of specific objectives may be found in Cooper et al. (1987) and Mager (1984).

The following guidelines summarize the process of selecting a target behavior:

1. Select only one individual or group target behavior to change at a time. This requires the establishment of priorities.

2. Analyze the potential target behavior for its frequency, duration, intensity, and type. The importance and pertinence of these variables change with the characteristics of the specific target behavior under consideration.

3. Consider the direction or course the behavior is to take during the change process. Is the behavior to be decreased or increased?

4. Determine whether the behavior is observable.

5. Determine whether the behavior is measurable in numeric terms.

6. Describe the target behavior in precise, descriptive terminology in all verbal and written communication.

The beginning behavior modifier is advised to use the checklist in Figure 4.1 to assist in the target behavior selection process. An additional copy of this checklist is provided in the back of the text.

COLLECTING AND RECORDING BASELINE DATA

Quantitative data collected before the behavior change intervention has been implemented is referred to as *baseline data*. The process of collecting preintervention or baseline data is frequently referred to as functional assessment. *Functional behavioral assessment* is the "identification of antecedent and consequent events, temporarily contiguous to the behavior, which occasion and maintain the behavior" (Lennox & Miltenberger, 1989, p. 304). Baseline data provide the foundation on which the behavior change process is established. These data are also used to determine the effectiveness of the intervention during the evaluation step of the behavior change process.

Target Behavior Selection Checklist

1. What is the target behavior to be modified? _____

    _____

    _____

    _____

2. Each characteristic of the behavior that should be considered in the target
    behavior selective process is listed below. An X should be marked by each
    characteristic as it is considered. The pertinency of these characteristics varies
    with the specific target behavior under consideration.

(X)	Characteristic	Comment
( )	Frequency	
( )	Duration	
( )	Intensity	
( )	Type	
( )	Direction	
( )	Observability	
( )	Measurability	

3. Restate the target behavior in precise and specific terminology. _____

    _____

    _____

    _____

    _____

Figure 4.1
Sample checklist to assist in the selection of a target behavior

In the Individuals with Disabilities Education Act Amendments of 1997 (IDEA 97), Congress required that an effort be made to understand the relationship between the individual student's learning and behavior. Knowledge of this relationship was seen as essential to planning the individual education plan (IEP). To respond to this mandate, the IEP team must address both the student's learning and the student's behavior. Thus, the team must conduct a functional behavioral assessment and plan and implement a behavior intervention plan (Buck et al., 2000; Fitzsimmons, 1998).

According to Buck et al. (2000), two major assumptions underlie the mandate in IDEA 97: (a) "Behavioral problems are best addressed when the cause of the behavior is known; and cause can be determined best when a functional assessment of the student's behavior is conducted" and (b) behavior intervention based on positive intervention strategies are more effective in changing maladaptive behavior than are punitive strategies (e.g., suspension). Such intervention strategies should be well thought out, implemented in a systematic fashion, and evaluated so that changes can be made when needed" (p. 4).

Buck et al. state that there are three reasons for previous failures that led Congress to mandate change:

1. School personnel often provide inappropriate interventions because they failed to identify the true cause of the disruptive behavior.

2. Behavioral interventions are often implemented haphazardly (e.g., lack of consistency, with little attention to the monitoring and evaluation of their implementation).

3. Disciplinary actions in schools have tended toward punitive rather than positive behavioral intervention plans.

The functional behavioral assessment is conducted to gather information about the student's behavior problem. The assessment focuses attention on the underlying motivation for the problem. As suggested by Fitzsimmons (1998), the function or purpose of the behavior often is not inappropriate; rather, the behavior itself is inappropriate. Therefore, to effectively assist the student, the focus of the intervention is on the purpose of the behavior rather than the symptoms of the behavior. For example, the purpose of a student's misbehavior may be to gain attention. Rather than trying to decrease his inappropriate outbursts and interruptions during class by punishment or deprivation, the appropriate intervention may be providing opportunities for the student to receive consistent, repeated, and legitimate attention during class. An effective intervention plan for this student, then, focuses on both increasing appropriate behavior and decreasing inappropriate behavior.

Fitzsimmons suggests five steps common to the functional behavior assessment:

1. Determine whether the problem behavior can be controlled by the usual classroom intervention strategies. If it cannot be controlled in this manner, then proceed to conduct a functional behavior assessment.

2. Translate the behavior problem into descriptive behavioral terms. Define the behavior so that it can be directly observed and quantified.

3. Analyze the student's behavior and other information about the student to determine the possible cause of the behavior.

4. Collect data and analyze the problem behavior by focusing on the behavior itself as well as its antecedents and consequences.

5. Formulate a hypothesis with regard to the problem behavior. The hypothesis will state a possible explanation for the behavior's occurrence. The hypothesis is then tested by consistently manipulating the variables suggested within it over a period of time. In effect, the practitioner is conducting a research study to test the significance of the proposed hypothesis.

A behavior intervention plan should be written and incorporated into the student's IEP. Scott and Nelson (1999, as cited in Jolivette et al., (2000) suggest a 10-step process for integrating functional behavioral assessment data into the behavioral intervention plan:

1. Determine the function of the desired behavior. A functional assessment of the behavior is conducted to determine the purpose of the learner's behavior problem.
2. Determine an appropriate replacement behavior. The alternative appropriate behavior(s) should serve to replace the purpose of the inappropriate behavior and be acceptable to others in the learner's environment.
3. Determine when the replacement behavior should occur. Determine when it is appropriate for the alternative behavior to occur and instruct the learner in the use of the behavior.
4. Design a teaching sequence. As in the instruction of academics, an instruction plan should be developed to teach the learner the alternative acceptable behavior.
5. Manipulate the environment to increase the probability of success. Arrange reinforcers within the environment to increase the probability the alternative behavior will occur and be positively reinforced.
6. Manipulate the environment to decrease the probability of failure. Arrange the environment to decrease any barriers to the occurrence of the alternative behavior.
7. Determine how positive behavior will be reinforced. Arrange the environment so that the alternative behavior will be reinforced with consistency. In addition, the environment must be arranged so that the alternative behavior will be reinforced, as necessary, with appropriate frequency and, as necessary, with artificial and natural reinforcers.
8. Determine consequences for occurrences of the problem behavior. Design strategies to be implemented when the learner exhibits the inappropriate behavior.
9. Develop a data collection system. Collect data on the frequency, intensity, and duration of both the inappropriate and the alternative behaviors. This system must also include the frequency, intensity, and duration of the problem behavior prior to the implementation of the intervention plan to teach the learner the alternative behavior.
10. Develop behavioral goals and objectives. These are similar to the goals and objectives developed to instruct in academic areas.

The plan should be positive in nature rather than negative. It should emphasize what the student can do rather than what he or she cannot do. It has been generally demonstrated that positive interventions have a more long lasting effect on student behavior than negative interventions.

The behavior intervention plan may include manipulation of variables that precede the observable behavior, instructing in alternative forms of appropriate behavior or providing reinforcement for appropriate behavior (Jolivette et al., 2000).

◆ *Example*

The behavior change program Mr. Dixon selected for Jean concerned increasing the amount of time Jean remained in her seat during history class. Mr. Dixon collected baseline data for 1 week. The data demonstrated that Jean usually remained in her seat an average of 10 minutes at a time before she was up and about the classroom. This information provided Mr. Dixon with the data he needed to determine the kind and characteristics of the reinforcement schedule to be implemented. In order to be sure Jean received immediate reinforcement for staying in her seat, a fixed interval schedule of 7 minutes was used.

The selection of the fixed interval schedule of 7 minutes was not a haphazard choice. It was based on the fact that Jean had demonstrated that she could, on the average, remain in her seat for 10 minutes without interference. Therefore, it was reasonable to select a 7-minute interval because that was a level of performance that Jean could easily attain. Consequently, she could be frequently reinforced for appropriate behavior.

If Mr. Dixon had not collected baseline data but had proceeded on a hunch, he might have selected a fixed interval schedule of 11 minutes. With this interval, there would be a strong possibility that Jean would be infrequently rewarded and that her behavior would not change significantly.

Reinforcement is initiated at a level of performance either above or below the baseline, depending on whether the behavior is to be increased or decreased. For instance, you want to work with a student on increasing the number of words he can read per minute. You know that the student can read 75 words per minute. To start at baseline or above baseline would usually mean waiting too long to get the appropriate behavior, and your behavior change program may not be effective. If, however, you start your reinforcement at a level below baseline, in this case, for example, at 65 words per minute, you have then established a level at which you can provide immediate success for the student and can begin the program on a positive note.

◆ *Example*

Ms. Waters has a very active, unpredictable child in her class named Emmet. Emmet is constantly yelling in the classroom, to the annoyance of Ms. Waters and the other members of the group. Ms. Waters initiated a behavior change program but did not collect baseline data since Emmet appeared to yell constantly. She withdrew attention from Emmet each time he yelled and praised him when he was not yelling.

After 2 weeks, Ms. Waters was convinced that no change had occurred in the frequency of the behavior. Emmet seemed to yell in class more frequently. Ms. Waters concluded that "this behavior modification stuff" only works in textbooks, and she abandoned the project. Emmet is still yelling in class.

It should be stressed that, generally, failure of an intervention lies not in the principles of reinforcement but in the application of those principles by the practitioner. In the preceding example, Ms. Waters would have been wise to collect baseline data.

Figure 4.2
Frequency of Emmet's yelling
behavior before and during the
intervention

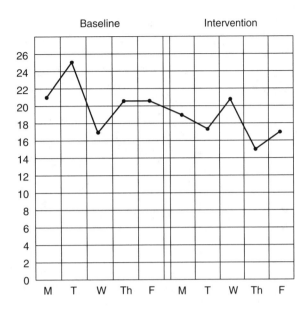

She would have been able to evaluate the effectiveness of the behavior change
process. Baseline data would have revealed that Emmet yelled in class on an average of 21 times a day. When the intervention was abandoned, the behavior was occurring only 18 times a day (Figure 4.2). The behavior was, in fact, changing in the
desired direction. However, without appropriate data, 18 yells a day sound very
much like 21 when you are immersed in a situation, as in the case of Ms. Waters.

There are a variety of methods for observing and recording baseline data behavior. According to Lennox and Miltenberger (1989), there are three categories of methods for collecting functional assessment data: (a) behavioral interviews, rating scales,
and questionnaires that depend on information from the individual whose behavior is
under consideration or an informant familiar with the individual; (b) direct observation
of the target behavior, including its antecedents and consequences; and (c) experimental manipulation of variables in the environment in which the behavior is exhibited. The efficiency of a particular technique varies with the expertise of the practitioner,
the characteristics of the behavior, and the setting in which the behavior occurs.

To obtain meaningful baseline data, the behavior modifier must engage in two
activities: counting the behavior and graphing or charting the behavior. *Counting
behavior* means enumerating the number of times the behavior occurs in a given period of time. *Graphing (charting) behavior* means preparing a visual display of the
enumerated behavior in graphic form.

These two processes are of paramount importance in the behavior change
process. When the number of occurrences or the average duration of the occurrences
of a behavior in a temporal framework are known, the behavior modifier can select
an efficient reinforcement schedule before implementing an intervention. Equally important is the application of the baseline data to the intervention evaluation process.
By comparing baseline data with intervention data, the teacher can determine the effectiveness of the reinforcer and the reinforcement schedule. Judgments can be made

regarding the responsiveness of the target behavior to the intervention; that is, is the behavior increasing, decreasing, or remaining unchanged?

The recommended method of collecting baseline data is direct observation in the environment in which the behavior occurs. The beginning behavior modifier is well advised to obtain observation data by means of a *time-sampling* technique.

A trained observer realizes that it is impossible to observe *all* the behavior occurring within the environment; neither is it possible to efficiently observe all the occurrences of a single behavior over an extended period. This is particularly true in a busy classroom with many students and a variety of activities occurring simultaneously.

With the time-sampling technique, the teacher first selects the behavior to be observed and then selects the periods of time that can be devoted to observing that behavior each day during the baseline period. Each occurrence of the target behavior during the observation period is tallied or recorded.

♦ *Example*

Joshua's teacher, Mr. Cates, wished to modify Joshua's hitting behavior during the 2-hour language arts period. With all his other teaching duties, he could not observe Joshua the full 2 hours for the 5 days required to collect reliable baseline data. Thus, Mr. Cates used a time-sampling technique; he observed Joshua's behavior during two 10-minute periods for each hour of the language arts period for 5 days. He designed a behavior-tallying sheet to record his observations (Table 4.2).

Mr. Cates noted several things as a result of this data-collecting effort:

1. Joshua hit other children a total of 32 times during the observation periods.

2. Mr. Cates observed only one-third of the total language arts period, that is, 20 minutes out of each 60 minutes. Thus, in all probability, Joshua hit others approximately 96 times during language arts that week.

3. Joshua hit others, on an average, approximately six times a day. However, he hit others less on Friday than on any other day of the week.

4. Joshua hit others more frequently with the passing of each observation period of the day.

Table 4.2
Baseline data: Joshua's hitting behavior

Time	Day					Time Total
	Mon.	Tue.	Wed.	Thur.	Fri.	
9:00–9:10	/	/		/	/	4
9:30–9:40	/	/	//	/	/	6
10:00–10:10	//	///	/	//	/	9
10:30–10:40	///	/	////	///	//	13
DAY TOTAL	7	6	7	7	5	32

Figure 4.3
Joshua's hitting behavior
(frequency)

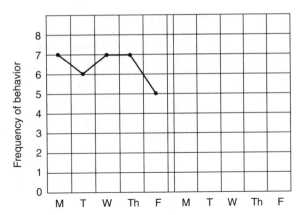

During the intervention phase of the behavior change program, Mr. Cates would isolate Joshua for 2 minutes each time he hit another child.

Before initiating the intervention, Mr. Cates transferred the baseline data to a graph to improve his visual image of the behavior (Figure 4.3).

Mr. Cates first made a chart for a 2-week period. His baseline data were entered in the section of the chart reserved for the first week. The remainder of the chart would be used for intervention data. He would enter the number of occurrences of hitting behavior during his observations each day of the intervention phase.

Mr. Cates used the horizontal axis of the chart for the days of the week and the vertical axis for the frequency of the behavior. He plotted the behavior and drew lines between the daily occurrences.

Horner, Sugai, and Todd (2001) state that the use of data is an essential part of developing and implementing a schoolwide system of discipline. They suggest that many teachers and administrators find data to be a "four-letter word" and avoid it if at all possible. A school discipline team's "efficency, precision, and effectiveness" is improved if its decisions are based on objective data collected on the individual and group problem behaviors it confronts and is responsible for resolving. In addition, data are used to monitor the general patterns of behavior within the school. Horner et al. offer four principles for making data useful in school and classroom: (a) Data should be used for making decisions, (b) data collection and use should emphasize simplicity and efficiency, (c) collected data should be applied to local problems, and (d) data collection and application systems should be designed to be used over time and in a cyclical manner.

When developing data systems, it should be a consequence of the problems confronting the local decision-making team and focus on resolving those problems. The focus of the system should be on a few key problems rather than a broad range of problems. The system should focus on important issues, and the quantity of data collected should be limited. Finally, those responsible for collecting data should analyze and summarize it for presentation to the team.

Table 4.3
Bucky's tantrums (duration and frequency)

Time			
Begin	**End**	**Total Minutes**	**Comments**
9:31	9:38	7	End of reading
11:03	11:12	9	Beginning of science
12:07	12:17	10	Lunchtime
2:30	2:39	9	Time to go home

Total occurrence for day: 4
Average duration: 9 minutes
Day: Monday

Although the same basic methods of counting and charting behavior are applied in all cases, certain modifications may be necessary, depending on the behavior under consideration.

In the example of Joshua's hitting behavior, the frequency of the behavior was the primary concern. The behavior itself was instantaneous; thus, the duration of the occurrences was not germane to the objective of the behavior change program.

However, if we were concerned with the duration of Bucky's tantrums, for example, we would focus our observation on both the frequency of occurrence and the duration of each occurrence. In this case, we would collect raw observation data in the manner shown in Table 4.3.

Table 4.3 is a tally log for Monday only, but the tally logs for the remaining 4 days of the baseline period are similar. The teacher, Mr. Wagner, is interested in decreasing both the frequency of the behavior and the duration of the behavior when it does occur.

Mr. Wagner has noted in the comments column that the tantrums occur when changes in group activities are taking place, such as at the end of reading period, at the beginning of science, at the beginning of lunchtime, and when it is time to go home.

The planned intervention is as follows:

1. Intervene before the transition period and assist Bucky through the potential tantrum period.

2. If a tantrum does occur, isolate Bucky immediately until 2 minutes after the tantrum ceases.

As a result of this baseline data-collecting procedure, Mr. Wagner designed two graphs to visually display the behavior. Figure 4.4 is concerned with the number of tantrums a day. Figure 4.5 represents the average duration of the tantrums.

Regardless of the specific target behavior being charted, the practitioner should remember that the *ordinate points* are generally located on the vertical axis of the

Figure 4.4
Bucky's tantrums (frequency)

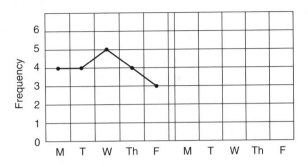

Figure 4.5
Average duration of Bucky's
tantrums

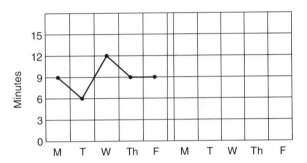

chart and the abscissa points on the horizontal axis. Ordinate points represent the behavior's frequency, duration, and percentage of occurrence. *Abscissa points* represent the hours, days, and sessions of observation (Axelrod, 1983).

To facilitate the data collection and graphing processes, Fabry and Cone (1980) and Shea and Bauer (1987) suggest that practitioners apply self-graphing procedures. Examples of these procedures are presented in Figures 4.6 and 4.7. By using these or similar procedures, the teacher can reduce the time and energy devoted to graphing.

If the practitioner wishes to record only the number of responses or behaviors, the system presented in Figure 4.6 is recommended. In this system, the total number of responses or behaviors exhibited by the student is circled for each day or time period. The circles are connected to form a graph.

In the example in Figure 4.6, Mr. Baden was interested in collecting and graphing data on the number of times Christina speaks without permission during industrial arts class. To begin, Mr. Baden completed the identifying information at the top and bottom of the form. During class, each time Christina spoke without permission, the appropriate number in the day's column was slashed. Next, Mr. Baden circled the highest slashed number for the day. He connected the circled numbers as the days passed and formed the graph in Figure 4.6.

A self-graphing event recording procedure is presented in Figure 4.7. To use this format, list the trial responses in the first column; note the dates in the other columns moving from left to right. As the student responds to each trial, make a slash over the corresponding number for the correct response. At the end of the session, the

Student __Christina__   Date Initiated __9/15/97__

Objective __Frequency of speaking in IA class without permission__

FREQUENCY OF BEHAVIOR

15	15	15	15	15	15	15	15	15	15	15	15	15	15	15	15
14	14	14	14	14	14	14	14	14	14	14	14	14	14	14	14
13	13	13	13	13	13	13	13	13	13	13	13	13	13	13	13
12	(12)	12	12	(12)	12	12	12	12	12	12	12	12	12	12	12
11	11	11	11	11	11	11	11	11	11	11	11	11	11	11	11
(10)	10	10	10	10	(10)	10	10	10	10	10	10	10	10	10	10
9	9	(9)	9	9	9	9	9	9	9	9	9	9	9	9	9
8	8	8	(8)	8	8	8	8	8	8	8	8	8	8	8	8
7	7	7	7	7	7	7	7	7	7	7	7	7	7	7	7
6	6	6	6	6	6	(6)	6	6	6	6	6	6	6	6	6
5	5	5	5	5	5	5	5	5	5	5	5	5	5	5	5
4	4	4	4	4	4	4	4	4	4	4	4	4	4	4	4
3	3	3	3	3	3	3	3	3	3	3	3	3	3	3	3
2	2	2	2	2	2	2	2	2	2	2	2	2	2	2	2
1	1	1	1	1	1	1	1	1	1	1	1	1	1	1	1

←   _criteria_ →

0	0	0	0	0	0	0	0	0	0	0	0	0	0	0	0
9/15	9/16	9/17	9/18	9/19	9/22	9/23									

DATES

Directions:
- Indicate behavior counted.
- Enter criteria line.
- Cross out one number each time the behavior occurs.
- Circle number of times the behavior occurs each date.
- Connect the circles to form graph.

Figure 4.6
Frequency data collection and graphing form

Student: Herm   Date Initiated: 1/15/98

Objective: Recognize safety words and phrases

TRIAL RESPONSES   DATES

		1/15	1/16	1/19	1/20	1/21	1/22	1/25	1/26	1/27	1/28
A	Stop	15	15	15	15	15	15	15	15	15	15
B	Go	14	14	14	14	14	14	14	14	14	14
C	Caution	13	13	13	13	13	13	13	13	13	13
D	Yield	12	12	12	12	12	12	12	12	12	(12)
E	Don't walk	11	11	11	11	11	11	11	(11)	(11)	11
F	Walk	10	10	10	10	10	10	10	10	10	10
G	Keep to right	9	9	9	9	9	9	9	9	9	9
H	Do not enter	8	8	8	8	(8)	(8)	8	8	8	8
I	Merge	7	7	7	(7)	7	7	(7)	7	7	7
J	No right on red	6	6	(6)	6	6	6	6	6	6	6
K	Right on red	(5)	(5)	5	5	5	5	5	5	5	5
L	4-way stop	4	4	4	4	4	4	4	4	4	4
M		3	3	3	3	3	3	3	3	3	3
N		2	2	2	2	2	2	2	2	2	2
O		1	1	1	1	1	1	1	1	1	1
P		0	0	0	0	0	0	0	0	0	0

Directions:
- Enter objective.
- Place a slash (/) over the number in the dated column for a correct response.
- At the end of the lesson, circle the number in the column that corresponds to the total correct responses (slashes) for the lesson.
- Connect the daily circles to make a graph.

Figure 4.7
Self-graphing event recording form

number corresponding to the total number of correct responses is circled. As sessions progress, the circles are connected to form a graph.

In the example in Figure 4.7, Mrs. Angie is teaching safety words and phrases to Herm using a predetermined sequence. If Herm responds correctly, the corresponding number in the day or session column is slashed. At the end of the session, the number of slashes is counted, and Mrs. Angie circles the appropriate number under the day's column. As the days or sessions progress, the circled numbers are connected to form a graph.

The methods of counting and charting behavior presented in this section are the ones used most frequently in the field, probably because of the ease with which the practitioner can visually perceive and evaluate the data and thus determine the status of the behavior at a given point in time.

O'Neill, Horner, Albin, Storey, and Sprague (1990) refer to the processes described in this section as the "functional analysis" of problem behavior or "an assessment process for gathering information that can be used to build effective behavioral support plans." They recommend three strategies that may be applied to conduct a functional analysis: (a) an interview with the individual whose behavior is to be modified or persons who know about the individual, (b) direct observation of the target behavior over an extended period of time and in various settings, and (c) manipulation of the setting or settings in which the target behavior may or may not be exhibited. O'Neill et al. provide a comprehensive plan for the functional analysis of problem behavior and a variety of practical protocols and forms. The reader is referred to their work for additional information on functional analysis.

Observer Reliability

Successful application of the behavior change process is dependent on the reliability with which target behaviors are observed or measured. If unreliable measurement procedures are used, then (a) behaviors that change may be recorded as stable, and (b) behaviors that are stable may be recorded as changed (Hall & Houten, 1983).

To increase confidence in their skills as observers, it is recommended that teachers conduct *interobserver reliability* checks. To do this, a second observer should be invited to observe and record the target behavior. This should be done occasionally during both the baseline and the intervention phase of the behavior change process. It is important that the second person observe the target behavior at the same time under the same circumstances and use the same definition of the behavior as the first observer.

By comparing the results of the two observations, using the following formula, an interobserver reliability percentage or quotient can be calculated. The closer to 100% the quotient is, the greater the confidence the practitioner has in the observation data. Hall and Houten (1983) suggest calculating interobserver reliability for interval data by dividing the number of intervals during which two observers agree by the total number of intervals they observed and multiplying the result by 100.

For example, Mrs. Sims and Mr. Horner observed Darlene's behavior together for a total of 20 5-minute intervals. Mrs. Sims observed the target behavior 20 times; Mr. Horner observed it 18 times. Using the preceding formula, their interobserver reliability quotient is

$$\frac{18}{18 + 2} \times 100 = 90\%.$$

Kerr and Nelson (1989) refer to this procedure as calculating "point-by-point reliability."

To obtain an interobserver reality quotient for frequency data, divide the frequency reported by the observer with the "lower" frequency by the frequency reported by the observer with the "higher" frequency and multiply the results by 100.

For example, Mr. Luther and Ms. Shanks were both observing Angel's frequency of cursing. They observed during the same time period. Mr. Luther recorded 12 curses; Mr. Shanks recorded 11. Using the formula, their interobserver reliability quotient is

$$\frac{11}{12} \times 100 = 91.66\%.$$

Kerr and Nelson refer to this procedure as calculating "total reliability."

IDENTIFYING REINFORCERS

A behavior modification intervention is only as effective as its reinforcer. Regardless of the intervention applied in a behavior change program, if the exhibition of the behavior is not reinforced, the behavior probably will not change. In a behavior change program, all factors may be carefully planned and the intervention precisely implemented, but if the child is not reinforced by the result of his or her behavior, little probability exists for a permanent behavior change.

♦ *Example*

Jean's third-grade teacher, Ms. Wildler, developed what she considered to be a foolproof intervention to reduce Jean's off-task behavior. She decided that for each 5-minute period that Jean was on task during language arts period, she would receive a small piece of fruit. Ms. Wildler implemented and monitored the intervention for 1 week. Jean's behavior did not change. During her observation, Ms. Wildler noted that each time Jean received a piece of fruit, she either gave it to another student or dropped it in the wastebasket. Jean did not like the pieces of apple and orange that Ms. Wildler was using as a reinforcer.

Remember: A reinforcer is not necessarily a desirable or undesirable consequence for a child merely because the child's teacher or parent believes it should be (Downing, Moran, Myles, & Ormsbee, 1991; Shea & Bauer, 1987; Smith & Rivera, 1993).

♦ *Example*

Mr. Jackson, the ninth-grade teacher at Edville Junior High School, was having difficulty getting his third-period social studies class to concentrate on their studies. He decided that he would begin to systematically reinforce their efforts by sending weekly praise notes to their parents. Mr. Jackson knew that every student liked to have notes of praise sent home. Rod, a class leader, became very agitated when he learned of Mr. Jackson's plan. Rod did not want his parents to know that he enjoyed school. His parents thought he should drop out of school and get a job.

A reinforcer is not necessarily desirable to all students.

♦ *Example*

Mrs. Karaker, an experienced practitioner of behavior modification, maintains a reinforcement menu of at least 10 items for her fifth-grade students. She knows the students have individual preferences and become bored with the same old reinforcer day after day. The only true test of the effectiveness of a specific reinforcer with a specific child is implementation—that is, to try it.

How can the teacher or parent identify potential reinforcers for the child whose behavior is to be modified? There are several procedures recommended for identifying reinforcers having a high probability of changing behavior in the desired direction. Among the available procedures are (a) preference scales, (b) preference lists, (c) interview with the child, (d) interview with the parent or teacher about the child, and (e) direct observation.

Preference Scales

Commercially available reinforcement *preference scales* are designed to assist the practitioner in eliciting and ranking the child's preferences. By means of pictures and questions, the teacher or parent presents the child with a variety of objects and activities, both tangible and social. The child selects from these potential reinforcers. The teacher or parent systematically guides the child through the process of selecting, comparing, and ranking the reinforcers. The practitioner may wish to review the literature for commercially available scales.

Preference List

A *preference list* (or reinforcement list), such as the one presented in the supplement at the end of this chapter, are frequently helpful to the teacher or parent who is having difficulty thinking of potential reinforcers. The preference list's greatest practical value to the practitioner is that it stimulates consideration of a broad spectrum of potential reinforcers; new reinforcers can be added to the list as the teacher or parent becomes aware of them.

Two reinforcement activities of current interest to students are computer time and the student newspaper. Hetfield (1994) discussed the use of a student newspaper to motivate learners with behavioral disorders. According to Hetfield, the newspaper can be used to motivate students, teach and reinforce academic skills, build self-esteem, promote positive social interaction in the classroom, and facilitate integration into the general classroom. Keyes (1994) offers suggestions for time on computer (TOC) to motivate reluctant learners. The TOC was employed within a classroom levels system (levels systems are discussed in Chapter 8). As students progress through the various levels, the TOC is extended.

The reinforcers listed in the supplement are suggestions for classroom use. Each child has unique personal likes and dislikes. The reinforcers must be selected in consultation with and by observation of the child whose behavior is to be changed.

Interview with Child

Interviewing a child to determine what he or she finds reinforcing is frequently productive. The interview should be structured, and the preference list may be used to stimulate discussion. The child is encouraged to express and discuss desires; he or she is asked questions such as "What kinds of things do you like to do?" "What are your favorite toys?" and "What do you like to do more than anything else?" The child's responses will be of great help in attempting to pinpoint those items and activities to be used as reinforcers. In addition, the interviewer has the opportunity to thoroughly explain the behavior change program and answer the child's questions.

There is evidence to indicate that when a child is involved in decision making concerning important elements of his or her program, the overall quality and rate of the program are enhanced (Raschke, 1979). Thus, involving the child in the selection of reinforcers enhances the probability that the intervention will be successful.

The use of the interview technique provides the child with an opportunity to learn to select reasonable and positive reinforcers. Many children initially have difficulty making reasonable selections because of a lack of experience in decision making. In this situation, the interview is in itself a learning experience for the child. The interview technique can be used with small groups as well as individuals.

The disadvantage of the technique is that it is time consuming, and its success depends on (a) the child's or group's ability to communicate with the interviewing adult and (b) the adult's skill as an interviewer.

In the interview situation, the following steps should be used as guidelines (Shea, Whiteside, Beetner, & Lindsey, 1974a, 1974b):

1. Establish rapport with the child or group
2. Explain the purpose of the session

3. Define and explain the meaning of individual and/or group reinforcers

4. Elicit suggestions for individual and/or group rewards:

   (a) Ask the child or group which rewards could be used as individual reinforcers. Record these suggestions. If working with a group, ask the individuals which suggested rewards could be used as group rewards.

   (b) Give the child or group an opportunity to add to the list of rewards.

   (c) Request that the child or each member of the group choose three rewards and rank them according to their desirability. If working with a group, determine the group's ranking of the rewards. Have the members vote to decide on the reward.

   (d) Make arrangements for another session at which the child or group may choose to add to or change the reinforcers. It is useful to record the reinforcers suggested by the child or group on the chalkboard.

Raschke (1981) published a procedure for designing reinforcement surveys that permit a child to choose personal reinforcers. The procedure is responsive to the needs and interests of the child and teacher in a specific instructional setting. To develop a survey, the teacher follows four steps: (a) select content items, (b) design a survey inventory, (c) administer the inventory, and (d) summarize the results.

The content of the inventory reflects not only the child's likes and dislikes but also what is practical and possible in the specific instructional setting. To assist in the selection of the survey's content, the teacher is encouraged to consult the list of potential reinforcers presented in the supplement.

The survey itself may take one of several forms: an open-ended format, a multiple-choice format, or a rank-order format. Examples of the open-ended format and multiple-choice format are presented on the following pages.

The administration of the survey includes very specific instructions that emphasize the confidentiality of responses and the fact that there are no right or wrong answers. From the information obtained, the teacher develops individual and group preference lists.

Reinforcement Assessment: Open-Ended Format

1. If I had 10 minutes free time during this class, I would most like to …
2. The favorite type of activity that I wish we would do more often in this class is …
3. My favorite seating arrangement in this class is …
4. My favorite place to sit in this class is …
5. My favorite way to learn new information in this class is …
6. My favorite instructional equipment to use in this class is …*
7. The person in this school I like most to praise me when I do good work is …
8. In this class, I feel proudest of myself when …
9. The thing that motivates me the most to do well in this classroom is …

Reinforcement Assessment: Multiple-Choice Format

1. The way I best like to learn about something new in this class is
    a. Lecture
    b. Books
    c. Pamphlets
    d. Films
    e. Tapes
    f. Small-group work
    g. Guest speakers

2. My favorite writing tool to use in this class is
    a. Magic Markers™
    b. Felt pens
    c. Colored pencils
    d. Colored chalk

3. My favorite seating arrangement in this class is
    a. Desks in rows
    b. Chairs at tables
    c. Desks randomly scattered

4. The special job I like to help the teacher with the most in this class is
    a. Handing out papers
    b. Putting away supplies
    c. Decorating a bulletin board
    d. Running the filmstrip projector
    e. Writing the assignment on the chalkboard
    f. Straightening up cupboards and bookcases

5. The best privilege I could earn in this class for good work would be to
    a. Sit anywhere I want in the class
    b. Help the teacher grade papers
    c. Put an assignment on the chalkboard
    d. Give the class announcements
    e. Pick a partner to work with*

Interview with Parent or Teacher

An interview with a parent or teacher can also be used in an effort to obtain and rank the child's reinforcers. Although less desirable than a direct interview with the

---

* From Raschke (1981, p. 93). Copyright 1981 by The Council for Exceptional Children. Reprinted by permission.

child, the parent or teacher interview can be helpful in determining which reinforcers have been applied successfully and unsuccessfully by others. It may also be used to determine the range of successful reinforcers within the child's response repertoire.

The parent or teacher interview is especially valuable to the behavior management consultant who is trying to determine the level of understanding and acceptance of behavior change techniques by the individual who works directly with the child.

The obvious disadvantage in applying this technique is that the parent's or teacher's level of sophistication as an objective observer is unknown. It should be recognized that the parent or teacher may not be of real assistance in the selection of potent rewards because of a distorted perception of the child's likes and dislikes. However, the use of the technique can be an excellent learning experience for parents and teachers; frequently, it can sensitize them to the importance of meaningful reinforcers for children. (This topic is discussed in detail in Chapter 9.)

Direct Observation

The most productive strategy for identifying effective reinforcers is direct observation. According to an old saying, "If you want to see a person do something well, observe the individual doing something he or she enjoys."

Direct observation requires the teacher to observe the child's self-selected activities in a variety of situations, such as on the playground, in the classroom, during structured time, and during free time, and to list those activities the child chooses. These self-selected activities and items can be used during the intervention as reinforcers (Mason & Egel, 1995).

♦ *Examples*

Ms. Maron observed that Marvin liked to congregate with his friends during recess to trade baseball cards. She decided to allow the boys to have an additional trading time after they finished their arithmetic lesson. The total arithmetic period was 40 minutes. After 30 minutes, the boys who had finished the assignment could go to a special area of the room and quietly trade cards. The longer Marvin took to complete the lesson, the less time he had to trade cards.

Mr. Dee knew that all 8-year-old boys like to play baseball. Mr. Dee wished to improve Jamie's performance in spelling. He told Jamie that each day that he got 80% of his spelling words correct, he could play baseball for 20 minutes on the playground. Mr. Dee was astonished when Jamie did not respond to this reward.

There were several reasons why Jamie did not respond, and Mr. Dee had failed to take them into consideration. Jamie had not only a visual-perception disability but also a gross motor disability, and these problems interfered with his skill in large-muscle activities. It was far more difficult to play baseball than to flunk spelling. Mr. Dee's fundamental error was that he did not include Jamie in the reinforcer selection process.

Different children value different consequences. It is nearly impossible to identify any event or item that will serve as a positive reinforcer for all children.

In the end, the potency of a reinforcer selected as a result of using any technique can be determined only by implementation. Many reinforcers, thought to be highly potent, fail to be effective with some children, whereas some reinforcers, discovered only on a teacher's hunch, prove to be most powerful in changing behavior.

A few additional suggestions for the selection and use of reinforcers may be useful:

1. Except for a few basic items such as food and water, no item or activity can be identified with certitude as an effective reinforcer before it has been demonstrated to be effective for a specific child. What is highly reinforcing for one child may not be for another.

2. With overexposure, even the most powerful reinforcer will lose strength and must be replaced. The teacher should provide a variety of reinforcers not only to prevent overexposure but also to satisfy the individual and his or her ever changing preferences. Many teachers provide a "menu of reinforcers" for their children. On any given day, a variety of items or activities are available to satisfy the diverse needs and interests of the children. They are permitted to select from this menu.

3. The task of observing the effects of existing reinforcers and searching for new reinforcers is a continuous process. A good reinforcement system is an ever changing blend of established and potential reinforcers.

4. Reinforcers should not be thought of only in terms of tangible items. There are many activities and privileges that are potent reinforcers. Frequently, teachers use a tangible reinforcer (with a social reinforcer) initially during the behavior change program. Later, they change the reward from the tangible reinforcer to a special activity or privilege (always keeping the social reinforcer). In the final stages of the behavior change process, the social reinforcer used alone should be adequate.

Although several methods for identifying reinforcers are discussed in this section, the two procedures most recommended are direct observation and a direct interview with the child. Both have proved effective for identifying reinforcers (Karraker, 1977).

The fact that a child is motivated by a specific reinforcer today does not necessarily mean the child will respond to that particular reinforcer next week. A change in performance may be the signal to initiate a new reward. The fact that Lisa correctly completed 25 addition problems on Monday to play with a puzzle, 27 problems on Tuesday to play with a puzzle, and 28 problems on Wednesday for the same privilege does not mean she will respond in a similar fashion on Thursday. To avoid this situation, a reward menu, as discussed in Chapter 5, is recommended. The menu allows the practitioner to systematically vary the rewards a child can work for on different occasions. With proficiency gained through practice in the techniques for changing behavior, the practitioner can predict when it is time to change reinforcers.

Schedules of reinforcement are discussed in Chapter 3; however, it should be reemphasized here that the schedule on which the reinforcement is delivered has considerable influence on the behavior change process.

Phasing Out Reinforcers

As stated previously, a goal of the behavior change process is to train an individual to respond to appropriate and occasional social reinforcers. Consequently, it is necessary that the behavior modification practitioner focus particular attention on *phasing out* the reinforcers over time. This task is accomplished primarily by changing from a fixed interval or ratio reinforcement schedule to a variable interval or ratio reinforcement schedule and by the systematic attenuating or lessening of the average frequency of reinforcer presentation. It must be remembered that a social reinforcer is always presented concurrently with a tangible reinforcer if tangible rewards are used.

Procedures applied to phasing out reinforcers are as follows:

Step 1:   Social and tangible reinforcers are presented simultaneously to the individual on a fixed reinforcement schedule. This statement assumes that tangible reinforcers are needed initially in the particular situation. This is not the situation in all cases.

Step 2:   Social reinforcers are continued on a fixed schedule, and tangible reinforcers are presented on a variable schedule. Tangible reinforcers are attenuated over time and are finally extinguished. Social reinforcers are presented simultaneously with tangible reinforcers during this step.

Step 3:   Social reinforcers are presented on a variable schedule. They are attenuated over time and are finally extinguished as the formal behavior change program is terminated.

♦ *Example*

Darlene was having considerable difficulty with her spelling assignments. On average, she was correctly spelling 4 of 10 words on the daily tests. In an effort to help her, Mr. Barea, Darlene's teacher, implemented a behavior modification intervention.

During the first phase of the program, each time that Darlene improved her score from the day before, she received verbal praise from Mr. Barea and a token worth 5 minutes of free time. She was never reinforced for attaining a score lower than her previous highest score.

When Darlene was consistently and correctly spelling 8 of 10 words, Mr. Barea implemented the next phase of the behavior change program. During this phase, Darlene was reinforced with free time less and less frequently. However, she was verbally praised each time she correctly spelled 8 of 10 words.

In the final phase, Mr. Barea phased out the free-time reinforcer completely and systematically lessened the social praise Darlene received to approximate that of the other students in the class.

Reinforcement Area

An area may be set aside in the classroom and home to serve as a reinforcement area. This area should be selected before a behavior change program is implemented and should contain those items needed to provide reinforcers. Among the items may be the following:

A table and chairs	Games (bingo, checkers, chess, cards)
A rug	Listening equipment (record player, tape deck, CD player)
Reading material (books, comics, magazines)	Viewing equipment (television, slide or filmstrip projector)
Art materials (clay, paint, paper, crayons)	

For additional examples, see the section on reinforcers in Supplement 1.

Obviously, the furnishings, materials, and equipment in a reinforcement area must be selected in response to the age, physical size, developmental levels, and interests of the students using the area. Figure 4.8 is an illustration of a classroom with a reinforcement area. It is recommended that the reinforcement area be a separate area of the classroom or home that is used exclusively for reinforcement. The area should never be used or associated with punishment, nor should the reinforcement area be used as a work area. The practitioner does not want the child to confuse positive reinforcement with punishment.

Figure 4.8
Classroom with reinforcement area

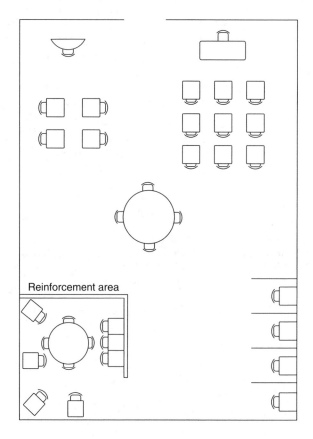

Reinforcement area

IMPLEMENTING THE INTERVENTION AND COLLECTING AND RECORDING INTERVENTION DATA

The next step in the behavior change process is selecting and implementing the intervention and collecting and recording intervention data. Chapters 5 and 6 are devoted to a detailed description of interventions applied to increase and decrease target behaviors.

Intervention data involve information collected on the effects of the intervention during the implementation phase. Equally as important as baseline data, intervention data provide a yardstick for comparing baseline behavior with new behavior. By comparing baseline data with intervention data, the teacher can determine the changes that have occurred as a result of the intervention. Figure 4.9 presents a comparison of Joshua's hitting behavior before and during the intervention.

In this graph, the target behavior shows an increase during the initial 2 days of intervention. The behavior then decreases to zero over the remaining days of the program.

The initial increase in the behavior (days 6 and 7) was probably a result of Joshua's testing of the teacher's response to his original behavior. In all probability, Joshua was confused by the fact that his previously effective response was no longer effective. Of course, this increase might also have been a result of the initial inefficiency of either the reinforcer or the practitioner. However, the initial increase in behavior, as discussed in Chapter 3, is normal and should be anticipated during the beginning days of the intervention.

The importance of continuing to count and chart the target behavior during the intervention can be readily seen on Joshua's graph. This procedure provides the practitioner with a visual image to be used in comparing the baseline and intervention behaviors. The data alert the teacher to the child's response to the intervention and thus to the overall effectiveness of the program at a particular point in time.

Figure 4.9
Frequency of Joshua's hitting behavior before and during the intervention

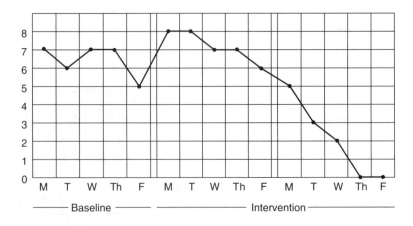

Prompting

Some children need assistance during the behavior change process. This assistance may be manual or verbal and is called *prompting*. Wolery, Ault, and Doyle (1992) define prompts as "any teacher behaviors that cause students to know how to do a behavior correctly" (p. 37). Prompts may include such activities as guiding a child's hand or foot in the completion of a task, moving the child's head to gain his or her attention, taking a child through a task by repeated precise verbal instruction, providing a verbal model for imitation, and providing printed or three-dimensional material that structures a task (Schloss, 1986). Prompts are used to increase the probabilities of success in a task. Prompting is applicable with several behavior change interventions discussed in Chapters 5 and 6.

According to Martin and Pear (1992), prompts are "supplemental stimuli that control the desired behavior but that are not a part of the desired final stimulus" (p. 126). There are various kinds of prompts that a parent or teacher may wish to apply during the behavior change intervention. These include verbal prompts (hints or cues), gestural prompts (motions made without touching the student to facilitate response), environmental prompts (the environment is altered to evoke the desired response), and physical prompts (physically guiding the student to the desired response).

Although prompts of various kinds may be a necessary component of the behavior change intervention initially, they must eventually be eliminated; the child must learn to complete the task independently. The gradual elimination of prompts is called *fading* (Panyan, 1980). Fading includes the reduction of the amount and quality of manual guidance, verbal assistance, and printed or three-dimensional material used to structure an activity. It is important that the practitioner consider the procedures to be used to fade the prompt before it is implemented.

♦ *Example*

Marie, a 6-year-old child, was enrolled in a motor therapy program in an effort to remediate her physical coordination problems. One of the objectives of her program was walking a 10-foot balance beam without assistance.

During the therapy program's assessment phase, Marie fell off the balance beam seven times in her effort to walk its length unaided. It was decided that during the initial stages of her motor therapy, Marie would be manually guided by a therapist. He would hold her right hand as she walked the beam.

With manual guidance, Marie learned to walk the 10-foot beam with efficiency within a few days. The therapist decided to fade the prompt (manual guidance) and applied the following schedule during the fading process:

1. The therapist reduced the firmness of his grasp on Marie's right hand.

2. The therapist grasped only one finger of Marie's hand.

3. The therapist positioned his hand in progressive steps approximately 6, 9, and 12 inches from Marie's right hand.

4. The therapist walked beside Marie with his hands at his side.

5. The therapist withdrew to the position he normally assumed to observe a person's efficiency on the balance beam.

EVALUATING THE EFFECTS OF INTERVENTION

Once the new behavior has been established at the acceptable level, the practitioner may question whether the observed changes were a result of the intervention or of an unknown intervening variable. This query cannot be responded to with exactitude. However, there is a procedure to test the effectiveness of the intervention. This is the process of extinction, or of reestablishing the baseline (Baseline 2). The process of reestablishing the baseline in this situation is as follows: If a behavior is thought to be maintained at a specific level by a reinforcer, the practitioner can evaluate the effectiveness of the reinforcer by withdrawing it.

◆ *Example*

Mr. Curtain had established Shirley's hand-raising behavior at an acceptable level. He then wondered whether the reinforcer applied in the intervention phase was the *factor* that had resulted in her change in behavior. The reinforcer was a smile and verbal praise each time Shirley raised her hand in class.

To check the potency of the reinforcer, Mr. Curtain withdrew it; that is, he ceased smiling at Shirley and praising her when she raised her hand in class. Within a few days, as demonstrated in Figure 4.10, Shirley's hand-raising response began to be extinguished. Because of the decrease in Shirley's hand-raising behavior, Mr. Curtain could assume that the reinforcer (smiles and verbal praise) was instrumental in increasing the hand-raising behavior. He had evaluated the effect of reinforcement on the behavior.

Reestablishing the baseline is not always an effective means of evaluating the potency of a reinforcer. If a behavior has been firmly habituated into the child's behavioral repertoire, it will not respond to extinction.

Establishing and then extinguishing a behavior is *not* a standard procedure applied in the behavior change process. However, this technique may assure new students of behavior modification that their efforts are effective in changing behaviors.

The use of Baseline 2 in an intervention is at the discretion of the practitioner. However, once a teacher or parent has determined that the reinforcer was instrumental in the behavior change program, it would be a disservice to the child not to reinstate it or not to return to the intervention state.

Meyer and Janney (1989) call for more practical measures of data collecting and thus the evaluation of the outcome of behavioral interventions in the classroom and

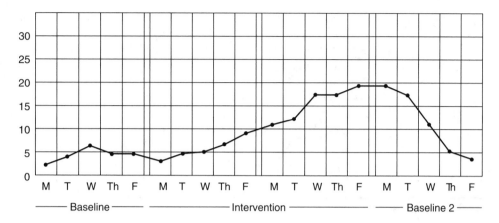

Figure 4.10
Frequency of Shirley's hand-raising behavior before and during the intervention and as a result of reestablishing the baseline (Baseline 2)

school setting. Their "user-friendly" measures include (a) the student's schedule of activities, which is evaluated periodically throughout the day; (b) a daily log of student behavior; (c) incident reports; and (d) alternative skill acquisition and excess behavior records. These measures of behavior change are suggested by Meyer and Janney because data collection is less arduous and less intrusive into the ongoing teaching-learning process. These same procedures can be used to supplement the baseline and intervention data collection strategies recommended in this chapter.

♦ SUMMARY

In this chapter, the steps for changing behavior are discussed. They are (a) selecting a target behavior, (b) collecting and recording baseline data, (c) identifying reinforcers, (d) implementing the intervention and collecting and recording intervention data, and (e) evaluating the effects of the intervention.

When selecting a target behavior, the practitioner should choose only one individual or group behavior to change at a time. The practitioner should analyze the potential target behavior in relation to its frequency, duration, intensity, and type; determine the direction the behavior is to take (whether it is to increase or decrease); determine whether the behavior is observable and quantifiable; and describe the behavior in precise, descriptive terminology. Collecting and recording baseline data allow an analysis of the changes in behavior that occur during the intervention.

A list of tangible and social reinforcers for application in the classroom and school are presented in Supplement 1. Consideration is given to consumable rewards, tangible and token rewards, games, activities, social rewards, and jobs. Two effective methods of identifying reinforcers are direct observation and an interview with the child.

Comparison of baseline and intervention data provides the practitioner with an evaluation technique for determining changes occurring in the target behavior as a result of intervention.

It is highly recommended that the new practitioner of behavior modification carefully follow each step in the behavior change process presented in this chapter.

♦ PROJECTS

1. Select five potential target behaviors and observe them. After observing the behaviors, discuss their characteristics in terms of frequency, duration, intensity, and type.

2. Collect and record accurate baseline data on two of the behaviors observed.

3. List 25 reinforcers that may be useful in modifying the behavior of children. Classify these as tangible or social reinforcers. At least 12 of the 25 reinforcers should be classifiable as social rewards.

4. Observe a child and develop a list of potential reinforcers for this child. Observe the child in a variety of situations.

   (a) As outlined in the text, interview the same child and develop a second list of reinforcers.

   (b) Interview the child's parent or teacher and develop a third list of reinforcers.

   (c) Compare the second and third lists of reinforcers. Can differences be noted between the reinforcers selected by the child and those selected by the child's teacher and parents?

5. Conceptualize and write a detailed description of an intervention to be applied to one of the behaviors observed in Project 1.

♦ REFERENCES

Alberto, P. A., & Troutman, A. C. (1990). *Applied behavior analysis for teachers* (3rd ed.). Upper Saddle River, NJ: Merrill/Prentice Hall.

Axelrod, S. (1983). *Behavior modification for the classroom teacher.* New York: McGraw-Hill.

Buck, G. H., Palloway, E. A., Kirkpatrick, M. A., Patton, J. R., & Fad, K. M. (2000). Developing behavioral intervention plans: A sequential approach. *Intervention in School and Clinic, 36*(1), 3–9.

Cooper, J. O., Heron, T. E., & Heward, W. L. (1987). *Applied behavior analysis.* Upper Saddle River, NJ: Merrill/Prentice Hall.

Downing, J. A., Moran, M. R., Myles, B. S., & Ormsbee, C. K. (1991). Using reinforcement in the classroom. *Intervention in School and Clinic, 27*(2), 85–90.

Fabry, B. D., & Cone, J. D. (1980). Autographing: A one-step approach to collecting and graphing data. *Education and Treatment of Children, 3,* 361–368.

Fitzsimmons, M. K. (1998). Functional behavioral assessment and behavior intervention plans. ERIC/OSEP Digest E571, pp. 1–3. (ERIC Document Reproduction Service No. ED 429 420)

Hall, R. V., & Houten, R. V. (1983). *The measurement of behavior.* Austin, TX: PRO-ED.

Hetfield, P. (1994). Using a student newspaper to motivate students with behavioral disorders. *Teaching Exceptional Children, 26*(2), 6–8.

Horner, R. H., Sugai, G., & Todd, A. W. (2001). "Data" need not be a four-letter word: Using data to improve schoolwide discipline. *Beyond Behavior, 11*(1), 20–22.

Jolivette, K., Scott, T. M., & Nelson, C. M. (2000). The link between functional behavioral assessment (FBA) and behavioral intervention plans (BIPs). ERIC Digest E592, pp. 1–4. (ERIC Document Reproduction Service No. ED 438 662)

Karraker, R. J. (1977). Self versus teacher selected reinforcers in a token economy. *Exceptional Children, 43*(7), 454–455.

Kerr, M. M., & Nelson, C. M. (1989). *Strategies for managing behavior problems in the classroom.* Upper Saddle River, NJ: Merrill/Prentice Hall.

Keyes, G. K. (1994). Motivating reluctant students: The time on computer program. *Teaching Exceptional Children, 27*(1), 21–23.

Lennox, D. B., & Miltenberger, R. G. (1989). Conducting a functional assessment of problem behavior in applied settings. *Journal of the Association for Persons With Severe Handicaps, 14*(4), 304–311.

Mager, R. F. (1984). *Preparing instructional objectives* (2nd rev. ed.). Belmont, CA: Pitman Learning Press.

Martin, G., & Pear, J. (1992). *Behavior modification: What it is and how to do it.* Upper Saddle River, NJ: Prentice Hall.

Mason, S. A., & Egel, A. L. (1995). What does Amy like? Using a mini-reinforcer assessment to increase student participation in instructional activities. *Teaching Exceptional Children, 28*(1), 42–45.

Meyer, L., & Janney, R. (1989). User-friendly measures of meaningful outcomes: Evaluating behavioral interventions. *Journal of the Association for Persons With Severe Handicaps, 14*(4), 263–270.

Morris, R. J. (1985). *Behavior modification with exceptional children: Principles and practices.* Glenview, IL: Scott, Foresman.

O'Neill, R. E., Horner, R. H., Albin, R. W., Storey, K., & Sprague, J. R. (1990). *Functional analysis of problem behavior: A practical assessment guide.* Sycamore, IL: Sycamore Publishing.

Panyan, M. C. (1980). *How to use shaping.* Austin, TX: PRO-ED.

Raschke, D. (1979). The relationship of internal-external control and operant reinforcement procedures with learning and behavior disordered children. (Doctoral dissertation, University of Wisconsin, 1979). *Dissertation Abstracts International, 40,* 4533.

Raschke, D. (1981). Designing reinforcement surveys—Let the students choose the reward. *Teaching Exceptional Children, 14,* 92–96.

Rusch, F. R., Rose, T., & Greenwood, C. R. (1988): *Introduction to behavior analysis in special education.* Upper Saddle River, NJ: Prentice Hall.

Schloss, P. J. (1986). Sequential prompt instruction for mildly handicapped learners. *Teaching Exceptional Children, 18*(3), 181–184.

Schopler, E., Reichler, R. J., & Lansing, M. (1980). *Individualized assessment and treatment for autistic and developmentally disabled children: Vol. II. Teaching strategies for parents and professionals.* Austin, TX: PRO-ED.

Scott, T. M., & Nelson, C. M. (1999). *Using functional behavioral assessment to develop effective behavioral intervention plans: A ten step process.* Lexington: University of Kentucky Press.

Shea, T. M., & Bauer, A. M. (1987). *Teaching children and youth with behavior disorders* (2nd ed.). Upper Saddle River, NJ: Prentice Hall.

Shea, T. M., Whiteside, W. R., Beetner, E. G., & Lindsey, D. L. (1974a). *Psychosituational interview.* Edwardsville: Southern Illinois University Press.

Shea, T. M., Whiteside, W. R., Beetner, E. G., & Lindsey, D. L. (1974b). *Selecting reinforcers.* Edwardsville: Southern Illinois University Press.

Smith, D. D., & Rivera, D. M. (1993). *Effective discipline.* Austin, TX: PRO-ED.

Wolery, M., Ault, M. J., & Doyle, P. M. (1992). *Teaching students with moderate to severe disabilities: Use of response prompting strategies.* White Plains, NY: Longman Publishing.

Sample Reinforcers

Preference List
Consumable Food Reinforcers

Apples	Jelly beans
Grapes	Small candies
Oranges	Mints
Raisins	Juice
Crackers	Fruit-flavored drink
Cookies	Milk
Popcorn	Soda
Potato chips	Ice cream
Peanuts	Lollipops
Gumdrops	Sugarless gum

Reinforcing Activities in Relation to the Consumable Foods

Distributing reinforcers

Cleaning the area after reinforcers have been distributed

Popping popcorn

Scooping ice cream

Baking cookies

Preparing snacks

Tangible Reinforcers Other Than Food

Tickets to games, movies

Personal grooming supplies

Toys, games, and so on from the class store

Special materials such as colored chalk, pencils, or felt-tipped pens

Token Reinforcers

Check marks and points

Happy faces and stars

Behavior and achievement charts

Individual behavior and achievement cards and bankbooks

Rubber-stamp marks of various designs

Gold stars next to child's name on the class chart

Trading stamps

Conservation stamps

Good-citizen tags and certificates

Social Reinforcers

Receiving verbal praise

Having photograph displayed

Getting personal time with the teacher, paraprofessional, counselor, or principal

Participating in small-group discussions

Having work and projects displayed

Participating in show and tell

Demonstrating a skill

Clapping and cheering by others when successful

Being leader or organizer of an event

Getting a hug, handshake, or pat on the back

Sitting next to the teacher at lunch

Playing with a classmate of choice

Sitting and talking with a friend (child or adult)

Time on the computer

Job Reinforcers

Conducting an auction in class	Taking the class roll
Passing out paper, pencils, and so on	Carrying messages to other teachers
Taking a note to the office	Serving as secretary for class meetings
Erasing the chalkboard	Raising or lowering the flag
Helping the teacher with a project	Emptying the wastebasket
Conducting a class raffle	Carrying the wastebasket while other
Being teacher for a lesson	children clean out their desks
Managing the class store	Distributing and collecting materials
Shopping for the class store	Operating a slide, filmstrip, or movie
Being messenger for the day	projector
Helping in the cafeteria	Using the overhead projector
Assisting the custodian	Recording own behavior on a graph
Cleaning the erasers	Teaching another child
Watering the plants	Helping the librarian
Running the photocopier	Telling the teacher when it is time to
Stapling papers together	go to lunch
Feeding the fish or other animals	Sharpening the teacher's pencils
Giving a message over the intercom	Opening the teacher's mail
Picking up litter on the school grounds	Sweeping the floor of the classroom
Cleaning the teacher's desk	Adjusting the window shades
Being lunch monitor	Being line leader
Working on class/school newspaper	

5

Methods of Increasing Behavior

Contingency contracting
Contract
Modeling
Positive reinforcement
Self-management
Shaping
Token economy

♦ **CHAPTER OBJECTIVES**

After completing this chapter, you will be able to do the following:

1. Characterize positive reinforcement.
2. Describe shaping.
3. Understand and exemplify modeling.
4. Define and explain contingency contracting.
5. Describe self-management strategies.
6. Identify and illustrate token economy.

◆ ◆ ◆

Judy, a second grader, is more socially mature than her peers. This social maturity is a result of her close association with her sister Joanne, who is a fifth grader. The girls spend most of their time playing together and with Joanne's friends. Judy thinks that second graders are babies and therefore does not associate with them at recess; she associates with them only when necessary in the classroom. Judy is not only socially mature for her age but intellectually mature as well.

Behavior problems are developing for Judy among her peers as well as among Joanne's friends. Joanne's friends often invite her to their homes for parties or to the movies. They do not invite Judy because they think she is too young. As Joanne gets older, Judy is finding herself alone more and more frequently. Not having anyone to play with upsets her greatly.

Maybe if Judy's parents knew more about behavior management, they might increase Judy's socialization with her peers.

Mr. Peterson is a basketball coach at William Tolbert Community College. Over the past 2 years, he has developed a winning basketball team and an excellent reputation as a coach. Mr. Peterson is employed by the college part time to coach and recruit basketball players. He is a full-time employee of a local high school where he teaches physical education. Because of overstaffing and declining budgets, the college is unable to offer Coach Peterson a full-time position.

Mr. Peterson is worried that additional budget cuts will eliminate his position at the college. He fears he will be replaced by the former basketball coach, who is teaching full time in the physical education department. If so, he believes he is developing a winning basketball team for another coach. He is so paranoid about the former basketball coach taking his team away from him that it is affecting his coaching and his relationship with the college faculty. Mr. Peterson dwells on one topic in all conversations: "I'm working day and night to build a team for someone else."

Maybe if the physical education department chairperson knew more about increasing behaviors, he would be able to help Coach Peterson be more positive toward his part-time position.

The six most common techniques applied in behavior modification interventions for increasing a target behavior are (a) positive reinforcement, (b) shaping, (c) contingency contracting, (d) token economy, (e) modeling, and (f) self-management. These basic methods should be of assistance to the beginning practitioner attempting to establish acceptable behaviors in children. The techniques are applicable with both individual and group behaviors.

POSITIVE REINFORCEMENT

Positive reinforcement, which is discussed in some detail in Chapter 2, is reviewed in this section. Positive reinforcement is known by various labels, such as positive attention, approval, social reinforcement, and rewarding. It is the process of reinforcing a target behavior in order to increase the probability that the behavior will recur. Positive reinforcement is the presentation of a desirable reinforcer after the behavior has been exhibited. The reinforcer tends to increase the frequency or duration with which the behavior is exhibited in the future. The advantages of positive reinforcement are (a) it is responsive to the child's natural need for attention and approval, and (b) it decreases the probability that the child will exhibit inappropriate behavior in an effort to obtain needed attention.

Two rules are essential for the effective application of positive reinforcement. First, when a child is initially exhibiting a new appropriate behavior, it must be positively reinforced each time it occurs. Second, once the target behavior is established at a satisfactory rate, the child's behavior should be reinforced intermittently.

To apply positive reinforcement, the teacher should follow these steps (Shea & Bauer, 1987):

Step 1: Carefully select a target behavior (do not attempt to reinforce every positive behavior a child exhibits).

Step 2: Observe the child's behavior to ascertain when he or she engages in the behavior.

Step 3: During the initial stage, reinforce the behavior each time and immediately after it is exhibited.

Step 4: Specify for the child the behavior that is being reinforced ("I like the _____" or a similar comment).

Step 5: When reinforcing, speak with enthusiasm and show interest in the child's behavior.

Step 6: When appropriate, the practitioner may become involved in the child's behavior, that is, give the child help.

Step 7: Vary the reinforcer.

Step 8: When appropriate, change to a variable reinforcement schedule.

A note of caution: Public reinforcement is unwelcome to some children under some circumstances. They may be embarrassed by positive reinforcement in the presence of peers, teachers, parents, and others.

Gross and Ekstrand (1983) studied increasing and maintaining rates of teacher praise and their effects on student behavior. They found that teacher positive reinforcement decreased student scolding, increased productivity, and increased teacher enthusiasm in the classroom.

According to Sutherland, Copeland, and Wehby (2001), teacher praise has been found to be an effective strategy for supporting both student learning and behavior.

However, they found that in classrooms serving learners with behavioral/emotional problems, teacher praise was quite infrequent. These authors suggested several guidelines for the use of effective praise:

1. Praise should be delivered immediately after the exhibition of the target behavior.
2. Praise should be delivered as unobtrusively as possible in order not to disrupt the flow of class activity.
3. Praise should be delivered in a manner that demonstrates that the teacher is sincere.
4. Praise by the teacher should include a statement of the positive behavior for which the learner is being praised.
5. Praise statements should be varied in words and gestures.
6. Praise during the beginning stages of learning a new behavior should be frequent, then should be less frequent as the behavior becomes habituated.
7. Praise is faded when the praised behavior becomes part of the learner's usual manner of behaving.

♦ *Examples*

Michael has extremely poor table manners. He not only eats with his hands and fingers but also eats very rapidly. His teacher, Ms. Vandan, is attempting to improve the boy's table manners by positively reinforcing Michael's use of a fork and placement of the fork on the plate between each bite of food.

Michael is pleased with the extra attention, and over a period of several weeks his table manners have dramatically improved. Ms. Vandan used first a continuous reinforcement schedule and then a variable schedule to help Michael.

Fourteen-year-old George, a member of the "Wild and Crazy Bunch," likes his math teacher, Ms. Chinn, very much. He enjoys receiving her attention, but sometimes it is a little annoying. This is especially true when Ms. Chinn makes a big show in front of the whole class of his successfully completing a difficult problem. It seems the other members of the "Bunch" hassle him after class when this occurs.

Brigham, Bakken, Scruggs, and Mastropieri (1992) researched the effects of positive reinforcement on group behavior. The subjects of their investigations were eight middle school students, five girls and three boys, in a self-contained special education class. The students were of low socioeconomic status and resided in the inner city. They were mildly mentally retarded and exhibited disruptive classroom behaviors.

The researchers applied cooperative behavior management strategies to promote positive classroom behavior. They investigated on-task behavior (e.g., attending to teacher, assignment, materials); off-task, active behavior (e.g., drumming fingers, tapping pencil, tapping feet, playing with objects, being out of seat); and off-task, passive behavior (e.g., looking out window, staring, sleeping). After 1 week of baseline, the class was divided into two teams. In the first study, the team exhibiting the highest level of on-task behavior was rewarded. This intervention was effective with all but one student. In the second study, which was implemented after a second baseline, both individuals and teams were rewarded for appropriate classroom behavior. Direct prompts were provided for one student. Both interventions were successful in decreasing inappropriate behavior for the group; the second intervention was effective with all students.

West et al. (1995) discussed the use of the "musical clocklight" to encourage positive classroom behavior in individuals and groups. The clocklight was applied as part of the Program for Academic Survival Skills (PASS). PASS is a management program for academic-related behaviors. It includes three components: (a) group reward contingency, (b) clearly stated classroom rules, and (c) a clocklight that signals students when the whole group is following the rules. The amount of time the total class is following the rules is recorded. Rewards are based on the percentage of available time that the whole group is following the rules.

The clocklight itself includes three components: the clock, the light, and recorded music. When the whole group is following the rules, the clock is running, the light is on, and music is being played in the classroom. The clocklight is not activated during instructional periods (i.e., lectures and discussions). Prior to implementation of PASS, classroom rules are discussed with the students and demonstrated by the teacher. During the program, teachers use praise techniques and corrective teaching methods with students.

In the applications of the clocklight in three middle school classrooms, West et al. found that classroom rule following, getting teacher's attention appropriately, and teacher satisfaction increased.

SHAPING

To initiate an intervention for the purpose of increasing a behavior, the teacher or parents need only wait until the target behavior is emitted by the child. When the behavior occurs, it must be immediately rewarded with a potent reinforcer.

However, suppose a situation arises in which the level of performance of the behavior is at zero or near zero. What can the teacher or parent do to establish the behavior? There are two alternatives:

1. Wait an undetermined length of time (in some cases, forever) for the behavior to naturally occur.
2. Use a behavior-shaping technique.

Shaping is the systematic, immediate reinforcement of successive approximations of the target behavior until the behavior is established (Shea & Bauer, 1987). It is used primarily to establish behaviors that have not been previously manifested in the individual's behavior repertoire (Cooper, Heron, & Heward, 1987). Just as the sculptor shapes and molds an object of art from clay, the practitioner shapes and molds a new behavior from an undifferentiated behavioral response. Shaping may also be used to increase infrequently exhibited behaviors. This technique is applicable to both learning and behavior problems.

The behavior-shaping process includes the following steps:

Step 1:   Selecting a target behavior

Step 2:   Obtaining reliable baseline data

Step 3:   Selecting potent reinforcers

Step 4:   Reinforcing successive approximations of the target behavior each time they occur

Step 5:   Reinforcing the newly established behavior each time it occurs

Step 6:   Reinforcing the behavior on a variable reinforcement schedule

Many of these steps are explained in Chapters 3 and 4. However, some of them require additional comments here for clarification.

The behavior selected for shaping must be carefully specified. The teacher or parent must be positive that the selected behavior is meaningful to the child in terms of the child's present life context and developmental level.

If the performance level of the target behavior is at zero, the teacher or parent must initiate the shaping process from the child's undifferentiated behavioral manifestations.

♦ *Examples*

Tommy's teacher, Ms. Allen, wishes to establish intelligible verbal responses in Tommy's behavioral repertoire. However, the child enunciates no understandable words. His entire verbal behavior consists of vocal noises, such as screeches, howls, and guttural sounds. The teacher must begin the shaping process with the manifested behavior, that is, vocal noise. She must reinforce successive approximations of intelligible verbal responses.

Jeff, a child with severe disabilities, was having great difficulty interacting appropriately on the playground during circle or ball games requiring running from one specific location to another. When he was required to engage in a game of this type, he ran about at random, dashing here and there, jumping up and down, and in general confusing himself and his playmates.

Mr. Speer, the physical education teacher, wished to modify this behavior. He realized he had to start the change process with the behavior presently being manifested by Jeff. He determined that Jeff did attend to the action of the game and attempted to play by the rules. In this effort to help Jeff, Mr. Speer modified the rules of the game; he established a "new rule" in which all team members ran hand in hand in pairs from one location to another. Jeff was Mr. Speer's partner until he was conditioned to the new running pattern. The game was played by the traditional rules after Jeff developed acceptable skills.

During the behavior-shaping process, the teacher or parent reinforces only those behavioral manifestations that most closely approximate the desired behavior.

♦ Example

Mr. Jackson designed a shaping intervention to increase the number of assigned math problems that Robert would successfully complete in his workbook during independent study. Robert never completed the 20 problems given for practice. However, baseline data revealed that Robert consistently solved the first 9 problems successfully in each practice section. He simply did not attempt the remaining 11 problems.

During the shaping process, Mr. Jackson reinforced Robert for *improvements* over his baseline of 9. Robert was rewarded for successfully completing 10 problems, 11 problems, 12 problems, and so on. Robert was *never* rewarded for completing a quantity of problems below his highest level of accomplishment. Within a short time Mr. Jackson's intervention, data confirmed the fact that Robert was consistently completing the 20 problems successfully. The reinforcer was phased out.

Reinforcing less than the existing baseline results in rewarding behavior in a direction of change that is the reverse of the proposed direction. Remember, *only* the *highest* approximations of the target behavior should be reinforced.

Another important consideration in the shaping process is the teacher's or parent's knowledge of how long to provide reinforcement at one level of performance before moving to the next level. Such a movement increases the demands on the child. Determining when to move on is the teacher's or parent's greatest dilemma. If reinforcement continues too long at a given performance level, the child's behavior may become so rigidly established that further progress will be difficult. However, if the practitioner insists that the child progress too rapidly from one level to the next, there is a great possibility that the new behavior will be extinguished.

Knowing when to progress from one level of performance to the next is of utmost importance. Unfortunately, this knowledge is part of the skill needed for behavior modification, and developing it is not easy. The teacher or parent develops this needed sensitivity and skill only with practice and experience in behavior shaping and through knowing the individual child.

The following two examples are presented to clarify the steps in the behavior-shaping process.

♦ Examples

Ms. Simpkins wished to increase Jim's letter identification skills. Jim could identify 7 of the 26 letters of the alphabet consistently. Before implementing a shaping intervention, Ms. Simpkins determined that gumdrops were an effective reinforcer for Jim.

During the intervention phase of the behavior change program, Jim was exposed to one new letter of the alphabet at a time. He was to learn each new letter before another letter was presented. Jim was reinforced with a gumdrop only if he identified the new letter and all previously identified letters. The new letter was always presented last in the daily sequence of letters. After he had learned a letter, it was presented randomly with all the other previously learned letters in the daily session.

This procedure was continued until Jim successfully identified all the letters in the alphabet.

Mr. Behe wished to increase Barry's in-seat behavior. Baseline data revealed that, on an average, Barry remained in his seat approximately 6 minutes. Mr. Behe had determined through observation that Barry enjoyed listening to story records. This activity was selected as a reinforcer for acceptable in-seat behavior.

During the intervention, a timer was placed on Barry's desk. He was told that each time he remained in his seat until the timer bell sounded, he would be allowed to go to the reinforcement area of the classroom and listen to his favorite story record for a specific number of minutes. (The reinforcement schedule Mr. Behe used to shape the in-seat behavior is presented in Table 5.1.)

Barry's behavior was shaped with little difficulty. However, during the 20-minute interval between reinforcement, Barry became bored. As a consequence, he remained at the 20-minute interval longer than the teacher had anticipated. At Barry's suggestion, Mr. Behe changed the reinforcer from story records to jigsaw puzzles.

According to Panyan (1980), there are two distinct types of behavior-shaping interventions: progressive and chain.

In forward shaping or chaining, the first component or link in the chain or series of links is taught first, the second link is taught second, and so on. In backward

Table 5.1
Reinforcement Schedule for In-Seat Behavior

Minutes of In-Seat Behavior	Minutes in Reinforcement Area
5	2
5	2
7	2½
8	2½
10	2½
15	3
20	3
25	3
30	3½
45	4
60	4
90	5
120	7½
150	10

shaping or chaining, the last component or link of a complex task or chain is taught to the individual first, the second-to-last component of the task is taught second, and so on. In other words, the components or links in the chain are taught in reverse order. Both forms of chaining are useful; their application depends on the particular task being taught, the individual being instructed, and other variables such as time and personnel availability.

◆ *Example*

Mr. McGinnis and Mr. Solomon were responsible for teaching their daughters, Angie and Beth, to make their beds before they left for school in the morning. Mr. McGinnis and Mr. Solomon were very busy in the morning and had little time to teach the task. Mr. McGinnis had a little more time in the morning because he was a professor of behavior management at the local university and left for work later than Mr. Solomon. Both men decided to use shaping.

Mr. McGinnis and Mr. Solomon analyzed the complex task of bed making into the following discrete steps:

STEP	TASK
1.	Remove the pillows
2.	Pull back the blanket and top sheet
3.	Smooth the bottom sheet
4.	Pull up the top sheet and smooth
5.	Pull up the blanket and smooth
6.	Fold the top of the top sheet over the top of the blanket
7.	Put the bedspread on the bed
8.	Fold the top one-fourth of the bedspread back
9.	Put the pillow on the top of the bed, above the fold in the bedspread
10.	Place the top one-fourth of the bedspread over the pillow
11.	Smooth and check

Mr. McGinnis used forward chaining to teach Angie to make her bed. During the teaching process, he and Angie proceeded from Step 1 to Step 11 in order. In the first session, Angie was required to complete Step 1 and was reinforced when the step was completed. After Angie completed Step 1, Mr. McGinnis completed making the bed (Steps 2–11). During the second session Angie completed Steps 1 and 2, was reinforced, and Mr. McGinnis completed making the bed.

Mr. Solomon used backward chaining to teach Beth to make her bed. He did this because he could reinforce "completed bedmaking" more frequently and, in addition, the teaching task would be quicker and the bed would look better. During the teaching process, Mr. Solomon and Beth proceeded from Step 11 to Step 1. In the first session, Mr. Solomon completed Steps 1 through 10, and Beth was required to complete Step 11 and was reinforced for making her bed. During the second session, Mr. Solomon completed Steps 1 through 9, and Beth completed Steps 10 and 11 and was reinforced. (By the way, both

Angie and Beth learned to make their beds each morning before departing for school. However, Beth appeared to enjoy the learning task more than Angie.)

In the progressive shaping intervention, the child is required to engage in a series of steps, each of which is a continuation and progression of the previously learned step or steps. Examples of this intervention are bathing, hand washing, putting on a sweater or socks, and so on.

A chain intervention is composed of two or more separate and distinct steps or skills that are learned and combined sequentially to complete a specific task (Alberto & Troutman, 1990). Examples of this intervention are tying shoes, polishing shoes, eating, buttoning clothing, and so on.

The following example and conceptual model summarize this discussion of the behavior-shaping process.

♦ *Example*

Five-year-old Stephen was nonverbal. His speech teacher selected the initiation of verbal exchanges with his preschool teacher as the target behavior. Baseline data revealed that Stephen's only verbal behavior consisted of babbling, yelling, and screaming. This behavior was frequent when he was in the company of adults he knew. However, he did not consistently emit this behavior in response to queries from others.

Stephen was observed by the speech teacher, who determined that he consistently responded to four tangible reinforcers: pickles, potato chips, prunes, and popsicles.

The behavior-shaping intervention was initiated on a daily basis for 30 minutes during the preschool sessions that Stephen attended at a local school. The effectiveness of the intervention was to be evaluated by means of direct observation of the behavior-shaping sessions and the boy's activities in the preschool classroom with his teacher and playmates.

Shaping began with undifferentiated, inconsistent verbal responses. Within a single school year, Stephen had progressed to initiating some verbal exchanges with others in both the shaping sessions and the preschool class. By the end of the year, he would ask his teacher for milk, juice, cookies, toys, and the like. Although he seldom played with his classmates, he did verbally object to their attempts to confiscate his toys and snacks.

Stephen's ascent up to the behavior-shaping ladder is presented in Figure 5.1. The steps of the ladder are self-explanatory with the possible exception of Steps 3 and 4. During these steps, Stephen consistently used specific verbal noises in place of words. For example, "ah" was used for the word "milk," "eh" was used for the word "no," and the like. Emphasis here was put on converting these emissions into meaningful words.

CONTINGENCY CONTRACTING

When we consider contemporary emphasis in the media on deferred-payment purchasing, we believe that every child should have some idea of the meaning of a contract. A *contract* is an agreement, written or verbal, between two or more parties,

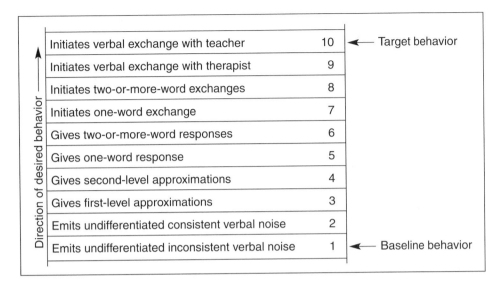

Figure 5.1
Behavior-shaping model (Stephen's verbal behavior)

individuals, or groups that stipulates the responsibilities of the parties concerning a specific item or activity. Contingency contracting in behavior modification parlance involves organizing events so that the learner gets to do that which he or she wishes to do after doing something that the parent or teacher wants him or her to do.

For purposes of this chapter, *contingency contracting* is defined as the process of contracting so that the child gets to do something he or she wants to do following completing something the parent or teacher wants the child to do.

We are all parties of contracts in daily living. Some of us are fortunate enough to have a written contract stating the terms of employment. This contract explains what duties we are to perform, for what period of time, and for what compensation. If we perform as specified in the contract, we cannot be fired under normal circumstances. A verbal contract exists between spouses. The terms of the contract state that they will love, honor, and respect one another until death (or divorce) does them part.

There are many lesser contracts in contemporary society, such as home loans and loans on automobiles, boats, and the like. Contracts such as these are indispensable to the efficient operation of the business system.

There are some contracts, seldom written, that are often taken for granted but nevertheless are indispensable in a complex urban society. Among these unwritten contracts are trust arrangements with utility services that the rubbish will be collected on certain mornings, the lights will go on when we turn a switch, or the water will flow when we open a faucet.

The use of contingency contracting as a behavior modification technique is based on a principle developed by Premack (1965). The Premack Principle suggests that behavior which is exhibited at a high frequency or rate of occurence can be used to increase a behavior that is exhibited at a low frequency or rate of occurrence. What Premack stated was an old and frequently used principle. For centuries, people have applied this principle to raising their children, teaching their students, and supervising their employees. *If you do X, then you can do or get Y.* This principle has often been referred to as "Grandma's law." Most persons remember the power of this law from childhood:

- "Eat your spinach, then you can have some ice cream."
- "Clean your room, then you can go to the movies."
- "Cut the lawn, then you can use the car."
- "Do your homework, then you can play computer games."

This same principle carries over to adult life:

- "Write 27 articles and 10 books, then you will be promoted to professor."
- "Don't join the union, then you will retain your job."
- "Don't make waves on the bureaucratic sea of calm, then you will be granted tenure."

Table 5.2 presents a series of *X* and *Y* statements found in the classroom.

Within the past several decades, teachers and parents have recognized the significance of individual differences caused by such factors as maturation, general knowledge, locus of control, and experience. Various instructional programs have been developed in response to these differences. Contingency contracting is one method that can be used to individualize instruction and behavior control to respond to the child's interests, needs, and abilities; it can be applied to the cognitive, affective, and psychomotor domains of learning.

In a study of the truancy behavior of students in an inner-city middle school, Hess, Rosenberg, and Levy (1990) demonstrated that contingency contracting can be applied effectively in conjunction with group counseling. Counseling and interviewing are discussed in Chapter 7.

According to Downing (1990), contingency contracts can be applied to teach new behavior, maintain existing behaviors, decrease inappropriate behavior, and promote enrichment and independent study for both individuals and groups.

Table 5.2
X, Then *Y*, Statements

X	Then	Y
Sit in your seat 2 hours		Get a 10-minute recess
Complete your term paper		Get an A
Be a "good" student		Receive a good report card
Volunteer for the football team		Receive recognition from the cheerleaders
Learn a letter of the alphabet		Immediately receive a gumdrop

According to Kelly and Stokes (1982), there are few published empirical studies on the use of contingency contracting in the schools. In his review of the research, however, Murphy (1988) cites school-based studies on contingency contracting and academic productivity, performance accuracy, study skills, school attendance, and social behavior. He suggests that contracting is an excellent method for facilitating self-management and academic and social development.

The advantages of contingency contracting are many. The method is positive; that is, the child takes an active role in deciding the type and amount of work required. Consequently, personal responsibilities are understood by the child. At regular intervals, the contract is reviewed for the child's reaffirmation. Accountability factors are built into this intervention. The teacher collects empirical data that indicate where the child was, where the child has progressed, and the child's current needs. The teacher can use this information to develop the program, instructional objectives, and developmental objectives with the child.

Downing (2002) discusses several potential applications for contingency contracting:

- To introduce and teach the learners new behavior
- To increase the frequency of an existing desired behavior
- To maintain and support the use and generalization of learner skills
- To decrease or extinguish learners' existing behavior
- To facilitate the completion of academic tasks
- To document the results of decision making, problem solving, and other interventions.

Downing offers the following step-by-step guidelines for implementing an individualized contingency contract:

1. Identify the area of concern
2. Describe the circumstances under which the behavior of concern occurs
3. Analyze the antecedent events that may trigger the behavior and the consequences that may increase the occurrence of the behavior
4. Determine which, if any, antecedents or consequences might be effective in decreasing the behavior
5. Develop a hypothesis to explain the student's behavior that you, as a practitioner, understand the behavior
6. Collect and summarize (perhaps in graphic form) the current level of the behavior
7. Develop behavioral objectives, based on the information or data collected in the previous step, that are specific, observable, and measureable
8. Identify the unsuccessful interventions that have been applied previously to change the behavior
9. Develop a list of potentially effective reinforcers that may be effective with the learner

10. Determine the consequence of the contract for the student if it is a failure. Determine whether there will be negative consequences and whether these will be natural or artificial

11. Determine who will be involved in agreeing on the terms of the contract and monitoring it

12. Evaluate the results of the contract

The teacher serves as contract manager, providing facts and explaining the principles. The teacher encourages the child to choose realistic limits. The teacher ensures that both the task and the reinforcer are fair to both parties of the contract (child and teacher).

When contingency contracting is first used with a child, small tasks and small reinforcers are most effective because they allow frequent reinforcement. Lengthy or complex tasks and small reinforcers defeat the motivational factors inherent in this intervention. If the task is more demanding than the reinforcer is desirable, the learner is not sufficiently motivated to perform. Likewise, the reinforcer should not be greater than the task warrants; otherwise, the instructional objective established for the child is difficult to obtain.

Initially, contracts may encourage and reward approximations of desired behavior. Short work periods are desirable because they permit frequent reinforcement. Low-achieving children usually require immediate reinforcers; consequently, short-term contracts (daily) are most appropriate. Higher-achieving children can usually delay reinforcements; therefore, long-term contracts (1 or 2 weeks) are feasible.

Some practitioners believe it is beneficial to separate the locations for task performance and reinforcer delivery. In this way, the learner equates the task performance as a means to a desirable end, that is, going to the reinforcement area. This also broadens the type and variety of reinforcers that can be made available to the students. Teachers are encouraged to establish a reinforcement area in their classroom. Reinforcement areas are discussed in Chapter 4.

The teacher must encourage the child to adhere to the contract for the designated period of time. The child should be cautioned that if the agreed-on task is not performed, the child will not receive the reinforcer. However, if the original contract is too difficult, a new contract must be written for the learner to perform successfully. Every effort should be made to ensure the success of the original contract.

The underlying principle of contingency contracting is constant; the learner, by making decisions concerning personal productivity, develops critical thinking skills, self-control, and the independence that increases productivity.

There are two types of contracts applicable in the classroom setting: verbal and written. Educators have generally found verbal contracts more useful than written contracts. The following are examples of verbal contracts that can be used in the classroom:

- "John, when you have completed eight addition problems correctly, you may play with the puzzles for the remainder of the period."

- "Mary, if you remain in your seat for 5 minutes, you may work in your coloring book for 10 minutes."

- "James, if you come to school on time tomorrow, you may be first in line for lunch."
- "Tom, if you don't hit anyone this morning, you may have an extra milk at lunch."
- "Mike, if you complete your seat work, you may watch *Sesame Street* on television."

Verbal contracts such as these are made daily in the classroom. They work effectively for both the teacher and the child.

Written contracts are more elaborate than verbal contracts. The elaborateness of the written contract depends on the child for whom it is designed. Contracts frequently lose their effectiveness when they include pseudolegal jargon, such as "the parties of the first part," "the parties of the second part," or "henceforth and forevermore." It is recommended that the teacher or parent use the contract format in Figure 5.2 or a similar one. An additional copy of the contract is provided in the back of the text.

Date _____

Contract

This is an agreement between _____
(Child's name)

and _____. The contract begins on
(Teacher's name)

_____ and ends on _____. It will be reviewed
(Date)   (Date)

on _____.
(Date)

The terms of the agreement are:

Child will _____

_____

_____

_____

Teacher will _____

_____

_____

_____

If the child fulfills his or her part of the contract, the child will receive the agreed-on reward from the teacher. However, if the child fails to fulfill his or her part of the contract, the reward will be withheld.

Child's signature _____

Teacher's signature _____

Figure 5.2
Contingency contract

Homme, Csanyi, Gonzales, and Rechs (1979) have suggested 10 basic rules for writing a contract for classroom use:

1. The contract payoff (reinforcer) should be immediate.
2. Initially, contracts should call for and reinforce approximations of target behavior.
3. The contract should provide for frequent reinforcers in small amounts.
4. The contract should call for and reinforce accomplishments rather than just obedience.
5. The performance should be reinforced after it occurs.
6. The contract must be fair to both parties.
7. The terms of the contract must be clear.
8. The contract must be honest.
9. The contract must be positive.
10. Contracting must be used systematically as an integral part of the ongoing classroom program.

In addition to the preceding rules, the practitioner should consider the following factors when developing and implementing a contract:

1. The contract must be negotiated and freely agreed on by both child and teacher.
2. The contract must include the target achievement or production level.
3. The reinforcer must be consistently delivered in accordance with the terms of the contract.
4. The contract must include the date for review and renegotiation.

One of the major functions of contingency contracting is to get children to the level of development at which they will initiate a contract instead of waiting for suggestions from the teacher.

The key to successful contracting is a negotiation session during which (a) the system of contracting is explained and discussed, (b) the contract is written, and (c) the contract is signed by the child and the teacher.

Negotiation should be systematic and precise. The teacher, as manager, has an obligation to ensure that the session is productive. It is recommended that the new practitioner use the following negotiation procedure (Shea, Whiteside, Beetner, & Lindsey, 1974):

1. Teacher establishes and maintains rapport with the child.
2. Teacher explains the purpose of the meeting by saying something such as, "I know you've been working hard on your schoolwork [reading, writing, spelling, arithmetic], and I'd like to help you."
3. Teacher gives a simple definition of a contract, explaining that a contract is an agreement between two people.

(a) Teacher gives an example of a contract such as, "When your mother takes your TV to the repair shop, the clerk gives her a ticket. The ticket is a contract between your mother and the repairman. He will repair and return the TV, and your mother will pay him."

(b) Teacher asks the child to give an example of a contract.

(c) If child cannot respond, the teacher gives another example and repeats Step 3b.

4. Teacher explains to the child that they are going to write a contract.

5. Teacher and child discuss tasks.

(a) Child suggests tasks for the contract.

(b) Teacher suggests tasks for the contract.

(c) Child and teacher discuss and agree on the specific task.

6. Teacher and child discuss reinforcers.

(a) Teacher asks the child which activities the child enjoys doing and which things he or she likes (see Chapter 4). The teacher may also suggest reinforcers.

(b) Teacher writes a reinforcer menu of suggested reinforcers.

(c) Child selects reinforcers for which he or she would like to work.

(d) Teacher and child rank the reinforcers in the child's order of preference.

7. Teacher and child negotiate the task-to-reinforcer ratio.

8. Teacher and child agree on the time to be allotted for the child to perform the task; for example, the child works 10 addition problems in 15 minutes to receive the reinforcer, or the child completes a unit of science and does the laboratory experiments in 2 weeks to receive an A.

9. Teacher and child identify the criteria for achievement; that is, the child will work the 10 addition problems in 15 minutes with at least 80% accuracy.

10. Teacher and child discuss evaluation procedures.

(a) Teacher discusses various types of evaluations with the child.

(b) Teacher and child agree on a method of evaluation.

(c) Teacher asks the child to explain the method of evaluation. If the child appears confused, the teacher clarifies the evaluation procedure.

11. Teacher and child negotiate delivery of the reinforcer.

12. Teacher and child agree on a date for renegotiation of the contract.

13. Teacher or child writes the contract. If feasible, the child should be encouraged to write it. Teacher gives a copy of the contract to the child.

14. Teacher reads the contract with the child as the child follows on his or her own copy.

15. Teacher elicits the child's verbal affirmation to the contract terms and gives affirmation.

Contract Work Sheet

Child _____

Teacher _____ Date _____

(X)	Tasks	Comments
( )	1. Establish and maintain rapport.	
( )	2. Explain the purpose of the meeting.	
( )	3. Explain a contract.	
( )	4. Give an example of a contract.	
( )	5. Ask the child to give an example of a contract; if there is no response, give another example.	
( )	6. Discuss possible tasks.	
( )	7. List child-suggested tasks: _____ _____ _____	
( )	8. List teacher-suggested tasks: _____ _____ _____	
( )	9. Agree on the task.	
( )	10. Ask the child what activities he or she enjoys and what items he or she wishes to possess.	
( )	11. Record child-suggested reinforcers.	
( )	12. Negotiate the task-to-reinforcer ratio.	
( )	13. Identify the time allotted for the task.	
( )	14. Identify the criterion or achievement level.	
( )	15. Discuss methods of evaluation.	
( )	16. Agree on the method of evaluation.	
( )	17. Restate and clarify the method of evaluation.	
( )	18. Negotiate the delivery of the reinforcer.	
( )	19. Set the date for renegotiation.	
( )	20. Write two copies of the contract.	
( )	21. Read the contract with the child.	
( )	22. Elicit the child's verbal affirmation and give your own affirmation.	
( )	23. Sign the contract and have the child sign it.	
( )	24. Congratulate the child (and yourself).	

Figure 5.3
Sample work sheet for contract negotiation

Date _____February 3, 2004_____

Contract

This is an agreement between _____Bob Wellrock_____ and _____Mr. Bare_____. The
                                        (Child's name)   (Teacher's name)

contract begins on _____2/9/04_____ and ends on _____2/11/04_____. It will be
                              (Date)   (Date)

reviewed on _____2/10/04_____.
                        (Date)

    The terms of the agreement are:

Child will ___spell with 90% accuracy the 20 assigned spelling words for Friday.___

Teacher will ___provide a ticket good for admission to the school movie on February 11, 2004.___

    If the child fulfills his or her part of the contract, the child will receive the agreed-
on reward from the teacher. However, if the child fails to fulfill his or her part of the
contract, the reward will be withheld.

Child's signature _____

Teacher's signature _____

Figure 5.4
Sample contract

16. Child and teacher sign the contract.

17. Teacher congratulates the child for making the contract and wishes the child success.

    A properly conducted negotiating session is complex and time consuming, particularly if the teacher has not previously introduced the concept of contracting in the classroom. Both the complexity and the time consumed by the negotiation process decrease as the student and teacher gain experience in contracting. As an aid to reducing confusion on the part of the teacher or the child and in an effort to facilitate the negotiation process, a contract work sheet is provided (see Figure 5.3). An additional copy of the work sheet can be found in the back of the text.

    The left-hand column of the work sheet should be checked as the practitioner and child complete each of the specified tasks. The tasks to be accomplished are specified in the middle column. The tasks are presented in logical order. It is strongly recommended that the order of presentation be followed during the session. The right-hand column of the work sheet is reserved for comments and notations.

    Three examples of contracts drawn from classroom experience are found in Figures 5.4 through 5.6.

    Contract forms need not be as formal as suggested by these procedures. Many home and school situations are responsive to less formal contracts. Examples of less formal contracts, developed by Kaplan and Hoffman (1990), are presented in the supplement at the end of this chapter.

Date _____April 6, 2004_____

Contract

This is an agreement between ____Russell Palmer____ and _____Mr. Davis_____. The
_____(Child's name)_____(Teacher's name)

contract begins on _____4/8/04_____ and ends on _____4/13/04_____. It will be
_____(Date)_____(Date)

reviewed on _____4/10/04_____.
_____(Date)

The terms of the agreement are:

Child will ____not engage in any fights during the school day for the period of the contract.____

Teacher will ___take the child to a Golden Gloves boxing match at the local arena.___

If the child fulfills his or her part of the contract, the child will receive the agreed-
on reward from the teacher. However, if the child fails to fulfill his or her part of the
contract, the reward will be withheld.

Child's signature _____

Teacher's signature _____

Figure 5.5
Sample contract

Date _____March 6, 2004_____

Contract

This is an agreement between _____Tom Hawk_____ and _____Mr. George_____. The
_____(Child's name)_____(Teacher's name)

contract begins on _____3/10/04_____ and ends on _____3/30/04_____. It will be
_____(Date)_____(Date)

reviewed on _____3/27/04_____.
_____(Date)

The terms of the agreement are:

Child will ___participate in a teacher-prescibed physical education program for 30 minutes a___

day during the period of the contract.

Teacher will ___provide one out-of-town basketball trip and admission to the game.___

If the child fulfills his or her part of the contract, the child will receive the agreed-
on reward from the teacher. However, if the child fails to fulfill his or her part of the
contract, the reward will be withheld.

Child's signature _____

Teacher's signature _____

Figure 5.6
Sample contract

SELF-MANAGEMENT

Cognitive behavior management is a term applied to a group of intervention strategies implemented to instruct learners in self-control. Through these interventions learners become increasingly aware of their cognitive processes and knowledge of how behavior influences academic and behavioral outcomes. The focus is on the evaluation of a learner's behavior and/or academic performance by the learner him- or herself rather than by the teacher. According to Swaggart (1998), cognitive behavior management includes (a) observational learning, (b) self-instruction, and (c) self-monitoring. Emphasis in this section is focused on self-monitoring or *self-management*. Observational learning is discussed in the section "Modeling" later in the chapter.

For the student, there are three phases of self-management (McConnell, 1999):

1. The student asks, "Was I on task?"
2. The student records the answer.
3. The student returns to the task.

Worksheets can be designed for the student to use to record and evaluate his or her responses. The interval used to monitor the target behavior vary according to the needs of the student. The length of the interval will be determined by the frequency, intensity, and duration of the behavior. Interval will also vary with the student's age and developmental level and the setting in which the student is functioning.

McConnell suggests a nine-step self-management procedure:

1. Identify the target behavior. Select a behavior that appears to have the most significant impact on the student's functioning.
2. Define the target behavior. Define the target behavior descriptively so that it can be observed.
3. Collect baseline data. These data are used to determine the design of the specific intervention to be implemented and to evaluate the results of the intervention.
4. Conduct conferences with the student. Confer with the student privately and explain the self-management procedure and its impact on the student's behavior. Discuss the target behavior and baseline data, present and model the appropriate behavior, gain the student's commitment to the self-management intervention, set appropriate goals for the intervention with the student, and select a potentially effective reinforcer. The conference should be positive.
5. Specify and describe the self-management procedure to be applied.
6. Instruct the student in the use of the self-management procedure to be applied. Provide the student sufficient practice so that he or she is comfortable with the procedure.
7. Implement the intervention.
8. Monitor the student's implementation of the procedure. Work with the student to improve, if necessary, the effectiveness of the intervention.

9. Conduct periodic follow-up of the student's behavior to ensure that the behavior is being maintained.

In a review of the research literature for a period of three decades, McDougall (1998) found that 240 self-management studies had been published. Only 14 of these focused on students with disabilities in the general school populations. These studies indicated a moderate to strong improvement in student performance after training. The research offers strong support for the effectiveness of self-management in inclusive environments.

McDougall and Brady (1998) found self-management procedures to be effective in increasing the fluency of mathematics students in the general education setting. Hutchinson, Murdock, Williamson, and Cronin (2000) found that self-recording, in combination with points and praise and encouragement, increased the on-task behavior and nondisruptive behaviors of a 6-year-old boy diagnosed as emotionally disturbed/behaviorally disordered who was on medication. Mathes and Bender (1997) studied the effects of self-monitoring to increase the on-task behaviors of learners with attention deficit hyperactivity disorder who were receiving medication. The three 8- to 11-year-old male subjects classified as having emotional/behavioral disorders demonstrated increased on-task behavior when self-monitoring was implemented with medication.

Snyder and Bambara (1997), using a multiple baseline research design, investigated the effectiveness of cognitive-behavioral self-management training package on the consistent use of specific classroom survival skills with three seventh- and eighth-grade male adolescents with learning disabilities. The results of the study demonstrated more consistent use of the survival skills by the subjects.

It appears that self-management techniques have the potential to facilitate the appropriate behavior and learning of students with disabilities.

TOKEN ECONOMY

When most of us think of learning, we recall our participation in formal educational systems, which involved acquiring knowledge by listening to teachers, having discussions, taking tests, and the like. This symbolic or verbal learning is essential to our development, but it is not the only kind of learning in which we participate. Human nature permits us to learn directly from experiences in our environment. It is through learning that we develop habitual ways of working our environment for reinforcers, that is, to obtain and sustain pleasure and to avoid discomfort and pain.

Although they differ in some ways, all learning environments are similar in that they are worked by individuals for reinforcers. Reinforcers may be defined as stimuli that induce changes in the person. These are positive reinforcers if they induce a pleasant state and negative reinforcers if they induce an aversive or painful state. Generally, we work the environment to acquire positive reinforcers and to avoid or escape negative reinforcers. Learning occurs by discovering behaviors that produce rewards and then repetitively working the environment to continue to obtain the reward. In general, the strength of a reinforcer is judged by the magnitude of the change it produces in the individual. The stronger or more desirable the reinforcers, the more quickly and easily the individual learns.

Learning environments generally provide feedback process cues that predict the presentation of delayed reinforcers. The immediacy of feedback, whether it is reinforcement per se or a process cue predictive of later reinforcement, is an important determinant of the rate of learning. In general, learning occurs more easily and more rapidly when feedback is immediate.

Learning environments vary in the consistency of feedback that they provide for the learner; the more consistent the feedback, the more quickly and easily the individual learns. Learning environments also vary in the degree to which individuals are allowed to set their own work rate. In other words, some environments allow individuals more freedom to work at a self-selected rate than others. Individuals learn more easily and quickly when they are free to set their own pace in working the environment for the desired reinforcer (Ayllon & McKittrick, 1982).

Many children are not able to function appropriately if they must wait an extended time for their reinforcer. In addition, there are some children who have not developed to the level at which social rewards alone are satisfactory reinforcers. In these cases, the use of a *token economy* has proved to be an effective behavior change intervention.

The tokens are usually valueless to the children when originally introduced to them. Their value becomes apparent as the children learn that tokens can be exchanged for a variety of reinforcers, such as being first in the lunch line, earning 10 minutes of free time, listening to CDs, watching television, purchasing a favored toy, and so on. This versatility makes the token system superior to many interventions.

It is an accepted fact that the child who is first in line for lunch today may not wish to be first in line next week. A properly administered token economy adjusts to this human tendency by providing a variety of rewards, that is, a reward menu.

When the teacher "sells" admission to a movie, use of Play-doh, or the like, the tokens rapidly take on value for the children. When the teacher states the price and asks a child to count out the needed quantity of tokens, they are engaged in a token economy.

In this manner, the tokens become potent reinforcers. They can be awarded over a period of time for acceptable effort and work. The system allows the teacher to structure the learning environment for positive reinforcement and to provide immediate feedback to the children via tokens. Hence, a moderately well run token exchange can promote direct learning regardless of the content of the activity.

We are all exposed to and use tokens daily. The most common form of token exchange is the use of currency to purchase various items and services. It is generally agreed (especially in today's economy) that money itself has no value; only the objects for which it is exchanged have real value. In the classroom, the token takes on the same meaning as currency has in the marketplace.

The classroom token economy suffers the same problems as the marketplace economy, that is, loss, theft, and counterfeiting. Some of these problems can be prevented by not using poker chips and other readily available objects for tokens.

Items that could be used include the following:

Check marks	Conservation stamps
Points	Trading stamps
Stars	Animal stickers
Smiling faces	Fairy tale character stickers
Point cards	Teacher-made tokens
Point tally forms	Play money

These tokens have several advantages over tokens made of rigid, hard materials, such as metal, plastic, and wood. They are made of soft, flexible materials, that is, paper, vinyl, or simple pen markings. They are less distracting to have in the classroom atmosphere because they neither rattle nor make noise if dropped on a hard surface. These characteristics eliminate much potential and actual distraction and confusion in the classroom. The tokens are easily glued to a paper, desktop, record card, or chart. They can be permanently affixed to various surfaces to minimize the incidence of misplacement, loss, or theft. However, they must be sufficiently distinctive to prohibit unauthorized duplication.

The following are the basic rules when establishing a token economy system for the classroom:

1. Select a target behavior. This topic is thoroughly discussed in Chapter 3 and does not warrant further elaboration here.

2. Conceptualize and present the target behavior to the child or group. It is a well-known fact that an emphasis on "what you can do" is more palatable to children (and adults) than an emphasis on "what you cannot do." Many unsuccessful behavior modification practitioners have determined their own failure by introducing a program by saying, "Now you boys and girls are going to stop that noise and fooling around in here. I have this new ... [and so on]." The children are immediately challenged; they prepare to defeat the teacher and defend their personal integrity.

3. Post the rules and review them frequently.

4. Select an appropriate token.

5. Establish reinforcers for which tokens can be exchanged.

6. Develop a reward menu and post it in the classroom. The children should be permitted to thoroughly discuss and consider the items on the menu. They should be encouraged to make their selections from among the items available. The children should not be permitted to debate the cost (number of tokens) of the various rewards after prices have been established.

7. Implement the token economy. Introduce the token economy on a limited basis initially. A complex, sophisticated system as an initial exposure confuses and frustrates the children. *Start small and build on firm understanding.* Explain the system to the children with great clarity and precision. Be patient and answer all the children's questions. It is better to delay implementation than create confusion and frustration.

8. Provide immediate reinforcement for acceptable behavior. The children will lose interest in the program if the process for obtaining the tokens is more effort than the reward is desirable. Many systems fail because the teacher neglects to dispense tokens at the appropriate time. Rewarding the children immediately reduces frustration and overconcern with the system. When the children are sure they will receive the tokens at the proper time, they can ignore the delivery system and concentrate on their work or behavior.

9. Gradually change from a continuous to a variable schedule of reinforcement. As discussed in Chapter 3, quick, unpredictable, or premature changes in a reinforcement schedule can destroy the program.

10. Provide time for the children to exchange tokens for rewards. If the token economy is a legitimate class program, time during the school day should be made available for the exchange. Time should not be taken from the children's recess, lunch, or free time.

11. Revise the reward menu frequently. Children, like adults, become bored with the same old fare day after day.

Rosenberg (1986) studied the effects of daily rule-review and rehearsal procedures on the effectiveness of a token economy with five disruptive and distractible elementary school-age students in a resource room program. He found that daily review of classroom rules resulted in an overall time-on-task improvement of 12% and a 50% reduction in disruptive talkouts. Shook, LaBrie, and Vallies (1990) demonstrated the effectiveness of a token economy in the regular classroom with the disruptive behaviors of two boys and one girl ranging in age from 6 to 7 years.

The token economy has worked very effectively in the classroom. Two reasons for its success are its lack of emphasis on competition with others and the fact that the reward menu provides sufficient variety to prevent boredom. Table 5.3 is an example of a reward menu for classroom use.

Table 5.3
Reward Menu

Reward	Time	Cost (Points)
Getting free time	10 minutes	20
Watching television	30 minutes	45
Reading comic books	5 minutes	15
Listening to CDs	10 minutes	20
Cutting and pasting	5 minutes	10
Purchasing modeling clay	—	55
Purchasing crayons	—	45
Purchasing coloring books	—	50
Finger painting	12 minutes	25
Playing with toys	10 minutes	25
Borrowing a book	48 hours	35
Borrowing a game	48 hours	50

The menu need not be lengthy or elaborate but should contain at least 10 items and activities. The children should exchange their tokens daily; they should not be allowed to take them home. If they are deferring their reinforcers and saving tokens, their tokens should be collected and recorded each day.

The number of tokens earned may be recorded on a point card or tally form. The teacher can affix the card or form to each child's desk and then either record or circle the points earned by the child. The points are totaled at the end of each day. The child may either delay the reward or accept it immediately.

In a discussion of token economy reinforcers, Raschke, Dedrick, and Thompson (1987) recommended the use of contingency packages to motivate reluctant learners. The packages are tangible reminders of potential reinforcers. They consist of three-dimensional displays designed specifically to advertise rewards. The packages should be novel, exciting, and age appropriate. Two packages described in detail by Raschke et al. included the "Flip-The-Lid-Robot," a multidrawered container in which each drawer holds various rewards, and "Touchdown Triumph," a football game board designed for adolescents. Raschke (1986) suggested a similar package using available classroom materials (construction paper, sponges, pipe cleaners) to make "delicious" incentives (hamburgers, french fries, ice cream cones) for display in the classroom.

In an effort to increase motivation and lessen the possibility of boredom among fifth-grade students they studied, Anderson and Katsiyannis (1997) developed and implemented a token economy based on an automobile driving and speedway theme. The economy included common items related to driving and auto racing, such as license plates, stop signs, stoplights, speeding tickets, and so on. The authors found the economy to be effective with their students.

Lyon and Lagarde (1997) suggested that teachers develop a "Graduated Reinforcement System" for use with individuals, small groups, and whole classroom groups at the upper elementary and secondary school levels. According to the authors, the system is easy for students to understand, allows the monitoring of both social and academic performance, simplifies record keeping, and eliminates differential points for each target behavior and differential prices for each reinforcer. Points are awarded by levels of performance, and groups of reinforcers are related to these various levels.

Clark (1988) recommended the use of "Behavior Tickets" to extend the token economy outside the classroom. The tickets can be used by involved adults in any class or area of the school in which the student works or plays. When the student leaves the classroom to go to the restroom, lunchroom, playground, or elsewhere, he or she is given a ticket. To earn points, the students must return to class with the ticket in one piece. If the student is caught misbehaving by another teacher, that teacher stops the student, requests the ticket, and tears it into two pieces. Missing tickets are considered to be torn tickets. This technique, according to Clark, has two advantages: (a) The student can be reinforced for appropriate out-of-classroom behavior, and (b) misbehavior can be addressed as soon as the student returns to the classroom. All tickets must be returned to the teacher at the end of the class period or day.

Of course, the system assumes that all adults in the school are trained in the technique and willing to participate.

Point Card									
Child's name _____ Date _____									
1	2	3	4	5	6	7	8	9	10
11	12	13	14	15	16	17	18	19	20
21	22	23	24	25	26	27	28	29	30
31	32	33	34	35	36	37	38	39	40
41	42	43	44	45	46	47	48	49	50
51	52	53	54	55	56	57	58	59	60
61	62	63	64	65	66	67	68	69	70
71	72	73	74	75	76	77	78	79	80
81	82	83	84	85	86	87	88	89	90
91	92	93	94	95	96	97	98	99	100

Figure 5.7
Point card for specific behavior

Examples of the point card and tally form to be used for specific behaviors are presented in Figures 5.7 and 5.8. Maher (1989) suggested a "punch-out" card for use as a behavior recording technique. The teacher punches a hole in the card when the student exhibits the appropriate behavior. Punching the card is paired with social and tangible reinforcement if tangible reinforcement is used.

The teacher, with little difficulty, may plan and implement a multipurpose token economy in the classroom. In this situation, the children earn tokens for a variety of appropriate behaviors as well as academic effort and academic success.

Tokens or points can be presented to the child for any or all of the following behaviors:

- Being present at the workstation on time
- Having appropriate work tools available for use
- Attending to the instructor's directions
- Exhibiting appropriate social behavior during the work period (raising the hand for attention, remaining at the work station, not talking without permission)
- Engaging in the assigned work task during the work period, that is, showing effort
- Correctly or satisfactorily completing the assigned work task
- Returning work tools to their appropriate place

Tokens are presented for various appropriate behaviors and withheld for inappropriate behaviors.

A point card for a multipurpose token economy is presented in Figure 5.9. Copies of each of the forms for recording points in a token economy are provided in the back of the text.

Point Tally Form

Child _____ Date _____

Monday																	
Tuesday																	
Wednesday																	
Thursday																	
Friday																	

TOTAL
Monday
Tuesday
Wednesday
Thursday
Friday
Week

Figure 5.8
Tally form for specific behavior

♦ *Examples*

Mr. Newman, a junior high school math teacher, was having difficulty with Charlie, who had developed the habit of counting and computing aloud while doing math assignments. At first, this behavior was not a serious problem, but then it began to distract many of the other students.

Mr. Newman decided to implement a token economy system to modify Charlie's behavior. He discussed the system with the class, established a set of rules, and developed a reward menu before implementing this intervention. (The reward menu is presented in

			Point Card for Multipurpose Token Economy			

Child _____ Day _____ Date _____

Work period	Readiness	Social behavior	Work effort	Work success	Teacher comments
9:00–9:15			*	*	
9:15–10:00					
10:00–10:30					
10:30–10:45			*	*	
10:45–11:30					
11:30–12:00					
12:00–1:00			*	*	
1:00–1:30					
1:30–2:45					
2:45–3:00			*	*	

*Points for work effort and work success are not available during these periods because of the nature of the activity: opening exercises, recess, lunch, and closing exercises.

Figure 5.9
Point card for multipurpose token economy

Table 5.4.) The token economy was used with the entire class and effectively modified the behaviors of Charlie and his peers.

Tokens were initially presented on a fixed interval schedule; as the group progressed, however, a variable interval schedule was introduced. Throughout the program, Mr. Newman conscientiously paired social rewards with the tokens.

Two physical education teachers were having problems with student participation in class. They were being bombarded with complaints such as headaches, back pains, sore toes, and sore ears. After discussing the token economy system between themselves and with their students, they decided to initiate a program to increase participation. A student delegation aided the teachers in developing the reward menu shown in Table 5.5.

Mrs. Thomas has been attempting to get Mary, her 16-year-old daughter, to share in the housekeeping. Mrs. Thomas has had very little success.

One day, Mary asked whether she and three of her friends could go into the city for dinner and the theater. The big evening was to be in 4 weeks. Mrs. Thomas said yes—if

Table 5.4
Mr. Newman's Reward Menu

Reward	Time (Minutes)	Cost (Points)
Checkers	10	15
Cards	10	15
Puzzles	15	20
Magazines	18	25
Chess	12	30
Model car kits	10	20
Comic books	5	10
Bingo	15	25
Quiet conversation	10	30

Table 5.5
Physical Education Class
Reward Menu

Reward	Time (Minutes)	Cost (Points)
Getting free time	15	50
Using trampoline	10	40
Shooting baskets	5	30
Acting as activity leader	—	25
Talking with friend	10	40
Playing badminton	10	30
Using trapeze	15	50
Sitting out an activity	—	100

Mary would pay for the trip by helping with the housekeeping. Mrs. Thomas made a list of tasks Mary was responsible for around the house. It included cleaning her room, washing and drying clothes, ironing, washing windows, cleaning the bathroom, helping with the cooking, and so on. Each task was assigned a specific point value. The points could be exchanged for money.

When the time for the trip arrived, Mary had sufficient money for the evening. In addition, she had an improved attitude about helping to take care of the house.

In these three examples, the token economy system proved to be effective in increasing participation. In two of the cases, the teachers changed the reward menu frequently in cooperation with their students throughout the duration of the program.

Frequently, the token economy intervention described in this section includes "response cost" procedures. This intervention is defined, discussed, and exemplified in the next chapter.

MODELING

One of the most common forms of human learning is accomplished through the processes of observation and imitation. All parents and teachers can relate a variety of acceptable and unacceptable behaviors exhibited by their children and students that are imitations of their own (the adults') personal acceptable and unacceptable behaviors. This form of learning at various times and by various theorists and practitioners has been called modeling, observational learning, identification, copying, vicarious learning, social facilitation, contagion, role playing, and so on (Bandura, 1969; Striefel, 1981). In this text, the term *modeling* is used to describe learning by observation and imitation.

As a behavior change method, modeling is the provision of an individual or group behavior to be imitated or not imitated by an individual. This is one of the oldest and most frequently applied methods of changing behavior.

Mothers and fathers, husbands and wives, teachers, and principals have been suggesting models to their sons, daughters, spouses, and students for generations:

- "Be a good boy like your brother John."
- "Why can't you be like George, an excellent father, a great lover, and a good provider?"
- "Mary, can't you be a good student like Eileen?"
- "Why can't you behave like the other boys and girls?"

Several state and national organizations exist for the purpose of providing children with acceptable social models. These organizations provide children with either the direct services of a live model or an abstract model inherent in their program and printed materials. Among these organizations are Big Brother and Big Sister, Boy Scouts and Girl Scouts, 4-H, and Little League.

According to Bandura (1969) and Clarizio and Yelon (1967), exposure to a model has three effects:

1. *Modeling effect or observational learning.* Children may acquire behavior from a model that was not previously a part of their behavioral repertoire. In this situation, the model performs a behavior that is imitated by the child in substantially identical form. Examples of the modeling effect are teaching a nonverbal child to verbalize in imitation of a model and teaching a child signing skills as a method of communication.

2. *Inhibitory and disinhibitory effects.* Modeling is not confined exclusively to the learning of new behaviors as in the preceding modeling effect. Modeling includes not imitating a model for the purpose of disinhibiting or inhibiting a behavior. For example, a child may observe and *not* imitate a peer who is punished or ignored for exhibiting a behavior. In this situation, the child may be said to be experiencing the other child's behavior and its consequences vicariously.

3. *Eliciting or response facilitation effect.* In this situation, the model's behavior is employed to facilitate the occurrence of a previously learned but dormant behavior

from the child. For example, a child may know that it is appropriate to say "Thank you" when given a cookie at snack time. However, this child may not say "Thank you" as a matter of common practice. Appropriate social responsiveness may be facilitated if all the children who receive cookies previous to this child during snack time say "Thank you."

Before implementing a modeling intervention, the teacher or parent should consider the following factors:

1. Is the child able developmentally and cognitively to imitate the model? Practitioners must be cognizant of the fact that some children are simply not ready to use modeling.
2. Will the child be rewarded for imitating the model? Some children are simply not intrinsically rewarded by performing behaviors that others consider acceptable.
3. Is the model "good"? Caution must be taken when a model is being selected for a child. Remember, what the model does in science class may be quite different from what this individual does in English, in shop, on the playground, at home, or behind the barn.
4. Is the model acceptable to the child? A model who is too good, too bright, too fast, or just plain obnoxious will be rejected by the child.

Modeling techniques can be effectively applied by teachers in an effort to change behavior only when consideration is given to these factors.

♦ Examples

Ms. Nyerges is a resource teacher for children with mental retardation. Dave and Carl work with Ms. Nyerges in the resource room for 1 hour each day. Until recently, Dave would usually attempt his assigned tasks, whereas Carl would seldom attempt his assigned tasks.

It was determined by Ms. Nyerges that both boys were reinforced by her attention. Therefore, she decided to use her attention as a reward they received for completing their work. Dave was reinforced by Ms. Nyerges's attention. She praised him each time he did his class work, attended to the appropriate stimulus, or completed an assigned task; she ignored Carl's inappropriate behavior.

After several sessions during which Dave's behavior was rewarded, Carl began to imitate Dave to receive Ms. Nyerges's attention. She immediately reinforced Carl whenever he exhibited the appropriate behavior.

The result of this intervention was a dramatic change in Carl's behavior. He is now completing his work to gain approval from Ms. Nyerges.

Mr. Cohen is an instructor of three boys and one girl in a class for children with behavioral disorders. The students' names are John, James, Charles, and Shirley. Of the four students, Charles is the most troublesome. Charles constantly moves about the room, exhibiting feelings of indignation at assignments and disrupting the activities of his classmates and Mr. Cohen. This behavior occurs throughout the school day. Originally, when the behavior occurred, the other children remained busy at their seats. On these occasions, Mr. Cohen would chase after Charles or provide him with attention for the unacceptable behavior he was exhibiting. The acceptable behaviors manifested by Shirley, John, and James were ignored. Lately, Shirley, John, and James have begun to move about the room and exhibit behaviors that disturb Mr. Cohen. They are imitating the behavior of Charles.

One can conclude that Shirley, John, and James are modeling Charles's behavior for the purpose of receiving attention from their teacher.

In both of these examples, the procedure of modeling is effective; in fact, it is effective in developing both appropriate and inappropriate behaviors. The consequence of behavior is again the key factor.

In too many classrooms, appropriate behavior is taken for granted. Modeling is a potentially effective preventive technique.

♦ SUMMARY

In this chapter, the practitioner of behavior modification is provided with an overview of the five common techniques used to increase appropriate behavior: (a) positive reinforcement, (b) shaping, (c) contingency contracting, (d) token economy, and (e) modeling.

Positive reinforcement is defined as the process of reinforcing an appropriate target behavior to increase the probability that the behavior will be repeated. Also known as positive attention, approval, social reinforcement, and rewarding, this technique requires two things: (a) During the initial stage, the target behavior must be reinforced each time it occurs, and (b) when the target behavior is established at a satisfactory rate, it should be reinforced intermittently.

Shaping is the reinforcement of successive approximations of the target behaviors that have not been previously manifested in the individual's behavioral repertoire. The steps in behavior shaping are (a) selecting a target behavior, (b) collecting baseline data, (c) selecting a reinforcer, (d) reinforcing successive approximations of the target behavior, (e) reinforcing the approximations immediately and continuously, and (f) changing to a variable reinforcement schedule.

Contingency contracting involves the completion of behavior X before reinforcement Y is given or allowed. This process is actively used in day-to-day living. Contracts may be verbal or written. Verbal contracts are commonly used in schools, but written contracts are appealing to the reluctant learner. When developing a contract, the practitioner should know the developmental level of the child or children with whom the contract is being negotiated. Contracting is more effective when the child is allowed to share in its development.

A token economy is a system of exchange. Children earn tokens that are exchanged for specific reinforcers. The tokens themselves are valueless; their value lies in the reinforcers for which they can be exchanged. There are a number of objects that can be used as tokens, such as check marks, points, smiling faces, stars, and other similar items. An important component of a token economy is the reward menu, which should be developed with the child or group.

Modeling, one of the oldest and most frequently applied methods of behavior change, has been effective in developing appropriate behaviors in children. Modeling is the provision of an individual or group behavior to be imitated or not imitated by the child.

♦ PROJECTS

1. Select a target behavior to change and describe how you would implement each step of shaping the behavior.

2. Write two examples of modeling as a technique for (a) increasing behaviors and (b) decreasing behaviors.

3. Develop and implement a contract for (a) an individual child in a class and (b) an entire class.

4. Develop a reward menu for your class.

5. Develop a token economy system.

♦ REFERENCES

Alberto, P. A., & Troutman, C. A. (1990). *Applied behavior analysis for teachers.* Upper Saddle River, NJ: Merrill/Prentice Hall.

Anderson, C., & Katsiyannis, A. (1997). By what token economy? A classroom learning tool for inclusive settings. *Teaching Exceptional Children, 29*(4), 65–67.

Ayllon, T., & McKittrick, S. M. (1982). *How to set up a token economy.* Austin, TX: PRO-ED.

Bandura, A. (1969). *Principles of behavior modification.* New York: Holt, Rinehart & Winston.

Becker, W. C. (1979). Introduction. In L. Homme, A. P. Csanyi, A. M. Gonzales, & J. R. Rechs (Eds.), *How to use contingency contracting in the classroom.* Champaign, IL: Research Press.

Brigham, F. J., Bakken, J. P., Scruggs, T. E., & Mastropieri, M. A. (1992). Cooperative behavior management strategies for promoting a positive classroom environment. *Education and Training of the Mentally Retarded, 27*(1), 3–12.

Clarizio, H. F., & Yelon, S. L. (1967). Learning theory approaches to classroom management: Rationale and intervention techniques. *Journal of Special Education, 1,* 267–274.

Clark, J. (1988). Behavior tickets quell misconduct. *Behavior in Our Schools, 1*(3), 19–20.

Cooper, J. O., Heron, T. E., & Heward, W. L. (1987). *Applied behavior analysis.* Upper Saddle River, NJ: Merrill/Prentice Hall.

Downing, J. A. (1990). Contingency contracting: A step-by-step format. *Intervention in School and Clinic, 26*(2), 111–113.

Downing, J. D. (Ed.). (2002). What works for me: Individualized behavior contracts. *Intervention in School and Clinic, 37*(3), 168–172.

Gross, A. M., & Ekstrand, M. (1983). Increasing and maintaining rates of teacher praise. *Behavior Modification, 7*(1), 126–135.

Hess, A. M., Rosenberg, M. S., & Levy, G. K. (1990). Reducing truancy in students with mild handicaps. *Remedial and Special Education, 11*(4), 14–19.

Homme, L., Csanyi, A. P., Gonzales, M. A., & Rechs, J. R. (1979). *How to use contingency contracting in the classroom*. Champaign, IL: Research Press.

Hutchinson, S. W., Murdock, J. Y., Williamson, R. D., & Cronin, M. E. (2000). Self-recording plus encouragement equals improved behavior. *Teaching Exceptional Children, 32*(5), 54–58.

Kaplan, P. G., & Hoffman, A. G. (1990). *It's absolutely groovy*. Denver: Love Publishing.

Kelly, M. L., & Stokes, T. F. (1982). Contingency contracting with disadvantaged youths: Improving classroom performance. *Journal of Applied Behavior Analysis, 15,* 447–454.

Lyon, C. S., & Lagarde, R. (1997). Tokens for success: Using the graduated reinforcement system. *Teaching Exceptional Children, 29*(6), 52–57.

Maher, G. B. (1989). "Punch out": A behavior management technique. *Teaching Exceptional Children, 21*(2), 74.

Mathes, M. Y., & Bender, W. N. (1997). The effects of self-monitoring on children with attention-deficit/hyperactivity disorder who are receiving pharmacological interventions. *Remedial and Special Education, 18*(2), 111–128.

McConnell, M. E. (1999). Self-monitoring, cueing, recording, and management: Teaching students to manage their own behavior. *Teaching Exceptional Children, 32*(2), 14–21.

McDougall, D. (1998). Research on self-management techniques used by students with disabilities in general education settings. *Remedial and Special Education, 19*(5), 310–320.

McDougall, D., & Brady, M. P. (1998). Initiating and fading self-management interventions to increase math fluency in general education classes. *Exceptional Children, 64*(2), 151–166.

Murphy, J. J. (1988). Contingency contracting in the schools: A review. *Education and Treatment of Children, 11*(3), 257–269.

Panyan, M. C. (1980). *How to use shaping*. Austin, TX: PRO-ED.

Premack, D. (1965). Reinforcement theory. In D. LeVine (Ed.), *Nebraska symposium on motivation*. Lincoln: University of Nebraska Press.

Raschke, D. (1986). "Delicious" incentives: A technique to motivate reluctant learners. *Teaching Exceptional Children, 19*(1), 66–67.

Raschke, D., Dedrick, C., & Thompson, M. (1987). Motivating reluctant learners: Innovative contingency packages. *Teaching Exceptional Children, 19*(2), 18–21.

Rosenberg, M. S. (1986). Maximizing the effectiveness of structured classroom management programs: Implementing rule-review procedures with disruptive and distractible students. *Behavioral Disorders, 11*(4), 239–248.

Shea, T. M., & Bauer, A. M. (1987). *Teaching children and youth with behavior disorders* (2nd ed.). Upper Saddle River, NJ: Prentice Hall.

Shea, T. M., Whiteside, W. R., Beetner, E. G., & Lindsey, D. L. (1974). *Contingency contracting in the classroom*. Edwardsville: Southern Illinois University Press.

Shook, S. C., LaBrie, M., & Vallies, J. (1990). The effects of a token economy on first grade students' inappropriate behavior. *Reading Improvement, 27*(2), 96–101.

Snyder, M. C., & Bambara, L. M. (1997). Teaching secondary students with learning disabilities to self-management classroom survival skills. *Journal of Learning Disabilities, 30*(5), 534–543.

Striefel, S. (1981). *How to teach through modeling and imitation*. Austin, TX: PRO-ED.

Sutherland, K. S., Copeland, S., & Wehby, J. H. (2001). Catch them while you can: Monitoring and increasing the use of effective praise. *Beyond Behavior, 11*(1), 46–49.

Swaggart, B. L. (1998). Implementing a cognitive behavior management program. *Intervention in School and Clinic, 33*(4), 235–238.

West, R. P., Young, K. R., Callahan, K., Fister, S., Kemp, K., Freston, J., & Lovitt, T. C. (1995). The musical clocklight: Encouraging positive classroom behavior. *Teaching Exceptional Children, 27*(2), 46–51.

Sample Contracts

Contract Your Way
Out of a

If I can squeeze through

_____

_____

_____

by _____
     (date)

then I will have a clean start to_____

_____

_____

_____   _____   _____
Squeezer   **Squeezee**   **Date**

Source: From It's Absolutely Groovy by P. Kaplan and A. Hoffman, 1990. Denver: Love Publishing Co.

I WILL **PLOW** THROUGH, and if

_____

_____

_____

by _____
     (date)

then _____

_____

_____

Contractor   Contractee   Witness

Source: From It's Absolutely Groovy by P. Kaplan and A. Hoffman, 1990. Denver: Love Publishing Co.

_____ and _____ will

PITCH IN

and help each other to

_____ by _____
                        (date)

When we are done, we will be able to _____

_____

_____

_____   _____
       Friend #1   Friend #2

_____ _____ _____
    Witness   Contractor   Date

Source: From It's Absolutely Groovy by P. Kaplan and A. Hoffman, 1990. Denver: Love Publishing Co.

I hereby agree to help

_____

by

_____
_____

on or before _____
When this pickle of a problem is
solved, we will be able to

_____
_____
_____

_____ _____
Pickle #1   Pickle #2

_____ _____
Pickler   Date

I hereby

to

_____
_____
_____

To do this, I will need _____
_____

When I deliver the finished
product, I will receive _____

_____
_____
_____

_____ _____
Builder   Supplier

Source: From It's Absolutely Groovy by P. Kaplan and A. Hoffman, 1990. Denver: Love Publishing Co.

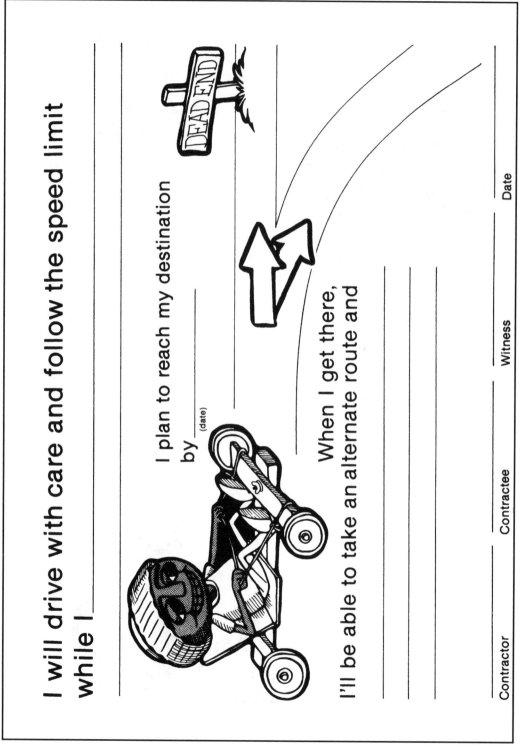

I will drive with care and follow the speed limit while I _____

I plan to reach my destination by _____
(date)

When I get there, I'll be able to take an alternate route and _____

| Contractor | Contractee | Witness | Date |

Source: From It's Absolutely Groovy by P. Kaplan and A. Hoffman, 1990. Denver: Love Publishing Co.

6 Methods of Decreasing Behavior

Desensitization
Differential reinforcement
Extinction
Loss of privileges
Punishment
Reprimand
Time-out

♦ **CHAPTER OBJECTIVES**

After completing this chapter, you will be able to do the following:

1. Describe the various forms of differential reinforcement and their application.

2. Describe extinction.

3. Explain reprimands.

4. Characterize loss of privilege.

5. Describe and exemplify time-out.

6. Explain the various forms of punishment and discuss their ethical implications.

7. Discuss desensitization techniques and their applications in the educational setting.

◆ ◆ ◆

Mrs. Hamilton dreaded coming to school today. It is raining, and her fourth-grade students will have to remain inside during recess. When the students do not get to go outside for recess, they seem to go crazy. As the recess period approaches, they become increasingly disruptive.

On this day, when the recess period arrives, Mrs. Hamilton tells the students that they are to engage in silent reading. They can choose any book from the classroom library. With little enthusiasm, each student selects a book. Within 5 minutes, the disruptive behavior begins. Charlie pinches George; Mary reports that Mike is pulling her hair; Fred and Martin are using their desks as drums; Gloria is blowing kisses at Larry; Sharon, Pat, and Carol are giggling; Walter is asleep; Mrs. Hamilton is angry.

Maybe if Mrs. Hamilton knew something about methods of decreasing disruptive behavior, her rainy-day recesses could be filled with sunshine.

Mr. Bell hates teaching, schools, students, other teachers, and, most of all, his principal, whom he refers to as "the superintendent's flunky." Mr. Bell never wanted to be a teacher. But after failing premed, prelaw, and biology, his college adviser counseled him into education. After completing college, Mr. Bell planned to teach a year or two and begin another career. That was 15 years ago.

At Washington High School, where he teaches physical science, Mr. Bell is viewed as the most negative person on the faculty. His colleagues tend to avoid him, especially in the faculty lounge, because of his constant complaining. He complains about the following: the school not being clean, teachers trying to act as young as their students, how dumb the students are, the limited exposure the faculty has to the world, a lack of materials with which to work, crime on the streets, drugs, sex, athletic program expenses, overpaid administrators, the do-nothing union, school board members being afraid of the superintendent, and so on.

Maybe if the faculty and principal knew something about methods of decreasing unacceptable behavior, the teacher's lounge would provide a positive and relaxing environment.

During the course of a single school day, a teacher may observe a number of behaviors that should be either decreased in frequency or eliminated. These may include the following:

- Rusty's incessant talking
- Richard's constant bullying
- Mary's endless complaining
- Barbara's inability to keep her hands off things and people
- Martin's thumb sucking

In this chapter, several methods of decreasing and eliminating behavior are discussed and exemplified. These are (a) differential reinforcement, (b) extinction, (c) reprimands, (d) loss of privileges, (e) time-out, (f) punishment, and (g) desensitization.

AVERSIVES IN THE EDUCATIONAL SETTING

During the past few years, several researchers have demonstrated concern with regard to the use of punishment—that is, aversive and behavior reduction strategies—in the educational setting (Drasgow, 1997; Rose, 1989; Yell, 1990).

Tobin and Sugai (1993) presented the findings of a research study to determine (a) educators' perceptions and attitudes about the relative aversiveness of various interventions and (b) the need for restrictions on aversive interventions that might be used in the educational setting. Their survey study was designed to be comparable to the works of Wood (1988) and Wood and Hill (1983).

Tobin and Sugai defined *aversive* as an unpleasant consequence, *intervention* as action by the teacher to decrease inappropriate behavior, and *restriction* as the degree of regulation to control the use of an intervention. Survey questionnaires were presented to 158 persons, and 126 responded. The respondents included general education teachers, special education teachers, administrators, teachers in alternative settings, and other educators (e.g., psychologists).

Ranking the interventions from the most to the least aversive, the respondents listed (a) mild electric shock, (b) exposure to ammonia, (c) wearing a negative sign, (d) hits and slaps, (e) tastes of hot sauce, (f) paddling, (g) tastes of lemon juice, (h) cloth restraints, (i) wearing an eye screen, and (j) exposure to water mist. The majority of respondents stated that restrictions on use should be placed on all these interventions except cloth restraints and water mist. In addition, the majority of the respondents recommended restrictions on (a) removal of the student from class to another class for the remainder of the term, (b) expelling or moving the student to a more restrictive educational environment, (c) suspension from school for a period of several days, (d) calling the police and pressing charges, and (e) using "stand up" to "sit down" repeatedly.

Among the least-aversive interventions, the respondents listed (a) talks with the student about the rules, (b) comments on the student's emotional state, (c) changing the student's seat, (d) changing the physical environment, (e) gestures and other signals to the student to stop, and (f) verbal warnings. The respondents placed no restrictions on the use of these interventions.

In a study conducted in New Zealand of the acceptability of various punishments, Blampied and Kahan (1992) surveyed 201 adults selected at random. The respondents were presented with four case studies depicting boys or girls having noncompliance behavior problems in home or school settings. They were invited to read the descriptions and prescribe punishment interventions to change the behavior. The results of the study, ranking the interventions from the most to the least acceptable, were (a) response cost, (b) social reprimand, (c) time-out, (d) overcorrection, and (e) physical punishment.

In their position paper on punishment, Skiba and Deno (1991) suggest that research demonstrates the long-term effectiveness of punishment. The controversy surrounding the use of the terms *punishment* and *aversive* is in large part due to the lack of a clear definition. They suggest that these terms have too long been associated with cruel and inhumane treatment in the minds of many persons. They call for the use of more precise terminology.

The authors of this text are in agreement with Simpson (1988), who suggested that if aversives are used in the educational setting, practitioners should implement the least-aversive method most likely to be effective for modifying the student's behavior. In addition, as will become evident in this chapter, the authors believe that restrictions should be placed on the use of aversive interventions and that some specific aversive interventions (e.g., physical punishment) are unacceptable for use.

DIFFERENTIAL REINFORCEMENT

Too often in school and home, the attention of teachers and parents is focused on the inappropriate behaviors rather than on the appropriate behaviors that children and youth exhibit. This unfortunate and generally ineffective and inefficient circumstance can be changed by applying differential reinforcement or positive reductive strategies. With the use of this group of strategies for modifying behavior, the practitioner "accentuates the positive" to "eliminate the negative" (Webber & Scheuermann, 1991, p. 13).

Differential reinforcement is defined as the process of reinforcing an appropriate behavior in the presence of one stimulus and, simultaneously, not reinforcing an inappropriate behavior in the presence of another stimulus. There are several types of differential reinforcement (Drasgow, 1997; Kerr & Nelson, 1989; Martin & Pear, 1992; Webber & Scheuermann, 1991): (a) differential reinforcement of zero rates of behavior (DRO), (b) differential reinforcement of incompatible behaviors (DRI), and (c) differential reinforcement of lower rates of behavior (DRL). The application of any differential reinforcement intervention requires the teacher to (a) identify and define the unacceptable behavior to be decreased or eliminated and (b) select and define an acceptable replacement behavior to increase.

When using the DRO strategy, the individual is reinforced for not exhibiting the target behavior during a specific period of time. Occurrences of the target behavior are ignored. Of course, the individual is reinforced for exhibiting appropriate behavior in other circumstances.

Brulle and Barton (1992) refer to DRO as differential reinforcement of other behaviors and define it as a schedule in which reinforcement is delivered if the client does not emit the target response for a specific interval.

♦ *Example*

Stacey, a student in Mr. Hicks's special class for students with behavioral disorders, had mild tantrums several times each day. This behavior interfered with Stacey's classroom activities and annoyed the other students and Mr. Hicks.

Mr. Hicks decided to implement a DRO intervention. He took baseline data for a period of 10 school days and determined that Stacey had a tantrum, on average, nine times each day. These occurred approximately every 35 minutes. Mr. Hicks discussed the DRO intervention with Stacey and the other students. He began reinforcing Stacey after each 30-minute period of tantrum-free behavior. When Stacey had a tantrum, it was ignored by Mr. Hicks and her classmates, who were reinforced for ignoring the behavior.

During the following 3 weeks, Mr. Hicks systematically extended the period of time Stacey had to be tantrum free to receive a reward. Within a month, the behavior was eliminated.

Among the behaviors to which DRO may be effectively applied are fighting, cursing (White & Koorland, 1996), name-calling, threats, talking back, and destruction of property. If a behavior is dangerous to self or others, causes serious destruction, or interferes excessively with the teaching-learning process, it cannot be ignored; an intervention other than DRO must be applied.

At times, it is necessary or desirable to decrease a behavior by systematically reinforcing a behavior that is in opposition to or incompatible with it. Such an intervention is called differential reinforcement of incompatible behaviors (DRI) (Kerr & Nelson, 1989).

For instance, Norman is a very talkative student and, to his teacher, appears to be constantly whispering and distracting others. After analysis of the situation by the behavior consultant assigned to help Norman and the teacher, it is suggested that the behavior, which is mildly disturbing to the teacher and other students, would decrease if the teacher and students ignored Norman's talking and reinforced his appropriate on-task behavior.

The assumption underlying the suggested intervention is that Norman wishes to be reinforced (receive attention) and will respond to the positive reinforcement received by remaining on task. The positive reinforcement will take the place of the negative reinforcement he is presently receiving for whispering and distracting others.

♦ *Example*

For a major part of the school year, Mr. Weber had been trying to decrease Wallace's random walking about the classroom. All efforts appeared to have been in vain. It seemed that the more effort Mr. Weber put forth to modify Wallace's out-of-seat behavior, the more frequent it became. Evidently, the attention Wallace received from Mr. Weber for being out of his seat was reinforcing.

As a last resort, Mr. Weber decided to attempt the technique of reinforcing incompatible behaviors. To remain in one's seat would be incompatible with walking about the classroom. Mr. Weber decided to positively reinforce Wallace's in-seat behavior and ignore his out-of-seat behavior. Initially, Wallace resisted the program. However, after a short time, the out-of-seat behavior decreased and was eventually eliminated. Figure 6.1 represents the data collected on Wallace's behavior.

There is no known explanation for the recurrence of Wallace's out-of-seat behavior on the 16th and 17th days of the intervention. One possible explanation is that because the target behavior had not been exhibited for 2 days, Mr. Weber acted as though the behavior

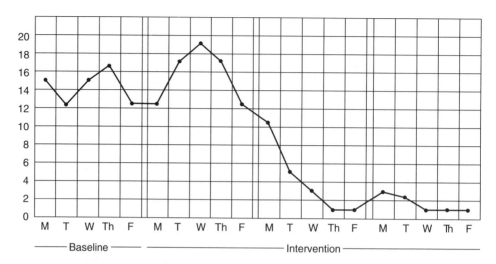

Figure 6.1
Frequency of Wallace's out-of-seat behavior before and during the intervention

had been eliminated. He may have altered his response to either the behavior he was rein-forcing or the behavior he was ignoring.

The classroom teacher could probably think of a number of other situations in which reinforcing an incompatible behavior might decrease target behavior.

♦ **Examples**

John cannot be looking at the teacher and looking out the window at the same time.

Paul cannot be standing in line for lunch and writing on his desk at the same time.

David cannot be mowing the lawn and watching television at the same time.

Additional examples of the behaviors to which the DRI intervention may be successfully applied are (a) following directions versus noncompliance, (b) name-calling versus using an appropriate or proper name, (c) talking at inappropriate times versus being quiet at appropriate times, (d) off task versus on task, (e) in seat versus out of seat, (f) sleeping in class versus not sleeping in class, (g) being tardy versus being on time, and (h) messy or incomplete work versus neat or com-plete work.

Another type of differential reinforcement is the differential reinforcement of lower rates of behavior (DRL) (Martin & Pear, 1992; Webber & Scheuermann, 1991). DRL may be applied with behaviors that (a) are habits, (b) do not need to be reduced rapidly, and (c) do not need to be reduced to zero. DRL is applied to gradually reduce the behavior by reinforcing progressively lower rates of the behavior.

♦ *Example*

Elmer was a "nail biter." He appeared to be constantly chewing his nails. For his behavior management project in Special Education 430 (Behavior Management in Special Education), Elmer decided to reduce and eventually eliminate his nail biting.

   He defined "nail biting" as any time his fingertips came in contact with his lips. During a week of baseline, Elmer found that his fingertips came in contact with his lips, on average, 97 times a day. Elmer decided that during the first week of intervention, he would be rewarded if he reduced his tips-to-lips contacts to an average of 80 times a day. He attained this goal and was reinforced. The next week he decided to reduce his tips-to-lips contacts to 65 times a day. Elmer was unsuccessful; he averaged 69 tips-to-lips contacts a day and was not rewarded. During the third week of intervention, Elmer remained at the goal of 65 and was rewarded. Elmer continued the program for the next 12 weeks of the semester and was successful in eliminating his nail-biting behavior.

   The DRL intervention may be applied to various behaviors, such as attention-seeking behavior, completing assignments, responding to teacher's or parent's questions, and hand raising.

   When implementing a differential reinforcement intervention, the behavior change process (as discussed in Chapter 4) requires the following steps:

1. Select the target behavior to be changed
2. Select a positive alternative to the target behavior
3. Select the appropriate differential reinforcement strategy (DRO, DRI, or DRL)
4. Determine the reinforcers to be used in the intervention
5. Determine the criteria for success
6. Implement the intervention
7. Evaluate the results of the intervention

   According to Webber and Scheuermann (1991), the use of a differential reinforcement strategy allows the practitioner to avoid punishment and its side effects and facilitates the teaching of prosocial behaviors.

EXTINCTION

The discontinuation or withholding of the reinforcer of a behavior that has previously been reinforcing the behavior is called *extinction*. This process is also known as systematic ignoring (Hall & Hall, 1980a). (This process is also discussed in Chapter 2.)

♦ *Example*

Timmy was constantly attempting to obtain Mr. Calm's attention in class by jumping up and down in his seat, frantically waving his hand, and whispering in a loud voice, "Mr. Calm, Mr. Calm, me, me, I know."

Mr. Calm knew he would have to change his name to Mr. Storm if this behavior did not stop or at least decrease in frequency. In an effort to retain his composure and aid Timmy, he commenced to study the situation.

Baseline observation data indicated that Timmy exhibited the target behavior an average of eight times per day, or 40 times during the 1-week baseline data-collecting phase. During this phase, Mr. Calm also collected data on his personal overt reactions to the unacceptable behavior. He discovered that 90% of the time, he responded to the behavior by either permitting Timmy to answer the question, telling the child to be quiet and sit still, or signaling his disapproval nonverbally. Regardless of his specific reaction, Mr. Calm realized that he was *attending to* Timmy's attention-seeking behavior.

Mr. Calm devised an intervention whereby he *would not* reinforce the behavior with his attention and would thus extinguish it. He would respond to Timmy only when he was exhibiting acceptable behavior in response to questions directed to the class.

As indicated in Figure 6.2, the behavior was extinguished within 2 weeks, although there were brief periods of regression thereafter.

Timmy's behavior (attempts to obtain attention) increased during the days immediately following the implementation of the intervention. This increase in the target behavior appeared to be an attempt by the child to defend his method for obtaining attention against the loss of effectiveness. This phenomenon, known as an "extinction burst," is discussed in detail in Chapter 3, and the reader is referred to that chapter for further clarification.

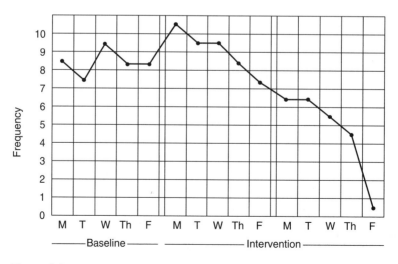

Figure 6.2

Frequency of Timmy's attention-seeking behavior before and during the intervention

As demonstrated in the case of Timmy, extinction techniques, when properly applied, result in a gradual decrease in the target behavior and its eventual elimination.

Extinction is only as effective as the teacher or parent is consistent and persistent in implementation of the intervention. The most effective approach to extinguishing behavior that has been previously reinforced is ignoring that behavior. This is easier said than done. Most of us are conditioned to the point that we find it difficult to ignore inappropriate behavior. But to ignore a behavior means exactly that—to totally and consistently ignore the target behavior. We are aware that there are some behaviors so serious that they cannot be ignored. However, if the individual is not inflicting pain on himself or others or disrupting the ongoing classroom program, then extinction may be the intervention of choice.

The following are some guidelines for those wishing to apply extinction:

- When the target behavior is exhibited, remain impassive; give no indication that you are aware of the behavior.
- Continue whatever activity you are presently doing.
- If the behavior persists, turn your back and walk away.

REPRIMANDS

Another form of punishment is the *reprimand* (Houten, 1980). To be reprimanded is to be scolded, "yelled at," "bawled out," or otherwise verbally chastised for exhibiting an inappropriate target behavior. Reprimands are useful when a child is engaging in behavior that necessitates immediate action because it is potentially harmful to self, others, or property.

It is suggested that reprimands be used selectively in response to specific behaviors. A reprimand should include a statement of an appropriate alternative to the inappropriate behavior (Bacon, 1990).

The following are some guidelines for the effective use of reprimands:

1. Be specific. Tell the child exactly what inappropriate behavior is being reprimanded.
2. Reprimand the behavior; do not derogate the child.
3. Reprimand immediately.
4. Be firm in voice and physical demeanor.
5. If either the child or others may be harmed by the behavior, remove the child.
6. If necessary, back up the reprimand with loss of privileges.
7. Encourage the child to behave appropriately and include a statement of the appropriate behavior in the reprimand.
8. Be calm.
9. When it's over, it's over. Do not keep reminding the child of past inappropriate behavior; avoid embarrassing the child in the presence of peers and others. To

this end, use nonverbal reprimands: shake your head "no," point your finger, frown, and so on.

10. Always observe the child's reaction to the reprimand to determine whether it is aversive.

♦ *Examples*

Margie! Turn off the lathe. Do not turn it on again until you have put on your safety glasses and removed that loose scarf from your neck. Please review the safety rules.

Donald! Sit up straight and put your feet on the floor while you are typing. Proper posture will help your concentration and prevent back pain and physical discomfort in the future.

Mary! Put on your seat belt. It is the law in Illinois and may save you from injury if we have an accident.

Herm! Close the windows when you turn on the air conditioner. This will save electricity, which is very expensive.

With regard to the effectiveness of verbal reprimands, intervention research results are mixed (Salend, Jantzen, & Giek, 1992). The efficacy of the verbal reprimand appears to be controlled by various conditions. According to Van Houten, Nau, Mackenzie-Keating, Sameoto, and Colavecchia (1982), the effectiveness of a reprimand is increased when (a) combined with nonverbal behavior generally associated with a verbal reprimand (e.g., pointing a finger) and (b) delivered in close proximity to the individual who is the target of the reprimand.

Wheldall (1991) researched the effectiveness of verbal reprimands with four teachers in general education classrooms. He concluded that reprimands should be given privately and within a positive context. In addition, reprimands should be used infrequently, and be specific to the unacceptable behavior.

LOSS OF PRIVILEGES

Unlike the vast majority of interventions discussed in this text, *loss of privileges* is a negative behavior management intervention, though its results may be positive. Loss of privileges is also known as deprivation of privileges or response cost. When the loss of privileges is applied, a portion of the child's present or future positive reinforcers is taken away following the exhibition of the target behavior.

This intervention is most effective when the privilege the child loses is a natural or logical consequence of the inappropriate behavior. For example, if a child refuses to work on assignments during class time, then the privilege of free time is lost. Likewise, if a child is late for the school bus, then he misses it. It is not always possible to impose natural consequences; thus, the teacher on occasion must impose an artificial consequence. In an artificial consequence, the relationship between the privilege lost and the behavior exhibited is arbitrary. It exists only because the teacher decides it will exist. Such artificial relationships must be carefully explained to the child.

When using loss of privileges, the teacher has several guidelines to follow:

1. Be sure the child understands the relationship between the target behavior and the privilege to be lost.
2. Be sure the child knows the punishable behavior and the consequence of exhibiting it.
3. When possible, use natural or logical consequences.
4. Apply the loss of privilege interventions fairly.
5. Avoid warning, nagging, or threatening.
6. Do not debate the punishable behaviors, the rules, or the punishment once these have been established.
7. Do not become emotionally involved. Do not feel guilty when the child loses a privilege. If the child knows the rules and the consequences of the behavior, then he or she has chosen to break the rule and suffer the consequences.
8. Be consistent.
9. Reinforce appropriate behaviors; do not emphasize inappropriate behaviors only.

♦ *Examples*

Patricia is head cheerleader at Saint Rudolph's High School. She greatly enjoys leading cheers at basketball and football games. Patricia was tardy for English class about three times a week. Her English teacher, Sister Mary, was very concerned that Patricia would fail the course if her attendance did not improve. Sister Mary talked to the principal, Sister Sharon, and they agreed to deprive Patricia of the privilege of cheering at one game for each time she was tardy for English class. The rule was explained to Patricia and implemented. After missing two games during the next 3 weeks, Patricia's tardiness ended.

Thomas, a salesperson for a major computer software firm, owned a 1990 Mercedes-Benz 535SEL and loved to drive down the interstate highways at 80 miles per hour. He was caught by the highway patrol on three occasions and fined. On the fourth occasion, the officer took away his driving privilege for 30 days. Thomas still enjoys driving fast but controls this urge.

Kevin, who is 17 years old, is allowed to stay out on Friday and Saturday nights until midnight. He consistently arrived home (and awakened his parents) at one or two o'clock in the morning. Needless to say, this behavior caused many heated discussions. It was finally agreed by Kevin and his parents that for each minute he was late arriving home, 5 minutes would be subtracted from the curfew time on the next evening he went out with his friends. After losing several hours during the course of the following few weeks, Kevin's behavior improved.

Proctor and Morgan (1991) (replicating the work of Witt & Elliott [1982]) researched the effectiveness of a response-cost raffle. The intervention was applied in a special education resource room to the behavior of four junior high school boys with mild to moderate behavior problems. At the beginning of each class, four slips of colored paper (raffle tickets) were placed on each student's desk. (Each student's ticket was a different color.) When a student exhibited an inappropriate behavior, the teacher removed a ticket and told the student the specific misbehavior. If the student responded negatively, the teacher removed another ticket. If the student continued to exhibit inappropriate behavior and responded negatively after all the tickets had been removed, then he was removed from the room. Five minutes prior to the end of class, the teacher collected all the remaining tickets. Two tickets were marked for a "group" reward. These and the other tickets were placed in an envelope. The teacher conducted the raffle, and the winning student selected a reward (e.g., soda, potato chips, free time) from a reinforcement menu. Or, if the winning ticket was designated as a "group" reward, the winner selected from among the group rewards (e.g., movie, group game, party).

The results of this research suggest that the response-cost raffle is an effective and efficient intervention for decreasing disruptive and inappropriate behavior.

TIME-OUT

In general, *time-out* is the removal of a child from an apparently reinforcing setting to a presumably nonreinforcing setting for a specified and limited period of time. Time-out is "time away from positive reinforcement" (Powell & Powell, 1982). According to Cuenin and Harris (1986), the definition of time-out includes two important factors: (a) Time-out is contingent on the exhibition of the target behavior, and (2) a discrepancy that is meaningful to the student exists between the time-in and time-out environments. Such removal can effectively decrease a target behavior (Hall & Hall, 1980b). Time-out is a frequently used behavior management intervention. In a questionnaire survey of preschool teachers and teachers of students with behavioral disorders in Kansas and Nebraska, Zabel (1986) found that 70% of her sample applied some form of time-out in the classroom. Teachers of young children used time-out more frequently than teachers of older children. Ruhl (1985) found that 88% of special education teachers surveyed used time-out with their students. In a similar study, Shapiro and Lentz (1985) found that 85% of school psychologists used time-out procedures.

Jones, Sloane, and Roberts (1992) compared the effectiveness of time-out and verbal reprimand ("Don't") interventions on the oppositional, aggressive behavior of three preschool children toward their siblings. Mothers of the children were trained and applied the interventions in the home. The researchers found the immediate time-out intervention to be more effective than the verbal reprimand.

Harris (1985) noted five types of time-out: (a) isolation, (b) exclusion, (c) contingent observation, (d) removal of reinforcing stimulus conditions, and (e) ignoring or extinction. Systematic ignoring or extinction was discussed in the previous section.

According to Lewellen (1980), there are three types of time-out:

1. *Observational time-out* is a procedure in which the student is withdrawn from a reinforcing situation by (a) placing him or her on the outer perimeter of the activity, where the child can see and hear the activity but not participate in it; (b) requesting the child to place his or her head on the desk (called "head-down"); (c) removing activity materials; or (d) eliminating or reducing response maintenance stimuli (e.g., room illumination).

2. *Exclusion* is a procedure in which the student leaves a reinforcing situation to a presumed nonreinforcing situation while remaining in the classroom. The student is not allowed to observe the group. An example is placing a screen between the student and the group.

3. *Seclusion* is a procedure that makes use of a "time-out room." In this situation, the student leaves the classroom and goes to an isolated room.

♦ *Example*

Benji is a very active first grader. The boy was having difficulty remaining in his seat and refraining from impulsive grabbing of persons and objects near him. He was also appropriating and ingesting his classmates' lunches. His teacher realized that these behaviors were interfering with Benji's classroom progress and that of his classmates. She attempted several procedures to help Benji control his behavior. Among these were verbal reprimands, ignoring the inappropriate behavior and reinforcing appropriate behavior, and peer pressure. Observation data revealed that none of these interventions were effective, although her efforts were sufficient.

A behavior management consultant observed Benji and recommended time-out as a potentially effective intervention. Together, the teacher and the consultant decided that *each time Benji left his seat, he was to be sent to time-out for 2 minutes.*

This intervention necessitated defining and specifying several factors:

1. Out-of-seat behavior was defined as any time Benji's posterior was not in contact with his chair.

2. When the unacceptable behavior did occur, the teacher's assistant was to escort Benji to the time-out area. Benji was to remain in time-out for 2 minutes; during this time, he had to be quiet.

3. After the time-out period, Benji would return to the group. There would be no discussion or reprimand.

4. Benji's desk and chair were relocated in the classroom to ensure that he would not participate in unacceptable behavior, such as grabbing people and lunches, without leaving his seat.

5. A time-out area was arranged in the corner of the classroom. The time-out area was constructed by rearranging two five-drawer filing cabinets. A chair was provided outside the area for the assistant who was to monitor Benji whenever he was in time-out.

The intervention was imposed, and although the behavior did not cease immediately, significant progress was observed during the first months, as indicated in Figures 6.3 and 6.4.

Figure 6.3
Frequency of Benji's out-of-seat
behavior before and during the
first week of intervention

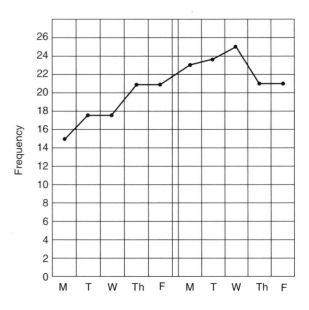

Figure 6.4
Frequency of Benji's out-of-seat
behavior during the fourth and
fifth weeks of intervention

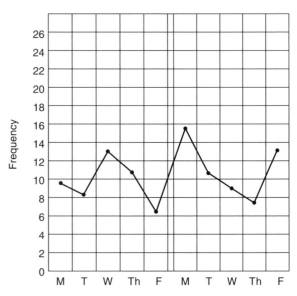

Benji's out-of-seat behavior was brought under control within a period of several months. However, it remains an occasional problem, so time-out procedures remain in effect.

Ribbon time-out is a nonexclusionary procedure (Foxx & Shapiro, 1978). It may be applied as an individual or a group contingency. While the individual or group is behaving appropriately, a ribbon or other symbol is visible (a ribbon may be worn by a child, or the group may see a ribbon on the bulletin board). While the ribbon is visible, positive reinforcement is available to the student or group. If the student or group act inappropriately, the ribbon is removed, and reinforcement is not available for a specific predetermined period of time. The ribbon is returned, and reinforcement is again available after the nonreinforcement time expires.

Salend and Gordon (1987) researched the effects of an interdependent group contingency ribbon time-out procedure to decrease the inappropriate verbalizations of two groups of students who attended a resource room. They found that the ribbon time-out procedure effectively decreased inappropriate verbalizations. In an earlier study, Foxx and Shapiro (1978) conducted an experiment using ribbon time-out with children with severe cognitive disabilities. They found that, on average, the children misbehaved 42% during baseline, 32% during a reinforcement-only intervention, and only 6% during the ribbon time-out condition.

A variation on the "removal of reinforcing stimulus condition" time-out is placing the stimulus (doll, toy) in time-out rather than removing the child to time-out. For example, a small child is playing inappropriately with a teddy bear (banging it on the floor, tearing its fur). The bear is taken from the child and placed on a shelf or in a basket visible to the child. The child is told that Mr. Bear is in time-out and will return when the child is ready to play properly. This procedure may be effective with very young and preschool children.

The time-out intervention includes the reinforcement of acceptable behavior. A child who is performing or approximating the desired behavior in the classroom should be reinforced for these efforts.

The effectiveness of time-out as an intervention is contingent on several factors (Cuenin & Harris, 1986):

- Characteristics of the individual child
- Teacher's consistent application of the intervention
- Child's understanding of the rules of time-out
- Characteristics of the time-out area
- Duration of time-out
- Evaluation of the effectiveness of the intervention

Characteristics of the Child

The practitioner must know the characteristics of the individual child before implementing a time-out intervention. For the acting-out, aggressive, group-oriented child, time-out may be very effective. Such children wish to be with the group and attended to by the teacher. Consequently, time-out is not rewarding. However, for a withdrawn, passive, solitary child who is prone to daydreaming, time-out may be inappropriate and would be contraindicated. These children may engage in their own little world while in the time-out area.

♦ *Example*

Cheryl, a 6-year-old girl, is in Mr. Roy's class for children with behavioral disabilities. Cheryl is quiet, shy, and withdrawn; she frequently engages in daydreaming.

Mr. Roy read about a new technique for behavior problems in a popular magazine. This technique was time-out. He decided to impose the intervention on Cheryl in an effort to force her to participate in class discussions and activities. He planned to put her in time-out each time she was inattentive in class.

Cheryl appeared to enjoy the opportunity to go to a time-out for 3 minutes. Her rate of inattentiveness increased dramatically immediately after the intervention was implemented. She evidently appreciated the opportunity to legitimately participate in her dream world.

This example is a stark illustration of misuse of time-out with a child whose behavior was reinforced by the intervention.

♦ *Example*

Richard, an 11-year-old boy in Ms. Jones's physical education class, was constantly arguing and fighting with his teacher and classmates about the rules of a game or how an activity should be conducted. This behavior occurred particularly when he was losing. Observation indicated that Richard truly enjoyed the activities and the company of his peers and Ms. Jones. However, the behavior was obtrusive and had to be eliminated for the sake of the group.

Ms. Jones selected time-out as a potentially effective intervention. Before the technique was imposed, it was decided that each time Richard started to argue or fight during class, he was to be sent to time-out. The time-out was out of view but not out of hearing of class activities. Under these conditions, Richard's disruptions were eliminated very rapidly.

Time-out in this situation was effective because Richard preferred to be with his classmates and teacher rather than in the less stimulating time-out area.

Consistency of Application

If time-out is to be applied as an intervention with a particular child, it must be used with consistency over a predetermined period of time (Brantner & Doherty, 1983). Frequently, teachers are inconsistent in their application of time-out. As a result, the child becomes confused, and the wrong behavior is reinforced. This situation is analogous to the confusion that results when, on Monday, Wednesday, and Friday, a child is forced to eat green vegetables under pain of death at the hands of Father, but on Tuesday and Thursday, Father is not so insistent. And on the weekend at Grandma's house, the child does not have to eat green vegetables at all.

Child's Understanding of the Rules

Children should know specifically what behaviors are not acceptable in their classrooms. In addition, they should know the consequence of exhibiting the forbidden behaviors. If time-out is to be used as an intervention, the rules for time-out should be communicated to the children; they should be posted and reviewed frequently. The rules assist the teacher in trying to remain consistent and fair in the application of the intervention.

Time-out should never be used whimsically with children; that is, one day a child is sent to time-out for talking in class, the next day for chewing gum, the next day for not completing a homework assignment, and so on. Such misuse will confuse the child and reduce the effectiveness of the intervention.

When time-out is imposed on the behavior of very young children, the teacher is often confronted with an additional problem. Frequently, it is impossible to communicate verbally to such children the rules governing time-out and its imposition. In this situation, it is necessary to initiate the program and demonstrate the intervention through implementation.

Time-out is not a technique that includes lecturing, reprimanding, or scolding before, during, or after the intervention. These techniques, although frequently used in everyday classroom exchanges, can provide unwanted reinforcement to the child. The teacher may wish to include a warning stage in the time-out procedures. When the inappropriate behavior occurs, the child may be redirected to the appropriate behavior. If within 10 or 15 seconds the child does not comply and return to task, then he or she is directed to time-out (Cuenin & Harris, 1986). Twyman, Johnson, Buie, and Nelson (1994) studied the effects of warning procedures to signal a more intrusive time-out contingency, that is, exclusionary time-out with nine elementary school students with behavioral disabilities. In the baseline condition, the students received three warnings before exclusionary time-out was imposed. In the experimental condition, students did not receive any warning prior to exclusionary time-out. They found that the number of exclusionary time-outs remained the same under both conditions, that is, baseline and experimental. The use of warnings was related to a decrease in appropriate contingent observation time-out behaviors, but not to the point where exclusionary time-out was imposed. The researchers suggest that warnings prior to the imposition of exclusionary time-out may result in more negative interactions between staff and students.

Time must be taken to explain why time-out is warranted, but the explanation should be brief and explicit. Going to time-out should not be a matter for debate between child and teacher. As the program continues, these explanations need only be reminders of the rules and consequences of exhibiting certain behaviors. Nelson and Rutherford (1983) noted two problems when a child is forced to go to time-out: (a) The physical contact may unwittingly reinforce the child's inappropriate behavior, and (b) the teacher may simply be unable to physically control the child.

♦ *Example*

Ms. Smith selected time-out as an intervention to decrease Elmo's talking in class. Each time Elmo talked out of turn in class, Ms. Smith would grab him by the arm and drag him to the time-out area. There she would proceed to babble at him (rather incoherently) for about 10 minutes. She would always conclude with the statement, "Now, be quiet for 2 minutes." She would then proceed to stare at Elmo for 2 minutes. At the end of that time, she would say, "Now, get back to your seat."

Ms. Smith's intervention is an example of the improper use of time-out. The results were as expected:

1. Elmo continued to talk out in class because, although he was not particularly interested in Ms. Smith's lectures, he was pleased with his classmates' reactions to her behavior.
2. Ms. Smith's classroom group certainly enjoyed the circus.
3. Ms. Smith suffered from nervous tension.

Characteristics of the Time-Out Area

Care must be taken in the selection of the time-out area. Teachers should avoid selecting an area that may appear nonreinforcing but is in effect reinforcing to children. For instance, placing a child in the corridor for time-out may be extremely reinforcing. In the hallway, the child has an opportunity to communicate with everyone who passes. In addition, the child is provided with a legitimate opportunity to get out of the classroom and assignments.

Another commonly used but generally ineffective area for time-out is the principal's office. The office has been demonstrated to be one of the most stimulating and reinforcing areas in the school for the majority of children. In the office, the child has an opportunity to observe piqued parents, out-of-sorts mail carriers, and anxious administrators in their natural human state. In addition, the child has opportunities to pick up the latest school news and gossip for dissemination among peers and teachers.

Bacon (1990) offers an excellent example of the misuse of time-out:

> On a school visit to observe a child who was being referred to our program for children with behavior problems, our team was greeted by a tall, nice-looking young man who pleasantly directed us to the school office, commented on the weather, and then resumed his class work. I assumed this must be the student council president or special office aide to be given so much responsibility. When we found the student's classroom, the teacher informed us that the problem student who could no longer be controlled by the school was sitting out at the front table at the entrance, "in time out." (p. 605)

Many administrators do not understand the concept of time-out, and on occasion the child is given various clerical tasks to perform in the office, such as stapling, folding, carrying messages, and making announcements. The child who is in time-

Figure 6.5
Classroom with time-out area: A, time-out area; B, bookcase; C, child's chair; D, supervisor's chair; E, library; F, science or game area; G, teacher's station; H, students' desks; I, discussion center

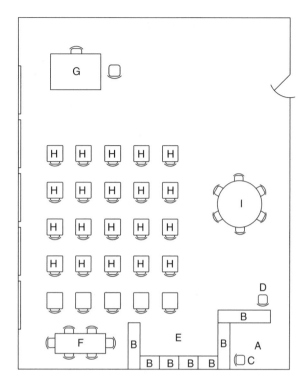

out just happens to be available when a body is needed to do something; the reason for the child's presence in the office is not considered when the task is assigned. An investigation of the use of the office for time-out would probably reveal that it is a far more attractive alternative for the child than sitting in the classroom reading, writing, or doing math problems.

The time-out area should be as nonreinforcing as possible and devoid of extraneous visual and aural stimulation. In most classroom settings, it is not necessary to construct a time-out room. A chair in an out-of-the-way corner of the classroom is adequate. In some settings, room dividers, screens, filing cabinets, or the backs of bookcases can be arranged to construct the walls of the time-out area. It is necessary to ensure that the area is supervised, safe, properly lighted, and ventilated. A chair may be placed in the time-out area. However, many children, especially young children, prefer to sit on the floor, and this practice should be permitted. The area should be (a) away from high traffic, (b) away from doors and windows, (c) out of the other children's view, and (d) within view of the observer.

It is recommended that a chair be placed outside the area for the observer-supervisor. A paraprofessional can serve as observer-supervisor if properly instructed. However, in cases where a paraprofessional is not available for this duty, the area must be in a location that permits the teacher to observe it from his or her teaching station. Figure 6.5 is a diagram of a time-out area in a classroom.

Duration of Time-Out

Time-out loses its effectiveness as an intervention if a child is left in the setting for too lengthy or too brief a period of time (Brantner & Doherty, 1983; Harris, 1985). Time-out should be limited to approximately 2 minutes after the child has quieted. Four or 5 minutes in time-out should be a maximum except under extraordinary circumstances. Never should a child remain in time-out for more than 10 minutes. Consistency in the duration of the time-out period is sought. It is strongly recommended that the teacher use an inexpensive, bell-type egg timer to ensure that the time limit of time-out is not violated. The timer alerts both teacher and child to the exact moment the time-out period expires. In addition, it reassures the child that the teacher is being fair in the application of the intervention.

Evaluation of Effectiveness

Records of time-out incidents should be recorded and analyzed by the teacher. Teachers should prepare a log such as the one in Figure 6.6. A copy of this log is provided in the back of the text.

The log should include (a) the time the child was sent or escorted to time-out, (b) the time the child returned to the activity, (c) any incidents during time-out, (d) the activity taking place just before the child was sent to time-out, and (e) the activity to which the child returned after time-out.

The log should be posted on the exterior wall of the time-out area. The teacher evaluates the overall effectiveness of the technique by studying the child's time-out record. In addition, the records, if closely analyzed, provide clues as to why time-out is an effective or ineffective intervention in a particular case.

♦ *Example*

Mr. Sherman was recently called to a day school for severely disturbed boys to consult on the case of Hector, a 14-year-old student. When Hector enrolled in the school 2 years ago, he was exposed to time-out as a behavior control intervention. During the following 2 years, time-out was effective in modifying much of Hector's behavior.

The boy had progressed to a point of being sent to time-out on an average of only once each day. However, he had never progressed beyond this point. His daily disruption prohibited his integration into a regular classroom.

Fortunately, at the day school, precise time-out records were maintained for all children and were available for study. An analysis of Hector's log indicated that he was in time-out each day immediately after the teacher announced that it was time for math. Although math time varied, it was discovered that Hector's disruptive time varied with it.

Mr. Sherman suggested that for Hector, time-out was more reinforcing than math; that is, it was the lesser of two evils. In an effort to test this hypothesis, Hector's math period was eliminated; Hector no longer went to time-out.

Time-Out Log

Child _____

Supervisor _____

Date _____

Time		Behavior before time-out	Behavior during time-out	Behavior after time-out
Enters	Leaves			

Figure 6.6
Data log to be posted at time-out area

Hector's skill in math has progressed acceptably under the guidance of a tutor. The tutor assists him individually during regular math periods.

It is highly recommended that the child return to the task that was interrupted by the time-out. Of course, the feasibility of the child's returning to the interrupted task will vary with the structure of the class schedule and activities. If the child is returned to and held responsible for the task being engaged in before time-out, the child learns that time-out cannot be used as a means of avoiding assignments he or she finds difficult or simply dislikes. This recommendation assumes that the assigned task is appropriate to the child's learning level and competency.

The following examples will further clarify the process of time-out.

◆ *Examples*

Ms. Drake was confronted with the problem of Donald striking other children in the stomach. She was so distressed by this behavior that she was about to reciprocate in kind. Ms. Drake had tried every intervention she knew to change the behavior (and a few she did not know she knew), but they only increased it.

At an in-service workshop, time-out as a technique to decrease inappropriate behavior was described. After absorbing the available knowledge about time-out and becoming somewhat comfortable with the concept, Ms. Drake implemented it in her classroom.

First, a set of "classroom rules of behavior" was presented to the children. Next, a time-out area was designed, and the concept of time-out was introduced and explained to the group.

The new rules included "Do not strike other children." Persons exhibiting this behavior would be in time-out for 3 minutes in an area located in a corner of the classroom. The area was screened off, devoid of visual stimuli, and unfurnished with the exception of a chair. A child in time-out could neither see nor be seen by classmates (see Figure 6.5). After the rules were communicated and apparently understood by all members of the class, time-out was implemented.

When Donald struck another child, he was quietly escorted to the time-out area for 3 minutes. After sitting quietly in the area for that period of time, Donald was asked why he was sent to time-out. If his response indicated that he understood the reason, he was instructed to return to his regular seat. However, if his response indicated that he did not understand the reason for being sent to time-out, it was briefly explained to him. He was then instructed to return to his seat. After several repetitions of the time-out routine, both Donald and Ms. Drake became aware of the potency of the intervention.

Donald's baseline and intervention data are presented in Figure 6.7.

Mr. Seltz had used every method possible to decrease Shauna's unacceptable burping behavior in the classroom. Finally, time-out was used as a technique to eliminate this behavior. Shauna was told that each time she burped in class, she was to go to the time-out area for 2 minutes. Mr. Seltz reinforced Shauna with attention and praise whenever she performed appropriately in the class. The baseline and intervention data for the behavior are presented in Figure 6.8. The data clearly indicate that Shauna preferred to cease burping rather than be placed in time-out.

As indicated in the examples, time-out can work effectively if it is properly applied. When implementing a program, the new practitioner of behavior modification should adhere closely to the suggestions in this section.

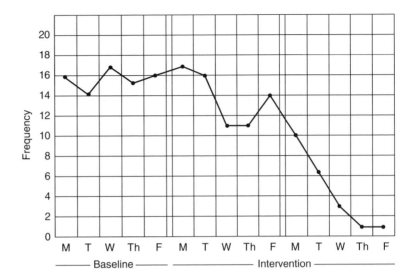

Figure 6.7
Frequency of Donald's striking
behavior before and during the
intervention

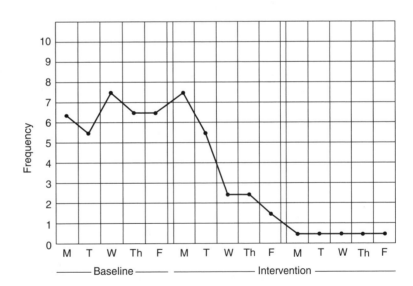

Figure 6.8
Frequency of Shauna's burping
behavior before and during the
intervention

PUNISHMENT

Briefly discussed in Chapter 3, *punishment* is perhaps the most misunderstood and
emotionally explosive of the behavior modification techniques. It is an intervention
used to decrease or eliminate an inappropriate behavior.

There are two distinct forms of punishment that the teacher or parent may consider for application with students. As commonly understood and applied by parents and teachers, punishment is the *addition* of an aversive stimulus (something

unpleasant) as a consequence of a behavior. Punishment of this form can be either physical or psychological. Examples are a spanking (physical punishment) or a scolding or reprimand, extra work, after-school detention, or an undesirable additional task (psychological punishment).

The other form of punishment is the *subtraction* of something the child perceives as desirable. Examples are the taking away of television privileges, late bedtime hours, freedom to leave the house, or tokens and points.

The subtraction of previously earned tokens or points in the token economy intervention presented in Chapter 5 is called *response-cost* and is discussed in another section of this chapter. In this situation, students are informed that not only can they earn points for privileges and goods but, if they exhibit specific unacceptable behaviors, they can lose points. A specific number of points are subtracted from the total for each transgression. In a word, the child is punished for exhibiting specific inappropriate behaviors.

Punishment by deprivation or response-cost is generally considered less harmful to the child and more effective intervention than the addition of physical or psychological aversive stimuli.

The short-term effectiveness of punishment for decreasing behaviors is difficult if not impossible to dispute (Wood, 1978). Punishment is *effective* for obtaining short-term goals. However, other interventions, such as extinction and ignoring the behavior, are probably more effective for attaining permanent long-range changes. Evans and Richardson (1995) urge that practitioners be trained in the alternatives to punishment, such as teaching students prosocial skills and implementing alternative interventions other than punishment as a consequence of inappropriate behavior.

During the past decade, parents and professionals have increasingly rejected the use of punishment in the effort to change the challenging behaviors of children. They have placed greater reliance on positive behavioral interventions. However, children with disabilities continue to be exposed to punishment. In the IDEA Amendments of 1997 (IDEA 97), Congress supports the use of positive behavioral interventions with learners with disabilities. Lohrmann-O'Rourke and Zirkel (1998), in a review of case law, found qualified support for the use of aversive interventions. Such supports appear to have not changed greatly since a review by Seiden and Zirkel (1989). Court decisions and administrative rulings continue the pattern of qualified support for the use of time-out and corporal punishment, among other aversive interventions, with some restrictions as governed by state statutes. In case law, the criteria for the use of aversive interventions are, in general, reasonable justification, the relationship of the intervention to the disability, the extent of intrusiveness and force required, the ineffectiveness of less restrictive interventions, the goals and objectives of the individualized education plan, parental consent, expert opinion, the norms or standards of practice, and federal, state, and local statutes and regulations. The use of aversive interventions are also restricted by such factors as duration of the intervention, documentation, monitoring, and safety.

Yell (1997) discussed the implications of IDEA 97 for special and general education teachers, administrators, and teacher educators. Among the provisions of IDEA 97, Congress demonstrated its concern with providing a safe school environment conducive to learning for all children. Congress also reaffirmed its commitment to a free appropriate public education for all learners with disabilities. Section 615(K) outlines provisions for the discipline of students with disabilities:

- With some exceptions, school officials may discipline learners with disabilities in the same manner as learners without disabilities.
- A proactive behavioral intervention plan, based on a functional behavioral assessment, is developed and becomes part of the individualized education plan.
- A review of the relationship between the student's disability and misconduct is conducted within 10 days. This procedure is called "manifestation determination."
- Standards for an interim alternative educational setting in which a student is placed are offered.
- With some exceptions, the student will "stay put" in his or her education placement, unless the parent or guardian and the state or local education agency agree otherwise, until a due-process hearing is conducted.

Maag (2001) and Wood and Lakin (1978) presented several reasons for avoiding the use of punishment:

1. It does not eliminate but merely suppresses behavior.
2. It does not provide a model for the desired acceptable behavior.
3. Aggression on the part of the practitioner presents an undesirable model.
4. The emotional results of punishment may be fear, tension, stress, or withdrawal.
5. The child's resulting frustration may result in further deviation.

In addition, physical punishment may result in physical harm to the child, although such harm is unplanned.

Punishment in the perception of the punished child is frequently associated with the punisher rather than with the unacceptable behavior. As a result, the punished child's reactions may be avoidance and dislike of the punisher rather than a change in behavior. Teachers who acknowledge that they are in effect behavioral models for their students will avoid assuming the role of punisher.

It may be helpful at this point to clarify some of the punishments that are frequently applied in school and homes. The following is a list of commonly used punishments:

- Denying participation in scheduled activities (games, field trips)
- Denying snacks (milk, cookies, candy)
- Physical punishment (paddlings, spankings, slaps)
- Verbal punishment (scoldings, reprimands, sarcasm, derogation, curses)
- Having the child stand apart from the others (in the corner, hallway)
- Having the child wear a sign ("I am a bad boy")

Members of the teaching profession seem to be very efficient in developing and applying harsh physical and psychological punishment. However, a variety of other methods of behavior reduction interventions are available for the teacher's use. Punishment, especially harsh and psychological punishment, should not be used in schools or classrooms. "All reasonable positive alternatives should have been considered, if not actually tried, before the decision is made to use an aversive procedure" (Wood, 1978, p. 120).

If punishment is to be used, the teacher or parent should adhere to the following guidelines:

1. Specify and communicate the punishable behavior to the children by means of classroom rules for behavior.
2. Post the rules where the children can see them; review them with the group frequently.
3. Provide models of acceptable behavior.
4. Apply the punishment immediately.
5. Apply the punishment consistently, not whimsically.
6. Be fair in using the punishment (what is good for Paul is good for Pauline).
7. Impose the punishment impersonally. Do not punish when you are angry or otherwise not self-controlled.

The following is an example of the misuse of punishment.

♦ *Example*

Paul, an 11-year-old boy in Ms. Woods's classroom, was frequently punching other boys during recess. Ms. Woods told Paul he would receive two swats with the paddle each time he hit another child.

Paul went to morning recess and within 10 minutes had punched three children and the playground supervisor. Paul was returned to the classroom. Nothing was said or done about his behavior.

At about 2:30 P.M., Mr. Brinks, the assistant principal, arrived at the classroom door. Paul was called into the hallway. Mr. Brinks struck him eight times with the paddle (two swats for each person). Ms. Woods observed the punishment as a witness.

After accomplishing this task, Mr. Brinks returned to his office without comment; Ms. Woods returned to the classroom without comment; Paul returned to his seat, crying and confused.

The absurdity of this example is that it happened at all and continues to happen.

♦ *Examples*

In the Meyers' kitchen is a cookie jar for petty cash. On the first day of each month, Mr. Meyer places $50 in bills and coins in the cookie jar. The rules for removing money from the jar are (a) that anyone can take up to $5 at any time for legitimate reasons and (b) that the purpose for which the money is used, the date, and the borrower's signature are written on a slip of paper and put in the cookie jar.

At the end of each month, Mr. Meyer totals the amount of the slips. The total is seldom $50 because their teenage son, Herman, takes $15 to $20 without putting a slip in the jar.

The Meyers have discussed this behavior with Herman several times without effect. It was decided that the next time the behavior occurred, Herman would no longer be allowed to take money from the petty cash fund. Herman considers his parents' action cruel and unusual punishment. However, he is complying with their wishes.

Mr. Sayers is a master at applying sarcasm and degradation. He is quick and devastating with his tongue, much to the discomfort of his students. His favorite epithets are "stupid," "dumbbell," "idiot," "meathead," and "dink."

One day, Rosemary was clowning around in English class. This behavior greatly disturbed Mr. Sayers. He grabbed 17-year-old Rosemary by the arm, shook her, and called her a "dink." The girl was very embarrassed and began to cry. Encouraged by her reaction, Mr. Sayers added a few more names to the list and caused the other students to laugh.

This is an example of a teacher losing self-control and perhaps causing psychological damage to a student. Mr. Sayers was unaware, or so he claimed, of the contemporary meaning of "dink." However, Rosemary and her peers were very aware of its meaning.

The authors are irrevocably opposed to the use of corporal punishment, whether it is paddling, slapping, spanking, or using a cattle prod or electric wand. We are opposed to psychological punishment, which at minimum can erode the already fragile self-concept of the developing child. If punishment must be implemented, two forms are preferred: loss of privileges and reprimands (Shea & Bauer, 1987).

In their discussion of corporal punishment, Evans and Richardson (1995) maintain that 27 states have abolished the use of corporal punishment in the schools either by state law or by regulations. Forty-six national professional and parent organizations have passed resolutions against the use of corporal punishment in the schools. They also note that corporal punishment is unevenly applied, with students with disabilities and African American and Hispanic American males from low-socioeconomic households receiving physical punishment more frequently.

DESENSITIZATION

Desensitization, the process of systematically lessening a specific, learned fear or phobic reaction in an individual, is a popular therapeutic technique developed by Wolpe in the 1960s.

The desensitization method consists of presenting to the imagination of the deeply relaxed patient the feeblest item in a list of anxiety-evoking stimuli repeatedly until no more anxiety is evoked. The next item of the list is presented and so on until, eventually, even the strongest of the anxiety-evoking stimuli fails to evoke any stir of anxiety in the patient. It has consistently been found that every stage of stimulus that evokes no anxiety when imagined in a state of relaxation will also evoke no anxiety when encountered in reality.[*]

As indicated by Wolpe (1982), the process of desensitization has been demonstrated to be an effective technique when applied to individuals with fears and anxieties related to public speaking, school attendance, participation in large groups, water, animals, heights, flying, test taking, and the like.

The process of systematic desensitization involves three phases or steps:

1. Training the subject in deep muscle relaxation
2. Constructing an anxiety-evoking hierarchy of stimuli
3. Counterposing relaxation and the anxiety-evoking stimuli

The importance of these three phases cannot be overemphasized; they are interdependent.

The practitioner is *not* encouraged to apply systematic desensitization on the basis of the information provided in this text alone. Teachers and parents should study other sources and obtain the services of a behavior therapy consultant before implementing a desensitization intervention.

The following reports of research are presented to clarify the procedures and effects of systematic desensitization under various conditions with a variety of problems.

Kravetz and Forness (1971) reported an experiment with a 6½-year-old boy who was unable to verbalize in the classroom. Psychiatric and medical reports did not reveal any known reason for his not talking in the classroom. The child's school progress was poor; however, test results indicated that he had above-average potential. A desensitization intervention of 12 sessions (two per week) was implemented to reduce the child's fear of speaking in class.

Deffenbacher and Kemper (1974) applied systematic desensitization in a program to reduce test-taking anxiety in 28 junior high school students. The group was composed of 12 girls and 16 boys. All the students had been referred by either a counselor, their parents, or a teacher. The test-taking anxiety-evoking stimulus hierarchy used with these students included the following:

- You are attending a regular class session.
- You hear about someone who has a test.
- You are studying at home. You are reading a normal assignment.
- You are in class. The teacher announces a major exam in 2 weeks.
- You are at home studying. You are beginning to review and study for a test that is a week away.
- You are at home studying, and you are studying for the important test. It is now Tuesday, 3 days before the test on Friday.
- You are at home studying and preparing for the upcoming exam. It is now Wednesday, 2 days before the test on Friday.

- It is Thursday night, the night before the exam on Friday. You are talking with another student about the exam tomorrow.
- It is the night before the exam, and you are home studying for it.
- It is the day of the exam, and you have 1 hour left to study.
- It is the day of the exam. You have been studying. You are now walking on your way to the test.
- You are standing outside the test room talking with other students about the upcoming test.
- You are sitting in the testing room waiting for the test to be passed out.
- You are leaving the exam room. You are talking with other students about the test. Many of their answers do not agree with yours.
- You are sitting in the classroom waiting for the graded test to be passed back by the teacher.
- It is right before the test, and you hear a student ask a possible test question that you cannot answer.
- You are taking the important test. While trying to think of an answer, you notice everyone around you writing rapidly.
- While taking the test, you come to a question you are unable to answer. You draw a blank.
- You are in the important exam. The teacher announces 30 minutes remaining, but you have an hour's work left.
- You are in the important exam. The teacher announces 15 minutes remaining, but you have an hour's work left.[*]

The desensitization treatment consisted of eight sessions (one per week) in groups of two to five students. The intervention effectively reduced test-taking anxiety.

Desensitization is a potent intervention that can be applied in a modified form by the teacher in the classroom. However, if desensitization is to be applied in the classroom, the following conditions must exist:

1. The teacher must have a positive interpersonal relationship with the child. The child must trust the teacher and be free to express fears in the teacher's presence.
2. The teacher must construct an anxiety-evoking stimulus hierarchy.
3. The teacher must be willing (and have adequate time) to accompany the child in the progression from the least to the most anxiety-evoking stimulus in the hierarchy.

Under normal classroom conditions, the desensitization process is time consuming. The teacher must be consistent and patient in the application of this intervention. It may be necessary to repeat some of the specific anxiety-evoking situations until their effect on the child has been eliminated.

♦ *Examples*

David, a 5-year-old boy in Ms. Philly's class for children with behavior problems, was afraid of dogs. Whenever the boy saw a dog, he would crawl under the nearest object or person and scream until the animal disappeared from view.

This behavior made it impossible for David to go out on the playground during recess with his peers, to walk to and from school, or to play outdoors in his neighborhood.

Desensitization was suggested as a possible intervention. Ms. Philly thought it was an excellent idea but suggested that implementation be deferred until she knew David better. A stimulus hierarchy was constructed, but the intervention was held in abeyance until 3 months after the beginning of the school year.

The following anxiety-evoking stimulus hierarchy was used to reduce David's fear of dogs:

1. Pictures of dogs were hung on the walls of the classroom. The pictures were initially placed as far away from David's desk as possible. As desensitization continued, they were moved nearer to David.
2. Pictures of dogs were observed by David in motion pictures and filmstrips.
3. Pictures of dogs were affixed to David's desk and notebook covers.
4. David observed dogs playing in the school yard from his classroom window.
5. David observed dogs playing in the school yard from the door of the school.
6. David observed dogs playing in the school yard as he stood at a distance that was systematically decreased.
7. David permitted dogs to walk past him in the school yard.

At *no time* during the desensitization process was David encouraged to touch or pet a dog. This precaution was taken simply because *some* dogs do bite *some* children.

During the desensitization process, Ms. Philly removed David from an anxiety-evoking situation whenever he manifested the slightest discomfort. The lessening of David's fear permitted him to tolerate dogs and to increase his interactions with his peers in the school yard and neighborhood.

Keith, an 8-year-old third-grade student, was enrolled in summer camp. Keith had a fear of water. Swimming lessons were a part of the camp program. Although swimming was not mandatory, it was encouraged. At the first suggestion of swimming or going to the pool, Keith would have a temper tantrum of considerable magnitude.

It was decided that Keith should overcome this irrational fear. The staff concluded that systematic desensitization would be an effective intervention.

The following stimulus hierarchy was constructed and applied during desensitization:

1. Swimming was announced to the group and discussed with Keith's peers. Keith did not attend swimming lessons but watched his peers, who were very happy and excited, get on the bus and depart for swimming.
2. Keith rode the bus to the pool and waited outside the building.
3. Keith rode the bus to the pool and waited outside the locker room.
4. Keith entered the locker room, put on his trunks, and remained in the locker room.

5. Keith, in trunks, observed the lesson from the pool observation room.

6. Keith observed the lesson from the poolside (approximately 10 feet from the water).

7. Keith observed the lesson from the edge of the pool.

8. Keith observed the lesson while sitting on the edge of the pool with his feet in the water.

9. Keith stood in the pool with his hands on the edge of the pool.

10. Keith walked in the shallow end of the pool with his hands on the edge of the pool.

Throughout this procedure, Keith was accompanied by his counselor, who provided positive reinforcement. As a result of this process and within 3 weeks, Keith began his swimming lessons. After 3 years, it was noted that the fear had not returned. Keith is an excellent swimmer.

♦ SUMMARY

In this chapter, several techniques used to decrease and eliminate inappropriate behavior are discussed and exemplified. The first technique is differential reinforcement, or the reinforcing of an appropriate behavior that is to be increased or exhibited and, simultaneously, extinguishing, by not directly addressing, an inappropriate behavior that is to be decreased or eliminated. Three types of differential reinforcement are discussed: differential reinforcement of zero rates of behavior, differential reinforcement of incompatible behaviors, and differential reinforcement of lower rates of behavior.

Extinction, the discontinuation or withholding of the reinforcer of a behavior that has previously been reinforcing the behavior, is discussed and exemplified. Reprimands or verbal aversives and their application and loss of privileges or response-cost are also discussed.

Time-out is a frequently misunderstood and misused behavioral intervention. Time-out is the removal of an individual from an apparently reinforcing setting to a presumably nonreinforcing setting for a specified and limited period of time. Several factors related to the effectiveness of time-out are (a) the characteristics of the individual, (b) the consistency of application, (c) the individual's understanding of the rules of behavior and time-out, (d) the characteristics of the time-out area, (e) the duration of time-out, and (f) the evaluation of the effectiveness of the intervention.

Punishment, the most familiar of the interventions discussed in the chapter, is the addition of an aversive stimulus or the subtraction of a desired reinforcer or privilege as a consequence of behavior. There are a number of serious concerns associated with the use of punishment. The major problem with the use of punishment to modify behavior is that punishment does not appear to eliminate inappropriate behaviors; instead, it appears to suppress inappropriate behaviors.

The chapter concludes with a discussion of desensitization, the process of systematically lessening a specific fear or phobia.

◆ PROJECTS

1. Joanie, a student in Mr. Jewel's class, is constantly asking, "What time is it?" She does this about 15 times a day. Mr. Jewel considers this to be attention-getting behavior and wishes to eliminate it. He usually responds to Joanie's request by telling her the time. Using the example of Joanie, (a) design four interventions for eliminating the behavior using the following intervention strategies and (b) discuss which of the interventions you think will be the most effective and the least effective.

   (a) Differential reinforcement

   (b) Reprimand

   (c) Extinction

   (d) Time-out

2. Write a brief essay (250 words or less) emphasizing the pros and cons of using punishment in home and school.

◆ REFERENCES

Bacon, E. H. (1990). Using negative consequences effectively. *Academic Therapy, 25*(5), 599–611.

Blampied, N. M., & Kahan, E. (1992). Acceptability of alternative punishments: A community survey. *Behavior Modification, 16*(3), 400–413.

Brantner, J. P., & Doherty, M. A. (1983). A review of time-out: A conceptual and methodological analysis. In S. Axelrod & J. Apsche (Eds.), *The effects of punishment on human behavior* (pp. 87–132). New York: Academic Press.

Brulle, A. R., & Barton, L. E. (1992). The reduction of maladaptive behaviors through DRO procedures: A practitioner's reference. *ICEC Quarterly, 41*(4), 5–10.

Cuenin, L. H., & Harris, K. R. (1986). Planning, implementing, and evaluating time-out interventions with exceptional students. *Teaching Exceptional Children, 18*(4), 272–276.

Deffenbacher, J., & Kemper, C. (1974). Systematic desensitization of test anxiety in junior high school students. *The School Counselor, 21,* 216–222.

Drasgow, E. (1997). Positive approaches to reducing undesirable behavior. *Beyond Behavior, 8(2),* 10–13.

Evans, E. D., & Richardson, R. C. (1995). Corporal punishment: What teachers should know. *Teaching Exceptional Children, 27*(2), 33–36.

Foxx, R. M., & Shapiro, S. T. (1978). The time-out ribbon: A nonexclusionary time-out procedure. *Journal of Applied Behavior Analysis, 11,* 125–136.

Hall, R. V., & Hall, M. C. (1980a). *How to use planned ignoring.* Austin, TX: PRO-ED.

Hall, R. V., & Hall, M. C. (1980b). *How to use time-out.* Austin, TX: PRO-ED.

Harris, K. R. (1985). Definitional, parametric, and procedural considerations in time-out interventions and research. *Exceptional Children, 51*(4), 279–288.

Houten, R. V. (1980). *How to use reprimands.* Austin, TX: PRO-ED.

Jones, R. N., Sloane, H. N., & Roberts, M. W. (1992). Limitations of "Don't" instructional control. *Behavior Therapy, 23,* 131–140.

Kerr, M. M., & Nelson, C. M. (1989). *Strategies for managing behavior problems in the classroom* (2nd ed.). Upper Saddle River, NJ: Merrill/Prentice Hall.

Kravetz, R., & Forness, S. (1971). The special classroom as a desensitization setting. *Exceptional Children, 37,* 389–391.

Lewellen, A. (1980). *The use of quiet rooms and other time-out procedures in the public school: A position paper.* Mattoon, IL: Eastern Illinois Area of Special Education.

Lohrmann-O'Rourke, S., & Zirkel, P. A. (1998) The case law on aversive interventions for students with disabilities. *Exceptional Children, 65*(1), 101–123.

Maag, J. W. (2001). Rewarded by punishment: Reflections on the disuse of positive reinforcement in schools. *Exceptional Children, 67*(2), 173–186.

Martin, G., & Pear, J. (1992). *Behavior modification: What it is and how to do it* (4th ed.). Upper Saddle River, NJ: Prentice Hall.

Nelson, C., & Rutherford, R. (1983). Time-out revisited: Guidelines for its use in special education. *Exceptional Education Quarterly, 3,* 56–67.

Powell, T. H., & Powell, I. Q. (1982). Guidelines for implementing time-out procedures. *The Pointer, 26,* 18–21.

Proctor, M. A., & Morgan, D. (1991). Effectiveness of a response cost raffle procedure on the disruptive classroom behavior of adolescents with behavior disorders. *School Psychology Review, 20*(1), 97–109.

Rose, T. (1989). Corporal punishment with mildly handicapped students. *Remedial and Special Education, 10*(1), 43–51.

Ruhl, K. (1985). Handling aggression: Fourteen methods teachers use. *The Pointer, 29,* 30–33.

Salend, S. J., & Gordon, B. D. (1987). A group-oriented time-out ribbon procedure. *Behavioral Disorders, 12*(2), 131–137.

Salend, S. J., Jantzen, N. R., & Giek, K. (1992). Using a peer confrontation system in a group setting. *Behavioral Disorders, 17*(3), 211–218.

Seiden, S. B., & Zinkel, P. A. (1989). Aversive therapy for handicapped students. *Education Law Reporter, 48,* 1029–1044.

Shapiro, E. S., & Lentz, F. E. (1985). A survey of school psychologists' use of behavior modification procedures. *Journal of School Psychology, 23,* 327–336.

Shea, T. M., & Bauer, A. M. (1987). *Teaching children and youth with behavior disorders.* Upper Saddle River, NJ: Prentice Hall.

Simpson, R. L. (1988). *Use of punishment with behaviorally disordered children and youth: Analysis of issues and recommendations for professional practice.* Position paper considered for adoption by the Executive Committee of the Council for Children with Behavioral Disorders, Reston, VA.

Skiba, R. J., & Deno, S. L. (1991). Terminology and behavior reduction: The case against "punishment." *Exceptional Children, 57*(4), 298–312.

Tobin, T. J., & Sugai, G. (1993). Intervention aversiveness: Educators' perceptions of the need for restrictions on aversive interventions. *Behavioral Disorders, 18*(2), 110–117.

Twyman, J. S., Johnson, H., Buie, J. D., & Nelson, C. M. (1994). The use of a warning procedure to signal a more intrusive timeout contingency. *Behavioral Disorders, 19*(4), 243–253.

Van Houten, R., Nau, P., Mackenzie-Keating, S., Sameoto, D., & Colavecchia, B. (1982). An analysis of some variables influencing the effectiveness of reprimands. *Journal of Applied Behavior Analysis, 15,* 65–83.

Webber, J., & Scheuermann, B. (1991). Accentuate the positive ... eliminate the negative. *Teaching Exceptional Children, 24*(1), 13–19.

Wheldall, K. (1991). Managing troublesome classroom behavior in regular schools: A positive teaching perspective. *International Journal of Disability, Development and Education, 38*(2), 99–116.

White, R. B., & Koorland, M. A. (1996). Curses! What can we do about cursing? *Teaching Exceptional Children, 28*(4), 48–52.

Witt, J. C., & Elliott, S. N. (1982). The response-cost lottery: A time efficient and effective classroom intervention. *Journal of School Psychology, 20*(2), 155–161.

Wolpe, J. (1961). The systematic desensitization treatment of neuroses. *Journal of Nervous and Mental Diseases, 132,* 189–203.

Wolpe, J. (1982). *The practice of behavior therapy* (3rd ed.). New York: Pergamon Press.

Wood, F. H. (1978). Punishment and special education: Some concluding comments. In F. H. Wood & D. C. Lakin (Eds.), *Punishment and aversive stimulation in special education: Legal, theoretical and practical issues in their use with emotionally disturbed children and youth* (pp. 119–122). Minneapolis: University of Minnesota Press.

Wood, F. H. (1988). Factors in intervention choice. In R. B. Rutherford, Jr., & J. W. Magg (Eds.), *Severe behavior disorders of children and youth* (Vol. 11, pp. 133–143). Reston, VA: Council for Children with Behavioral Disorders.

Wood, F. H., & Hill, B. K. (1983). Aversiveness and frequency of use of commonly used interventions for problem behavior. In R. B. Rutherford (Ed.), *Severe behavior disorders of children and youth* (Vol. 6, pp. 28–34). Reston, VA: Council for Children with Behavioral Disorders.

Wood, F. H., & Lakin, K. C. (1978). The legal status and use of corporate punishment and other aversive procedures in schools. In F. H. Wood & K. C. Lakin (Eds.), *Punishment and aversive stimulation in special education: Legal, theoretical and practical issues in their use with emotionally disturbed children and youth* (pp. 3–27). Minneapolis: University of Minnesota Press.

Yell, M. L. (1990). The use of corporal punishment, suspension, expulsion, and time-out with behaviorally disordered students in public schools: Legal considerations. *Behavioral Disorders, 15*(2), 100–109.

Yell, M. L. (1997). The IDEA Amendments of 1997: Implications for special and general education teachers, administrators, and teacher trainers. *Focus on Exceptional Children, 30*(1), 1–19.

Zabel, M. K. (1986). Time-out use with behaviorally disordered students. *Behavioral Disorders, 12*(1), 15–21.

7

Psychodynamic Behavior Management

Behavior influence techniques
Expressive media
Life-space interview
Reality therapy
Social skills curriculum

After completing this chapter, you will be able to do the following:

1. Describe and exemplify the application of life-space interviewing, reality therapy, and classroom conferencing.

2. Understand the application of the expressive media in behavior management.

3. Explain the application of the behavior influence techniques in the management of behavior.

4. Characterize the application of social skills curriculum.

◆ ◆ ◆

Jack, a 13-year-old seventh grader, is enrolled in Mr. Bird's junior high resource room for students with adjustment difficulties. Jack functions well in the academic areas. He performs above grade level in all subjects. However, his social behavior is creating difficulties for Jack, his classmates, and his teachers. Jack's unacceptable social behaviors have caused him to be ignored by some students, overtly rejected by others, and used as a scapegoat by a few.

Essentially, Jack believes that he is unacceptable to (unwanted by) his peers. He appears to believe that others are making fun of him or rejecting him when they are being overtly friendly. When Jack feels he is being rejected, he immediately attempts to escape his discomfort. He escapes by putting his head in his lift-top desk and closing the top, placing an open book over his face, placing his backpack over his head, walking the hallways sideways with his face to the wall, and so on.

Mr. Bird recognizes that eventually this behavior will affect all facets of Jack's functioning, including academics. Mr. Bird realizes that he is not a trained psychotherapist. However, he wishes to assist Jack in a practical manner with his unacceptable overt social behavior in the classroom and school.

Mrs. Lietner, a sixth-grade teacher, is watching 12-year-old Wendell and his classmate Tommy shooting baskets in the school yard. They are playing "21," and Tommy is winning 16 to 10.

Suddenly and for no observable reason, Wendell throws the basketball in Tommy's face with great force. When Tommy recovers, he begins to chase Wendell. Wendell runs around the playground for a few minutes and then begins to climb over the fence with Tommy in hot pursuit. As Wendell climbs the fence, his shirt catches on a wire and tears. He immediately runs to Mrs. Lietner and reports that Tommy tore his shirt.

Mrs. Lietner calls both boys to her side. Each is asked to review the incident. They are encouraged to verbally reconstruct the game, Wendell's throwing of the basketball into Tommy's face, the chase, fence climbing, and the torn shirt. During the discussion, it becomes apparent to Mrs. Lietner that Wendell fails to see any connection between his behavior, Tommy's behavior, and the torn shirt.

The teacher recognizes that this incident is similar to many others in which Wendell has been involved throughout the year. He appears unable to perceive the relationship between his actions and their consequences.

Mrs. Lietner recognizes her need for a behavior management intervention to assist Wendell.

Several behavior management interventions derived from the psychodynamic model are presented in this chapter. Four categories of interventions are discussed. These are counseling techniques, the expressive media, behavior influence techniques, and social skills curriculum. The counseling techniques discussed are the life-space interview, reality therapy, and classroom conferences. The expressive media include free play, puppetry, role playing and psychodrama, creative movement, dance and physical activities, music, the written word, the spoken word, bibliotherapy, art therapy, and others. The behavior influence techniques reviewed are planned ignoring, signal interference, proximity control, interest boosting, tension reduction through humor, hurdle helping, program restructuring, support from routine, direct appeal, removing seductive objects, antiseptic bouncing, and physical restraint. The chapter concludes with a discussion of social skills curriculum.

Several important psychodynamic interventions employed by professionals in the mental health disciplines are not presented in this text because of their complexity and special training requirements. These include individual and group psychotherapy, directive and nondirective counseling, psychoanalysis, and family therapy.

Jones (1992) asserted that recent research and theory in classroom management and therapeutic interventions with students with behavior disorders support a deemphasis on control procedures, such as those presented in Chapters 4 and 5. He calls for the incorporation of insight-oriented interventions, such as those presented in this chapter, into school-based programs for learners with behavior problems.

Before studying the remainder of this chapter, the reader is urged to review the theoretical framework underlying the psychodynamic model, presented in Chapter 2.

COUNSELING TECHNIQUES

Teachers frequently limit their ability to help children with behavior problems by excluding various counseling and other psychoeducational interventions that are available to them (Nichols, 1986). Many of the methods discussed in this chapter are frequently not applied by teachers because these methods have traditionally been seen to be within the purview of the psychologist, psychiatrist, counselor, and social worker. However, the methods presented here have been carefully selected and explained to enable the teacher to apply them to students with behavior problems. Methods that require specialized training are noted.

Life-Space Interview

The *life-space interview* is a here-and-now intervention built around a child's direct life experience. It is applied by a teacher or other practitioner significant in the child's life space. The interviewer has a definite role and power influence in the child's daily life. The life-space interview technique is imposed to structure an incident in the child's life to enable the child to solve the problems confronting him or her. The interviewer's role is facilitator.

According to Redl (1959), the life-space interview technique may be applied for either of two purposes: clinical exploitation of life events or emotional first aid on the spot.

In the first situation, *clinical exploitation of life events,* the interviewer uses an actual incident to explore with the child habitual behavioral characteristics. This is an effort to use the incident to attain a long-range therapeutic goal previously established for the child by a clinical or individualized educational program team.

When the life-space interview technique is employed for the exploitation of life events, the interviewer assists the child in increasing conscious awareness of distorted perceptions of existing realities, pathological behavior characteristics, hidden social and moral values and standards, or reactions to the behaviors and pressures of the group. The interviewer uses the technique to discuss with the child more personally productive and socially acceptable means of solving problems. This particular application of the life-space interview requires training and experience.

♦ *Example*

Jack, who was introduced to the reader at the beginning of this chapter, is an excellent example of the application of the life-space interview for the clinical exploitation of life events. Jack's bizarre methods of escaping from what he perceived to be rejections were habitual behavioral characteristics. The unacceptable behavior was repeated several times each day.

The staff discussed and agreed that life-space interviewing was an appropriate intervention in Jack's case. Each time Jack engaged in the behavior, he was immediately removed from the setting in which the behavior occurred by a supportive teacher.

The incident was verbally reconstructed and discussed, and a plan for a more acceptable response by Jack to a peer's smile, wave, and so on was agreed on by Jack and the supportive teacher. Jack returned to the setting in which the behavior was manifested and continued his daily schedule.

Over time and after many life-space interviews, Jack increased his capacity to differentiate between social acceptance and rejection.

The life-space interview technique also provides a child with *emotional first aid on the spot* in times of stress. The purpose of the life-space interview technique in on-the-spot first aid is to assist the child over a rough spot in the road in order to continue an activity. The interview is imposed to (a) reduce the child's frustration level, (b) support the child in emotionally charged situations, (c) restore strained child-teacher and child-child communications, (d) reinforce existing behavioral and social limits and realities, or (e) assist the child in efforts to find solutions to everyday problems of living and emotionally charged incidents, such as fights and arguments.

♦ *Example*

John and Thomas, both 11-year-old fifth-grade students, were on a camping trip with their teacher and classmates. The boys were in the process of erecting their two-person tent before the evening meal.

During the process of erecting the tent, John shouted at Thomas, "Come on, stupid. Get the stakes in right. Boy, am I sick of you. You're slow. Hurry up. I'm hungry. We can't eat until you get this dumb tent up."

Thomas proceeded to tell John, "Do it yourself, big mouth. I don't care if I ever eat. Besides, I'm not sleeping in there with you anyway."

Both boys were extremely frustrated after a long day of backpacking. They began fighting.

Mr. Wise recognized that emotional first aid on the spot by means of a life-space interview was needed. He stopped the fight and allowed the boys to calm down before begin-

ning the interview. During the interview, each boy reconstructed the incident as he perceived it, listened to Mr. Wise's perception of the incident, and agreed to try again with a
specific plan of action. The tent was erected quickly, and the evening meal was eaten.

As in any counseling situation, the application of the life-space interview is dependent on a variety of variables: the purpose and goal, the specific environment,
the training and experience of the teacher, and especially the child and the particular problem or difficulty.

The application of the life-space interview technique in the school is a decision
involving all members of the team responsible for the child. When the technique is
adopted for use, it should be used with consistency by all personnel under the supervision of trained and experienced professionals.

Fagen (1981) outlined a series of steps that occur during the life-space interview.
This is not a rigid series of steps; on occasion during an interview, some steps are
omitted and others reordered.

Generally, the interview begins as a result of a specific incident in the individual's
(or group's) actual life space. The interviewer encourages those involved in the incident to state their personal perceptions of it. At this time, the interviewer must determine whether this is an isolated happening or a significant part of a recurring theme.

The interviewer *listens* to those involved in the incident as they reconstruct it,
accepting their feelings and perceptions without moralizing or attacking. Although
individual perceptions of the incident are accepted, the interviewer may suggest alternative perceptions for consideration.

The interview process then moves into a resolution phase. This phase should be
nonjudgmental in tone. Many conflicts and confrontations are resolved at this point,
and the interview is terminated.

However, if the problems are not resolved, the interviewer may offer his or her
view of the happening as it is related to the situation in which the individual or individuals find themselves. Finally, those involved and the interviewer develop an acceptable plan to deal with the present problem and similar problems in the future.

Several guidelines for interviewer behavior have been offered by Brenner (1969):

1. *Be polite.* If you do not have control of your emotions, do not begin the interview.

2. *Talk with, never at or down to,* the individual being interviewed. Positive interpersonal communication is essential to the success of the interview.

3. When you are unsure of the history of the incident, investigate. *Do not conduct
   an interview on the basis of second- or thirdhand information or rumors.*

4. *Ask appropriate questions* to obtain a knowledgeable grasp of the incident.
   However, do not probe areas of unconscious motivation; limit the use of "why"
   questions.

5. *Listen to the individual* and attempt to comprehend his or her perception of the
   incident.

6. Encourage the individual to ask questions. Respond to questions appropriately.

7. When the individual is suffering from apparent shame and/or guilt as a result of the incident, *attempt to reduce and minimize these feelings.*

8. *Facilitate the individual's efforts to communicate* what he or she wishes to say. If the individual is having difficulty communicating, provide help.

9. *Work carefully and patiently* to develop a mutually acceptable plan of action for immediate or future implementation.

There is limited empirical research available. DeMagistris and Imber (1980) and Reilly, Imber, and Cremins (1978) researched the effectiveness of the life-space interview in educational settings. Reilly et al. found that in the resource room, the interview decreased inappropriate behavior. DeMagistris and Imber conducted a study in a self-contained special class with eight boys with behavioral disorders and found that academic performance improved and inappropriate behavior decreased. Naslund (1987) reported a study conducted at the Rose School in Washington, D.C., using the life-space interview technique with 28 elementary-school-age students with emotional disturbances. The study was in a crisis intervention program that applied the life-space interview as a basic intervention strategy. The study focused on frequency of use, reasons for referral, type of interview, and changes in these factors over an academic year. Naslund stated that the results were significant. Caution should be exercised in generalizing the findings of these studies because of sample limitations and research design.

Fecser and Long (1997) discussed the application of life space crisis intervention (LSCI) during classroom conflicts. They presented a six-step process for the implementation of LSCI in the classroom:

1. Crisis occurs: An effort is made to drain off or reduce the emotions surrounding the incident by acknowledging the feelings of the individual(s) involved.

2. Time line: The practitioner, using affirming and active listening techniques, attempts to determine the perspective of the involved individual(s).

3. Central issue: The underlying or core issue of the conflict is determined, and appropriate LSCI strategies are applied.

4. Insight: The involved individual(s) are helped to recognize the self-defeating behaviors active in present and similar conflicts and to change them.

5. New skills: The individual(s) involved are taught new skills that will enable the resolution of similar conflicts in the future.

6. Generalization: The generalization or transfer of the newly learned skills to other settings and circumstances by those involved is facilitated.

Fecser and Long also discuss the conflict cycle through which the student progresses. This is a four-phase cycle that includes (a) a stressful incident, (b) student feelings, (c) student's observable behavior, and (d) adult/peer reaction. When a stressful incident occurs, the student's irrational beliefs are activated. These irrational beliefs tend to trigger the student's feelings. Negative feelings drive the resulting inappropriate behavior. The inappropriate behavior results in reaction from peers and/or adults. These others in the environment respond to the student's inappropriate behavior and may do so by mirroring them. Negative reactions to the inappropriate behavior generally escalates the problem and often ends in a power struggle. The student may lose the "battle" in a particular incident but may "win" the war by having his or her irrational beliefs and negative feelings affirmed.

In a discussion of life-space interviewing introduced by Wood (1990), Gardner (1990a, 1990b) and Long (1990) generally disagree on its applications and effectiveness. Gardner finds little empirical research reported in the literature. He suggests that the life-space interview should be employed in conjunction with the principles of behavior and in response to positive behaviors rather than negative behaviors, which may be unwittingly reinforced. He suggests that by using the life-space interview, the practitioner may be condoning inappropriate feelings and behaviors. In addition, Gardner notes that it is difficult to train professionals in the proper use of the life-space interview.

Long presents himself as a "radical believer in the power and effectiveness of life-space interviewing." He generally agrees that there is inadequate research on the life-space interview. He suggests that the life-space interview was designed to be reactive and not proactive. He states that the interview does take time from academics but that this is essential for the benefit of the individual. He also states that it does focus on negative behaviors but that this is its purpose. Long agrees that training is essential and time consuming.

Wood and Long (1991) published the first text devoted exclusively to the life-space interview. Their book *Life-Space Intervention: Talking With Children and Youth in Crisis* provides an extensive, in-depth discussion of the life-space interview, the philosophy on which it is based, its uses and applications, its principles of operation, and its application with general and specific problems. Wood and Long offer a detailed discussion of the 50-year history of the development of the life-space interview and its field validation. This book is highly recommended for those interested in applying the life-space interview in the school setting.

Reality Therapy

Glasser (1969, 1990) offers a unique perspective on mental health and the treatment of mental illness. His thesis is a departure from traditional Freudian and neo-Freudian theoretical frameworks that mental health is a state of contentment and mental ill health a state of discontent. From the *reality therapy* point of view, mental health is the ability to function competently in the environment, whereas mental illness is incompetence.

An individual in need of psychiatric assistance is unable to fulfill essential psychological needs. The objective of reality therapy is to lead the individual toward competent functioning in the environment. This technique is designed to help the individual grapple successfully with the tangible and intangible aspects of the real world and as a result be able to fulfill personal needs.

According to Glasser (1990), human beings have two basic psychological needs: (a) to love and be loved and (b) to feel worthwhile to self and others.

To feel worthwhile to self and others, an individual must maintain satisfactory standards of behavior. The individual who fails to maintain acceptable standards suffers pain or discomfort. This discomfort is *mental illness,* that is, lack of responsible involvement with significant others in the environment. A mentally ill person desiring to return to the state of mental health, that is, responsible and competent functioning, must have someone whom he or she genuinely cares about, and the person must believe that the feeling is mutual. With the development of this theory, Glasser (1986) identified five basic needs—one is physiological, and the others are psychological. These needs are (a) survival, (b) love and belonging, (c) power, (d) freedom, and (e) fun.

In reality therapy, the process of therapy and the process of teaching are identical. The therapist's or teacher's primary objective is to teach the mentally ill person responsible behavior. Responsibility is the ability to fulfill one's personal needs in a manner that does not deprive other individuals of their ability to fulfill their personal needs.

According to Glasser's thesis, learning to be a responsible person is not a natural developmental process. Individuals are taught to be responsible through involvement with responsible and significant others. This involvement with others includes love and discipline. The majority of individuals learns to be responsible from loving and disciplining parents or guardians and others, such as teachers.

In summary, reality therapy is the process of teaching an irresponsible individual to face existing reality, to function responsibly, and, as a result, to fulfill personal needs.

For the individual with mental illness, the therapeutic process includes the following:

- Involvement with an acceptable person who is perceived by the person with mental illness as caring about him or her. The quality of the involvement must be sufficient to permit the ill individual to face existing reality and begin to view his or her personal behavior as irresponsible.

- A therapist who is accepting of the individual and maintains involvement with the individual while rejecting irresponsible behavior.

- The learning of responsible means of fulfilling personal needs in reality. This learning process is a cooperative activity that may include direct instructions, discussions, conversations, and planning sessions relative to any element of the individual's present lifestyle.

Reality therapy processes assume that the therapist is an acceptable and accepting person. The therapist, who may be a teacher, is also assumed to be appropriately trained and experienced in reality therapy techniques.

In an educational program, reality therapy's goal is to guide individuals toward more responsible behavior. This goal is attained by means of the reality therapy interview.

Guidelines for teachers engaged in the interview are as follows:

1. Be personal. Demonstrate that you are a person who cares about the individual and who is interested in his or her welfare.

2. Focus the therapeutic process on present behavior, not on past behavior. Accept the individual's expressed feelings, but do not probe into unconscious motivation. Ask "what," "how," and "who" questions. Limit the asking of "why" questions.

3. Do not preach, moralize, or make value judgments about the individual's behavior.

4. Help the individual formulate a practical plan to increase responsible behavior. Planning is a cooperative effort.

5. Encourage the individual to overtly make a commitment to the mutually agreed-on plan.

6. Do not accept excuses for irresponsible behavior. When a plan fails or cannot be implemented, develop another.

7. Do not punish the individual for irresponsible behavior. Allow the individual to realize the logical consequences of irresponsible behavior unless the consequences are unreasonably harmful.

8. Provide emotional support and security throughout the therapeutic process.

Because it is primarily verbal in nature, reality therapy is perhaps most appropriately used with upper elementary school children and adolescents who are capable of carrying on meaningful verbal transactions with others. It probably has limited application with persons who are identified with severe emotional disorders or developmental disabilities.

♦ *Example*

Kyle, a 10th-grade student at Greenwood High School, had superior academic potential. However, he was failing several subjects. It became evident that Kyle's future relative to graduation and college was being affected by his behavior.

Mr. Germaine, Kyle's favorite teacher, decided he must help the young man. He did not want Kyle to jeopardize his future. Mr. Germaine decided to use the reality therapy approach with Kyle. After all, he and Kyle were friends, he cared about the young man, and he knew Kyle could improve with help.

In their first session, it was found that Kyle would not work in any subject areas if he did not like the teacher. If the teacher was too demanding, unfriendly, and so on, Kyle just gave up—he refused to study.

Kyle recognized that his behavior was harmful only to himself. He and Mr. Germaine developed a plan of action. During the next few months, they met regularly to monitor Kyle's progress. Kyle learned to accept responsibility for his behavior. His grades improved dramatically.

Glasser (1969) and Heuchert (1989) suggested reality therapy principles for application with classroom groups. In an effort to reduce the emphasis in schools on competition and achievement, he proposed reality therapy meetings to teach decision making, social responsibility, and cooperation. These purposes are accomplished through social-problem-solving, open-ended, and educational-diagnostic meetings. The social-problem-solving meeting is focused on individual and group problems in classroom and school. Open-ended meetings are discussions of any thought-provoking questions related to the members of the group or the group itself. Educational-diagnostic meetings focus on the content of the educational program in which the group is involved.

Few empirical research studies of the effect of reality therapy have been conducted. In general, studies lack experimental rigor and yield mixed results. Cook (1972, in Shearn & Randolph, 1978) reported no significant changes in positive or negative behaviors of sociometrically underchosen adolescents exposed to reality therapy. Hawes (1970, in Shearn & Randolph, 1978) reported significant gains in the self-concept of black children in reality therapy. However, Glick (1968, in Shearn & Randolph, 1978) reported no significant changes in self-concept and self-responsibility of emotionally disturbed boys in residential school. However, significant changes in self-esteem were reported.

Scheaf (1972, in Shearn & Randolph, 1978) noted no significant changes in the reading achievement of delinquents involved in reality therapy. Shearn and Randolph (1978), using a four-group experimental design, studied the effects of reality therapy on the task-oriented behaviors and self-concept of fourth-grade students; results were not significant. In a follow-up study of adolescents who had successfully left a facility using reality therapy and contingency management procedures, most of the students were found to be moderately successful young adults; only 1 of the 18 subjects returned to the facility, and only 4 were unemployed 2 to 4 years after leaving the program despite substantial deficits in academic skills (Leone, 1984).

Classroom Conference

McIntyre (1987) developed a method of classroom conferencing specifically designed for teachers of students with behavioral problems. The "long talk" is an easily implemented classroom conferencing procedure and is especially responsive to a variety of interpersonal interaction and counseling styles. The long talk is applied to help students analyze their behavior and develop better self-control.

The steps in classroom conferencing are to (a) meet, (b) review, (c) discuss respect, (d) discuss typical behavior, (e) devise another response, and (f) reconvene.

The teacher should *meet* privately with the student as soon as possible after the behavioral incident. During the conference, the student is requested to *review* the incident. The teacher should clarify the student's perception to ensure that both student and teacher are discussing a common perception. The teacher may make corrections in the student's perception on the basis of first-person knowledge of the incident. Next, the teacher and student *discuss respect* to clarify what actions and feelings resulting from the incident were right and wrong and whose rights and privileges were violated. Student and teacher *discuss typical behavior* during the next step of the conferencing process. The student is helped to see the inappropriateness of the behavior and is informed that it is unacceptable.

In the fifth step, student and teacher *devise another response*. The student is requested to suggest alternative ways of responding in similar situations in the future. All suggested alternatives are accepted and written on paper. The student is asked to select the alternative he or she will use in the future. The alternative's use in various situations is discussed. The pros and cons of the alternative are discussed. If the alternative that the student selects is unrealistic, he or she is requested to select another. Student and teacher discuss why the first alternative is unrealistic. The teacher may assist students who are unable to generate alternatives.

In the final step, student and teacher *reconvene* to review student progress and performance and engage in further planning, as necessary. Behavior change takes time, and a series of conferences is often necessary.

EXPRESSIVE MEDIA

The *expressive media* refer to interventions that encourage and permit children to express personal feelings and emotions through creative activities with minimal constraints.

All human beings have feelings and emotions that must be expressed in some manner if mental health is to be maintained. A child's feelings and emotions, positive and negative, can be expressed verbally and physically. Frequently, children (and adults) unconsciously express their feelings and emotions in socially unacceptable ways. This can result in conflicts with others and may have negative impact on the individual's self-concept.

The expressive media, applied in an appropriate environment and under competent guidance, can be an acceptable and legitimate means for expressing positive and negative feelings and emotions. Adults frequently reduce personal stresses and frustrations in verbal exchanges with trusted friends and relatives or by means of avocations, hobbies, games, projects, trips, sports, vacations, and so on. For children who are generally less capable in verbal communications and less in control of their personal lifestyle, the expressive media are an opportunity to reduce stresses and frustrations without danger of conflict with others.

The media can provide many benefits for children. Not only are they beneficial in the affective domain, but they provide a variety of cognitive and psychomotor learning benefits.

If the media are to be used as a behavior management technique, the child must be provided with opportunities to find a personally satisfying medium of expression. The individual must be provided with consistent, repeated opportunities to express feelings and emotions through the chosen medium.

Cheney and Morse (1972) summarized the value of the expressive media for children as follows:

> This group of interventions supports and develops the child's expressive abilities. Such techniques serve to mobilize the child's internal resources in a number of ways: they facilitate involvement through activity rather than retreat and withdrawal; they provide acceptable channels for cathartic release; they serve as means of both externalizing the child's conflicts and communicating his feelings about them to others (though both the signal and response may be nonverbal, and nonconscious and not discussed); many

of the expressive media seem to embody inherent "therapeutic" qualities. For children with verbal inhibitions the whole "language" may be nonverbal. (p. 352)

Axline (1947) suggested several principles for play therapy that are applicable by teachers using the expressive media. The therapist must develop a warm relationship with the child, built on accepting the child exactly as he or she is. The therapist establishes a feeling of freedom in the relationship so that the child expresses his or her feelings. The therapist must be sensitive to the feelings of the child and reflect those back to facilitate insight. The relationship is built on respect and a belief that the child can change his or her behavior. The only limits established in this setting are those necessary to assist the child in becoming aware of responsibility in his or her relationships.

When using the expressive media for therapeutic purposes, the individual's activities should not be prescribed, though some limitations and structure in their application relative to time, place, specific medium, and behavioral extremes are necessary.

Minimal limits must be established and communicated to the child either verbally or by demonstration (Ginott, 1959). These limits involve (a) time; (b) the use and location of materials and equipment; (c) the prevention of the destruction of facilities, equipment, and materials; and (d) restrictions to ensure the safety of the child and the teacher. The remainder of this section describes various kinds of expressive media.

Free Play

Play therapy as described by Axline (1947) is difficult, if not impossible, to initiate in the classroom because of (a) restrictions inherent in the classroom setting, (b) the traditional role of the teacher, and (c) the teacher's lack of training in play therapy.

However, free-play sessions can be provided for individuals or groups. If a free-play program is instituted, sessions should be scheduled with regularity. Play materials and equipment, located in the designated free-play area, should be "primitive" or basic materials that the child or group can use to create an environment in which to express feelings and emotions. Complicated toys and games, although entertaining, may restrict the child's creative activities. These complex items often require the child to be passive rather than active during the sessions.

Martin, Brady, and Williams (1991) examined the effects of social toys and isolate toys on the free-play behavior of preschool children with and without disabilities in integrated and segregated settings. Social toys were those that generally encouraged interpersonal transactions, that is, balls, dress-up clothes, toy trucks and cars, wagons, puppets, and similar items. Isolate toys—those that an individual generally plays with alone—included picture books and story books, puzzles, paper, crayons, paints, and so on. They found that under social toy conditions, children engaged in social behavior more frequently than during any other condition. The incidence of social play was higher in integrated groups than in segregated groups. The researchers concluded that the types of toys are setting events for the social behavior of preschool children; toys are a viable and nonintrusive method of promoting social interaction between children with disabilities and children without disabilities.

In a free-play session, a child is invited to play with any of the materials in the play area and is encouraged to select materials of interest. Activity is restricted only by the limits previously discussed. The teacher's role is that of observer and activity facilitator.

◆ *Example*

Elmer, a 6-year-old child with a severe emotional disorder, is assigned full time to Mr. Parker's special class. Elmer was severely withdrawn. He was unable to interact verbally or nonverbally with Mr. Parker and his classmates. He spent his days quietly sitting at his desk unless physically moved from activity to activity and location to location.

Mr. Parker believed that a daily 30-minute free-play period might decrease Elmer's withdrawal. Mr. Parker believed that if Elmer would begin playing with the objects in the free-play area of the classroom, he would, in time, begin relating to his classmates and teacher.

During the first several sessions of free play, Mr. Parker, with great enthusiasm, demonstrated to Elmer the use of the various play objects and manually guided Elmer through simple activities. Elmer was introduced to the sandbox, water table, dollhouse, tools, dishes, toy animals, trucks and cars, and so on.

After several weeks of free play, Mr. Parker observed that Elmer was quietly and carefully manipulating some of the toys without encouragement. He was particularly interested in the dolls, dollhouse, hammer, and pegboard.

As the months progressed, Elmer began playing and talking with the toys with vigor. Before the end of the school year, Elmer was silently playing with one of his classmates and occasionally talking to Mr. Parker.

Puppetry

Puppets may help children express feelings and emotions. Many children who cannot communicate with others directly will do so through a puppet.

Many language development and affective education programs have successfully implemented puppetry into their programs. Perhaps the child feels safe and secure in the world of puppets, which can be manipulated and managed to express personal needs and moods.

Experience in clinical, classroom, and camp settings has demonstrated that sophisticated puppets and puppet stages are unnecessary. Simple hand puppets, which often are created and constructed by the children and may be personal possessions, are effective (D'Alonzo, 1974). The puppet stage may be a tabletop and a cardboard box decorated by the children.

Children enjoy not only playing spontaneously with puppets but also creating and producing puppet shows. Children who are not involved directly in the puppet show can profit from this activity. They respond to and converse with the puppet being manipulated by a teacher or peer.

Caputo (1993) recommends using puppet theater in the classroom with learners with behavior problems to help them master a variety of nonthreatening issues and to develop rational solutions for their problems. He suggests that puppets motivate learners and facilitate communication on the most basic of levels. In addition, through puppet theater, learners can help peers master problem-solving skills.

Caputo (1995) recommends combining puppets, problem-solving strategies, and rationale-emotive therapy to assist children with behavior problems. The central theme of rationale-emotive therapy is that disturbed feelings and behavior result when individuals apply irrational beliefs and irrational problem-solving strategies to real-life situations. According to Caputo, emotional reactions and behavior problems are caused by the manner in which the individual views life events rather than by the events themselves. Consequently, the focus of intervention is to help the individual with the behavior problem to recognize his or her irrational beliefs and ways of thinking and then to assist the individual to substitute more rational beliefs and problem-solving strategies. Puppets are recommended to facilitate this therapeutic process with children.

♦ *Example*

Mary Lou, a shy kindergarten student, was unable to communicate verbally with her classmates and teacher during the first 3 months of the school year. Mary Lou was not a disruptive child; she was always smiling and cheerful, followed directions, and completed all tasks not requiring verbalization. Her mother reported that she was very verbal at home. In addition, Mary Lou's mother said that her daughter enjoyed kindergarten.

Mrs. Holtz, the kindergarten teacher, believed that puppet play might help Mary Lou overcome her shyness. Mary Lou and her teacher worked together to make and decorate personal puppets. When the puppets were complete, Mrs. Holtz and Mary Lou held semiprivate play sessions for 15 minutes each day. After several days, Mary Lou's puppet began talking to Mrs. Holtz's puppet. As other children joined the puppetry group, Mary Lou's puppet cautiously talked to other puppets. Before the Easter break arrived, Mary Lou was very talkative in school. Her puppet was seldom used.

Role Playing and Psychodrama

Role playing and psychodrama are potentially valuable therapeutic interventions for use with children. Psychodrama was originally developed for therapeutic purposes by Moreno (1946). These techniques are based on the assumption that individuals may gain greater understanding of their behavior if they act out various aspects of their lives (Newcomer, 1980). Warger (1985) and Warger and Weiner (1987) recommend creative drama for children whose play development may be slow as a consequence of a disability. It is an excellent method for enhancing skills critical to learning and developing social skills, and it can be readily individualized.

According to Raths, Harmin, and Simons (1978), role playing can assist an individual in the clarification of feelings and emotions as they relate to existing reality in three ways:

1. It can focus on real occurrences. An incident may be reenacted and the participants told to attend to the feelings aroused; or an incident may be reenacted with
   the participants changing roles and attending to the feelings aroused by these
   new roles. An individual may be directed to deliver a soliloquy to re-create an
   emotionally loaded event. Emphasis here is on expressing feelings that were hidden or held back when the event first occurred.

2. It can focus on significant others. The individual may portray a significant person in his or her life about whom a great amount of conflict is felt.

3. It can focus on processes and feelings occurring in new situations. Directions for
   this type of role playing may be very specific, with the participants provided with
   special characters and actions; or direction may be vague, allowing the participants to form their own characters.

Anderson (1992) recommends the use of selected theater rehearsal techniques
with African American students identified as behaviorally disordered.

Role-playing and psychodrama techniques have been incorporated into several
social skills and affective education programs concerned specifically with the learning of values and standards.

♦ *Example*

Thomas, a 15-year-old 10th grader, was quite overweight. He was the class scapegoat.
His classmates were constantly making fun of his size. They called him "porky," "fatso,"
"pig," "slob," "tubby," and so on. Each day, someone came up with a new name to call him.

Thomas was a sensitive young man, and whenever he was called a name, he withdrew. Frequently, the teacher saw tears in his eyes.

Mrs. Minup was very concerned about Thomas's mental well-being and his classmates' lack of consideration and compassion for Thomas and other children who were different. She believed that role playing might be a method of helping the whole class,
including Thomas, gain insight into their behavior.

Without including obesity, Mrs. Minup conducted a series of role-playing activities with
the class. The students role-played their reactions and feelings to roles concerned with
height, complexion, race, religion, and so on.

As the students began to empathize with the feelings of the characters they were role
playing, Thomas became more accepted and less of a target of their hurtful behavior.

Drama, as a therapeutic technique, can be used with students for several purposes
in the educational setting (Creekmore & Madan, 1981; Necco, Wilson, & Scheidmantel,
1982; Newcomer, 1980). Among these are the following:

- To assist in finding solutions, making decisions, and assuming responsibility for
  personal social-emotional problems

- To assist in affective education, increasing feelings and emotions, and improving communication skills

- To assist in solving problems associated with normal child and adolescent development
- To facilitate group cohesiveness
- To facilitate experimentation with adult roles
- To aid in the conceptualization of abstracts in subject matter such as language and science
- To offer entertainment and recreation opportunities
- To offer the teacher opportunities to observe students in various situations

Newcomer (1980) cautions teachers to apply drama therapy with care. Student preparation includes a clear understanding of the purpose, objectives, and benefits of drama. Rules and regulations should be explained. Participation is always voluntary and devoid of personal criticism.

Creative Movement, Dance, and Physical Activities

As a therapeutic intervention, creative movement, dance, and other physical activities have the capacity to assist children in expressing their feelings and emotions in an acceptable manner (Chace, 1958). This can be accomplished in a variety of ways, such as imitating nature or animals or by expressing the feelings of others or expressing personal feelings under varying circumstances. During creative movement sessions, the child can express past, present, and even future feelings and emotions. These activities encourage the child to externalize personal feelings and begin to deal with them.

Movement activities can be conducted with or without music (Hibben & Scheer, 1982). On occasion, voices, hand clapping, feet stamping, recorded environmental sounds, and rhythm instruments are used to facilitate sessions.

♦ *Example*

At camp R&R, the staff noticed that the preteen group known as the "cool persons" was the most "uptight" of all the groups. Children in this group appeared afraid to "let go," to have a good time, or to relax. They appeared concerned about making mistakes in front of their peers.

Ms. Taphorn, a dance enthusiast, suggested that a daily early morning session of creative movement might relax the group and develop cohesiveness. During the sessions, in which Ms. Taphorn and the staff participated, the group became trees, grass, wind, rain, sun, and flowers. They acted out sadness, happiness, joy, sorrow, excitement, fear, and so on.

Within a few days, the "cool persons" were acting as "happy cool persons." The campers began to relax and enjoy each other's company.

In a research brief, Zabel (1988) suggested that available research tends to support physical exercise as an adjunctive therapy. Physical activities have been used to provide both aerobic activity and therapeutic restructuring of the environment (Lane,

Bonic, & Wallgren-Bonic, 1983). Group "walk-talks" have demonstrated the production of healthy levels of fatigue and improved peer relationships among adolescents (Lane et al., 1983). Daily jogging programs have decreased disruptive behaviors among behavior-disordered children (Allen, 1980; Hoenig, Shea, & Bauer, 1986). Anderson (1985) reported positive effects from the "A.M. Club," a jogging club for junior high school students with behavioral disorders. Evans, Evans, Schmid, and Pennypacker (1985) studied the relationship between jogging and touch football and specific behaviors in adolescents with behavioral disorders. The data indicated that a decrease in talk-outs and an increase in problems completed were associated with vigorous exercise. Yell (1988) studied the effects of jogging on the talk-outs and out-of-seat behavior of elementary school students with behavioral disorders. A decrease in the inappropriate behaviors following jogging was found in five of six students.

Music

It is an accepted fact in contemporary society that people are affected by music. We are exposed to mood-modifying music in restaurants, factories, supermarkets, department stores, banks, and so on. Presumably, this music has some effect on our behavior and moods (Roter, 1981).

Music is applied as a therapeutic intervention for children in several ways (Lament, 1978; Purvis & Samet, 1976):

1. Children enjoy listening to recordings.
2. Music is an effective tool for reducing excitement and activity levels after high-interest, strenuous activities.
3. Young people enjoy producing music. Although every child cannot play a piano or guitar, most children can learn to enjoy singing and participating in a rhythm band.

Through music, children can express feelings and emotions in an acceptable way.

♦ *Example*

Mr. Binckly used music for two purposes in his class for behavior-disordered acting-out elementary school boys. Music was used (a) to calm the group after vigorous outdoor activity and (b) to allow the group to express pent-up energy and aggression.

After outdoor activities, the class devoted 5 minutes to sitting quietly and listening to calming music. Mr. Binckly found this an excellent way to help the group make the transition from recess and physical education to academics.

In addition, Mr. Binckly used music to channel the students' energy after a test or long period of seat work. On such occasions, the group would sing a few songs. No effort was made to perfect the technique.

Music as therapy has several advantages for children. It encourages personal freedom and interpretation and provides "a unique personal experience that has its own meaning for each individual" (Thursby, 1977, p. 77). Music responds to the needs of individuals within a broad range of ages, intellectual abilities, social and educational experiences, and emotional characteristics. Music encourages self-subordination through cooperation and encourages self-discipline and self-directed behavior (David & Newcomer, 1980).

In a discussion of the advantages of music as an integral component of the Developmental Therapy curriculum for severely emotionally disturbed children, Wood (1976) suggested that for such children,

> communication must be established as a basis for trust if there is to be subsequent growth; and of all the ways to communicate, perhaps music is the most universal.... Whatever form the disturbance takes, and whatever the age of the child, there is a way to reach each child through music in order to begin the gradual movements toward healthier responses. (p. vii)

Michel (1985) suggested that music therapy techniques may be of assistance even though a trained music therapist is not available. Music can be used by the teacher as part of a child's education program, as an adjunct to daily programming, and to teach specific subject matter (Duerksen, 1981). As part of a child's education, music may be used for the following purposes (David & Newcomer, 1980; Ferolo, Rotatori, & Fox, 1984; Ferolo, Rotatori, Macklin, & Fox, 1983; Hibben & Scheer, 1982; Lament, 1978):

- To facilitate cognitive development through increasing abstract thinking, increasing attending, and providing practice for conceptual skills
- To facilitate affective development and social skills and encourage social interaction
- To increase psychomotor skills, coordination, body image, position in space, movement skills, and auditory and visual discrimination
- To assist in the development of self-concept, to develop self-reliance, and to provide an opportunity to be successful
- To provide creative experiences and increase expressive skills and to provide an expressive outlet for "blowing off steam"

There are several adjunctive uses of music in the educational setting (David & Newcomer, 1980; Duerksen, 1981). Music may be used to manage the behaviors of individuals and groups, to produce a relaxing atmosphere, or to serve as a distraction for children and youth. Musical activities may serve to motivate students: They can be used as reinforcement for improved behavior, completed work, or other target behaviors. Music may serve both as a form of communication and as an aesthetic outlet for some children and youth with behavior disorders.

Music may also be used to teach subject matter (Duerksen, 1981; Thursby, 1977). For instance, it can provide musical background and context for academic subject areas. Music can also be used to inspire creative writing, art, and storytelling.

In whatever its applications, it is important to remember that the goals of music therapy are not to teach specific musical skills and knowledge but to assist the student in reaching nonmusical developmental goals.

The Written Word

Few studies have been conducted on the therapeutic benefit of writing as an intervention for children, although writing has been repeatedly demonstrated to be a useful therapeutic intervention for adults. It seems logical that children can express personal feelings and emotions through written communications. By writing and at times sharing with others that which is written, it is possible to externalize personal conflicts and frustrations (Levinson, 1982). According to Dehouske (1982),

> The written word is a modality for self-expression, self-exploration, and problem solving. Through story writing, students reveal their perceptions, attitudes, coping skills, and problem-solving strategies. Story-writing tales can be structured to encourage students to explore the decision-making process and identify behavioral alternatives and consequences. (p. 11)

Writing for therapeutic benefit is not concerned with any particular format. Concern is focused entirely on content. The written forms may include poetry, stories, essays, articles, books, journal entries, and so on.

♦ *Example*

For a teenager, Michael had several serious problems on his mind. Not only was he concerned about himself and his future, but he was concerned about his parents, who were separated and considering divorce.

Michael had great difficulty talking about his problems to anyone, including parents, teachers, and friends. The school counselor suggested that Michael might keep a journal in which he could write about his concerns and his feelings. The counselor told Michael not to be concerned about spelling, grammar, handwriting, and so on—just write what he wished. The counselor offered to discuss these writings with Michael *if and when* Michael wished.

Michael wrote a daily journal. He did not discuss the content with the counselor but did report that it helped to write about his problems and reread his daily entries.

The Spoken Word

Although many children are not developmentally or emotionally prepared to enter formal verbal therapy, they frequently enjoy and profit from communicating verbally. Communications may take the form of group storytelling sessions or conversations and discussions with teachers. In each of these, the child is encouraged to express feelings and emotions.

Bauer and Balius (1995) found the interaction between the reader (child) and listener (teacher) in storytelling to be beneficial in treating behavioral and emotional problems. In storytelling, there is a connection between emotional and academic development through communication. They suggest a combination of bibliotherapy and storytelling with young children to ameliorate behavior problems. Bibliotherapy is discussed in the next section of this chapter.

♦ *Example*

Mr. Blackside believed that a special camp was a setting in which emotionally disturbed campers could express their feelings.

It was suggested that the campers' aggressions, in part, could be channeled into evening campfire discussions and storytelling sessions. During these sessions, the campers were encouraged to review the day's activities. They were encouraged to discuss their arguments, fights, and hurt feelings.

Newcomer (1980) suggests that the therapeutic benefit of the spoken word is greatest if creative, original materials are emphasized. The teacher helps the children create stories and cast themselves as characters in the story. The story may be acted out by the children with emphasis on the affective content.

Bibliotherapy

Bibliotherapy is an indirect intervention that uses the interaction between the reader and literature for therapeutic purposes. It is a tool for helping children deal with their problems through reading literature about characters who possess problems similar to their own (Adderholdt-Elliot & Eller, 1989; Sridhar & Vaughn, 2000). This intervention can be applied with children and youth to encourage them to fulfill their needs, relieve pressures, and improve mental and emotional well-being (Russell & Russell, 1979). McCarty and Chalmers (1997) suggest that bibliotherapy is effective not only in the treatment of behavior problems but also in the prevention of behavior problems.

According to Gladding and Gladding (1991), there are two kinds of bibliotherapy. The first, originating in the 1930s, is a collaborative effort of librarians and counselors. In this form of bibliotherapy, counselors prescribe reading material (suggested by librarians) to clients who are experiencing emotional difficulties. The clients respond directly to the materials, and change is brought about through insight, catharsis, or copying the behavior characteristics in the literature.

The second kind of bibliotherapy is "interactive bibliotherapy." Interactive bibliotherapy emphasizes that the processes of growth, change, and healing are centered not so much in reading appropriate material as in guided dialogue between the client or group and the counselor about the materials. This process involves several phases: identification, catharsis, and insight (Bauer & Balius, 1995; Halsted, 1988). During the first phase (identification), the student identifies with the character(s) in the reading material and recognizes similarities between him- or herself and the character(s). In the next phase (catharsis), the student lives through the situations presented in the reading material and shares feelings with the character(s). Finally, the student develops insight, becoming more aware of the motivations and rationalizations in his or her personal behavior and situation.

Richards, Gipe, and Callahan (1997) recommend holistic literacy lessons to help students with language disabilities enhance their reading comprehension and social understanding. Holistic literacy lessons are designed to connect reading, writing, listening, speaking, and thinking. In addition, they facilitate interpersonal interaction, collaboration, and cooperation among students.

For bibliotherapy to be effective, the child must be able to read, be motivated to read, and be exposed to appropriate materials. Literature that is selected by the teacher and child, focuses on the child's needs, is at the appropriate level, is realistic, and accurately represents the characters in the story (Cianciolo, 1965) is most effective. Adderholdt-Elliot and Eller (1989) recommend using bibliotherapy with students who are gifted.

Hoagland (1972) indicates that bibliotherapy works as a three-phase process. First, the children identify themselves in the literature—they must perceive themselves as a part of the story or as a character. Second, children become emotionally involved in the story and the problem it presents. Finally, they arrive at a greater understanding of themselves and their problems by identifying with the characters or situations in the story. As previously mentioned, Bauer and Balius (1995) suggest a form of bibliotherapy based on storytelling by the teacher or therapist.

Learning activities used to facilitate bibliotherapy include the following:

1. Writing a summary of the book for discussion
2. Dramatizing, role-playing, or presenting skits or puppet shows about the message in the literature
3. Making artworks that represent characters and situations in the literature

McCarty and Chalmers (1997) see bibliotherapy as including several phrases: read, reflect, discuss, and follow-up. First, the student reads the book (or other form of literature). This can be done aloud or silently. Next, the student is encouraged to reflect on the literature. Third, the literature is discussed with the teacher either individually or in a small or large group. Finally, follow-up activities are conducted (i.e., art activities, dramatization, or written responses).

Though more research is needed on the effects of bibliotherapy, Schrank and Engels (1981), in a review of the extant research, concluded that it was an effective intervention.

Harms, Etscheidt, and Lettow (1986) suggested the use of poetry as an aid to helping children recognize and explore their feelings and emotions. Poetry is generally brief and concise, and it explores a broad range of topics and events. It can help the child in several ways: creating mental images, responding to varied perspectives, reciting, exploring rhythmic activity, and enacting stories. Children can also express their feelings and emotions by writing poetry.

Sridhar and Vaughn (2000) recommend bibliotherapy for all students to enhance their reading comprehension, self-concept, and behavior. They offer lists of selected books for preschool through second-grade students and second- through fourth-grade students. Prater (2000) is an additional resource, presenting a list of 46 frequently recommended books for the instruction of students about learners with disabilities. McCarty and Chalmers (1997) also list readings focusing on the topics of abuse and neglect, anger, differences, and families.

Art Therapy

Art productions, from the young child's scribbling to the young adult's realistic drawings and paintings, are expressions of self. Art as a therapeutic treatment medium is a growth-oriented experience that benefits children in many ways: communication, socialization, creativity, self-expression, self-exploration, and manipulation of the environment (Williams & Wood, 1977).

Children should be afforded opportunities to express their feelings and emotions through the two-dimensional arts. These productions may be finger paintings, pencil drawings, watercolors, oil, tempera, and so on. Teachers should remember that their personal perceptions of the form and content of a child's art production are secondary. The important element is the child's perceptions and feelings.

The three-dimensional arts are more limited than the two-dimensional arts for classroom use because of the nature of the materials and equipment. They are, nevertheless, valuable therapeutic tools. In three-dimensional art forms, the child can externalize feelings and emotions through the manipulation of clay, plaster, sand, wood, plastic, and a variety of other materials. Arts-and-crafts projects are included in this group of therapeutic interventions.

Omizo and Omizo (1988) implemented an art therapy program for adolescents with learning disabilities. The intervention consisted of 12 sessions of 45 to 60 minutes within a 6-week period. Students, under the guidance of their teachers, engaged in activities using common art materials (crayons, clay, paint). In interviews at the conclusion of the program, teachers reported that students were better behaved and that they behaved in ways indicating enhanced self-esteem. The teachers reported that they enjoyed working with students in art therapy and that they themselves felt better as well.

♦ *Example*

Mrs. Fingerling believed that children would express their feelings and emotions through the two- and three-dimensional art forms if encouraged to do so. She established an art center in the classroom. The center included the materials and equipment needed for painting with various media, drawing, sculpting, molding, and so on. She scheduled 45 minutes of art activities 3 days each week. The period was scheduled at the end of the day so that those children wishing to continue their work could remain for an extra few minutes. To introduce the program, Mrs. Fingerling systematically demonstrated the use of various media. Each child was encouraged to choose his or her medium. They were encouraged to experiment and produce objects meaningful to them.

Photography and Videotaping

Minner (1981) suggested photography as an adjunctive therapy for children with behavioral disorders and other disabling conditions. This medium is useful not only for its therapeutic benefit but also to stimulate creativity. Minner suggested two activities in which photography can be used effectively: a slide-tape presentation and a visual arts gallery. Both activities are responsive to individualization.

Production of a slide-tape presentation involves several steps:

1. Selecting a topic. This can be a collaborative activity involving students and teacher.

2. Taking photographs, which involves selecting specific subjects and learning to operate the camera, lights, light meter, and other equipment.

3. Preparing the script, which involves arranging the slides, writing the script, selecting and recording music, taping the script, and operating the equipment.

The school or classroom visual arts gallery, another beneficial outcome of photography, can include unusual and creative photographs that are framed and titled and may be changed periodically or seasonally to project special themes. Students may share the gallery—which may be in the classroom or in another location in the school—with peers, teachers, administrators, and parents.

Raschke, Dedrick, and Takes (1986) suggested videotape feedback as a therapeutic tool. Videotaping can be used to help students with behavior problems become more aware of their behavior and develop more appropriate ways of interacting. They suggest three techniques: behavioral rehearsal, self-control training, and reality replay.

Behavioral rehearsal engages the student in role-playing simulations of situations involving interpersonal relations. Playback sessions are devoted to teacher and student analysis of the tape and discussion. Through discussion, the student is helped to grow in understanding of behavior, its antecedents and consequences, and alternative ways of behaving.

Self-control training using videotape feedback can be helpful in the areas of on-task behavior, disruptive behavior, and academic productivity. Using feedback, students can be trained in self-assessment, self-monitoring, and self-reinforcement.

Reality replay can be a valuable therapeutic tool for students who are unable to see the antecedents and consequences of their behavior. During playback, the students can clearly see both their appropriate and inappropriate behaviors and their antecedents and consequences. They may become aware of the coping mechanisms they use to justify or rationalize their behavior and discuss more appropriate and productive coping mechanisms.

Falk, Dunlap, and Kern (1996) investigated the effects of self-evaluation by means of videotaped feedback on the appropriate and inappropriate peer interactions of students with externalizing and internalizing behaviors. The students who were identified as emotionally/behaviorally disordered were members of a general education classroom. Consequently, all the experimental sessions included students without identified behavior problems. As a result of the videotaped feedback, substantial increases in appropriate interactions for students with internalizing behavioral problems were found, as were substantial decreases in inappropriate interactions for students with externalizing behaviors.

Lonnecker, Brady, McPherson, and Hawkins (1994) studied the relationships between videotaped self-assessment, self-modeling, discrimination training, and behavioral rehearsal on the cooperative classroom behaviors of two second-grade students with learning and behavior problems. Intervention was effective in helping the students (a) acquire cooperative classroom behaviors, (b) generalize the behaviors to other settings, and (c) maintain the behaviors in both training and generalization settings. In addition, the videotapes reduced inappropriate behavior in the training and generalization settings. Finally, the researchers found a reduction in the variability of the behaviors exhibited by the students.

Holaday (1994) experimented with self-as-a-model videotape viewing to reduce inappropriate behaviors of 26 students from five self-contained classes for students with emotional/behavioral disorders. The students were in experimental (18 students) and control (8 students) groups. Self-as-a-model tapes, 4 to 6 minutes in duration, show the student doing his or her "best" in the classroom. Inappropriate behaviors were edited from the tapes. The tapes are viewed by the student each day for 10 consecutive days. It is expected that during the day, the student will model the "best" behavior on the tape. Although no significant results were found, Holaday asserts that the method does have strong face validity and that further experimentation is needed.

Broome and White (1995) suggest a variety of classroom applications for videotapes:

- Providing a permanent record for antecedent-behavior-consequence analysis
- Providing self-monitoring of behavioral strengths and weaknesses
- Evaluating the behavioral strength and weaknesses of others
- Providing reality replay of facial expressions, body language, expressions of feelings, tone of voice, and other hard-to-define performance criteria
- Providing motivation and enthusiasm for group sessions
- Adding vitality to simulations and role plays
- Reinforcing shared experiences
- "Catching" unobserved misbehavior or adaptive behavior
- Providing a less intrusive consequence for misbehavior
- Providing parents and others a realistic perspective of student and classroom behaviors
- Building cooperation and trust
- Developing a plan for inclusion

Teachers are cautioned to use videotape feedback in a nonjudgmental manner with students.

Pet-Facilitated Therapy

Pets have been used in a variety of settings to facilitate therapeutic goals. Pet-facilitated therapy has been applied with children with emotional disturbances, children with physical handicaps, geriatric patients, depressed veterans, and psychiatric patients. A variety of animals have been used in therapy, including dogs, cats, rabbits, and horses. Other common classroom pets may be used in the program.

Polt and Hale (1985) described a pet-facilitated therapy program for children with developmental delays at the Hope Center in Denver. A dog and a cat were cotherapists in the program. The goals of the program were to give children experience with animals and their needs and care and to respond to the individual child's therapeutic goals. Among the individual goals sought in the Hope Center program were (a) overcoming fear of animals, (b) increasing self-confidence, (c) developing nurturing skills, (d) improving reality orientation, (e) increasing self-esteem, and (f) learning to cooperate with others.

To implement a pet-facilitated therapy program, several steps must be taken. First, staff commitment to the program is sought in a meeting that encourages the expression and discussion of questions and concerns. Parents should participate in this meeting and their permission for their child's participation must be obtained. Next, animals must be selected with great care. Obedience-trained, people-oriented, docile animals are used in the program. Both individual and group program goals should be developed. The individual goals should be developed in response to the child's individualized education program. At least weekly sessions should be scheduled; more frequent sessions are desirable.

Murry (1996), in a review of the selected research, suggests that animal-assisted therapy is beneficial for students with emotional/behavioral disorders. She offers implementation guidelines from the Delta Society, an independent nonprofit corporation concerned with pet-assisted therapy. The organization, located in Reston, Virginia, offers general information, materials for teachers to use in the classroom, training sessions, and pet certification programs. The society's guidelines for teachers wishing to implement a therapy program are as follows:

- Inform the school administration of the "what" and "why" of the program you wish to implement
- Check local and state laws and regulations; check insurance coverage and potential liability
- Choose animals with care and carefully match children and animals
- Provide constant supervision for the benefit of the children and the animals
- Model appropriate human-animal interaction. (If you are uncomfortable around animals, do not engage in pet-assisted therapy.)
- Consider the health and well-being of both the children and the animals
- Establish and enforce rules with regard to the pet-assisted therapy program and the interaction between the children and animals

Teachers are urged to obtain appropriate training before engaging in pet-assisted therapy.

BEHAVIOR INFLUENCE TECHNIQUES

Psychodynamic theorists and practitioners recognize that many of the counseling and expressive media techniques do not immediately change unacceptable behaviors to acceptable behaviors. Techniques of behavior management are needed that can be implemented to interfere with ongoing unacceptable behaviors in the classroom, resource room, school, or playground.

Teachers have a responsibility to interfere with behaviors when they do the following:

- Present a real danger
- Are psychologically harmful to the child and others
- Lead to excessive excitement, loss of control, or chaos
- Prohibit the continuation of the program
- Lead to destruction of property
- Encourage the spread of negativism in the group
- Provide opportunities to clarify individual and group values, standards, and social rules
- Lead to conflict with others outside the group
- Compromise the practitioner's mental health and ability to function

Redl and Wineman (1957) suggested 12 behavior management interventions or *behavior influence techniques* compatible with the psychodynamic framework for the management of surface behaviors. The work of Redl and Wineman has been expanded by Long and Newman (1961, 1965) and Shea, Whiteside, Beetner, and Lindsey (1974). The behavior influence techniques are planned ignoring, signal interference, proximity control, interest boosting, tension reduction through humor, hurdle helping, program restructuring, support from routine, direct appeal, removal of seductive objects, antiseptic bouncing, and physical restraint.

Planned Ignoring

At one time or another, most children engage in unacceptable behavior in an effort to gain the attention of their classmates, teacher, and parents. These unacceptable behaviors are legion in number and may include pencil tapping, body movements, hand waving, whistling, snorting, desktop dropping, book dropping, and so on. Such behavior, although relatively benign, is annoying to others.

Planned ignoring may be used to eliminate many of these behaviors. The teacher using this technique simply ignores the disruptive behavior. No response is made when the behavior occurs. It is generally true that when attention-seeking behaviors are ignored, they become nonfunctional and decrease in frequency. Of course, the child is reinforced when he or she exhibits appropriate behavior (Bacon, 1990).

Signal Interference

There are a variety of nonverbal techniques that a teacher may use to interfere with unacceptable behaviors (Bacon, 1990). Nonverbal techniques or signals, such as eye contact, a frown, finger snapping, toe tapping, book snapping, light flicking, and so on, can alert a child or group to their unacceptable behavior. Often, nonverbal behavior influence techniques help the disruptive child "save face" with his or her peers, and thus the disruption is not escalated. They also save the shy child from unnecessary embarrassment.

Conversely, nonverbal signals can be used to reinforce acceptable behaviors in the classroom.

Proximity Control

Very frequently, the proximity of an authority figure (teacher, parent, police officer) results in the discontinuation of unacceptable behaviors. Even college professors find it useful to walk about the classroom in an effort to reduce the level of conversation and side comments.

In addition, proximity can have a positive effect on children experiencing anxiety and frustration. The physical presence of a teacher available to assist has a calming effect on troubled children.

Shores, Gunter, and Jack (1993) suggested that teacher movement in the classroom may effectively control student disruptions by bringing the teacher into closer proximity to all students, thereby increasing the effectiveness of their interactions. Gunter, Shores, Jack, Rasmussen, and Flowers (1995) reviewed the literature and empirical research on the effectiveness of teacher/student proximity control to improve student behavior in general and special education classrooms. They concluded that proximity is generally defined as being within 3 feet of the student and supported with brief interactions with the student. In addition, the proximity of students to other students may have an effect on the control of behavior. It appears that if one student is reprimanded or positively reinforced, this interaction impacts nearby students. Gunter et al. recommend that teachers monitor their movement about the classroom in an effort to increase their proximity to all students. Finally, they recommend that teachers move about the room during seat-work activities.

Interest Boosting

Most persons become bored with routine and difficult tasks. Interest tends to wane with time. The teacher who observes a child losing interest or becoming bored with a task should make an effort to boost the child's interest. This may be accomplished by offering to help, noting how much work has been accomplished, noting how well done the completed part of the task is, discussing the task, and so on. Interest boosting may help the child reorganize a task and mobilize his or her energies to complete it.

Tension Reduction Through Humor

Humor has been used to reduce tension, frustration, and anxiety for as long as human beings have been laughing. Children, quite naturally, become tense when engaged in significant tasks. The prudent teacher will apply humor in an effort to help children relax and place their tasks in perspective when they become frustrated. A joke or a humorous comment will frequently reduce tension. Caution must be used to be sure the humor is not harmful to any individual.

Hurdle Helping

Hurdle helping is a technique applied to assist a student who is experiencing difficulty with a specific task. Hurdle helping may simply be an encouraging word from the teacher, an offer to assist with a specific task, or the making available of additional materials and equipment. Help is provided before the child becomes disruptive or simply gives up on the assignment.

Program Restructuring

Occasionally teachers, especially new teachers, are so committed to a lesson, task, or schedule that they will continue regardless of student response. Prudent teachers are sufficiently observant to recognize when a lesson or activity is going poorly; they are flexible. Before the class becomes disruptive or loses all interest, the teacher either restructures the lesson or postpones it until a more appropriate time.

Support From Routine

All persons, including children, like to know their daily schedule. We appreciate being able to plan our day and knowing where, when, why, and with whom we will be at various times. It appears to be especially important to children with behavior problems that they be provided with a schedule and a routine.

The teacher is wise to announce and post the day's schedule in the classroom. Changes in the schedule should be announced in advance if possible. The children should be reminded of future special events. It is equally important to post and review classroom rules. Rules, schedules, and routines are discussed extensively in the next chapter.

Direct Appeal

Many times during an unacceptable behavior incident, the teacher can quickly and effectively resolve the problem through direct appeal to the students' sense of fairness. The direct appeal is derived from the following:

1. The teacher's personal positive relationship with the individual or group
2. The consequences that will result if the unacceptable behavior continues
3. The effect of the behavior on the student's peers
4. The teacher's authority over the student and group

Many teachers neglect this approach to influencing behavior in favor of more indirect interventions. They neglect to simply and forcefully state, "Stop this behavior because ...."

Removal of Seductive Objects

Frequently, misbehavior occurs because the student has available some object of attention that is distracting. Young children bring small toys, games, and other objects to the classroom that distract them. Older children are distracted by books, magazines, combs, keys, and so on. When the teacher finds that these objects are keeping the child from the assigned task, the objects should be confiscated until after class or school. The confiscation should be kind and firm. Discussion is not necessary. It is more effective if children are trained to routinely store such objects in an appropriate place before school and until it is time to use them.

Antiseptic Bouncing

When a student becomes agitated and frustrated with an activity and before he or she is physically or verbally disruptive, it is prudent to remove the student from the work setting (Bacon, 1990). This removal is called antiseptic bouncing. It is viewed as a positive behavior influence technique and not as a punishment. Antiseptic bouncing, properly applied, provides the student with an opportunity to avoid embarrassment, calm down, reorganize thought, and begin the task anew.

Physical Restraint

Perhaps no children are more concerned with their physical and emotional well-being—and perhaps their continued existence—than children who have lost control of themselves in a tantrum. These children feel totally and absolutely helpless. They simply cannot control their physical and verbal behaviors. On such an occasion, physical restraint is not only necessary but a kindness. The child is held until calm. The teacher communicates physically and verbally to the child in a calm voice or whisper. The teacher communicates to the child, "You are safe; I will protect you; I will not let you harm yourself." After the child regains control, the teacher may wish to discuss the incident with the child. They may plan ways the child can avoid similar problems in the future.

Because of the controversial nature of restraint and physical contact with children, it is prudent to discuss the use of such methods with the school administrator and ascertain school and district policies with regard to their use. Parental permission must be obtained if physical restraint is to be used to manage children's behavior.

The behavior influence techniques discussed in this section are effective in the control of directly observable behaviors. They should be a part of the behavior management method of all teachers. The techniques are most effective when used with consistency.

SOCIAL SKILLS CURRICULUM

Often, students with behavior problems are viewed by peers, teachers, parents, and others as socially incompetent. They engage in behavior excesses, such as cursing, shouting, arguing, and disrupting. They either have not had the opportunity to learn or have not learned, when given the opportunity, appropriate social skills (Carter & Sugai, 1989).

A *social skills curriculum* is designed to help students focus on increasing their awareness and understanding of personal emotions, values, and attitudes through educational activities (Edwards & O'Toole, 1985; Epanchin & Monson, 1982; McGinnis, Sauerbry, & Nichols, 1985). These activities lead to improvement of the students' interpersonal problem-solving skills. Neel (1988) suggests that social skills training would better prepare all children to live in our complex society.

Goldstein, Spafkin, Gershaw, and Klein (1983) list 50 social skills in six categories needed by children and youth to enhance their social functioning. The categories are beginning and advanced social skills, skills for dealing with feelings, skill alternatives to aggression, skills for dealing with stress, and planning skills. The social skills curriculum most compatible with the psychoeducational framework, discussed previously in this chapter, is the "Psychoeducational Curriculum for the Prevention of Behavioral and Learning Problems" (commonly referred to as the "self-control curriculum") by Fagen, Long, and Stevens (1975). The self-control curriculum was designed as a preventive intervention for use with all children.

This curriculum is based on the assumption that a common denominator for disruptive behaviors of children with behavior and learning problems is a lack of self-control. To function effectively, children must develop the capacity to control their behavior, even when frustrated. According to Fagen and Long (1976), self-control is understood to be an individual's capacity to exercise control over and regulate personal behavior in a manner which is flexible and realistic in a given situation. An important objective of the curriculum is the reduction of students' anxiety over losing self-control by increasing the skills and confidence they have in their ability to regulate their impulsive behavior. Morse (1979) indicated that the self-control curriculum advocates inserting a cognitive pause between an impulse and its expression. It trains students to use cognitive processes to balance personal behavioral options in terms of their experiences and goals.

In the curriculum, the learning of each specific skill is accomplished through a variety of activities. Through learning the skills, the authors predict growth in the student's capacity to direct and regulate personal action in given situations. Activities that make up the curriculum include games, role playing, lessons, and discussion. Activities are implemented in small, developmental steps and include positive feedback. Short, regular training sessions are advised. Andersen, Nelson, Fox, and Gruber (1988) suggested procedures for integrating a social skills curriculum with cooperative learning and structured learning teaching methods.

There are a variety of social skills and affective education curricula available in the literature. The practitioner must give careful consideration to the appropriateness of a particular program for the children for whom it is to be applied. Schumaker, Pederson, Hazel, and Meyen (1983) suggest five questions for practitioners to address when selecting a social skills curriculum:

1. Does the curriculum promote social competence?
2. Does the curriculum accommodate the learning characteristics of the students for whom it is to be applied?
3. Does the curriculum target the social skills deficits of the students for whom it is to be applied?
4. Does the curriculum provide training in situations as well as in skills?
5. Does the curriculum include instructional methodologies found to be effective with the population of students for whom it is to be applied?

Carter and Sugai (1989) developed a comprehensive procedure for the analysis of a social skills curriculum. Analysis includes giving consideration to instructional strategies, grouping, individualization, cost-effectiveness, instructor training, field test results, student assessment and evaluation, and maintenance and generalization training. These authors designed a useful curriculum analysis checklist and decision-making grid.

Nelson (1988) notes that research indicates that a social skills curriculum does promote the acquisition of socially appropriate behaviors by students with disabilities. However, there is little research evidence that social skills instruction is effective over time and across settings.

Zaragoza, Vaughn, and McIntosh (1991) analyzed 27 studies on the effects of social skills training on school-age children. They were cautiously optimistic with regard to the positive effects of social skills interventions with learners identified as behaviorally disordered. The participants, when compared with nonparticipants, felt better about themselves, and their teachers and parents felt better about them. In the vast majority of the studies, their peers' feelings about them did not change.

Gresham and Elliott (1990) conceptualized social competence within a two-dimensional model of social skills and interfering problem behaviors. Social skills are defined as socially acceptable learned behaviors enabling individuals to either act effectively with others and avoid or escape socially unacceptable behaviors exhibited by others. These behaviors are organized into five response groups: cooperation, assertion, responsibility, empathy, and self-control. Interfering behaviors include behaviors that are internalizing and overcontrolled (e.g., anxiety, fear, social withdrawal) and those that are externalizing or undercontrolled (e.g., aggression, disruption, impulsivity). This model views social behavior from a competing behaviors framework in which social skills either are not learned or are performed because of the presence of stronger, competing, or interfering problems. Gresham (1998) proposed a modification in the model in which social skills deficits are classified as either acquisition, performance, or fluency deficits. Acquisition refers to either the absence of knowledge of how to execute particular social skills or a failure to discriminate when certain social behaviors are appropriate. Social performance deficits represent the presence of social skills in a behavioral repertoire but failure to perform these behaviors at acceptable levels in specific circumstances. Fluency deficits stem from a lack of exposure to sufficient models of behavior, insufficient rehearsal or practice of the skills, or low rates or inconsistent delivery of reinforcement for performance.

Using this model and based on years of research experience, Gresham (1998) reviewed past and present conceptualizations and summarized narrative and meta-analytic reviews of social skills training outcome studies. He found a modest positive effect as a result of social skills training and suggests that social skills training is a relatively weak intervention. These weaknesses in social skills training can be attributed to (a) the use of socially invalid and insensitive outcome measures, (b) failure to match social skills interventions to specific social skills deficits, and (c) failure to program for functional generalization. He makes recommendations for restructuring and improving social skills training interventions: improve assessment, match social skills interventions to specific problems, and program for functional generalization using a contextual approach.

Sabornie and Beard (1990) suggest that instruction in social skills for students with mild disabilities be provided on the basis of an individual's assessed needs. If a student needs instruction, then that instruction should be structured and frequent. They found two general approaches to instruction in social skills: (a) manipulation of antecedents and consequences related to social behavior and (b) application of a "packaged" curriculum. They urge practitioners to evaluate a packaged curriculum before purchasing it.

Armstrong and McPherson (1991) suggest that instruction in social skills is most effective when it is a collaborative home-school or parent-teacher-student activity. They suggest that such collaboration will facilitate generalization.

Allsopp, Santos, and Linn (2000) suggest a collaborative approach to instructing social skills to learners with social skill deficits. Steps in the program include forming a team of two or more teachers who are interested in participating in a program, targeting the prosocial skills students need to learn, reducing the skills into teachable steps, developing an instructional plan that includes a teaching strategy, determining the instructional setting and collaborative roles, delivering instruction, and providing opportunities for student practice, reinforcement, and self-monitoring.

Elksnin and Elksnin (1998) suggest several strategies for instruction social skills to learners with learning and behavior problems. They discuss how to select students for training, which social skills to use, teaching discrete skills and problem-solving routines, and helping students generalize skills across settings and situations.

In their study of a prevention program for Head Start, kindergarten, and first-grade students with behavioral problems, Kamps, Tankersley, and Ellis (2000) reported reduced inappropriate behaviors, including aggression, grabbing, out-of-seat behaviors, and negative verbal statements. There was improved compliance with teacher directions and significantly more time engaged in positive interactions with peers during free time and play groups. The comparison group, which did not receive social skills training with reinforcement, peer tutoring, and parent support, maintained or increased their level of inappropriate behaviors. Another social skills program (Presley & Hughes, 2000) used peer instruction, self-instruction, and a traditional anger control program with students.

Quinn, Kavale, Rutherford, and Forness (1999) conducted a meta-analysis of 35 studies on the effects of social skills interventions for students with emotional-behavioral disorders. The pooled mean effect of the studies demonstrated that for the average student with emotional-behavioral disorders, a modest outcome gain occurred. A slightly greater gain was found in studies that focused on measuring and teaching specific social skills.

Social skills training programs should be responsive to the needs of students and parents from culturally and linguistically diverse backgrounds. Such sensitivity becomes more and more essential as the demographics of the nation change (Rivera & Rogers-Adkinson, 1997).

♦ SUMMARY

In this chapter, a variety of behavior management interventions derived from psychodynamic theory is discussed. Counseling techniques, life-space interviewing, and reality therapy interviewing, for use by the teacher with minimal training, are discussed in detail.

The expressive media are presented as indirect behavior management interventions. The expressive media include free play, puppetry, role playing and psychodrama, creative movement and dance, music, the spoken and written word, bibliotherapy, art therapy, and others. They are recommended as therapeutic interventions that encourage children to express their positive and negative feelings and emotions in an acceptable manner.

Several behavior influence techniques are discussed as interventions teachers may apply when a student's surface behavior interferes with daily function. (These interventions *must* be applied in circumstances that endanger the student, teacher, peers, and property.)

The chapter concludes with a discussion of social skills curricula that may be applied to instruct students in socially appropriate behaviors.

In the next chapter, attention is focused on interventions derived from environmental and biophysical theories.

♦ PROJECTS

1. Write a brief essay (300 words) on the advantages and disadvantages of the psychodynamic behavior management interventions.

2. Conduct a life-space interview with a classmate. Invite your other classmates to evaluate your performance.

3. Conduct a reality therapy interview with a classmate. Invite your other classmates to evaluate your performance.

4. Conduct a library research study of one of the expressive media as a behavior management intervention. Report your findings in a formal presentation to your classmates.

5. Discuss the advantages and disadvantages of the behavior influence techniques for the teacher.

6. Research the literature on the self-control curriculum and report your findings to your class.

♦ REFERENCES

Adderholdt-Elliot, M., & Eller, S. H. (1989). Counseling students who are gifted through bibliotherapy. *Teaching Exceptional Children, 22*(1), 26–31.

Allen, J. I. (1980). Jogging can modify disruptive behaviors. *Teaching Exceptional Children, 12*(2), 66–70.

Allsopp, D. H., Santos, K. E., & Linn, R. (2000). Collaborating to teach prosocial skills. *Intervention in School and Clinic, 35*(3), 141–146.

Andersen, M., Nelson, L. R., Fox, R. G., & Gruber, S. E. (1988). Integrating cooperative learning and structured learning: Effective approaches to teaching social skills. *Focus on Exceptional Children, 20*(9), 1–8.

Anderson, E. (1985). A. M. Club. *Teaching: Behaviorally Disordered Youth, 1,* 12–16.

Anderson, M. G. (1992). The use of selected theater rehearsal technique activities with African-American adolescents labeled "behavior disordered." *Exceptional Children, 59*(2), 132–140.

Armstrong, S. W., & McPherson, A. (1991). Homework as a critical component in social skills instruction. *Teaching Exceptional Children, 24*(1), 45–47.

Axline, V. M. (1947). *Play therapy.* Boston: Houghton Mifflin.

Bacon, E. H. (1990). Using negative consequences effectively. *Academic Therapy, 25*(5), 599–611.

Bauer, M. S., & Balius, F. A., Jr. (1995). Storytelling: Integrating therapy and curriculum for students with serious emotional disturbances. *Teaching Exceptional Children, 27*(2), 24–28.

Brenner, M. B. (1969). Life-space interview in the school setting. *American Journal of Orthopsychiatry, 33,* 719–719.

Broome, S. A., & White, R. B. (1995). The many uses of videotape in classrooms serving youth with behavioral disorders. *Teaching Exceptional Children, 27*(3), 10–13.

Caputo, R. A. (1993). Using puppets with students with emotional and behavioral disorders. *Intervention in School and Clinic, 29,* 26–30.

Caputo, R. A. (1995). Puppets, problem-solving and rationale emotive therapy. *Beyond Behavior, 6*(2), 15–18.

Carter, J., & Sugai, G. (1989). Social skills curriculum analysis. *Teaching Exceptional Children, 22*(1), 36–39.

Chace, M. (1958). Dance in growth or treatment settings. *Music Therapy, 1,* 119–121.

Cheney, C., & Morse, W. C. (1972). Psychodynamic interventions in emotional disturbance. In W. C. Rhodes & M. L. Tracy (Eds.), *A study of child variance: Vol. 2. Interventions.* Ann Arbor: University of Michigan Press.

Cianciolo, P. J. (1965). Children's literature can affect coping behavior. *Personnel and Guidance Journal, 43*(9), 897–903.

Cook, J. H. (1972). *The effects of small group counseling on the classroom behavior of sociometrically underchosen adolescents.* Unpublished doctoral dissertation, University of Georgia.

Creekmore, N. N., & Madan, A. J. (1981). The use of sociodrama as a therapeutic technique with behavior disordered children. *Behavioral Disorders, 7*(1), 28–33.

D'Alonzo, B. (1974). Puppets fill the classroom with imagination. *Teaching Exceptional Children, 6*(3), 141–144.

David, D., & Newcomer, P. L. (1980). Art and music therapy. In P. L. Newcomer (Ed.), *Understanding and teaching emotionally disturbed children* (pp. 391–408). Boston: Allyn & Bacon.

Dehouske, E. J. (1982). Story writing as a problem solving vehicle. *Teaching Exceptional Children 15*(1), 11–17.

DeMagistris, R. J., & Imber, S. C. (1980). The effects of life-space interviewing on the academic and social performance of behavior disordered children. *Behavioral Disorders, 6*(1), 12–25.

Duerksen, G. L. (1981). Music for exceptional students. *Focus on Exceptional Children, 14*(4), 1–11.

Edwards, L. L., & O'Toole, B. (1985). Application of self-control curriculum with behavior disordered students. *Focus on Exceptional Children, 17*(8), 1–8.

Elksnin, L. K., & Elksnin, N. (1998). Teaching social skills to students with learning and behavior problems. *Intervention in School and Clinic, 33*(3), 131–140.

Epanchin, B. C., & Monson, L. B. (1982). Affective education. In J. L. Paul & B. C. Epanchin (Eds.), *Emotional disturbance in children: Theories and methods for teachers* (pp. 405–426). Upper Saddle River, NJ: Merrill/Prentice Hall.

Evans, W. H., Evans, S. S., Schmid, R. E., & Pennypacker, H. S. (1985). The effects of exercise on selected classroom behaviors of behaviorally disordered adolescents. *Behavior Disorders, 11*(1), 42–51.

Fagen, S. A. (1981). Conducting an LSI: A process model. *Pointer, 25*(2), 9–11.

Fagen, S. A., & Long, N. J. (1976). Teaching children self-control: A new responsibility for teachers. *Focus on Exceptional Children, 7*(8), 1–10.

Fagen, S. A., Long, N. J., & Stevens, D. J. (1975). *Teaching children self-control: Preventing emotional and learning problems in the elementary school.* Upper Saddle River, NJ: Merrill/Prentice Halll.

Falk, G. D., Dunlap, G., & Kern, L. (1996). An analysis of self-evaluation and videotape feedback for improving the peer interactions of students with externalizing and internalizing behavioral problems. *Behavioral Disorders, 21*(4), 261–276.

Fecser, F. A., & Long, N. J. (1997). Life space crisis intervention: Using conflict as opportunity. *Beyond Behavior, 8*(1), 10–15.

Ferolo, M. A., Rotatori, A. F., & Fox, R. (1984). Increasing visual attention by music therapy programming for sensory stimulation with profoundly retarded children. *ICEC Quarterly, 33*(2), 17–21.

Ferolo, M. A., Rotatori, A., Macklin, F., & Fox, R. (1983). The successful use of behavior modification in music therapy with severely/profoundly retarded people. *ICEC Quarterly, 32*(2), 30–34.

Gardner, R., III (1990a). Life-space interviewing: It can be effective, but don't … *Behavioral Disorders, 15*(2), 111–119.

Gardner, R., III (1990b). Sincere but sincerely wrong: A reply to Nicholas Long. *Behavioral Disorders, 15*(2), 125–126.

Ginott, H. G. (1959). The theory and practice of therapeutic interventions in child treatment. *Journal of Consulting Psychology, 23,* 160–166.

Gladding, S. T., & Gladding, C. (1991). The ABCs of bibliotherapy for school counselors. *The School Counselor, 31,* 7–13.

Glasser, W. (1969). *Schools without failure.* New York: Harper & Row.

Glasser, W. (1986). *Control theory.* New York: Harper & Row.

Glasser, W. (1990). *Reality therapy: A new approach to psychiatry.* New York: Borego Press.

Glick, B. H. (1968). *The investigation of changes in self-concept, social self-esteem, and academic self-responsibility of emotionally disturbed boys who participate in open-ended classroom meetings.* Unpublished doctoral dissertation, Syracuse University.

Goldstein, A. P., Spafkin, R. P., Gershaw, N. J., & Klein, P. (1983). Structures learning: A psychoeducational approach for teaching social competencies. *Behavioral Disorders, 8*(3), 161–170.

Gresham, F. M. (1998). Social skills training: Should we raze, remodel, or rebuild? *Behavioral Disorders, 24*(1), 19–25.

Gresham, F. M., & Elliott, S. N. (1990). *Social skills rating system.* Circle Pines, MN: American Guidance Services.

Gunter, P. L., Shores, R. E., Jack, S. L., Rasmussen, S. K., & Flowers, J. (1995). On the move: Using teacher/student proximity to improve students' behavior. *Teaching Exceptional Children, 28*(1), 12–14.

Halsted, J. W. (1988). *Guiding gifted readers.* Columbus, OH: Ohio Psychology Publishing.

Harms, J. M., Etscheidt, S. L., & Lettow, L. J. (1986). Extending emotional responses through poetry experiences. *Teaching: Behaviorally Disordered Youth, 2,* 26–32.

Hawes, R. M. (1970). *Reality therapy in the classroom.* Unpublished doctoral dissertation, University of the Pacific.

Heuchert, C. M. (1989). Enhancing self-directed behavior in the classroom. *Academic Therapy, 24*(3), 295–303.

Hibben, J., & Scheer, R. (1982). Music and movement for special needs children. *Teaching Exceptional Children, 14*(5), 171–176.

Hoagland, J. (1972). Bibliotherapy: Aiding children in personality development. *Elementary English, 15,* 390–394.

Hoenig, G. K., Shea, T. M., & Bauer, A. M. (1986). Jogging and children with behavior disorders: Effects on self-doubting and aggressive behaviors. *ICEC Quarterly, 36*(4), 16–21.

Holaday, M. (1994). Self-as-a-model videotapes: An experimental study with guidelines on how to make videotapes for students. *Beyond Behavior, 5*(2), 19–23.

Jones, V. F. (1992). Integrating behavioral and insight-oriented treatment on school based programs of seriously emotionally disturbed students. *Behavioral Disorders, 17*(3), 225–236.

Kamps, D. M., Tankersley, M., & Ellis, C. (2000). Social skills interventions for young at-risk students: A two-year follow-up study. *Behavioral Disorders, 25*(4), 310–324.

Lament, M. M. (1978). Reaching the exceptional student through music in the elementary classroom. *Teaching Exceptional Children, 11*(1), 32–35.

Lane, B., Bonic, J., & Wallgren-Bonic, N. (1983). The group walk-talk: A therapeutic challenge for secondary students with social-emotional problems. *Teaching Exceptional Children, 16*(1), 12–17.

Leone, P. (1984). A descriptive follow-up of behaviorally disordered adolescents. *Behavioral Disorders, 9*(3), 207–214.

Levinson, C. (1982). Remediating a passive aggressive emotionally disturbed pre-adolescent boy through writing: A comprehensive psychodynamic structured approach. *The Pointer, 26*(2), 23–27.

Long, N. J. (1990). Comments on Ralph Gardner's article "Life-space interviewing: It can be effective, but don't …" *Behavioral Disorders, 15*(2), 119–125.

Long, N. J., & Newman, R. G. (1961). A differential approach to the management of surface behavior of children in school. *Bulletin of the School of Education, 37,* 47–61.

Long, N. J., & Newman, R. G. (1965). Managing surface behavior of children in school. In N. J. Long, W. C. Morse, & R. G. Newman (Eds.), *Conflict in the classroom: The education of emotionally disturbed children* (pp. 352–362). Belmont, CA: Wadsworth.

Lonnecker, C., Brady, M. P., McPherson, R., & Hawkins, J. (1994). Video self-modeling and cooperative classroom behavior in children with learning and behavior problems: Training and generalization effects. *Behavioral Disorders, 20*(1), 24–34.

Martin, S. S., Brady, M. P., & Williams, R. E. (1991). Effects of toys on the social behavior of preschool children in integrated and nonintegrated groups: Investigation of a setting event. *Journal of Early Intervention, 15*(2), 153–161.

McCarty, H., & Chalmers, L. (1997). Bibliotherapy: Intervention and prevention. *Teaching Exceptional Children, 29*(6), 12–17.

McGinnis, E., Sauerbry, L., & Nichols, P. (1985). Skill-streaming: Teaching social skills to children with behavior disorders. *Teaching Exceptional Children, 17*(3), 160–167.

McIntyre, T. (1987). Classroom conferencing: Providing support and guidance for misbehaving youth. *Teaching: Behaviorally Disordered Youth, 3,* 33–35.

Michel, D. E. (1985). *Music therapy: An introduction to therapy and special education through music* (2nd ed.). Springfield, IL: Charles C. Thomas.

Minner, S. (1981). Using photography as an adjunctive and creative approach. *Teaching Exceptional Children, 13*(4), 145–147.

Moreno, J. L. (1946). *Psychodrama.* Beacon, NY: Beacon House.

Morse, W. C. (1979). Self-control: The Fagen-Long curriculum. *Behavioral Disorders, 4,* 83–91.

Murry, F. R. (1996). Animal-assisted therapy: You think you have animals in your class: Animals helping students with EBD. *Beyond Behavior, 7*(3), 10–13.

Naslund, S. R. (1987). Life-space interviewing: A psychoeducational intervention model for teaching pupils insight and measuring program effectiveness. *The Pointer, 31*(2), 12–15.

Necco, E., Wilson, C., & Scheidmantel, J. (1982). Affective learning through drama. *Teaching Exceptional Children, 15*(1), 22–24.

Neel, R. S. (1988). Implementing social skills instruction in schools. *Behavior in Our Schools, 3*(1), 13–18.

Nelson, C. M. (1988). Social skills training for handicapped students. *Teaching Exceptional Children, 20,* 19–23.

Newcomer, P. L. (1980). *Understanding and teaching emotionally disturbed children.* Boston: Allyn & Bacon.

Nichols, P. (1986). Down the up staircase: The teacher as therapist. *Teaching: Behaviorally Disordered Youth, 2,* 1–13.

Omizo, M. M., & Omizo, S. A. (1988). Intervention through art. *Academic Therapy, 24*(1), 103–106.

Polt, J. M., & Hale, C. (1985). Using pets as "therapists" for children with developmental disabilities. *Teaching Exceptional Children, 17*(3), 218–222.

Prater, M. A. (2000). Using juvenile literature with portrayals of disabilities in your classroom. *Intervention in School and Clinic, 35*(3), 167–176.

Presley, J. A., & Hughes, C. (2000). Peers as teachers of anger management to high school students with behavioral disorders. *Behavioral Disorders, 25*(2), 114–130.

Purvis, J., & Samet, S. (1976). *Music in developmental therapy.* Baltimore: University Park Press.

Quinn, M. M., Kavale, K. A., Rutherford, R. B., & Forness, S. R. (1999). A meta-analysis of social skills interventions for students with emotional or behavioral disorders. *Journal of Emotional and Behavioral Disorders, 7*(1), 54–64.

Raschke, D., Dedrick, C., & Takes, M. (1986). Videotape feedback as a therapeutic tool. *Teaching: Behaviorally Disordered Youth, 2,* 14–19.

Raths, L. E., Harmin, M., & Simons, S. B. (1978). *Values and teaching.* Columbus, OH: Merrill.

Redl, F. (1959). The concept of the life-space interview. *American Journal of Orthopsychiatry, 29,* 1–18.

Redl, F., & Wineman, D. (1957). *The aggressive child.* New York: Free Press.

Reilly, M. J., Imber, S. C., & Cremins, J. (1978). *The effects of life-space interviews on social behaviors of junior high school special needs students.* Paper presented at the 56th International Council for Exceptional Children, Kansas City.

Richards, J. C., Gipe, J. P., & Callahan, T. (1997). The Little Red Hen meets Peter Rabbit: Enhancing the reading comprehensive and social understanding of young students with language disabilities. *Teaching Exceptional Children, 29*(3), 71–73.

Rivera, B. D., & Rogers-Adkinson, D. (1997). Culturally sensitive interventions: Social skills training with children and parents from culturally and linguistically diverse backgrounds. *Intervention in School and Clinic, 33*(2), 75–80.

Roter, J. (1981). Music, a therapeutic intervention for emotionally disturbed youth. In F. H. Wood (Ed.), *Perspective for a new decade: Education's responsibility for seriously disturbed and behaviorally disordered children and youth* (pp. 154–162). Reston, VA: Council for Exceptional Children.

Russell, A. E., & Russell, W. A. (1979). Using bibliotherapy with emotionally disturbed children. *Teaching Exceptional Children, 11,* 168–169.

Sabornie, E. J., & Beard, G. H. (1990). Teaching social skills to students with mild handicaps. *Teaching Exceptional Children, 23*(1), 35–38.

Scheaf, W. A. (1972). *The effects of paired learning and Glasser-type discussions on two determinants of academic achievement and on reading achievement of male delinquents.* Unpublished doctoral dissertation, Case Western Reserve University.

Schrank, F., & Engels, D. (1981). Bibliotherapy as a counseling adjunct: Research findings. *Personnel and Guidance Journal, 60*(3), 143–147.

Schumaker, J. B., Pederson, C. S., Hazel, J. S., & Meyen, E. L. (1983). Social skills curricula for mildly handicapped adolescents: A review. *Focus on Exceptional Children, 16*(4), 1–16.

Shea, T. M., Whiteside, W. R., Beetner, E. G., & Lindsey, D. L. (1974). *Microteaching module: Behavioral interventions.* Edwardsville: Southern Illinois University Press.

Shearn, D. F., & Randolph, D. L. (1978). Effects of reality therapy methods applied in the classroom. *Psychology in the Schools, 15,* 79–83.

Shores, R. E., Gunter, P. L., & Jack, S. L. (1993). Classroom management strategies: Are they setting events for coercion? *Behavioral Disorders, 18,* 92–102.

Sridhar, D., & Vaughn, S. (2000). Bibliotherapy for all: Enhancing reading comprehension, self-concept, and behavior. *Teaching Exceptional Children, 33*(2), 74–82.

Thursby, D. D. (1977). Everyone's a star. *Teaching Exceptional Children, 9*(3), 77–78.

Warger, C. L. (1985). Making creative drama accessible to handicapped children. *Teaching Exceptional Children, 17*(4), 288–293.

Warger, C. L., & Weiner, B. B. (Eds.). (1987). *Secondary special education: A guide to promising public school programs.* Reston, VA: Council for Exceptional Children.

Williams, G. H., & Wood, M. M. (1977). *Developmental art therapy.* Baltimore: University Park Press.

Wood, F. H. (1990). When we talk with children: The life-space interview (Special Section). *Behavioral Disorders, 15*(2), 110–126.

Wood, M. M. (1976). Foreword. In J. Purvis & S. Samet (Eds.), *Music in developmental therapy* (pp. vi–viii). Baltimore: University Park Press.

Wood, M. M., & Long, N. J. (1991). *Life space intervention: Talking with children and youth in crisis.* Austin, TX: PRO-ED.

Yell, M. L. (1988). The effects of jogging on the rates of selected target behaviors of behaviorally disordered students. *Behavioral Disorders, 13*(4), 273–279.

Zabel, R. H. (1988). Research in brief. *Behavior in Our Schools, 2*(3), 9.

Zaragoza, N., Vaughn, S., & McIntosh, R. (1991). Social skills interventions and children with behavioral problems: A review. *Behavioral Disorders, 16*(4), 260–275.

Environmental and Biophysical Behavior Management

◆ CHAPTER OBJECTIVES

After completing this chapter, you will be able to do the following:

1. Discuss group composition and process, discussion groups, and class meetings.
2. Describe and exemplify the several antecedents to effective management.
3. Explain milieu therapy.
4. Design a levels system.
5. Define expulsion, suspension, and in-school suspension.
6. Characterize the several biophysical interventions.
7. Understand the educator's role in biophysical intervention.

◆ ◆ ◆

Jack and his gang were loitering near the front door of Hooverville High School planning their Monday morning activities. By general consensus, their target for the day was to be Marcie Meek. Jack conducted a discussion during which the group of five boys decided how to make life miserable for Marcie. They agreed to whistle and catcall at her in the corridors. They were going to tell everyone they met that Marcie was "easy." Finally, every time she was called on during class, they would grumble and sigh.

Jack and the gang were of considerable concern to the whole school population, especially to Mr. Whiteburn, assistant principal for discipline. It appeared that Jack and his friends selected a different student or teacher each day as a target for their hostility. Each of the boys had been referred to Mr. Whiteburn several times during the year for disciplining. He had punished them, individually and as a group, many times without success. He had even called their parents.

Although the group's behavior was disruptive, it was not severe enough to result in expulsion or suspension.

Mr. Whiteburn knows that the group's behavior must be redirected from negative to positive goals before the boys become involved in a serious incident. He must seek out a means to help the gang plan and carry out appropriate activities.

Six-year-old John was being observed by the first-grade teacher, Mrs. Prime. As she observed John, he climbed over the worktable, ran to the toy box, and threw several blocks, trucks, and dolls on the floor. Next John ran around the room touching each child and the four walls.

After this, he returned to his seat at the worktable, grabbed his crayon, and scribbled on his worksheet for about 10 seconds. While he was scribbling, John was wiggling in his chair and tapping his feet.

Suddenly, John fell to his hands and knees and began crawling to the toy box. He climbed into the box and threw the remaining toys on the floor. Having accomplished this, John returned to the worktable. John's hyperactive behavior continued throughout Mrs. Prime's 1-hour observation session.

That afternoon, in discussion with John's mother and preschool teacher, Mrs. Prime learned that John's behavior during the observation session was typical of his behavior at home and in preschool. Both the preschool teacher and John's mother reported using a variety of behavior modification interventions without success. John appeared unable to control his activity; he appeared driven.

Mrs. Prime knows that she must have some assistance if John is to attend her first-grade class. He simply cannot succeed in school unless his behavior is managed.

In this chapter, a variety of behavior management interventions derived from environmental and biophysical theories are reviewed and exemplified. The environmental behavior management interventions include strategies related to group composition and processes, the classroom setting, and class meetings. In addition, the antecedents of effective management and in-school suspension, suspension, and expulsion are discussed in the first section of this chapter. The section concludes with a review of milieu therapy and the levels system.

The second section of this chapter is devoted to a discussion of biophysical strategies, such as medication and diets. This section concludes with discussion of the educator's role in biophysical interventions.

It should be noted that, for the most part, environmental interventions focus attention on the manipulation of groups and the environment rather than on individual students.

Several environmental and biophysical interventions employed by professionals in the medical and mental health disciplines are not presented in this chapter because of their complexity and the training requirements necessary for implementation. The reader is urged to review the theoretical frameworks underlying the environmental and biophysical models, presented in Chapter 2, before studying this chapter.

ENVIRONMENTAL INTERVENTIONS

Group Composition

Several behavior management interventions are closely associated with classroom and activity groups. Some specific management techniques employed as a part of these *environmental interventions* are discussed in Chapter 7 as counseling techniques and throughout this text as behavior modification interventions. However, when the group is a significant part of a child's overall behavior management program, two important topics must be considered in the selection and imposition of these management techniques: group composition and group processes.

Grouping children on the basis of school records and admission data is a difficult task. It is a process that of necessity involves the cooperation of all persons familiar with the children.

Among the variables to be considered during the grouping process are (a) age; (b) sex; (c) interests; (d) disabling conditions, if any; (e) personality traits; (f) the degree, intensity, and kind of behavior problems, if any; and (g) group experiences and skills. When grouping children, an effort is made to avoid extremes in group composition while at the same time attempting to form a "balanced" group. In the organization of groups, the adult members of the group, such as the teacher and paraprofessional, are considered group members.

Rockwell and Guetzloe (1996) suggest that the dynamics within a group are affected by the number of students in the group, the severity of their disorders, and their social and academic compatibility.

Guidelines to avoid extremes in group (and subgroup) composition are as follows:

1. Children of greatly different ages are not placed in the same group.

2. Children without common interests are not placed in the same group.

3. An individual is not placed in a group that lacks a like-sex peer.

4. A child with a severe disability is not placed in a group of children without disabilities or with mild disabilities if the placement prohibits either from participating in important activities. However, if adequately trained personnel are available to assist, the curriculum can be modified and this potential limitation circumvented.

5. Children with potentially conflicting personality traits and behavior problems are not placed in the same group.

6. An unskilled child is not placed in a group composed of individuals who are highly skilled and experienced in group processes. This placement is permissible only if the group members, including the adults, are aware of the child's lack of skill and experience in groups and agree to facilitate the child's integration.

7. An individual who is not ready or willing to participate in group activities is not placed in a group environment. Reference here is to children with severe behavior and learning problems who lack skills needed for meaningful group participation. Frequently, these individuals remain in the group but do not become "functioning" members.

Grouping is a difficult process because the staff must deal with intangible variables that defy precise measurement. However, the group can have a positive impact on student behavior. Using a nonintrusive management technique to control acting-out behavior, Stainback, Stainback, Etscheidt, and Doud (1986) reaffirmed the belief that peer modeling affects student behavior. They studied the differences in the acting-out behavior of a student in a well-behaved group and in a disruptive group. They noted a significant decrease in acting-out behavior in the well-behaved group.

Group Process. Rockwell and Guetzloe (1996) urge educators to become familiar with the stages of group development and their implications for the management of instructional activities in classes for learners with behavior problems. Their suggestions are based on the work of Maslow's (1962) hierarchy of basic human needs and the developmental stages of Erikson (1963).

According to Rockwell and Guetzloe, students with behavioral disorders begin the school year at Stage 1 of the group developmental process. At this stage, the students focus on satisfying physiological needs and establishing a sense of safety and trust. These needs must be met before the group can move to the next stage. Deviant behaviors at this stage include tantrums, low frustration tolerance, fighting, power struggles, and verbal and physical aggression.

Stage 2, according to Rockwell and Guetzloe, begins when most of the members of the group are responding appropriately most of the time. The group members focus on the need for belonging to the group and socialization activities. Group thinking appears to shift from "me against them" to "us against them." Aggression decreases dramatically, and assistance to others in the group becomes spontaneous. There are fewer and fewer conflicts during Stage 3. Students are now capable of problem solving. The group process focuses on developing self-respect and respect for others and self-actualization.

The group process itself can be of therapeutic benefit to some children. Loughmiller (1965) used self-governing, problem-solving groups in the camp setting. Also applicable in the school setting, these groups are set up to expose students to a wide range of successful interpersonal experiences. These experiences encourage participation, responsibility, and cooperation in activities.

In this intervention, children and teachers are responsible for their daily activities within predetermined limits established by the administration. The members find themselves in a situation where majority rule prevails. Each individual is responsible for his or her personal behavior and for the behavior of the group (Shea, 1977).

Some limits on the group's behavior and activities are imposed by an administrator or other nongroup authority figure rather than by the teacher, who is a member of the group. However, the group members may impose, by means of majority rule, additional limits on behavior and activities. The limits imposed by the administrator are few in number and are concerned with dining and work schedules, attendance at assemblies, transportation, health, safety, and the like. These limits must be imposed by the administration if it is to meet its responsibilities to the members of the group.

Any social cosmos requires certain routines (Morse & Wineman, 1957). Without routines, limits, and prescribed ways of behaving, anarchy would result, and the group would disintegrate. Thus, the group, as a group, decides (a) the limits to be set on social interaction, (b) how extreme behaviors are to be managed if they occur, (c) how activities and schedules of events are to be developed and executed, (d) who is to be responsible for various phases of daily living, and (e) how problems and conflicts are to be resolved.

The problem-solving process becomes a part of the group's daily life. When conflicts or unfamiliar problems occur that prohibit the group from attaining its immediate goals, problem solving is initiated. During the problem-solving process, the group attempts to develop alternative solutions to the circumstances confronting it. The members have two major tasks: (a) identifying and clarifying their problem and (b) discussing (evaluating) and agreeing on one or more solutions to the problem. The agreed-on solution can be imposed either immediately or in similar situations in the future. In addition to these tasks, the members of the group must deal with the positive and negative social-emotional behaviors that naturally occur during the problem-solving process.

Morse and Wineman (1957) recommended the application of life-space interview techniques in the group on a regular and emergency basis. Discussed in Chapter 7 as a counseling technique, the life-space interview may focus on a variety of critical group-process issues:

- Existing social realities that prohibit group desires

- Existing defense or coping mechanisms that the group and its members unconsciously apply for protection against those who are not members of the group

- Techniques for application by the members to admit mistakes, misdeeds, and asocial behaviors

- Ways to use the group as a setting in which emotions and frustrations may be expressed and the limits on such expression

- Ways to strengthen the group's and the individual's self-concept, especially after conflicts, frustrations, and failures

- Procedures for identifying, clarifying, and agreeing to mutually acceptable solutions to common problems

As a group member, the educator's role is important if group behavior management interventions are to be effectively applied in the classroom and school. The teacher must be a model of "give and take" democratic leadership and must be willing to permit the members of the group to make meaningful decisions, implement programs, and realize the consequences of their actions.

The teacher allows the logical consequences of the group's decisions and actions to occur. At the same time, however, the teacher protects the group from repeated or excessive failure and individual members from physical and psychological harm.

Discussion Groups

Anderson and Marrone (1979) described the use of therapeutic discussion groups in public school classes for students with emotional problems. As a result of 12 years of experience with more than 6,000 children, they concluded, "We cannot imagine a program for emotionally handicapped students that would not fit the proven, cost-effective methodology of therapeutic discussion groups in the classroom" (p. 15).

After a period of experimentation during which students were involved in individual therapy, therapeutic discussion groups, or nontherapeutic treatment, it was concluded that the group model benefited the children and teachers in several ways. Teachers benefited by receiving support through teamwork with mental health professionals. In addition, they received training in psychodynamic theory and techniques that enhanced their understanding of student behavior. For students, the group provided structured time for communication and affective education. The goal of the therapeutic discussion groups was to change behavior. Through the group, appropriate student behavior could be reinforced and empathy, concern, and caring encouraged. Group discussion also increased the opportunities for early intervention with children who had potential problems. Group techniques were applied successfully with psychotic, passive-aggressive, and depressed children.

When implemented, group sessions of 30 to 60 minutes are conducted weekly with the psychologist or psychiatrist, teacher, paraprofessional, and social worker present. The group sits in a circle, and meeting length varies according to the age and needs of the children. Pre- and postmeeting sessions are conducted by the mental health consultant with the teacher to evaluate the session and to discuss concerns, needs, and behaviors of the children. Group sessions then become a standard part of each student's program.

Anderson and Marrone suggest the following group discussion guidelines:

1. Children may speak on any topic. Physical aggression and obscene language are inappropriate.
2. Confidentiality is stressed.
3. Discussion may be initiated or facilitated by centering on a specific student interest, need, positive behavior, or similar topic.

4. After several weekly meetings, when the team has an understanding of each student's needs, the following therapeutic progression is applied:

 (a) Help each student recognize his or her ineffective behavior.

 (b) Help the student explore and recognize the feelings behind the ineffective behaviors.

 (c) Identify the source of the feelings.

 (d) Connect these feelings with the student's actions and their consequences.

 (e) Facilitate the student's commitment to change.

 (f) Plan alternative behaviors with the student.

 (g) Support the student's efforts to change.

 (h) Recognize the new behavior and encourage it.

There are several prerequisites for the successful implementation of groups in the public schools. Anderson and Marrone maintain that a belief in the use of therapeutic discussion groups and administrative support are essential. The program must also have a competent mental health consultant (psychiatrist, clinical psychologist, case worker, counselor) who accepts the team concept.

Class Meetings

Class meetings can be instituted as a part of the normal classroom procedure. Meetings can be called to deal with the common problems of living and learning in a group setting. Over a period of time, the members of the class learn, with guidance, to seek solutions to problems through verbal transactions with peers and the teacher. During class meetings, members grow in understanding of themselves and others. They learn to conceptualize problems from another's point of view. Coleman and Webber (1988) recommended working with adolescents in groups to reduce teacher-student conflicts and to enhance student self-control.

Three kinds of meetings for classroom application have been suggested by Harth and Morris (1976) and Morris (1982).

Open Meeting. This meeting is called to permit an individual to express covert feelings. The individual is given an opportunity to state to the group the frustrations and feelings that the individual believes are the result of another member's actions. This other member, or antagonist, may be a peer or the teacher. Any member of the group may request an open meeting. The session is generally conducted by a peer.

♦ *Example*

Billy's ninth-grade class was responsible for planning and conducting the all-school assembly for the Christmas holiday. It was the most important activity of the school year for the class. Each member of the class had a role to play in the program.

Unfortunately for Billy, he was absent from school with the flu on the day his class planned the program. Neither the teacher nor his fellow students remembered to assign a function to Billy. Consequently, he was very frustrated and angry. He was angry with the teacher and his peers. He was hurt and sad because he was a forgotten person. After all, it was not his fault that he got the flu and his mother made him stay at home.

Billy's teacher, Mr. Jetro, had always suggested to his students that if they had a concern about the group, they should request a class meeting. At the meeting, they could express and discuss their concern with the group.

Billy asked Mr. Jetro for a meeting. At the meeting, he stated his personal concerns. As a result of his action, Billy not only was assigned a role in the assembly but also was given an apology by the program chairperson and teacher for their oversight.

Problem-Solving Meeting. This meeting focuses primarily on potential problems. It may be called by any member of the class. Topics include such items as tardiness, disorganization, lack of follow-through on previous commitments, group responsibilities, distractions in the classroom, lack of time to complete assignments, and the like. During the meeting, a solution to the problem is sought by the group. The agreed-on solution is implemented.

♦ *Example*

Mr. Kaat always tells his senior honors German classes that if they are honestly overburdened by the class assignments, they may request a class meeting to discuss the problem. On one particular occasion, Mr. Kaat assigned the class a 10-page technical translation and a term paper just 3 days before midyear examinations. The students believed that they were severely overburdened and would, as a result, do inadequate work on the translation, the term paper, and the examination. They were also concerned about having sufficient time to prepare for their other examinations.

A problem-solving meeting was called at which a more realistic schedule was agreed to by Mr. Kaat and the class.

Decision-Making Meeting. This meeting focuses primarily on program and curriculum decisions. It gives the program direction: What is to be done? How is it to be accomplished? Where? When? Who is responsible? Why? The decision-making meeting is an excellent medium for involving all members of a class in the curriculum planning.

♦ *Example*

Mrs. Picoff was faculty adviser for the Blaskit Island High School Future Teachers Society. She was very concerned about the group's future because of lack of interest on the part of the members. The principal had told her that he was considering disbanding the group because they did not plan or complete any projects of benefit to the school or community.

Mrs. Picoff called the officers and members of the group together for a problem-solving meeting. At the meeting, she presented the problem confronting the group. As a consequence, the members planned an annual schedule, assigned responsibilities to various members, and established a feedback mechanism to ensure that each person met his or her responsibilities.

These class meetings are designed to find practical solutions to real problems. In addition, the class meeting intervention has significant potential as a preventive technique if consistently and appropriately applied. Ziont and Fox (1998) presented practical guidelines for teachers wishing to facilitate group classroom meetings. They suggested that classroom meetings be used to provide information to students on getting along with others, communication skill enhancement, improving interpersonal relationships, and a variety of current topics (living in addictive and disorganized families, divorce, abuse, step families, death and dying, living with AIDS, suicide, and violence) and crisis. Group meetings may be implemented as a vehicle to facilitate behavioral therapy, reality therapy, life-space interviewing, and bibliotherapy. These interventions were discussed in the previous chapter.

The format of the problem-solving group meeting, suggested by Ziont and Fox (citing Thompson & Rudolph, no date), includes the following:

1. Establishing a therapeutic relationship among the members of the group
2. Defining the problem or problems confronting members of the group
3. Exploring previous interventions and their effectiveness
4. Deciding on alternative interventions to address the problem
5. Developing a plan of action, including setting goals
6. Implementing the new plan
7. Homework
8. Evaluating and reporting results of the intervention to the group

The authors suggest that to be an effective group leader, the teacher must be an active listener; reflect on thoughts, perceptions, and feelings of others; seek clarification of poorly understood concepts of others; use questioning strategies; summarize the discussion at the appropriate times; offer brief minilectures; and encourage and support the members of the group.

Antecedents of Effective Management (Organizing for Instruction)

The *antecedents of effective management* are discussed in this section. The effective classroom is planned and organized to facilitate instruction and behavior management (Montague, Bergerson, & Lago-Delello, 1997). Prior to beginning the school day or year, the teacher must take into consideration a broad range of factors to enhance the probability that learning will occur in the classroom. Among those factors that must be given consideration are space utilization and storage, including procedures for the use of classroom and nonclassroom space, facilities, materials, and equipment. The teacher must develop procedures for individual and small- and whole-group activities, beginning and ending the school day or period, transitions, housekeeping, interruptions, visitors, fire drills, and various other activities. The teacher must consider classroom rules for behavior and develop schedules. Cues or prompts to be used in the classroom should also be planned.

Stephen W. Smith, in an interview with Brownell and Thomas (2001), suggested that the best way to eliminate problem behaviors in the classroom is to take a proactive approach to classroom management. One of the most important factors in the elimination of behavior problems is being proactive. Being proactive necessitates that many professionals revisit their views about punishment and consider strategies to build more positive, proactive environments in which the opportunities to misbehave are diminished. Effective classroom environments require a positive culture that reinforces values, such as respect and fairness, and that makes students feel welcome and successful. This is a daily priority for teachers who are concerned and care about their students.

In a discussion of guided dramatization, Brown, Althouse, and Anfin (1993) suggest that to function successfully with peers in integrated settings, children with disabilities need appropriate social skills that are based on both cognitive ability and experience. They urge teachers to adapt environmental props and settings to each child's specific disabilities in order to give the child the support needed to become productively involved in classroom activities. Murdick and Petch-Hogan (1996) discuss alternative intervention strategies for application with educational and behavioral problems in inclusive classes prior to evaluating students for special education services. They suggest strategies designed to increase the probability that students with disabilities will remain in the general education classroom. Their suggestions focus on manipulating the antecedents of behavior and learning, such as the physical setting; the daily schedule; the instructional delivery system, including preinstruction, during instruction, and postinstruction variables; the management plan; and classroom rules. They also recommend that teachers analyze methods (verbal and nonverbal) used to communicate with students.

The more thoroughly a classroom facility and program are planned, the greater the probability of success for both children and teacher. Though the majority of behavior management research focuses on the effects of manipulating the consequences of behavior, Wheldall (1991) reports some positive results from research that focuses on the effects of manipulating the antecedents of behavior. Munk and Repp (1994) did a review of the research literature on instructional variables that may decrease behavior problems in the classroom. The focus of their review was on positive or nonaversive strategies for reducing and preventing problem behaviors. The review centered on the antecedents of instruction. Among the variables that they suggested may decrease problem behaviors are (a) student choice of task, (b) variation in tasks, (c) instructional pace, (d) interspersal of high-probability tasks, (e) partial- versus whole-task training, (f) decreasing task difficulty, and (g) multielement package. This section is devoted to an overview of the antecedents to effective instruction and classroom management. The suggestions presented are general and must be modified to respond to the needs of a particular classroom situation.

Space, Materials, and Equipment. Teachers begin the school year by planning for the use of the space, materials, and equipment that they have been assigned. They must give consideration to the use of the space shared with others, such as hallways, lunchroom, playground, library, and music room (Evertson et al., 1981).

Walls, Ceilings, and Bulletin Boards. These are valuable spaces that can be used to display a variety of materials, such as schedules, rules, seasonal and topical items, calendars, study assignments, housekeeping assignments, charts, maps, and so on. It is prudent not to overdecorate; space should be reserved for student work and current items. Students can profit from helping to plan displays for bulletin boards. Material displayed on walls, ceilings, and bulletin boards should be changed periodically so that students will not become desensitized to it.

Floor Space. The use of floor space will vary with the size of the room, the number of students and their characteristics, and the activities to be conducted. The room must be arranged to ensure that the teacher can observe all areas in which students will be working and that the students will be able to see the teacher and work materials that the teacher is using for instruction. Student desks and tables should be arranged away from high-traffic areas. If tables are used instead of or in addition to desks, then space for storage of student materials must be planned. Space must be planned for individual and small- and whole-group activities. If learning centers (reading, mathematics, science) are used, then space must be planned to include these areas. Centers that generate a high degree of activity and noise should not be located near centers that require a high degree of student concentration. All needed materials and equipment should be located in the appropriate center.

   The teacher must plan where common items, such as plants, pet cages, fish tanks, bookcases, and storage cabinets, will be located in the classroom. The teacher's desk, files, and other equipment must be located where they are easily accessible yet do not interfere with activities. Every effort should be made to maintain traffic lanes in the classroom; this will prevent confusion as students move about the room. If the classroom is serving students with physical disabilities or visual impairments, free traffic lanes must be maintained and space organized to ensure accessibility.

Storage Space. There are various kinds of supplies, materials, and equipment used in the classroom—everyday supplies and materials, infrequently used supplies and materials, student supplies and materials, and teacher supplies and materials, as well as the personal items of students and teacher. The teacher must plan for their storage and use.

   Everyday supplies and materials, such as pencils, paper, and chalk, should be stored in an easily accessible location. The teacher may wish to locate these items where they are available to students. Students' instructional materials, such as texts, workbooks, dictionaries, and study guides, may be stored in students' desks, bookcases, or filing trays and cabinets. Infrequently used items, such as seasonal and topical materials, should be stored in the back of cupboards. Equipment such as overhead projectors, record players, and movie projectors should be stored in a safe place when not in use but accessible to electrical outlets. Students should have a private place to store personal items, such as clothing, gym shoes, lunch boxes, and prized possessions. The teacher must have private space for his or her briefcase and other personal items as well as personal instructional materials and equipment. It is essential that the personal and private space of all—students and teacher—not be violated.

Procedures. The teacher is responsible for developing a variety of classroom and nonclassroom procedures designed to ensure that students will learn and behave effectively and efficiently. The teacher must be sure that these procedures are compatible with school policy.

1. *Student Use of Classroom Space and Facilities.* Procedures should be established to facilitate the care of students' desks and storage areas. Procedures are established for the number of students permitted in various areas of the room at one time and for the use of the drinking fountain, sink, pencil sharpener, restroom, and other shared facilities within the classroom. Procedures for the use and care of common and personal instructional materials must be developed, and procedures should be made with regard to students' and teachers' personal space and possessions.

2. *Student Use of Nonclassroom Space and Facilities.* Procedures should be developed for the use of nonclassroom space and facilities, such as restrooms, drinking fountains, offices, library, media room, resource rooms, and other areas. Procedures must be developed for students leaving the classroom and the movement of individual students and groups of students throughout the school building. Playground activities procedures must be developed. These procedures should facilitate fair play and safety and maximize enjoyment. Special procedures are frequently needed for the lunchroom because of the large number of students in the facility and the limited time available to eat.

3. *Whole-Group, Small-Group, and Individual Activities.* Procedures for a variety of individual and small- and whole-group activities must be established by the teacher. Procedures are developed for the conduct of discussions, the answering of questions during class, talking among students, out-of-seat behavior, and so on. Students should be instructed about the cues and prompts the teacher will use to attain student attention. Procedures are developed for making assignments to work groups, assigning homework, distributing supplies and materials, turning in work, returning assignments, and completing missed assignments. Students should know what they are expected to do when they have completed a task and have unscheduled time available.

   Small-group activities require procedures. Students must know the cues the teacher uses to begin and end small-group activities, what materials to bring, and behavioral expectations. Students who are not in a particular small group must know what is expected of them during other students' small-group activities.

Students working individually must know how to obtain their work, where they are to work, what work to do, how to signal for assistance, and what to do when their work is complete.

Teachers are prudent to establish standard procedures for beginning and ending the school day or period. It is important to begin and end the day on a positive note. Students should know what behaviors are appropriate and inappropriate during this time. Students should also know the procedures for reporting after an absence, tardiness, and early dismissal.

Procedures are developed for the selection and duties of classroom helpers. These activities should be shared by all students. Finally, procedures should be established for conduct during classroom interruptions and delays; for fire, tornado, and earthquake drills; and other infrequent and unplanned occurrences.

4. *Rules.* Rules of behavior are needed in all classrooms. According to Joyce, Joyce, and Chase (1989), a *rule* is "the specification of a relation between two events and may take the form of instruction, direction, or principle" (p. 82). Students follow rules to obtain reinforcers. These reinforcers may be artificial (grades, points, free time) or natural (getting the correct answer, praise, self-satisfaction). Teachers use various kinds of rules to organize classroom instruction and conduct. Rules usually are designed to apply to those activities and occurrences that are not governed by classroom and nonclassroom procedures discussed in the previous section.

Rules should be few in number. They should be brief and understandable to the students and positively stated. They should communicate expectations rather than prohibitions. However, it may be necessary to state rules that prohibit specific behaviors.

Rules are best developed through the collaborative efforts of students and teacher (Murdick and Petch-Hogan, 1996; Thorson, 1996). When students are involved in developing rules, the rules become "our rules" rather than "the teacher's rules." When rules are set collaboratively, they may be changed only through discussion and consensus (Cheney, 1989). Rules should be posted in a highly visible location in the classroom and reviewed with the students frequently (Blankenship, 1986). During the initial weeks of the school year, the rules should be reviewed daily.

Rademacher, Callahan, and Pederson-Seelye (1998) suggested a five-step procedure for planning effective classroom rules:

(a) Create rules and procedures based on cooperative and productive learning behaviors

(b) Identify specific student behavior for rule compliance

(c) Define teacher responsibilities for rule compliance

(d) Establish logical positive and negative consequences for compliance

(e) Develop communication among teacher, students, and parent

Criteria for an effective rule include making the rule acceptable to both students and teacher; begin each rule with an action word; state rules in positive terms; focus on observable behaviors that are associated with well-established classroom procedures; relate rules to work and safety; rules should be general and applicable in many situations and settings; sequentially ordered rules should be few in number; and rules should be posted.

Rademacher et al. recommend the following rules for the positive classroom:

(a) Enter classroom quietly

(b) Begin work on time

(c) Stay on task

(d) Complete work on time

(e) Follow directions at all times

(f) Listen while others speak

(g) Use appropriate language

(h) Keep hands, feet, and objects to self

The teacher must give students repeated examples of the behaviors that a student demonstrates when following the rules. The function of a rule is to encourage appropriate behavior and prevent inappropriate behavior. Teachers are responsible for enforcing classroom rules with fairness and consistency (Rieth & Evertson, 1988). Rules are not made to aid the teacher in catching students acting inappropriately.

Four or five rules are more than adequate to govern classroom behavior. They should be general—but not so general as to be meaningless. Rules must be sufficiently objective to be exemplified by the teacher.

Examples of general rules are the following:

• Be polite and helpful

• Keep your space and materials in order

• Take care of classroom and school property

Some teachers have certain highly specific rules. Examples of specific rules are the following:

• Raise your hand before speaking

• Leave your seat only with permission

• Only one person in the restroom at a time

Such specific rules should be few in number and carefully explained to the students.

Joyce et al. (1989) remind teachers that students whose behavior is rule governed (under the control of reinforcers) may become insensitive to environmental conditions that make rule following inappropriate. To prevent the development of environmental insensitivity due to rule following, they suggest that students (a) be exposed to contingencies incompatible with specific rules, (b) be provided various tasks for meeting the objective of the rule, (c) be exposed to natural contingencies for appropriate classroom behavior, and (d) be overtly aided to make transitions from rule-governed behaviors that were in effect in previous environments.

In an article directed primarily to parents, Seid (2001) suggests that rules are essential to raising children and the smooth functioning of the home and other settings. Because there is no magic number of rules for the effective and efficient function of the home, Seid suggests three basic steps to ensure harmony. First, set family priorities that focus generally on safety, health, appropriate behavior, rights, and values. Next, tailor the message; that is, set rules that make sense to the child and respond to the parents' priorities. Finally, ensure cooperation by explaining to the children the reason for the rule and the consequence for breaking the rule. Children should also be made aware of the positive consequences for obeying the rule.

Cuing. *Cuing* is the process of using symbols to communicate essential messages between individuals. The use of cuing reduces interruptions in ongoing classroom activities, and the symbols facilitate structure and provide routine (Legare, 1984; Olson, 1989). Cuing is a proactive, preventive behavior management intervention (Slade & Callaghan, 1988).

There are various cues or help signs that can be used in the classroom. Such cues are most effective if developed collaboratively by students and teacher at the beginning of the school year.

Among the many cues that may be implemented are the following:

- Students place a sign or flag in a holder on their desks when assistance is needed.

- Students write their name on the chalkboard when help is needed.

- Students take a ticket (as in the supermarket deli) when help is needed.

- Students use a cardboard symbol such as the letter "R" for restroom, "P" for pencil, or "W" for water in place of frequently asked questions.

- Teachers use a traffic signal to control noise levels (red = too loud, yellow = caution, green = noise level is OK).

- Teachers turn on or off the lights to signal the beginning and end of activities.

In addition, teachers may use body language, hand signals, smiles or frowns, and schedules as cues (Rosenkoetter & Fowler, 1986). The design and use of cues is limited only by imagination. Of course, cues should not be used in lieu of appropriate verbal communication.

Transitions. *Transitions* are the movement from one activity to another. According to Rosenkoetter and Fowler (1986), transitions are complex activities that frequently result in classroom disruptions. They should be carefully planned to minimize the loss of instructional time. Effective transitions teach children self-management skills.

In a study of 22 classes (15 regular and 7 special education) for young children (4 and 5 years old), Rosenkoetter and Fowler found that, on average, 18% of the school day was devoted to transitions. Special education and regular education classes differed with regard to the management of transitions. Regular teachers used more cues than special teachers. Special teachers used children's names as cues: regular teachers used group names. Individual cues in the regular classes were rare; when special teachers used group cues, they would follow with individual cues. Special teachers employed one- or two-step directions; regular teachers employed three- or four-step directions. Special teachers often used proximity control. It was noted that in the special class, children were frequently not held responsible for their materials and were not taught group movement.

The authors discussed the implications of these differences for the inclusion of children from special to regular classes. They suggested several guidelines for special teachers wishing to facilitate transition behaviors:

- Visit the mainstream class to determine transition rules
- Plan for transitions and use shaping to assist in the learning of appropriate behavior
- Evaluate existing transition behaviors to determine whether students need more or less assistance
- Move from individual to group cues
- Use a variety of cues
- Teach lining up and moving in line behaviors
- Teach children how to ask for assistance

Teachers may use the following activities to facilitate transitions (Shea & Bauer, 1987):

- Model appropriate transition behaviors
- Signal or cue the beginning and ending of activities
- Remediate transition difficulties, such as slowness and disruptiveness
- Observe student performance during transitions and, if the student is having difficulties, repeat the rules and practice until they are firmly established behaviors
- Reinforce quick and quiet transitions

Effective transitions are essential to maximize engaged time in the classroom.

Schedules. Scheduling is an important teacher function. Rosenshine (1977) found that student learning increases when teachers allocate considerable time for instruction and maintain a high level of task engagement. To develop an effective *schedule,* two important variables are considered: allocated time and engaged time (Shea & Bauer, 1987). Englert (1984) describes allocated time as the amount of time scheduled for a specific subject or activity. Engaged time is the amount of time the students are actually participating in the subject or activity. To increase engaged time, teachers must plan the schedule with care, begin and end activities on time, facilitate transitions from activity to activity, and assign scheduled activities as a first priority rather than engaging in spontaneous, alternative activities.

Scheduling is a dynamic process—a continuous and creative activity (Gallagher, 1988; Murdick and Petch-Hogan, 1996). Schedules must be revised throughout the school year in response to emerging student needs and changing behaviors as well as the demands of the curriculum. Two important kinds of scheduling are overall program scheduling and individual program scheduling.

Schedules are based on individual and group priorities. After the teacher determines priorities, available time, personnel, and materials must be fitted into those priorities. Shea and Bauer (1987) suggested the following step-by-step process for schedule development:

1. Using each student's individualized education program or personal educational records as a database, complete a 3-by-5-inch index card for each goal for each student. On the card, write the student's name, current level of functioning, and short-term objectives with reference to the goal.

2. Group students by sorting the cards by goals and functional levels.

3. Choose a specific schedule format. Reproduce the schedule format on a standard sheet of paper. In the left-hand column, write the time periods available for scheduling.

4. Write the "given" activities (lunch, recess, art, music, speech therapy) on the schedule. A resource room teacher must write in the givens imposed by other teachers' schedules. Write in the times needed for transitions. Write in the times needed for data recording, communicating with others, and preparing for instruction.

5. Write group activities on the schedule. Adjust these until there are no conflicts with other scheduled activities.

6. Review and discuss the proposed schedule with others serving the students (regular or special teachers, therapists, parents) to minimize conflicts.

7. Establish procedures for periodically evaluating the schedule.

Another variable considered when developing schedules is the length of time of the activity periods. As a rule, it is more effective to begin the school year with brief activity periods and gradually lengthen them as the year progresses; the students then learn the schedule and become involved in the learning process.

Clees (1995) evaluated the effectiveness of students' self-recording of teachers' expectancies. Four middle-school students (two males, two females) with disabilities (three learning disabled, one behavior disordered) were included in the study. They were given a schedule with headings for three general education classes, one special education class, and locker time. Under each heading were listed the expected behaviors for that period. Among the expectancies listed on the schedule are the following:

• Bring necessary materials to class

• Begin class on task

- Turn in completed assignments
- Complete all classwork
- Write assignments in assignment book

The study investigated the differences between student behavior during two conditions: (a) carrying the schedule without self-recording and (b) carrying the schedule and self-recording whether teacher expectancies were met. Carrying the schedule without self-recording had no discernible effect on student behavior. Self-recording, however, was effective across students in increasing the percentage of expectancies met.

Milieu Therapy

Milieu therapy is a clinical concept, and although it varies in ease of application, it can be applied in any setting in which children function. In varying degrees, this intervention can be applied in residential settings, day schools, special classrooms, regular classrooms, and camp settings.

According to Long, Morse, and Newman (1965), "Milieu implies the total environment a child lives in, the whole culture that surrounds him, in other words, everything that is done to, with, for, or by an individual in the place where he finds himself" (p. 217).

According to Redl (1959), a specific milieu is not "good" or "bad" for an individual in itself; its effects on the person or group are dependent on their needs in interaction within the milieu. Redl further indicated that no single aspect of the environment is more important than any other aspect. The importance of the various discrete aspects of the environment are dependent on the needs of the individual or group living in that particular setting.

Because it is not possible, a priori, to design with certitude a therapeutic milieu for an individual, milieu therapy is a continuous process throughout the child's placement in a particular setting. The staff must be constantly alert to the impact of the milieu on the individual and adjust it when necessary. Although these adjustments may appear simple when presented in a written statement, such environmental manipulations are difficult tasks that require personnel who are observant and sensitive to the needs of the individual and the group.

Redl (1959) identified several critical elements in the milieu; these elements are presented here as questions that persons responsible for a particular milieu must ask themselves:

- *Social structures:* What are the roles and functions of various individuals and groups in the milieu? What is the role of the therapist? Of the teacher? Of the administrator? Of the children? Are staff members parent surrogates? Are they like brothers and sisters? Are they confidants? Are they friends? Are they authority figures? Are they servants? Who is in charge here? Staff? The children? Administrators? No one? Are there open or closed communication channels between staff and children? Between children and staff? Among staff personnel? Among the children?

- *Value systems:* What values and standards are consciously and unconsciously being communicated among and between the children and staff? Sympathy? Empathy? High expectations? Low expectations? Like? Dislike? Acceptance? Rejection? Trust? Mistrust?

- *Routines, rituals, and regulations:* Are routines, rituals, and behavioral regulations and limits facilitating or frustrating the goals of a program for the individual?

- *Impact of group processes:* What is the impact of the natural group processes on individuals and subgroups? On the total group? Are individual group members cast in the role of a leader? A follower? An antagonist? A scapegoat? An isolate? A mascot or pet? A clown? Can the individual at his or her present stage of development function effectively in a group setting such as this milieu provides?

- *Impact of the individual's psychopathological characteristics:* What are the effects of behaviors on the individuals themselves and on others? Are these effects positive? Are they negative? Do they result in aggression? In withdrawal? In respect? In pity? In fear?

- *Personal attitudes and feelings:* What are the staff's attitudes and feelings toward each other and the children? What is the impact of these attitudes and feelings on their behavior and on the behavior of others (staff and children)? Is the impact positive? Is it negative? Is it neutral? Is it productive? Is it destructive?

- *Overt behavior:* Regardless of the individual's intentions, what are group members really doing to each other? What is their overt behavior? Is their relationship helpful? Is it harmful? Is it supportive? Is it personal? Is it vindictive?

- *Activities and performance:* Is the activity program, including its structure, designed to facilitate the developmental process? Is it productive? Is it constructive? Is it busywork? Is it tedious? Is it frustrating? Is it boring? Is it wasteful? Is it negative? Is it destructive?

- *Space, equipment, time, and props:* Are space, equipment, time, and props available to adequately conduct the activities in the program?

- *Effects of the outside milieu:* What is the effect of information, visits, news, telephone calls, and the like from persons on the outside on the individual or group?

- *Limits and enforcement:* Are the behavioral limits within which the individual and group must function established? Are these limits reasonable? Are they enforced? Are they enforced consistently and fairly? How are extremes of behavior handled?

- *Program responsiveness:* Is the total milieu adequately and objectively monitored to ensure recognition of nontherapeutic elements? Is the structure of the milieu sufficiently flexible and responsive to allow and encourage modification to reduce or neutralize nontherapeutic elements?

The questions listed under each of the preceding variables that compose a milieu may be systematically responded to by educators wishing to evaluate the therapeutic quality of the program in which they teach.

The therapeutic milieu in any setting, residential or day, must be continuously monitored, discussed, evaluated, and manipulated for the benefit of the child. For example, Kern, Delaney, Clarke, Dunlap, and Childs (2001) applied assessment-based curricular modifications to improve the behavior of two 11-year-old fifth-grade boys in a self-contained public school class for students with emotional/behavioral disorders. Functional assessments were conducted to identify instructional and curricular variables associated with undesirable behavior during problematic academic assignments. The results of assessment led to individualized modifications of assignment variables. Analyses verified that the modifications resulted in decreased problem behavior and increased task engagement for each boy.

Levels Systems

A *levels system* is an organizational framework designed to shape students' social, emotional, and academic behaviors (Bauer, Shea, & Keppler, 1986). Rather than an intervention technique or strategy derived from a single theoretical perspective, a levels system offers a structure within which various interventions may be applied. The interventions implemented in a levels system range in theoretical construct from behavior modification (token economy, positive reinforcement, contingency contracts) to psychodynamic (social skills curriculum, group and individual counseling, expressive media interventions). The selection of the interventions is based on the practitioner's skills and the functioning level of each student concerned.

The purpose of a levels system is to increase student responsibility for personal, social, emotional, and academic performance. A student's progress through the various levels is dependent on his or her measurable behavior and achievement. As the student progresses through the levels, the behavioral expectations and privileges change (Bauer & Shea, 1988).

Levels systems originated in residential settings. In 1971, the Holy Cross Program in New York City used a levels system in an adolescent substance abuse program. A four-level system that included a token economy was used to provide students with positive reinforcement and frequent feedback about their performance, to increase their tolerance for delayed gratification, and to develop their reliance on self as a source of reinforcement (Coughlan, Gold, Dohrenwend, & Zimmerman, 1973). Levels systems have also been applied with incarcerated adolescents (Reid, 1979) and in residential treatment facilities (Gable & Strain, 1981; Mitchell & Cockrum, 1980; Rosenstock & Levy, 1978).

The few classroom adaptations reported in the literature appear to be derived from institutional systems. Gersten (in Swanson & Reinert, 1984) described demonstration classrooms for adolescents at the University of Northern Colorado in which a five-level system was applied. Recently, levels systems have been suggested for application during the process of phasing out token economies without interrupting student progress (LaNunziata, Hunt, & Cooper, 1984). Mastropieri, Jenne, and Scruggs (1988) developed a levels system for application in a special education high school resource program. They found that existing literature suggests that levels systems facilitate student self-reinforcement and self-management, the durability and generalization of intervention gains, and the fading of other management structures, such as a token economy.

Barbetta (1990) developed a group-oriented adapted levels system (GOALS) to facilitate classroom management and instruct children with behavior disorders in social skills. GOALS applies peer-group functioning as criteria for earning privileges. The benefits of this levels system to the students are that (a) behavior is mediated by peers, (b) opportunities are provided to serve as change agents for peers, and (c) opportunities are provided each day to work toward a common goal with peers. The system permits the teacher to function more as a behavior consultant than as an authoritarian and to devote time usually expended on behavior management to other activities.

The success of GOALS is dependent on four steps: (a) developing group identity among small groups of students; (b) developing commonly accepted classroom rules and expectations; (c) instructing students in the giving of positive comments, cues, and hints to peers; and (d) teaching procedures for the daily monitoring and evaluation of the system. Through the use of a points system and bonus points, the students earn privileges at various levels of functioning. Barbetta recommends GOALS as a means of harnessing and using the power of the peer group as an effective means of producing academic and social change.

To demonstrate this approach to behavior management, this section presents a levels system that has been used in the public school setting. The discussion of levels systems concludes with several guidelines for practitioners wishing to design a levels system appropriate for the students and environment in which they work.

Pals. The Personal Adjustment Level System (PALS, Hinsdale Illinois South High School), a five-level system for secondary students, is designed to increase self-motivation and academic achievement. The goal of the system is reintegration into the mainstream of regular education. Small-group and individual counseling sessions are an integral part of the program. All students on Levels I through IV are required to attend group sessions. Students who fail to attend the group remain at Day 1 of their present levels. Initial level placement is determined by a student support team. There are minimum lengths of stay at each level. Students can earn bonus days for appropriate behavior or lose days for suspension and inappropriate behavior. Requirements and incentives for PALS levels are presented in Table 8.1.

The levels system presented here demonstrates the diversity of this approach to managing students' behavior. Analysis indicates that PALS provides a framework within which various therapeutic interventions and behavior management strategies can be applied. Though they differ in specifics, each system contains (a) a description of each level, (b) criteria for movement from one level to another, and (c) specific behaviors, expectations, restrictions, and privileges for each level. Typically, levels systems are comprised of four to six levels. There is considerable variation in

Table 8.1
PALS

Length of Stay	Requirements	Incentives
Level I 20 days (or as contracted with teacher)	Personal goal-setting conference Personal IEP conference Learn school rules, PALS rules, daily routine Log in journal daily Keep record of assignments Participate in weekly group therapy Maintain appropriate behavior 70% of the time Complete 65% of assignments Participate in required class activities Document "helping others" project on a weekly basis Maintain stable attendance Progress on 60% of IEP goals Contained for all classes except PE Pass 75% of classes	In-school field trips One cafeteria pass per week Off-campus lunch with teacher Break time with teacher Bonus days Free time in class Food privileges in classroom

Level II
30 days
	Log in journal three times each week
	Personal IEP conference to review objectives and
	    program
	Participate in weekly group therapy
	Complete 75% of assignments
	Maintain appropriate behavior 75% of the time
	Participate in required class activities
	Attend regular class for one to three classes
	Maintain stable attendance
	Progress on 75% of IEP goals
	Pass all classes
		In-school field trips
		Bonus days
		Two cafeteria passes per week
		Two off-campus lunches with the
		    teacher
		Free time in class

Level III 40 days	Log in journal weekly Participate in weekly group therapy Complete 85% of weekly assignments Maintain appropriate behavior 90% of the time Integration into four academic classes and PE Document "helping others" project Maintain stable attendance Progress on 90% of IEP goals Pass all classes Participate in required class activities	Three cafeteria passes per week Up to four outside lunches with the teacher Food privileges in classroom In-school field trips Outside field trips Bonus days Free time in class
Level IV 50 days	Maintain stable attendance Complete 90% of assignments Maintain appropriate behavior 90% of the time Integration into all classes Pass all classes Progress on 100% of IEP goals to criteria Contact with special teacher daily	Free time in class Cafeteria passes Off-campus lunch and breakfast with the teacher Food privileges in classroom In-school field trips Outside field trips Bonus days

Length of Stay	Requirements	Incentives
Level V (Exit) 25 days	No progress notes from regular teachers Pass all classes Integration into all classes Maintain appropriate behavior 100% of the time Maintain stable attendance	(Student is monitored only. Beginning at day 15, special teacher begins arrangement for permanent regular educational placement.)

Source: Adapted from Personal Adjustment Level System, Hinsdale Illinois South High School. Adapted by permission.

the criteria for movement from level to level. All levels systems have a procedure for evaluating student fulfillment of expectations. This procedure may be a point system, a group meeting of staff and/or students, or minimum stay guidelines.

Designing a Levels System. Practitioners wishing to design a level system will find the following guidelines helpful.

Step 1:   Determine the usual entry-level behaviors of the student population. As an alternative, an "assessment level" may be written into the system. During a brief assessment period (several days), a student's functioning can be evaluated and compared with the expectations for the various levels. Then the student may be placed at an appropriate level rather than being required to progress through levels that are inappropriate to the student's present functioning.

Step 2:   Determine the terminal behavior expectations for the students. Expectations should be expressed positively ("If you are on time, you will be awarded two points") as opposed to negatively ("If you are late, you will lose two points").

Step 3:   List at least two but no more than four sets of behavioral expectations of approximately equal distance between the expectations listed in Steps 1 and 2.

Step 4:   Write the sets of graduated expectations on separate sheets of paper. Label them "Level I" through "Level IV."

Step 5:   Consider including a disciplinary or ground level. If such a level is appropriate for the students, describe expectations for this level on a separate sheet of paper.

Step 6:   Determine the privileges appropriate for students beginning the program, that is, students at Level I.

Step 7:   Determine the privileges appropriate for students preparing to terminate the program, that is, students at the highest level.

Step 8:   For each level in Step 3, list appropriate privileges evenly distributed among levels. Remember to reduce the amount of direct supervision provided for the students as they progress through the levels.

Step 9:   Consider the following questions to determine the length of stay for each level and movement among levels:

      (a) Will a minimum length of stay be required at each level?

      (b) How frequently will a student's status be reviewed? Weekly or bi-weekly meetings to review placement may be appropriate.

      (c) Who will review a student's status? Involving students in the evaluation process can be beneficial. Student involvement encourages the development of self-control and decision-making skills. Involving other students provides positive peer support, which is particularly beneficial at the secondary school level.

      (d) What level of appropriate behavior will be required to remain at the various levels?

      (e) What self-monitoring and teacher monitoring procedures are needed?

Step 10:   Determine the appropriate communication systems among staff, parents, and students. A successful levels program requires frequent, positive communication. Communications may be facilitated by group meetings, individual conferences, written notes, or forms.

Step 11:   Determine needed augmentive systems. It may be desirable within the levels system to use various augmentive systems, such as contingency contracts or a token economy.

Caution should be exercised in planning and implementing a levels system. Expectations should be expressed positively. For example, rather than "stops hitting," the same expectation can be expressed positively by saying "keeps hands to self." The latter statement not only is positive but suggests to the student the appropriate alternative behavior.

If a disciplinary or ground level is included in the system, then offenses and their consequences should be reasonable, carefully explained, and fairly administered.

The number of days at each level should be realistic. The student should not be required to remain at a level for so many days that he or she becomes frustrated and begins to resist or "drop out" of the system.

A behavior expectations checklist, such as the one presented in Figure 8.1, may be developed for each level. The checklist is designed for use with Level III of PALS. The checklist is reviewed frequently by student and teacher. It is a reminder to the student of his or her duties, responsibilities, expectations, and consequences. In addition, the checklist is an excellent guide for use in student-teacher conferences.

Reisberg, Brodigan, and Williams (1991) discuss several characteristics of the effective levels system that must be carefully considered during planning:

1. Clearly define the levels or steps in the system

2. Clearly define the desired observable and specific behaviors students must exhibit to progress through the system

3. Clearly define the inappropriate behaviors and their consequences that prohibit the student from progressing through the system

---

Requirements

_____ 1. Weekly journal entry

_____ 2. Weekly group therapy

_____ 3. Complete 85% of assignments

_____ 4. Appropriate behavior 90% of time

_____ 5. Integrated for four classes and PE

_____ 6. Document "helping others" project

_____ 7. Maintain attendance

_____ 8. Progress on 90% of IEP goals

_____ 9. Pass all classes

_____ 10. Participate in all required class activities

Beginning date:

Projected completion date:

Special notes:

Student's signature: _____

Teacher's signature: _____

Figure 8.1
Behavior expectations checklist

4. Clearly define the reinforcers the student may earn at each level

5. Clearly define the criteria for placement and movement within the system

6. Provide procedures for the continuous evaluation and measurement of student performance

7. Include a complementary system within the levels system, such as a token economy

8. Implement procedures to facilitate frequent communication among all parties

Rosenberg (1986) cautions that simply putting a system in place is not enough; a periodic, brief review of the rules with the students maximizes the effectiveness of a management system.

A significant benefit of a levels system is that its structure and routine provide security for students. The system provides workable limits with a theoretical flexibility that allows a levels system to respond to individual and group needs.

The advantages of a levels system parallel those of the positive peer culture (Carducci, 1980): (a) It delivers the teacher from the embattled "me against them" position; (b) it encourages the teacher to respect the strengths and abilities of the students; (c) it lends itself to specific classroom approaches such as grouping, students helping students, and individualized interventions; and (d) it provides a means for dealing with students' defense mechanisms, such as projection and rationalization, by placing the responsibility for personal behavior on the student.

Articles by Scheuermann, Webber, Partin, and Knies (1994) and Scheuermann and Webber (1996) question the compatibility of levels systems and special education laws. The authors suggest that to date there is little research to support the effectiveness of levels systems and that certain components of the levels systems strategy may violate laws protecting children and youth with disabilities. Scheuermann et al. state that levels systems, as presently understood, impact negatively on the individualized education mandate as required by law. The levels systems they studied restricted individualized programming in the areas of access to the general education setting, target behaviors, entry into the levels system, criteria for advancement through the levels, behavioral sequences, and downward movement. They offer suggestions for the individualization of levels systems and a levels system evaluation checklist.

Farrell, Smith, and Brownell (1998) conducted a large-scale survey to ascertain the extent of level system use, the characteristics of teachers and students using level systems, the characteristics and procedures in the levels systems, teacher perceptions of level system effectiveness, and teacher satisfaction with level systems. A randomly selected research sample of 200 teachers of learners with emotional/behavioral disorders was surveyed. This included 136 (68%) of teachers of students with emotional/behavioral disorders and 64 (32%) of teachers of students with severe emotional/behavioral disorders. The sample crossed grade levels and service settings.

The researchers found that level systems were implemented at every grade level and with every model of service delivery. Teachers of students with hyperactivity and attention deficit were more likely to use level systems than others. Level system interventions were used more frequently in special classes and special schools than in less restrictive settings. Teachers stated that their knowledge of level systems was a consequence of personal creativity and information from other professionals rather than reading the literature. However, the researchers found that the level systems implemented by the teachers were like those suggested in the literature.

The survey results suggest that although students can be successful within the level system, it does not prepare them for life outside the system's purview. In addition, it was indicated that teachers working in restrictive settings may be unable to incorporate into their system those components necessary to facilitate integration of students into general education settings.

The teachers recognized that level systems and their application did raise some questions about their use in responding to individual student needs. They also recognized the legal concern with regard to level systems. However, in general, the teachers express satisfaction with level systems despite their relative ineffectiveness in achieving the important goal of integration into the general education setting.

EXPULSION, SUSPENSION, AND IN-SCHOOL SUSPENSION

Recently, disciplinary removal through expulsion, suspension, and in-school suspension has been discussed in the literature as it applies both to students with disabilities and to regular students. There is considerable controversy surrounding the use of these behavior management procedures (Bacon, 1990; Editor, 1995; Lieberman, 1996). Several court decisions impact on their use with regular and special education students (Yell, 1990).

Hindman (1986) and Center and McKittrick (1987) define *expulsion* as the removal of a student from school for more than 10 days and *suspension* as the removal of a student from school for no more than 10 days. *In-school suspension* is the removal of a student from regular or special education class but not from the school.

"Generally so long as students' constitutional rights are not infringed upon (*Tinker v. Des Moines Independent Community School District,* 1969), and discipline is meted out with appropriate procedural due process (*Goss v. Lopez,* 1975), school officials' handling of student disciplines has not been altered through the judicial process" (Bartlett, 1988a, 1988b). The message in this quote is applicable to students in the regular class and general school population. However, as a consequence of various court decisions, it is not always applicable to students in special education (Shea, Bauer, & Lynch, 1989).

The implementation of expulsion with students with disabilities is limited by Public Law 94–142 (Morris, 1987). Except in circumstances in which the student is a threat to the life and well-being of self or others, students with disabilities may be expelled or suspended only if the following criteria are met: (a) the procedures are included as disciplinary options in the student's individualized education plan, (b) the procedural requirements of Public Law 94–142 are adhered to, and (c) the use of the procedures does not result in a permanent cessation of educational services (Grosenick et al., 1982). In most circumstances, expulsion is considered a change in educational placement and cannot be imposed on students with disabilities.

According to the U.S. Supreme Court, suspension is considered to be not only a necessary tool to maintain order in school but also a valuable educational device. Short-term suspension is permitted if the behavior for which the student is suspended is not directly linked to the disability. In this situation, the suspension is not considered a change in educational placement. However, the linkage between the disability and the behavior must be established or not established prior to the imposition of the suspension unless the student is dangerous to self or others. However, the general 10-day rule applies, and parents must be notified and agree to the suspension.

Center and McKittrick (1987) offer guidelines for those establishing school policy on expulsion and suspension. Policy should include clearly defined expectations for student behavior. Behavioral expectations are generally presented in a policy handbook that is made available to administrators, teachers, parents, and students. The handbook should include the rules, the consequences for violation, and the student's due-process rights. A standard procedure should be developed and implemented consistently in all cases in which expulsion and suspension may be considered as disciplinary options. The imposition of these disciplinary procedures is a team process and should never be done unilaterally.

Morgan-D'Atrio, Northup, LaFleur, and Spera (1996) conducted two studies on the use suspension in a large urban public school (1,150 students). The first study was concerned with the extent of disciplinary problems in the school, the use of suspension as a disciplinary strategy, and the procedural integrity of the school's disciplinary policy. They found that 65% (745) of the students were referred to the principal's office for discipline during the 1993–1994 school year. A random sample of 150 students was studied. The sample represented a total of 979 disciplinary referrals. Referral ranged from 1 to 43 per student with a mean of 6. Ninety-four of the 150 (62%) students were suspended at least once. Reasons for suspension included cutting class, tardiness, disobedience, not attending time-out room, fighting, profanity, disrespect, disturbing the classroom, leaving campus, leaving class, and others. Of the 94 suspended students, 39 (42%) were suspended once and 55 (58%) more than once. With regard to the integrity of the school disciplinary policy, it was found that 45% of the actions taken did not correspond with any of the disciplinary consequences in written school policy. About 20% of the suspensions actually violated school policy.

The purpose of the second study, conducted by Morgan-D'Atrio et al., was to ascertain the extent of academic deficits, social skills deficits, and other adjustment problems within the sample of students with recurrent suspensions and to determine the extent of individual differences among that group. The sample included the high school students from the first study and an additional sample for a middle school with approximately the same demographics. Twenty-four randomly selected students were studied. The results of this study were that 22% of the students had social skills deficits, 30% had social skills and academic deficits, 22% had academic deficits, and 26% had no deficit. The deficits of the middle school students were not significantly different. The authors, while recognizing the limitations of the studies, suggested that "it may be a prudent investment of time and resources to practice a more prescriptive approach to the development of treatment alternatives to suspension that can at least begin to answer the classic assessment question of what treatment for what problems for which students" (p. 199).

Farmer (1996) describes the search for alternatives to suspension in a middle school in which more than 3,000 disciplinary referrals resulted in 1,300 placements in in-school suspension and over 400 out-of-school suspensions during a single school year. The teachers and administrators, as a result of frustration with the present disciplinary policies and procedures, designed an alternative. The new system included (a) an honor-level discipline system that emphasized student responsibility and (b) proactive discipline behavior and assistance for students to assume responsibility for their behavior.

In-school suspension has not been tested in the courts, and its use with students with disabilities is becoming more frequent in schools. Center and McKittrick (1987) suggest that school policies established for expulsion and suspension be used for in-school suspension.

In-school suspension has several advantages over expulsion and suspension:

- It eliminates the probability that the student will be unsupervised during the school day.

- As a form of segregation from the general school population, it decreases the probability of disruption in the school.
- With an effective learning program, it can be a useful educational experience.

Those wishing to implement an in-school suspension program must develop policies, curriculum, and management guidelines. The following is a summary of policies suggested by Center and McKittrick:

- The 10-day rule should be applied.
- Age range among students should be no more than 3 years or three grades.
- A maximum enrollment should be set, perhaps 12 to 15 students. An experienced and qualified teacher should be assigned to each group.
- Specific criteria should be set for assignment to the program.
- Placements should be for a predetermined and specific period of time. The placement period should be uniform for particular offenses.
- Placement should begin on a specific day of the week.
- Students should be required to meet specific criteria for return to their regular school program.
- Failure to successfully complete in-school suspension should result in a hearing to consider other disciplinary procedures.
- Policy should be established for multiple placements within a school year.
- Acceptance or continuation of participation in other school programs (special groups, cocurricular activities, special studies) should be contingent on successful participation in the program.

In-school suspension should not be viewed as simple detention. Students should not be allowed to sit passively for an hour a day for several days and then return to their regular program. In-school suspension should be a valuable learning experience.

There are two general approaches to curriculum in the in-school suspension program. In the first approach, the student may continue studying his or her regular curriculum. This approach is frequently difficult and requires the regular and in-school suspension teachers to coordinate their activities. It is particularly difficult in the secondary school, where a student may be instructed by many teachers. This approach requires the in-school suspension teacher to be familiar with a broad range of curricula.

The second approach to in-school suspension curriculum is the stand-alone curriculum, which includes two options: (1) the learning skills program and (2) the functional academics program. In the learning skills program, the student studies generic learning strategies, such as listening skills, reading skills, study skills, and time management. In the functional academics program, the student studies daily living skills or work skills (e.g., budgeting, interviewing for a job, using credit, maintaining home and auto).

The in-school suspension program must include a behavior management program. Management should be positive and emphasize appropriate interpersonal and work skills. It could be a multipurpose token economy such as that presented in Chapter 5.

The effectiveness of any in-school suspension program is greatly dependent on the teacher assigned to the program. The teacher must be a highly skilled instructor and behavior manager and must be able to relate positively and productively with students.

In-school suspension is often used with other interventions (Bacon, 1990). In a comparison of the effects of in-school suspension combined with counseling and in-school suspension used alone, Hochman and Woerner (1987) found that students in in-school suspension used alone were 13 times more likely to return to in-school suspension and 15 times more likely to be referred to the principal's office. According to Miller (1986), the attendance of adolescent truants improved in an intervention that combined in-school suspension with counseling, bibliotherapy, writing therapy, and contingency contracting.

Stage (1997) conducted a study of the effects of three types of in-school suspension on disruptive classroom behavior and the impact of management strategies on assignment to in-school suspension. Thirty-six students with behavioral disorders enrolled in a residential school were studied. The students ranged in age from 12 to 17. Three types of in-school suspension were imposed:

- A time-out procedure whereby the student was sent to a vacant classroom for one class period (exclusion time-out)
- A longer time-out with the requirement to complete an academic assignment
- An in-school suspension with a counseling procedure

The researchers reported no apparent effects of in-school suspension on disruptive classroom behavior since there were no systematic differences in disruptive behavior in the in-school suspension phase of the study. The rate of student disruptive behavior remained rather constant across all phases of intervention, suggesting that no type of in-school suspension, as defined in this study, is more effective than another. It is suggested that the teacher's use of aversive contingencies in the classroom served to create conditions for students to wish to escape (i.e., enter in-school suspension). No direct or indirect evidence that a coercive behavior cycle was in place was found. The authors suggested that the effectiveness of in-school suspension may rely on sufficient positive social reinforcement within the ongoing classroom environment.

BIOPHYSICAL INTERVENTIONS

In this section, several *biophysical interventions* are discussed. In the majority of these interventions, the educator plays an important supportive role to that of the physician and other medical personnel. Consequently, an analysis of the educator's functions in referral, collaboration and reporting, the modification of classroom structure and curriculum content, the obtaining of permission to administer medication, and the safeguarding and administering of medication is presented as a conclusion to the discussion of the biophysical behavior management interventions.

In addition to the educator's "need to know," the biophysical techniques are reviewed because some of the behavior problems of children may be a direct result of biophysical or biophysical-environment interactions. In addition, the social-emotional (secondary) effects of many biophysical disabilities on the individual's lifestyle are of direct concern to educators.

The biophysical frame of reference implies that the source of an individual's behavior problem is an organic defect. There are two known causes of biophysical defects in unborn and newborn children: environment and heredity. Environmental factors of special importance to the health of the child are maternal factors (metabolic disorders, maternal age, number and frequency of pregnancies) and factors that affect the mother during pregnancy (viral diseases and infections, venereal disease, drugs, alcohol, tobacco, diet, injuries). In addition, the larger environment may have an effect on the child as a consequence of pollution, radiation, and the like.

Heredity, or the transmission of the characteristics or traits of the parents to the child, is a factor in some birth defects. Hereditary characteristics are transmitted from parents to child by chromosomes. Chromosomes are present in every human cell, including the ovum and sperm. Chromosomes are composed of genes—the units of heredity. The inherited characteristics of a child are determined by the composition and manner in which the gene-carrying chromosomes from the parents combine at the time of conception. There are approximately 4,000 disorders known to be caused by genetic defects. Among the most commonly known disorders are Down syndrome, sickle cell disease, cystic fibrosis, and hemophilia. Because genetic disorders are permanent, chronic, and complex, they tend to evoke labeling. As a consequence, they impact on the lifestyle of both the individual and the family (Costello, 1988).

It is generally agreed that birth defects are best reduced or controlled by preventive rather than curative techniques. Among the curative interventions available are chemical regulation, corrective surgery, and rehabilitation through training.

Chemical regulation includes such familiar interventions as medication and diet. Corrective surgery is frequently effective in reducing the debilitating effects of clubfoot, cleft lip and palate, and some vision, hearing, and speech problems, among others. Cosmetic surgery is a valuable aid in reducing the effects of observable deformities on the individual. Rehabilitation and training services have a significant positive impact on the lives of people with mental retardation, visual and hearing impairments, speech disorders, physical disabilities, learning disabilities, or emotional/behavioral disorders.

Diet

There is considerable activity and publicity on the effects of *diet* control on the hyperactive behaviors of children. Feingold (1973, 1985) hypothesized that naturally occurring salicylates and artificial food additives may cause the hyperkinetic syndrome in children who have a genetically determined predisposition.

Elimination of these substances from a child's diet would eliminate the symptoms of the hyperkinetic syndrome. Feingold claims that 48% of his patients were effectively treated by the diet and that symptoms can be reversed within a few hours if the diet is broken. Cook and Woodhill (1976) supported Feingold's claim in a clinical study of 15 hyperkinetic children. The parents of 10 children were "quite certain" and those of three others "fairly certain" that their child's behavior improved with the diet and relapsed when the diet was broken. Cook and Woodhill cautioned against the generalization of their finding because the sample was limited and the study did not meet rigorous research standards.

In a study of 59 children, Brenner (1977) reported that of 32 children able to tolerate the diet, 11 showed marked improvement as reported by teachers, parents, and physicians. Eight other children were judged "probably improved." No changes were reported in 13 children. In a control group of 27 children not on the diet, only 2 were improved without medication after 8 months. Brenner noted that the placebo effect could not be ruled out in the study.

Weiss et al. (1980) conducted a challenge study of 22 children with regard to behavioral response to artificial food colors. Of the 22 children, 20 displayed no convincing evidence of sensitivity to the color challenge as reported by parents. Swanson and Kinsbourne (1980) studied the effects of food dyes on children's laboratory learning performance. In the study, 20 children were classified as hyperactive, 20 were not. Both groups were challenged with food dyes. The performance of the hyperactive children was impaired on the days they received food dyes. Performance of the nonhyperactive children was not affected.

In a review of the pertinent empirical investigations with regard to the Feingold diet, Baker (1980) concluded that the differential results reported by Feingold, parents, and others using the diet may be due to variables other than the eliminated substances. He found that in properly controlled studies, the positive effects of the diet evaporated. At this time, the debate remains unsettled as to whether a diet intervention is truly effective. In a review of the research, Pescara-Kovach and Alexander (1994) concluded that there is no connection between food additives and behavior. They suggest that there is a need to educate the public about these findings.

Medication

Although behavior-modifying medications have been prescribed for children and youth with behavior disorders since the late 1930s (Wilson & Sherrets, 1979), the treatment-evaluation process remains complex. At present, approximately 2% to 3% of all schoolchildren are receiving psychopharmacologic medication to modify their behavior. Sweeney, Forness, Kavale, and Levitt (1997) estimate that between 15% and 20% of children in special education are receiving one or more behavior-modifying medications. The physician must not only be concerned with the individual child's personal status but also evaluate the child's environment, potentially biased evaluations of those associated with the child, and the actual and potential effects of other interventions being applied with the child, such as special education.

Several reviews have been published (Epstein & Olinger, 1987; Forness, Kavale, Sweeney, & Crenshaw, 1999; Forness, Sweeney, & Toy, 1996; Sweeney et al., 1997) describing the use of medication with children, particularly in the treatment of attention deficit hyperactivity disorder. These reviews are summarized in the following paragraphs.

Central Nervous System Stimulants. *Central nervous system stimulants* are the most commonly used psychiatric medications in children and adolescents and are most often used with individuals with attention deficit/hyperactivity disorders (Wilens, 2002). The sought-for positive effects of the stimulants are (a) increased controlled physical activity; (b) increased goal directedness; (c) decreased impulsivity and disruptiveness; (d) decreased distractibility; (e) increased attending; (f) improved performance, cognition, and perception; (g) improved motor coordination; (h) improved cooperation; and (i) decreased negative and increased positive behavior. The effectiveness of stimulants medications have been supported by many controlled studies and are usually well tolerated by children and youth. Decrease of appetite and sleep disturbance are among the most common side effects. Though weight and height growth has been shown to be slowed among prepubertal children who receive continuous treatment with stimulants, ultimate height and weight does not seem to be affected (National Institute of Mental Health, 1998).

The most common medications—methylphenidate (Ritalin) and dextroamphetamine (dexidrine)—are short acting, with children and youth demonstrating changes in their behavior within 30 minutes of taking the medication. The peak of the medication's effectiveness is usually between 1 and 4 hours after administration. Because of this short-term effect, many parents are opting for slow-release versions of these medications, the effects of which usually last from 2 to 6 hours. Other medications used include pemoline (Cylert) and combined amphetamines (Adderall). Cylert takes effect within 1 or 2 hours and may last up to 8 hours, and Adderall typically works in 45 minutes and lasts 6 to 8 hours (Wilens, 2002). These medications work with individuals with attention deficit/hyperactivity disorder by restoring the delicate levels of neurotransmitters in the brain. The "paradoxical effect" (calming produced by a stimulant) is caused by boosting serotonin levels in the brain, reducing restlessness, impulsivity, and difficulty concentrating (Gainetdinov et al., 1999).

Antianxiety and Antipsychotic Drugs. *Antianxiety and antipsychotic drugs* are prescribed for calming effects. Trade names include Mellaril, Thorazine, Librium, Haldol, and Equanil, among others. Mellaril and Thorazine are the most frequently prescribed tranquilizers for children.

Desired positive effects of tranquilizers are increased calmness and improved behavior and social functioning. Possible negative effects include nausea, drowsiness, dry mouth and nasal congestion, nervousness, rashes, increased appetite, and weight gain.

Anticonvulsants and Antihistamines. *Anticonvulsants* are used to treat children whose behavior and learning problems are complicated by seizures. Trade names for these medications include Dilantin, Mysoline, and Valproic Acid, among others.

Antihistamines are used to counteract the effects of various allergies. Trade names include Benadryl, Vistaril, and Phenergan. According to Renshaw (1974), these medications are exceptionally safe. They are often prescribed for their sedative effects on children in pain and as a nighttime sedative.

According to the American Academy of Child and Adolescent Psychiatry (1999a), medications are primary prescribed for the treatment of bedwetting, anxiety, attention deficit hyperactivity disorder, obsessive-compulsive disorder, depressive disorders, eating disorders, bipolar disorder, psychosis, autism, severe aggression, and sleep problems. The use of medication should always be within a comprehensive treatment plan (American Academy of Child and Adolescent Psychiatry, 1999a, 1999b; Forness et al., 1999; Gorton, 1996). Medication is not a "quick fix."

In summary, teachers should remember that although properly prescribed and monitored medication can have a beneficial effect on the child, it cannot (a) compensate for "lost" years of learning, (b) provide the discipline needed to develop acceptable functioning, (c) improve the self-esteem needed for self-acceptance, (d) provide the love the child needs for normal development, or (e) reverse essential deficits, such as mental retardation and cerebral palsy (Renshaw, 1974).

Educator's Role in Biophysical Interventions

The educator plays an important supportive role to medical personnel in the application of biophysical interventions. Howell, Evans, and Gardiner (1997) suggested several guidelines for teachers of students taking stimulant medications. These guidelines for obtaining optimal benefit from medication include the following:

- Ensure that the decision to use medication is made appropriately
- Establish direct communication among all concerned parties
- Plan who will receive the medication and how the medication will be administered
- Promote student responsibility for personal behavior
- Alert student to the potential for change as a consequence of medication
- Help student explain to others about medication
- Provide student with appropriate and positive reminders to take medication
- Set realistic goals for behavior change
- Teach student prosocial behaviors to replace inappropriate behaviors
- Monitor the effects of medication on academic behavior, social interactions, and adverse side effects

The supportive role includes (a) referral, (b) collaboration with and reporting of observations to the physician, (c) modification of classroom structure and curriculum content to meet the needs of the child, (d) obtaining permission to administer medication, and (e) safeguarding and administering medication to the child in school.

Referral. The educator is not in a position by experience, training, or function to refer a child directly to a physician. Neither is the educator in a position to suggest to a physician the prescribing of medication for a specific child. In addition, the educator should not attempt to coerce parents to accept any particular biophysical treatment.

It is proper for teachers to inform parents of a child's problems. The school initiates contact with medical personnel on behalf of a particular child only with parental consent. It is suggested that an educator not directly involved with the child in school serve as a contact person and intermediary between the teacher and parents during the referral process (Report of the Conference on the Use of Stimulant Drugs in the Treatment of Behaviorally Disturbed Young Children, 1971).

Collaboration With and Reporting of Observations to the Physician. A primary role of the teacher in biophysical interventions is the provision of current and objective feedback to the physician on the observable effects of the treatment on the child's behavior and learning (Wilson & Sherrets, 1979). The majority of the present-day medications are experimental substances, the effects of which on a particular child cannot be predicted with exactitude. Thus, meaningful feedback to the prescribing physician will assist in maximizing the positive effects of medication. The teacher, a trained observer who is with the child throughout the day, is in an excellent position to observe the effects of the medication and report, through proper channels, to the physician.

Modification of Classroom Structure and Curriculum Content. During the biophysical treatment process, especially during the beginning weeks, the child's behavior and learning styles may change radically. Consequently, it will be necessary for the teacher to modify, as necessary, both classroom structure and curriculum content to respond to the child's needs. Classroom structure may have to be increased or decreased to permit the child to adjust to his or her "new" behavior. The curriculum may have to be changed to allow the child to learn the knowledge and skills neglected during the "lost" years.

Obtaining Permission to Dispense Medication. The educator must obtain permission to dispense medication in the school when medical personnel (physician and/or nurse) are not available. A child should not be dismissed from school because medical personnel are not immediately available to administer medication. In some circumstances, teachers may dispense medication with proper permission. However, school personnel must investigate and adhere to their state's laws and regulations governing the dispensing of medication in the schools. In some cases, the school may need legal advice. A permission form suggested by Renshaw (1974) is shown in Figure 8.2.

Safeguarding and Administration of Medication. In a survey of 149 teachers who were members of the Illinois Council for Children with Behavioral Disorders, Epstein (1989) found that 49% of the schools represented by the teachers did not have a policy on medication practices in their schools. He urged all schools to develop a reasonable and comprehensive policy. When medication is dispensed in the school, the guidelines on the following pages should be used:

School Medication Consent and Directions Form

Parent permission: Date: _____

Child _____   Birthdate _____

Address _____   Phone _____

School _____   Grade _____   Teacher _____

_____

I hereby consent for the above-named school to supervise the medication
prescribed below by my physician for my child.

Parent's signature _____

Physician's direction: Date _____

Child _____

Medication and instruction _____

_____

Doctor requests teacher's comments:

Please observe the following _____

Phone _____   Best time to call _____

_____
Physician's signature

_____
Physician/Clinic Name

_____
Address

Figure 8.2
School medication consent and directions form

Source. From *The Hyperactive Child* (p. 127) by D. C. Renshaw (Chicago: Nelson-Hall Publishers, 1974).

1. Proper permission forms, completed by parents and physicians, should be obtained and filed in the child's record folder (see Figure 8.2).
2. All medications should be stored in a central location. This facility should be clean, ventilated, and lighted and should contain a locked cabinet. A water tap is needed. A refrigerator is necessary for some medications.
3. All medications must be properly labeled with the child's name and the physician's name. The label should include directions for use.

Medication Log

Child's Name	Date	Time	Medication	Person dispensing medication	Notes

Figure 8.3
Medication log

4. All medications, including new prescriptions and refills, received from and returned home should be logged in and out of the school. Medication should be inventoried frequently. One individual from the school's faculty or staff should be appointed to inventory the medication and function as a contact person in all communications with parents, physicians, and other medical personnel in relation to medication.

5. A responsible adult must be present when a child takes a medication.

6. A log, to be filled in each time a child takes medication, should be affixed to the wall in the medication center. This form is presented in Figure 8.3. The completed forms should be retained in a file.

♦ SUMMARY

In this chapter, several biophysical and environmental interventions of relevance to the teacher interested in a broad understanding of behavior management are presented.

The careful reader will note that significant overlap exists between the behavior management interventions presented in this and the previous chapter. The educator should seek to synthesize the various conceptual frameworks (theories) and their interventions into a personal perspective of behavior management.

♦ PROJECTS

1. Write a brief essay (300 words) on the following topics:
   (a) The advantages and disadvantages of the environmental interventions.
   (b) The advantages and disadvantages of the biophysical interventions from the educator's point of view.
2. Discuss the role of the educator in biophysical interventions.
3. Invite a physician or nurse to discuss biophysical interventions with your class.
4. Survey your community and school to ascertain which, if any, of the environmental interventions discussed in the chapter are applied to assist children with behavior problems.
5. Using the questions presented under the critical elements in the milieu, interview a teacher and principal to determine the character of the milieu in which they function.

♦ REFERENCES

American Academy of Child and Adolescent Psychiatry (1999a). Psychaitric medication for children and adolescents (Part 1: How medications are used). *Facts for Families, 21.*

American Academy of Child and Adolescent Psychiatry (1999b). Psychiatric medication for children and adolescents (Part II: Types of medication). *Facts for Families, 29.*

Anderson, N., & Marrone, R. T. (1979). Therapeutic discussion groups in public school classes for emotionally disturbed children. *Focus on Exceptional Children, 12*(1), 1–15.

Bacon, E. H. (1990). Using negative consequences effectively. *Academic Therapy, 25*(5), 599–611.

Baker, R. W. (1980). The efficacy of the Feingold K-P diet: A review of pertinent empirical investigations. *Behavioral Disorders, 6*(1), 32–35.

Barbetta, P. M. (1990). GOALS: A group-oriented adapted levels system for children with behavior disorders. *Academic Therapy, 25*(5), 645–656.

Bartlett, L. (1988a). Doe v. Honig and school discipline. *Behavior in Our Schools, 2*(3), 10–11.

Bartlett, L. (1988b). To expel or not to expel: Discipline of special education students from a legal perspective. *Behavior in Our Schools, 2*(2), 14–16.

Bauer, A. M., & Shea, T. M. (1988). Structuring classroom through levels systems. *Focus on Exceptional Children, 21*(2), 1–12.

Bauer, A. M., Shea, T. M., & Keppler, R. (1986). Levels systems: A framework for the individualization of behavior management. *Behavioral Disorders, 12*(1), 28–35.

Blankenship, C. S. (1986). Managing pupil behavior during instruction. *Teaching Exceptional Children, 19,* 52–53.

Brenner, A. (1977). A study of the efficacy of the Feingold diet on hyperkinetic children. *Clinical Pediatrics, 16,* 652–656.

Brown, M. H., Althouse, R., & Anfin, C. (1993). Guided dramatization: Fostering social development in children with disabilities. *Young Children, 48*(2), 68–71.

Brownell, M. T., & Thomas, C. W. (2001). An interview with Stephen W. Smith: Strategies for building a positive classroom environment by preventing behavior problems. *Intervention in School and Clinic, 37*(1), 31–35.

Carducci, D. J. (1980). Positive peer culture and assertiveness training. *Behavioral Disorders, 5*(3), 156–162.

Center, D. B., & McKittrick, S. (1987). Disciplinary removal of special education students. *Focus on Exceptional Children, 20*(2), 1–10.

Cheney, C. O. (1989, August). First time in the classroom? Start off strong! *Exceptional Times, 4.*

Clees, T. J. (1995). Self-recording of students' daily schedules of teachers' expectancies: Perspectives on reactivity, stimulus control, and generalization. *Exceptionalities, 5*(3), 113–129.

Coleman, M., & Webber, J. (1988). Behavior problems? Try groups! *Academic Therapy, 23*(3), 265–275.

Cook, P. S., & Woodhill, J. M. (1976). The Feingold dietary treatment of the hyperkinetic syndrome. *Medical Journal of Australia, 2,* 85–89.

Costello, A. (1988). The psychosocial impact of genetic disease. *Focus on Exceptional Children, 20*(7), 1–8.

Coughlan, A. J., Gold, S. R., Dohrenwend, E. F., & Zimmerman, R. S. (1973). A psychobehavioral residential drug abuse program: A new adventure in adolescent psychiatry. *International Journal of Addiction, 8*(5), 767–777.

Editor. (1995). Court: No services needed in short-term suspension. *The Special Educator, 11*(3), 1, 6.

Englert, C. S. (1984). Measuring teacher effectiveness from the teacher's point of view. *Focus on Exceptional Children, 17,* 1–14.

Epstein, M. H. (1989). *Survey of teachers of children and adolescents with behavior disorders on the use of medication.* De Kalb: Northern Illinois University Press.

Epstein, M. H., & Olinger, E. (1987). Use of medication in school programs for behaviorally disordered pupils. *Behavioral Disorders, 12*(2), 138–145.

Erikson, E. (1963). *Childhood and society* (2nd ed.). New York: W. W. Norton.

Evertson, C. M., Emmer, E. T., Clements, B. S., Sandford, J. P., Worsham, M. E., & Williams, E. L. (1981). *Organizing and managing the elementary school classroom.* Austin: Research and Development Center for Teacher Education, University of Texas.

Farmer, C. D. (1996). Empowering discipline: Proactive alternatives to school suspension. *Journal of Emotional and Behavioral Problems, 5*(1), 47–51.

Farrell, D. T., Smith, S. W., & Brownell, M. T. (1998). Teacher perceptions of level system effectiveness on the behavior of students with emotional and behavioral disorders. *Journal of Special Education, 32*(2), 89–98.

Feingold, B. F. (1973). Food additives and child development. *Hospital Practice, 8,* 11.

Feingold, B. F. (1985). *Why your child is hyperactive.* New York: Random House.

Forness, S. R., Kavale, K. A., Sweeney, D. P., & Crenshaw, T. M. (1999). The future of research and practice in behavioral disorders: Psychopharmacology and its school implications. *Behavioral Disorders, 24*(4), 305–318.

Forness, S. R., Sweeney, D. P., & Toy, K. (1996). Psychopharmacologic medication: What teachers need to know. *Beyond Behavior, 7*(2), 4–11.

Gable, R. A., & Strain, P. S. (1981). Individualizing a token economy system for the treatment of children's behavior disorders. *Behavioral Disorders, 1,* 39–45.

Gainetdinov, R. R., Wetsel, W. C., Jones, S. R., Levin, E. D., Jaber, M., & Caron, M. G. (1999). Role of serotonin in the paradoxical calming effect of psychostimulants on hyperactivity. *Science, 283,* 397–401.

Gallagher, P. A. (1988). *Teaching students with behavior disorders* (2nd ed.). Denver: Love Publishing.

Gorton, C. P. (1996). Medication that affects behavior. *Pennsylvania Journal on Positive Approaches, 1*(1), 1–5.

Goss v. Lopez, 95 S. Ct. 729 (1975).

Grosenick, J. K., Huntze, S. L., Kochan, B., Peterson, R. L., Robertshaw, C. S., & Wood, F. (1982). *National needs analysis in behavior disorders working paper.* Columbia: Department of Special Education, University of Missouri.

Harth, R., & Morris, S. M. (1976). Group processes for behavior change. *Teaching Exceptional Children, 8*(4), 136–139.

Hindman, S. E. (1986). The law, the courts, and the education of behaviorally disordered students. *Behavioral Disorders, 11*(4), 280–289.

Hochman, S., & Woerner, W. (1987). In-school suspension and group counseling: Helping the at-risk student. *National Association of Secondary School Principals Bulletin, 71*(501), 93–96.

Howell, K. W., Evans, D., & Gardiner, J. (1997). Medications in the classroom: A hard pill to swallow? *Teaching Exceptional Children, 29*(6), 58–61.

Joyce, B. G., Joyce, J. H., & Chase, P. N. (1989). Considerations for the use of rules in academic settings. *Education and Treatment of Children, 12,* 82–92.

Kern, L., Delaney, B., Clarke, S., Dunlap, G., & Childs, K. (2001). Improving the classroom behavior of students with emotional and behavioral disorders using individualized curricular modification. *Journal of Emotional and Behavioral Disorders, 9*(4), 239–247.

LaNunziata, L. J., Hunt, K. P., & Cooper, J. O. (1984). Suggestions for phasing out token economy systems in primary and intermediate grades. *Techniques, 1,* 151–156.

Legare, A. F. (1984). Using symbols to enhance classroom structure. *Teaching Exceptional Children, 17,* 69–70.

Lieberman, H. A. (1996). The court corner: Suspension/expulsion: The "10-day rule." *Missouri Innovations in Special Education, 24*(2), 2–3.

Long, N. J., Morse, W. C., & Newman, R. G. (1965). Milieu therapy. In N. J. Long, W. C. Morse, & R. G. Newman (Eds.), *Conflict in the classroom: The education of emotionally disturbed children* (4th ed.). Belmont, CA: Wadsworth.

Loughmiller, C. (1965). *Wilderness road.* Austin: University of Texas, Hogg Foundation for Mental Health.

Maslow, A. (1962). *Toward a psychology of being.* Princeton, NJ: Van Nostrand.

Mastropieri, M. A., Jenne, T., & Scruggs, T. E. (1988). A levels system for managing problem behaviors in a high school resource program. *Behavioral Disorders, 13*(3), 202–208.

Miller, D. (1986). Effect of a program of therapeutic discipline on the attitude, attendance and insight of truant adolescents. *Journal of Experimental Education, 55*(1), 49–53.

Mitchell, J. D., & Cockrum, D. L. (1980). Positive peer culture and a level system: A comparison in an adolescent treatment facility. *Criminal Justice and Behavior, 7*(4), 399–406.

Montague, M., Bergerson, J., & Lago-Delello, E. (1997). Using prevention strategies in general education. *Focus on Exceptional Children, 29*(8), 1–12.

Morgan-D'Atrio, C., Northup, J., LaFleur, L., & Spera, S. (1996). Toward prescriptive alternatives to suspension: A preliminary evaluation. *Behavioral Disorders, 21*(2), 190–200.

Morris, P. (1987). The restricted use of traditional disciplinary procedures with handicapped youngsters. In A. Rotatori, M. Banbury, & R. Foxx (Eds.), *Issues in special education.* Mountain View, CA: Mayfield.

Morris, S. M. (1982). A classroom process for behavior change. *The Pointer, 26*(3), 25–28.

Morse, W. C., & Wineman, D. (1957). Group interviewing in a camp for disturbed boys. *Journal of Social Issues, 13*(1), 23–31.

Munk, D. D., & Repp, A. C. (1994). The relationship between instructional variables and problem behavior: A review. *Exceptional Children, 60*(5), 390–401.

Murdick, N. L., & Petch-Hogan, B. (1996). Inclusive classroom management: Using preintervention strategies. *Intervention in School and Clinic, 31*(3), 172–176.

National Institute of Mental Health. (1998). Diagnosis and treatment of attention deficit hyperactivity disorder. NIH Consensus Statement. Available: *http://consensus.nih.gov/cons/110/110_statement.htm.*

Olson, J. (1989). Managing life in the classroom: Dealing with the nitty gritty. *Academic Therapy, 24,* 545–553.

Pescara-Kovach, L. A., & Alexander, K. (1994). The link between food ingested and problem behavior: Fact or fallacy? *Behavioral Disorders, 19*(2), 142–148.

Rademacher, J. A., Callahan, K., & Pederson-Seelye, V. A. (1998). How do your classroom rules measure up? Guidelines for developing an effective rule/management routine. *Intervention in School and Clinic, 33*(5), 284–289.

Redl, F. (1959). The concept of the life-space interview. *American Journal of Orthopsychiatry, 29,* 1–18.

Reid, I. (1979). Developing a behavioral regime in a secure youth treatment centre. *Bulletin of the British Psychological Society, 32,* 207.

Reisberg, L., Brodigan, D., & Williams, G. J. (1991). Classroom management: Implementing a system for students with BD. *Intervention in School and Clinic, 27*(1), 31–38.

Renshaw, D. C. (1974). *The hyperactive child.* Chicago: Nelson-Hall.

Report of the Conference on the Use of Stimulant Drugs in the Treatment of Behaviorally Disturbed Young School Children. (1971). *Journal of Learning Disabilities, 4,* 523–530.

Rhodes, W. C., & Gibbins, S. (1972). Community programming for the behaviorally deviant child. In H. C. Quay & J. F. Werry (Eds.), *Psychopathological disorders of childhood.* New York: Wiley.

Rieth, H., & Evertson, C. (1988). Variables related to the effective instruction of difficult-to-teach children. *Focus on Exceptional Children, 20,* 1–8.

Rockwell, S., & Guetzloe, E. (1996). Group development for students with emotional/behavioral disorders. *Teaching Exceptional Children, 29*(1), 38–43.

Rosenberg, M. S. (1986). Maximizing the effectiveness of structured classroom management programs: Implementing rule-review procedures with disruptive and distractible students. *Behavioral Disorders, 11*(4), 239–248.

Rosenkoetter, S. E., & Fowler, S. A. (1986). Teaching mainstreamed children to manage daily transitions. *Teaching Exceptional Children, 19,* 20–23.

Rosenshine, B. (1977). Review of teaching variables and student achievement. In G. D. Borich & K. S. Fenton (Eds.), *The appraisal of teaching: Concepts and process.* Menlo Park, CA: Addison-Wesley.

Rosenstock, H. A., & Levy, H. J. (1978). On the clinical superiority of the level system. *Journal of the National Association of Private Psychiatric Hospitals, 9*(3), 32–36.

Scheuermann, B., & Webber, J. (1996). Level systems: Problems and solutions. *Beyond Behavior, 7*(2), 12–17.

Scheuermann, B., Webber, J., Partin, M., & Knies, W. C. (1994). Level systems and the law: Are they compatible? *Behavioral Disorders, 19*(3), 205–220.

Seid, N. (2001). How to set rules your kids won't break. *Parents, 76*(9), 108–110.

Shea, T. M. (1977). *Camping for special children.* St. Louis: Mosby.

Shea, T. M., & Bauer, A. M. (1987). *Teaching children and youth with behavior disorders* (2nd ed.). Upper Saddle River, NJ: Prentice Hall.

Shea, T. M., Bauer, A. M., & Lynch, E. M. (1989, September). *Changing behavior: Ethical issues regarding behavior management and the control of students with behavioral disorders.* Paper presented at the CEC/CCBD Conference, Charlotte, NC.

Slade, D., & Callaghan, T. (1988). Preventing management problems. *Academic Therapy, 23,* 229–235.

Stage, S. A. (1997). A preliminary investigation of the relationship between in-school suspension and the disruptive classroom behavior of students with behavioral disorders. *Behavioral Disorders, 23*(1), 57–76.

Stainback, W., Stainback, S., Etscheidt, S., & Doud, J. (1986). A nonintrusive intervention for acting-out behavior. *Teaching Exceptional Children, 19*(1), 38–41.

Swanson, H. L., & Reinert, H. R. (1984). *Teaching strategies for children in conflict.* St. Louis: Mosby.

Swanson, J. M., & Kinsbourne, M. (1980). Food dyes impair performance of hyperactive children on a laboratory learning test. *Science, 207*(28), 1485–1486.

Sweeney, D. P., Forness, S. R., Kavale, K. H., & Levitt, J. G. (1997). An update on psychopharmacologic medication: What teachers, clinicians, and parents need to know. *Intervention in School and Clinic, 33*(1), 4–21, 25.

Thorson, S. (1996). The missing link: Students discuss school discipline. *Focus on Exceptional Children, 29*(3), 1–12.

Tinker v. Des Moines Independent Community School District, 393 U.S. 503, 89 S. Ct. 733, 21 L. Ed. 2d 721 (1969).

Weiss, B., Williams, J. H., Margen, S., Abrams, B., Citron, L. J., Cox, C., McKibben, J., & Ogar, D. (1980). Behavioral responses to artificial food colors. *Science, 207*(28), 1487–1488.

Wheldall, K. (1991). Managing troublesome classroom behavior in regular schools: A positive teaching perspective. *International Journal of Disability, Development, and Education, 38*(2), 99–116.

Wilens, T. E. (2002). The stimulant medications for attention-deficit/hyperactivity disorder. Washington, DC: National Association for Mental Illness.

Wilson, J. E., & Sherrets, S. D. (1979). A review of past and current pharmacological interventions in the treatment of emotionally disturbed children and adolescents. *Behavioral Disorders, 5*(1), 60–69.

Yell, M. L. (1990). The use of corporal punishment, suspension, expulsion, and timeout with behaviorally disordered students in public schools: Legal considerations. *Behavioral Disorders, 15*(2), 100–109.

Ziont, P., & Fox, R. W. (1998). Facilitating group classroom meetings: Practical guidelines. *Beyond Behavior, 9*(2), 8–13.

 **9**

Parent Education and Home-School Collaboration

Attitudes (in psychosituational interview)
Behavior (in psychosituational interview)
Daily report cards
Environments/situations (in psychosituational interview)
Expectations (in psychosituational interview)
Home reinforcers
Integrative framework
Parent education
Passport
Psychosituational assessment interview
Teacher-Parent Communication Program (TPCP)

After completing this chapter, you will be able to do the following:

1. Analyze the integrative framework or perspective of parent education and education.
2. Understand the need for and desirability of parent education.
3. Characterize the reactions, problems, and needs of parents of children with behavioral problems and other disabilities.
4. Explain the purpose and objectives of parent behavior management education.
5. Implement assessment strategies used to aid parents conducting a behavior change program.
6. List potentially effective reinforcers available in the home.
7. Implement techniques to facilitate parent-teacher collaboration.

◆ ◆ ◆

Mr. and Mrs. Wagnal arrived at the counseling center for their appointment with Dr. Murphy promptly at 3 P.M. They were visiting the center to consult with Dr. Murphy, a psychologist, concerning the behavior problems of their 3-year-old son, Dennis. Dennis is their first child.

The Wagnals were disturbed about Dennis because of his poor eating habits, his lack of interest in other children, his frequent tantrums, and his toilet-training problems. They reported that Dennis would eat only pickles, potato chips, chocolate candy, white bread, and frankfurters. He drank only water and cola. Needless to say, the Wagnals were concerned about Dennis's physical and emotional well-being.

Mrs. Wagnal stated that she had tried "everything" in an effort to bladder-train Dennis. She had placed him on a rigid drinking schedule to control his liquid intake, she had awakened him every hour throughout the night to take him to the bathroom, she had set an egg timer to remind her to take him to the bathroom each hour throughout the day, and she had even purchased a musical potty chair. All this had no influence on the boy's behavior.

The Wagnals' greatest concern was Dennis's behavior toward other children. Whenever another child of Dennis's age visited the home, Dennis would ignore the other child until he or she began playing with one of his toys. When the other child touched his possessions, Dennis immediately had a tantrum. He would kick and scream until the other child was removed from the home.

The Wagnals were desperate for help. Neither parent had relatives to whom they could turn for help with Dennis.

The Wagnals realized their need for some education and counseling if they were to help Dennis.

Mr. and Mrs. Mitchell arrived at Room 210 of Collinsdale Junior High School promptly at 7:30 P.M. They were to confer with Mr. Boyle, their 13-year-old daughter Eileen's homeroom teacher. This was the first time they had been summoned to conference because of one of their children.

Neither parent was anxious to visit with Mr. Boyle. Eileen's last report card contained two Fs, three Cs, and a B. Her conduct grades were at the bottom of the school's 5-point scale. In addition to the report card, the Mitchells had received a dozen or more negative notes from Eileen's teachers.

They had yelled and hollered, scolded and punished, and even grounded Eileen during the preceding 3 months without effect. The Mitchells realized that without cooperation from their daughter's teachers, they could not successfully help her.

There must be some techniques available for implementation to increase the consistency with which the home and school could manage Eileen's behavior and academic performance.

After studying the literature on parent education and training from a variety of theoretical and methodological perspectives, Clements and Alexander (1975) concluded, "Extensive research demonstrates unequivocally that children learn more, adjust better, and progress faster when parent education is effected" (p. 7).

Parent education is an integral part of a successful home-school management program. According to Beale and Beers (1982), there are three broad categories from which to work with parents: (a) parent education, (b) parent collaboration, and (c) parent-teacher communication. These categories may be rephrased as (a) "teach them what they need to know," (b) "work with them," and (c) "I talk, you talk, we talk, and I listen, you listen, we listen."

The primary purposes of this chapter are to present a systematic methodology designed to facilitate (a) the effectiveness with which parents manage their children's behavior in home and community settings, (b) collaboration between the parents and teacher in the implementation of effective behavior management interventions on behalf of the child for whom they have a shared responsibility, and (c) the teacher's efforts to plan and conduct a parent behavior management training program.

The parent education perspective presented here is but one of many discussed in the literature. Extensive references to other approaches—such as those developed by Bauer and Shea (2003); Croft (1979); Dunst, Trivette, and Deal (1988); Ehly, Conoley, and Rosenthal (1985); Kroth and Otteni (1985); Seligman (1979); Shea and Bauer (1985, 1991); and Winton (1986) as well as references to several other methods of conducting parent education and training—are presented at the end of the chapter. The reader will find these references an excellent point of departure for a comprehensive study of parent education and training.

NEED FOR COLLABORATION

There remains among present-day regular and special education teachers, as well as educational administrators and other professionals, skepticism concerning the need for and desirability of school-sponsored programs for parents. Our experience, however, as parents and educators, indicates that parent education and training is a necessary component of a comprehensive school service program (Courson & Hay, 1996; Shea & Bauer, 1991).

Clements and Alexander (1975) agree:

> It is unnecessary to revisit the already proven axiom that parents are effective change agents in the lives of exceptional children. It is, perhaps, equally as extravagant to indulge in outlining the boundaries of social and academic learning and perpetuate the pseudo-issue of who governs which set of constructs when, in reality, these are shared and interactive responsibilities. We must instead face an important issue in the third quarter of the twentieth century; parents are moving both physically and intellectually back into the mainstream of American education. (p. 1)

The question is not whether parent education is needed but how educators can effectively and efficiently conduct parent programs for the ultimate benefit of all children. Clements and Alexander suggest that the teacher is the school-based professional primarily responsible for parent services. All teachers in general and special education must acknowledge their responsibility and take steps to provide appropriate programs with parents.

Gardner (1974) maintains that cooperative home-school endeavors are more effective in responding to the needs of children with behavior problems than are school endeavors alone. The Pathfinder School (Susser, 1974) perceives parents and educators as partners. According to Susser, success in the classroom is lasting only if there is 24-hour-a-day follow-through; the approach of school and home, teacher and parent, must be consistent. Karnes and Zehrbach (1972) have suggested that programs for children with disabilities can be significantly improved if parents are meaningfully involved in them.

Opinions relative to the need for and desirability of programs for parents are not exclusively the domain of professionals. Many parents are aware of their need for education and training. Stigen (1976) writes repeatedly of her need for assistance through meaningful education and training. She discusses the inadequacy of the guidance and supportive services for parents offered by hospitals, schools, clinics, and other social service agencies.

Kratoville (1975a, 1975b) and Jogis (1975), both parents of children with disabilities, have described their need for sensitive, practical assistance in their role as primary therapist for their children. These parents noted a lack of meaningful assistance and understanding of their problems by professionals in hospitals, schools, clinics, and community agencies. They report an obvious lack of training and sensitivity of professionals toward parents.

The opinions of the parents and professionals just cited and those of many others, including parents and teachers involved primarily with children with disabilities, lead to the following conclusions (Shea & Bauer, 1991):

1. Both parents and professionals recognize the need for parent education and training.

2. Parent programs are desirable because they not only respond to the needs of the parents but also have a significant positive effect on the children.

3. The teacher, a specialist in instructional processes and behavior management techniques, is the logical professional to coordinate and conduct parent programs in cooperation with the school counselor, psychologist, or social worker.

4. Children benefit most when the behavior management approaches of the home and school are consistent.

5. Parent programs must be practical, concrete, specific, and meaningful to the parents.

Although the literature cited is concerned primarily with children administratively classified as disabled, the conclusions drawn from the literature are relevant to all children and their parents. "Normal" children also have problems and are frequently a behavior management concern to their parents.

PARENTS' REACTIONS, PROBLEMS, AND NEEDS

The parents of a child with a problem are first and foremost human beings, and like all human beings, they react as individuals to the problems of loved ones. A particular parent's reaction is in large part determined by that individual's personal characteristics, life experiences, education and training, expectations, socioeconomic circumstances, and a variety of other variables. The parent's reaction is influenced by the characteristics of the child and the specific problem and by the educator's and others' reaction to the problem (Shea & Bauer, 1991).

Educators should keep in mind that parents with problem children are not necessarily "problem parents." They do not necessarily need personal counseling. The majority are normal persons who are responding in a normal manner to unanticipated trauma.

Ross (1964) discussed parental reactions to the birth or diagnosis of a child with disabilities from a psychoanalytic perspective. The recognition of a disability in a child causes an increase in the parents' level of anxiety. This anxiety appears to be caused by recognition of the unanticipated discrepancy between the parents' expectations for the child and the child in reality. In their efforts to control anxiety, the parents employ one or more of a broad range of personal coping mechanisms. These mechanisms are used to regain emotional equilibrium, which has been threatened by the crisis. Although coping mechanisms are applied for positive reasons, that is, the regaining of emotional equilibrium, they may be destructive to the individual parent and child if they are overused or if they become habitual. According to Ross, counseling and similar supportive therapeutic services are required to aid parents in dealing with their initial anxiety and consequent reactions resulting from their child's problem.

A crisis reaction to a child's problems is not the exclusive province of parents of children classified as deviant, special, or disabled (Gordon, 1976). Emotional reactions to problems with a child are a natural human response for any parent confronted with a crisis or perceived crisis. In addition, all parents do not employ the same coping mechanisms. Parental reactions are as varied as the individual parents confronted with a crisis situation (Gordon, 1976).

Among the coping mechanisms parents may apply in response to their recognition of a problem with their child are the following:

- *Self-doubt:* The parents may doubt their worth as human beings and as parents. Their self-worth may be in doubt because of a perceived inability to give birth to or raise a child according to their expectations and the expectations of society.

- *Unhappiness and mourning:* The child's problem is perceived as so severe that the parents' joy of life is gone. It is impossible for them to smile, laugh, converse, or take an active part in any of life's common pleasures. This parental reaction has been compared to the mourning that occurs after the death of a loved one.

- *Guilt:* Because of the uncertain cause of their child's problem, many parents feel guilty. They believe that the child's problem is their fault. At times, parents will go to extreme lengths to find a reason for the child's difficulty and may discover some insignificant personal behavior or incident in the past on which to place blame.

- *Denial:* The parents may react to the child's problem by denying its existence. They reason that if the existence of the problem is denied, they do not have to concern themselves with it.

- *Projection:* Many parents who recognize the existence of a problem may blame it on another person. They may blame the child's difficulty on a physician, nurse, caseworker, counselor, baby-sitter, or teacher. Occasionally, they will project blame onto their spouse or other children.

- *Withdrawal:* The parents may react to the child's problem by withdrawal, believing that they can find a solution if they give the problem sufficient time and personal consideration. In some cases, withdrawal leads to depression requiring professional attention.

- *Avoidance and rejection:* To some parents, the birth or diagnosis of a child with a disability is so traumatic that they avoid contact with the child; they are unable to feed, clothe, or play with the child.

- *Embarrassment and social isolation:* Many parents of children with disabilities are embarrassed. In some cases, this embarrassment leads to social isolation. Neither parent nor child leaves the home for shopping, walks, visits, or entertainment.

- *Hostility:* Some parents report feelings of hostility and, on occasion, overt anger toward others who stare or ask questions about the child. The object of this hostility and anger may be anyone: a passenger on a bus, a person in the street, a friend, a neighbor, a relative, or a child.

- *Overdependency and helplessness:* The parents may react with overdependency on their spouse, a child, a relative, or a professional.

- *Confusion:* Most parents are confused by the child's problem. They are confused about the cause of the problem, its normal course, and its treatment. Such confusion is largely a result of a lack of factual information and guidance.

- *Frustration:* Many parents who have decided on a course of action that is appropriate for their child become frustrated in their efforts to obtain services. They are confronted with insensitive and inadequately trained professionals. They are frustrated by the lack of appropriate services in the community.

The educator must recognize that many of the foregoing reactions are not under a parent's conscious control. Parents must be aided in dealing with their reactions before they can fully participate in and benefit from collaborative activities.

Teachers realize that they need a variety of communication and instructional skills. They must learn to listen to the meaning behind the parents' words as well as to the words themselves. They must be sensitive to the parents' feelings. They must be able to empathize with the problems confronting the parents and child. Although parent educators must approach their task with honesty and forthrightness, they must not be cruel; give the impression that the parents, child, and problem are hopeless; or indicate that they have all the answers. Parent educators must have sufficient confidence in their teaching ability to permit parents to develop confidence in them—and, through them, in themselves. Teachers must recognize the limits of their knowledge and skills when working with parents. Generally, teachers are neither counselors nor therapists. As a consequence, they must refer parents to the appropriate individuals and agencies for services that are beyond the scope of their professional expertise. However, teachers are educators and can provide services to parents from an educational perspective.

AN INTEGRATIVE FRAMEWORK

The ecological contexts that affect children with a behavior problem are described in detail in Chapter 2. The reader is encouraged to review the sections in that chapter on traditional models of human behavior, the integrative framework, and Figure 2.6 before studying this section.

The *integrative framework* stresses that the understanding of human development and behavior requires examination of the contexts of interactions in several settings (Bronfenbrenner, 1977). The mesosystem—the interrelations among the major settings the child inhabits at a particular point in life—includes both home and school. To effectively respond to student needs, the teacher must involve those in the mesosystem (parents, siblings, and surrogate parents) in the child's behavior management program.

The integrative or systems approach invites consideration of the joint impact of two or more settings on one another. School and home jointly impact on children with behavior problems. The subsystems that are significant when working with children and their families include parent-child, parent-teacher-child, teacher-child, sibling-child, and sibling-parent-child (Shea & Bauer, 1987). According to Bronfenbrenner (1977), the design of an ecological intervention for an individual functioning in more than one setting should take into account the possible subsystems and effects that exist or could exist across settings. Consequently, programming with parents in behalf of children should take several subsystems into account. Those to be examined by teachers collaborating with parents in behalf of children with behavior problems include the following:

- Nature and requirements of the parents' work
- Neighborhood, health, and community services
- School and community relations
- Informal social networks
- Patterns of recreational and social life
- Family type (traditional or neolocal nuclear family, blended family, extended family, one-parent family, and so on)

- Delegation of child care to others outside the home
- Existence and character of explicit and implicit societal values with reference to parenting, children, disability, and behavior

By examining the child and the parents and family with reference to these ecological factors, the teacher can develop, in collaboration with the parents, an individualized behavior management program responsive to the needs of the child and parents.

PARENT TRAINING PURPOSES

McDowell (1976) has classified parent programs under three headings: (a) informational, (b) psychotherapeutic, and (c) education.

The *informational* program is designed primarily to present knowledge to parents about a variety of topics. Among the focuses of such informational programs are (a) child-raising techniques; (b) child development; (c) educational program designs, objectives, and procedures; (d) the causes, effects, and treatment of disabilities; and (e) techniques of behavior management. The primary purpose of these parent programs is the transmission of information.

The *psychotherapeutic* strategy is employed to assist parents in efforts to deal with personal feelings and conflicts related to the child's problem and its impact and contingencies. It is assumed that parents must adjust emotionally before they can plan and implement an action program.

Parent education programs are designed to assist parent efforts to effectively interact with and manage the behavior of their children. In an examination of the research on parent behavioral training, Graziano and Diament (1992) concluded that there is significant evidence that education has a positive effect on the functioning of both children and parents. It was especially effective with children who are noncompliant or oppositional or who have specific problems, such as phobias. Through education, parents gained in knowledge and management skills and demonstrated attitudinal improvement.

The program for parent-teacher cooperation in child management presented in this chapter can be classified as a parent education program. It focuses primarily on education and implementation of behavior management techniques as an effective and efficient means of managing behavior. As a consequence of this focus, the program is limited in its effectiveness with those parents in need of psychotherapeutic or basic informational services.

Objectives

The objectives of the parent education program presented in this chapter are the following:

- To increase the parents' knowledge of the techniques of behavior modification

- To increase the parents' skills in the application of behavior modification techniques in the management of their children's behavior
- To provide both the parents and the teacher with a common perspective of child behavior management and facilitate collaborative child behavior management efforts

These objectives are attained by instructing the parents in behavior modification techniques and by assisting the parents' application of these techniques in home and home-school behavior management interventions.

The steps in the behavior change process applied in the parent education program are identical to those presented in Chapter 4. These steps are repeated here for reader convenience. Those wishing to review in depth the steps in the behavior change process are referred to Chapter 4. The steps are as follows:

Step 1:   Selecting a target behavior

Step 2:   Collecting and recording baseline data

Step 3:   Identifying appropriate reinforcers

Step 4:   Implementing an intervention and collecting and recording intervention data

Step 5:   Evaluating the effects of intervention

It must be remembered that in parent education, the teacher is generally once removed from direct observation of the child's behavior in the home setting; thus, the teacher must rely on the parents' observations and reports. Consequently, assessment strategies must be implemented to facilitate the parents' selection and objectification of a target behavior.

In addition, reinforcers applied in the home setting differ somewhat from those available and applicable in the school; thus, attention is given to the parents' recognition and application of home reinforcers.

Selecting and Assessing the Target Behavior

To be of practical assistance to parents wishing to improve their behavior management skills, the educator must obtain specific information about the child's behavior. The information needed includes the following (Blackham & Silberman, 1980):

- The history of the problem
- Specific areas of conflict
- A description of the behavior that makes it receptive to direct observation and measurement
- The identity of the person or persons present when the behavior occurs
- Reinforcers that appear to maintain the behavior

- The roles and responsibilities of the parents and other family members in the child's life
- Parental expectations and behavior requirements and the reasonableness of these expectations and requirements
- Methods presently used to change the behavior
- Reinforcers that are available or that can be made available in the home
- Observational data on the rate or frequency of the behavior

Blackham and Silberman have suggested four methods for obtaining data on parent-child interactions and problem areas:

1. Direct observation of the child and other family members in the home
2. Direct observation of the child and other family members in the clinic or school setting
3. Parental observation of the child's interaction within the family at home and the reporting of the resultant data to the educator
4. A personal interview with the parents and child

As a result of the administrative organization of the school, the first two methods are not feasible; that is, the teacher is usually unable to spend the needed time observing parent-child interaction in either the home or the school. A possible exception may be in school- and home-based preschool programs. The third and fourth methods are most practical and can be implemented by means of the psychosituational assessment interview.

Psychosituational Assessment Interview. The *psychosituational assessment interview* is primarily an information-gathering technique. The interview focuses on obtaining from the parent or parents descriptive data about the child's behavior and the circumstances surrounding it.

The psychosituational interview technique was designed by Bersoff and Grieger (1971) and applied by Shea, Whiteside, Beetner, and Lindsey (1974). The purpose of the interview is to analyze the unacceptable behavior and uncover the antecedents and consequences that elicit, reinforce, and sustain it. This information about the child is obtained from the parent or parents and contributes to decisions concerning interventions to modify the behavior.

By means of the interview, it is possible to determine to what extent the behavior is reinforced and maintained by the environment and to what extent it may be modified by the manipulation of the environment. Thus, the primary aspects of the setting in which the behavior occurs are analyzed. These aspects are (a) the child's behavior, (b) the environmental variables surrounding the behavior, and (c) the attitudes and expectations of the parents.

Behavior refers to the actual behaviors for which the child was referred, including the antecedents and consequences of that behavior, that is, teacher, parental, and peer responses. *Environments* and *situations* refer to the specific places and circumstances in which the behavior occurs, including the presence of significant others. *Attitudes* refer to the beliefs and feelings of the referring agent, that is, the parent or parents.

A parent's concern about a child's behavior may be based on irrational ideas and attitudes that lead to unwarranted *expectations,* demands, and feelings—all of which may result in inappropriate actions toward the child following exhibition of the target behavior. *Expectation* has a dual meaning: It refers to the specific performance that the adult would like the child to achieve (short-term goals) and to the long-range aspirations that the adult has for the child.

The four major tasks to be accomplished during the interview are (a) defining the target behavior(s), (b) explicating specific situations in which the behavior occurs, (c) uncovering the contingencies (antecedents and consequences) that seemingly sustain the behavior, and (d) detecting any irrational ideas, if any, that make it difficult for the parent or parents to objectively understand, accept, and modify the behavior.

Defining the target behavior involves analyzing the following: (a) its *frequency rate,* or the number of times the behavior occurs within a particular time period; (b) its *intensity,* or the strength or force of the behavior; and (c) its *duration,* or the length of time that the behavior is maintained. A careful analysis of the problem within a behavioral framework helps delineate and define it so that it becomes remediable. This process helps the parents check their perceptions and focus on the relevant problem.

Obtaining information about the specific situations in which the behavior occurs is important because behavior is considered a function of interaction between the learned response of the child and the situation in which the behavior occurs. This information helps the interviewer plan the intervention.

Exploring the antecedents and consequences of the behavior is the next interviewer task. The parents must be aware that *they are part of the problem* and may have a role in sustaining the behavior.

Finally, the interviewer must be aware of the parents' irrational and unrealistic ideas about the child. The following irrational ideas of parents are frequently apparent:

1. The notion that the child is infallible and has wide-ranging competence. When the parents' expectation is that the child is competent in all respects, inefficiency in one or two areas of functioning is regarded as general failure.

2. The maintenance of absolutistic and unreasonable expectations of the child. These ideas are usually expressed in "ought" and "should" terms. A parent may say, "He should be able to sit longer" or "He ought to know better."

3. The feeling that it is helpful to become angry over the child's misbehavior. This feeling may lead to guilt and anxiety on the part of the parents that may further interfere with parent-child interactions.

4. The belief that the child is blameworthy and needs to be punished for misdeeds. The failure to accept things as they exist inhibits rational problem solving.

It is recommended that both parents be present at the interview. A joint interview is desirable because differing perceptions and inconsistencies in parental behavior management strategies can be uncovered. It also allows the interviewer to gauge the amount and frequency of mutual support that the parents provide to each other.

The interview may be a single session or a series of sessions. If the interviewer is concerned primarily with obtaining data in an effort to design an intervention that includes parental participation, two or three sessions may be sufficient. However, frequently the strategy can be applied in an ongoing intervention program.

To assist the parent, the interviewer may suggest that the parents gather behavioral data. A form for this purpose is presented in Figure 9.1, along with instructions for completing the form.

The following are specific interviewer tasks:

1. Establish rapport with the parent or parents.

   Example Questions

   - How are you doing today?
   - Did work go well today?
   - Would you care for something to drink? Coffee? Tea? Soda?
   - Is that seat comfortable enough?

2. Have the parents specify the target behavior(s), that is, the specific behavior(s) that is disturbing to them. Explore the frequency, intensity, and duration of the behavior.

   Example Questions

   - What exactly does the child do that you find unacceptable or annoying?
   - What exactly does the child do that makes you say he or she is hyperactive, nonresponsive, or disobedient?
   - What else does the child do that makes you say he or she is hyperactive, non-responsive, or disobedient?
   - In the course of an hour (day), how often is the child hyperactive, nonre-sponsive, or disobedient?

3. Have the parents delineate the specific situations and environments in which the behavior occurs. Establish where the behavior takes place and who is present when the behavior occurs.

   Example Questions

   - Where does this behavior occur? In the house? In the yard? On the play-ground? In a store?
   - Does it occur when the child is working on a particular project? With a par-ticular group? While watching TV? When getting ready to go to bed? When getting up in the morning?
   - Who is present when the behavior occurs? Mother? Father? Brothers? Sisters? Playmates? Visitors?

Behavior Log Form

Target behavior _____

Child _____

Observer _____

Date (2)	Time		Antecedents (4)	Consequences (5)	Applied Interventions (6)	Comments (7)
	Begins (3)	**Ends (3)**				

INSTRUCTIONS

(1) Complete the top portion of the form, that is, the target behavior to be observed, the child's name, and the observer's name.

(2) Write *day* and *date* of the first observation in first column: for example, M/8/3 or Th/11/13.

(3) Upon each occurrence of the target behavior, write the time it begins and ends in the second and third columns, respectively. If the target behavior is nearly instantaneous, write the time of the occurrence in the second column.

(4) Upon each occurrence of the target behavior, write what happened immediately *before* the behavior (antecedents) in the fourth column.

(5) Upon each occurance of the target behavior, write what happened immediately *after* the behavior (consequences) in the fifth column.

(6) In column 6, write what you or another person interacting with or supervising the child did to either *encourage* or *discourage* the behavior. If there was no reaction to the behavior, it should be noted in this column.

(7) In column 7, write any comments you have regarding the occurrence of the behavior that is out of the ordinary. For example, child was tired, grandmother was visiting, bad day in school, marital conflict occurring, and so on.

It is recommended that a behavior log be maintained for a minimum of 1 week before an intervention is implemented.

Figure 9.1
Parents' behavior log for home use

4. Explore the contingencies that may stimulate and sustain the behavior. Determine what happens immediately before and after the behavior occurs, that is, the antecedents and consequences of the behavior.

   Example Questions

   - What happens just before the behavior occurs?
   - What happens just after the behavior occurs?
   - What do you usually do when the child engages in this behavior?
   - How do other people indicate to the child that the behavior is unacceptable?

5. Attempt to determine the ratio of positive-to-negative interactions between the child and the parents.

   Example Questions

   - Is your relationship with the child usually pleasant or unpleasant?
   - Do you usually praise his or her accomplishments?
   - Do you reprimand the child's failures and ignore his or her success?

6. Explore the methods the parents use for behavior control. Explore the type of punishment and the conditions for application.

   Example Questions

   - Do you punish the behavior?
   - How do you punish inappropriate behavior?
   - Who is responsible for administering the punishment?
   - Do you always use a specific method of punishment?
   - Which other methods do you use?

7. Determine to what degree the parents are aware of how praise or punishment is communicated and its effect on the child's behavior.

   Example Questions

   - Can the child tell when you are angry? How?
   - Can the child tell when you want him or her to stop doing something? How?

8. Explore the manner in which expectations and consequences are communicated by the parents to their child.

   Example Questions

   - Are the rules you expect the child to follow clearly spelled out?
   - Does the child know what you expect him or her to do?

9. Detect irrational and unrealistic ideas that make it difficult for the parents to understand, accept, or modify the child's behavior. Be alert for and explore irrational ideas that may be expressed by the parents. Restate irrational ideas but avoid reinforcing them.

10. Conclude the session by restating the unacceptable behavior and presenting the desirable behavior. You may suggest that the parents keep a log of the child's behavior. (Refer to Figure 9.1.) Explain to the parents how the log should be used. You may suggest one or two techniques for changing the behavior. (This is only done if additional sessions are prohibited.) Make arrangements for a future meeting.

Home Reinforcers

In this section, a list of potentially effective *home reinforcers* is presented. These have been found useful to parents needing suggestions for reinforcers they may apply at home. Additional suggestions are presented in extensive lists of reinforcers in Chapter 4.

Consumable Food Reinforcers

Fruits	Cookies
Candies	Cake
Snack foods	Crackers
Gum	Milk
Ice cream	Soda
Yogurt	Juice

Reinforcing Activities in Relation to Food Reinforcers

Baking cookies or a cake with a parent

Preparing dinner with a parent

Operating a toaster, mixer, or other appliance

Washing dishes or operating the dishwasher

Setting the table for snack time

Serving snacks

Cleaning the table after snack time

Tangible Reinforcers

Pencils or pens

Colored, broad-tipped markers

Erasers

Money to purchase desired items

Records

Surprise gifts

Toys

Games

Coloring books

Pads of paper

Books

Jewelry

Clothing

Pets

Pet supplies

Token Reinforcers

Points

Stars

Chips

Play money

Check marks

Working on a project with a parent

Visiting a parent's place of work

Joining and participating in a club or tea

Game Activity Reinforcers

Playing outdoors alone with friends or a parent

Participating in organized sports

Flying a kite

Participating in table games: checkers, backgammon, cards, and so on

Playing computer games

Social Reinforcers

Smiles

Hugs

Pats

Kisses

Attention from parents

Compliments about activities, efforts, appearance

Reinforcing Activities

Reading or looking at books, magazines, catalogs

Using the home computer

Watching television

Getting additional playtime

Going to the zoo

Fishing

Caring for a pet

Spending the night with a friend or relative

Shopping with a parent

Having a friend spend the night

Going to the movies

Using the stereo

Getting telephone privileges

Receiving help from a parent on a homework assignment or chore

Attending a recreational activity or sporting event

Attending or having a party

Staying out later than usual

Accompanying parents instead of remaining with a sitter

Driving the family car

Going for ice cream, hamburgers, french fries

Taking lessons (music, dance, swimming)

Using the family typewriter or computer

Listening to a story as a parent reads

Parent Education Program

The *parent education* program presented here has two objectives: (a) to train parents in the theory and application of behavior modification principles and practices and (b) to assist parents' efforts to systematically modify selected target behaviors exhibited by their children. Although not a primary objective of the program, a benefit derived by many parents is mutual support and understanding of their child management problems from the other members of the group and the educator.

The program includes these three phases: preparation, instruction, and follow-up.

Preparation Phase. Before beginning the instructional phase of the education program, the educator should conduct one or more psychosituational interviews with each parent or couple. The objective of these interviews is (a) to determine the parent or parents' needs, interests, and readiness to participate in a formal education program and (b) to clarify at least one child behavior they wish to modify.

The individual interview sessions are an excellent time for the educator to discuss the program objectives, organization, and requirements and to invite the parents' participation.

Instruction Phase. The instruction phase of the parent education program includes eight weekly sessions. The $1\frac{1}{2}$-hour sessions are divided into two 40-minute segments and a 10-minute break.

The first 40-minute segment is devoted to brief formal presentations by the educator on the principles and practices of behavior modification. The remainder of this segment is devoted to a question-and-answer session, group discussion, and practice exercises and activities.

The 10-minute break is devoted to informal discussion. Coffee, tea, milk, and soft drinks as well as snacks can be served. These items may be furnished by the educator or by the parents.

The second 40-minute segment of the weekly session is devoted to planning, implementing, and evaluating the parents' behavioral intervention programs. These programs are concerned with the behaviors selected during the preparation phase. During this second segment, time is devoted to participants' reports of their interventions. All members of the group are expected and encouraged to question, discuss, and make suggestions for improving the interventions. A positive and helpful attitude must be maintained by all participants throughout this segment. Maintaining a positive tone in the group is a primary function of the educator.

Meetings are conducted in a mutually agreed-on location. The educator's or participants' home is *not* recommended, in large part to avoid potential competition or inconvenience to the participants. A school, YMCA, YWCA, or community center is an excellent location for meeting. The facility must be accessible. If necessary, car pools can be arranged among the participants. In some cases, child care services will be needed. The meeting room should ensure the group's privacy. Appropriate adult furnishings are necessary. A worktable should be available.

Group membership is limited to 12 to 14 persons, excluding the educator. Teachers of the parent-members' children can become group members. Groups are open to both mothers and fathers. Participation by both parents is desirable.

Attendance should be regular because of the cumulative nature of the material. If parents are unable to attend a particular session, the educator or another parent must update them in an individual session. However, absences should be discouraged for the sake of group cohesion.

The educator functions as an instructor and group facilitator during weekly sessions. Although the educator's function as an instructor remains relatively constant throughout the program, parents should be permitted and encouraged to make instructional presentations. The educator's function as group facilitator should diminish as the instructional phase progresses and the participants begin to assert leadership.

Occasionally, a team of two educators may present the education program. This is an excellent idea, particularly if one assumes the functions of instructor and the other the functions of facilitator. Of course, success in team teaching assumes professional compatibility, that is, fundamental agreement on the subject matter and instructional methods.

Any person who is knowledgeable of the principles and practices of behavior modification, child behavior, and group processes can serve as an educator. This includes parents, regular and special education teachers, college instructors, counselors, psychologists, nurses, social workers, and others.

The instructional materials needed for the parent education program are in this text, especially the worksheets at the back. Each participant should have a copy of the text.

Follow-Up Phase. Contacts with the parents should not be terminated at the end of the 8-week education program. It is suggested that the educator develop a follow-up plan, maintaining periodic contact with the group and with individual members to reinforce their efforts and assist in the planning and implementation of additional interventions. Contact can be maintained by individual interviews, telephone conversations, and monthly meetings.

The periodic reinforcement offered the participants during the follow-up phase will increase the probability that the skills learned during the education program will not fall into disuse.

Sample Lesson Plan. The reader will find a sample lesson plan in this section. The lesson includes information on goals, content, instructional methods, and activities for a $1\frac{1}{2}$-hour lesson that is divided into two 40-minute instructional segments and a 10-minute break. The first segment is devoted to formal instruction in behavior modification; the second segment is devoted to the practical application of behavior modification by the participants. The lesson plan also includes suggested resources, evaluation strategies, and home-study assignments for the participants.

LESSON 1: INTRODUCTION TO BEHAVIOR MODIFICATION

Goals

1. To familiarize participants with the models of causation of human behavior and with the behavior change process
2. To enable participants to exemplify each of the principles of behavior modification
3. To enable participants to complete two or more target behavior selection checklists correctly
4. To enable participants to accurately observe and record a target behavior

Content

1. Models of causation of human behavior
2. Principles of behavior modification
3. Overview of the behavior change process
4. Selecting a target behavior
5. Observing and recording a target behavior

Instructional methods

1. Lecture
2. Discussion

3. Demonstration

4. Completion of a target behavior selection checklist

5. Recording the target behavior rate or frequency

Activities

1. Segment A (40 minutes)

   (a) Introduction of the educator and individual participants

   (b) Overview of the course organization and content

   (c) Brief lecture on contemporary theories of causation of human behavior

   (d) Brief lecture or overview of the behavior change process

   (e) Lecture on the principles of behavior modification; each participant requested to cite a personal example of each principle (may be written)

   (f) Examples of target behaviors presented and explanation of the target behavior selection process; demonstration of how to complete a target behavior selection checklist; each participant requested to select a target behavior and complete a target behavior selection checklist

   (g) Procedures for observing and recording target behaviors presented, exemplified, and discussed

2. Break (10 minutes)

3. Segment B (40 minutes)

   (a) Target Behavior 1 (home behavior)

      (1) Each participant (or mother and father) presents to the group the target behavior selected during the psychosituational assessment interview of the course preparation phase. Participants also present and discuss the data that they recorded on the behavior log form.

      (2) Each participant completes a target behavior selection checklist on Target Behavior 1.

      (3) Each participant transfers the data on the behavior log form to an appropriate tally form (see Table 4.2).

Resources

1. Segment A

   (a) Parent educator and individual participants

   (b) Chapter 9: Preparation phase of program and lesson titles

   (c) Chapter 2: Models of human behavior

   (d) Chapter 4: Entire chapter

   (e) Chapter 3: Principles of reinforcement

(f) Chapter 4: Selecting a target behavior; target behavior selection checklist (back of text)

(g) Chapter 4: Collecting and recording baseline data

2. Break
3. Segment B
   (a) Target Behavior 1
      (1) Behavior log form (back of text)
      (2) Target behavior selection checklist (back of text)
      (3) Chapter 4: Collecting and recording baseline data

Evaluation

1. Quiz on written examples of the principles of reinforcement
2. Completed behavior log form, target behavior selection checklist, and tally form

Home Assignment

1. Observe and record baseline data on Target Behavior 1
2. Read:
   (a) Chapter 3: Consequences of behavior; schedules of reinforcement
   (b) Chapter 4: Collecting and recording baseline data

The following are suggested subsequent lesson titles:

Lesson 2: Consequences of behavior

Lesson 3: Selecting effective reinforcers

Lesson 4: Strategies to increase behavior, part I

Lesson 5: Strategies to increase behavior, part II

Lesson 6: Strategies to decrease behavior, part I

Lesson 7: Srategies to decrease behavior, part II

Lesson 8: Ethical and effective application

HOME-SCHOOL COLLABORATION

During the implementation phase of a home-school behavior change intervention, the parents and educator need to communicate precisely and frequently to ensure the integrity of the program. Although it is possible to use telephone conversations and handwritten notes to communicate, the parents and teacher may find these methods imprecise and inordinately demanding of time.

In this section, several aids to parent-teacher collaboration that appear to minimize inconvenience for both parties are presented.

Passport

Courson and Hay (1996) and Schmalz (1987) recommended a home-school notebook for parents and teachers who wished to communicate on a daily basis on the behavior of the student in both home and school. The *passport* (Runge, Walker, & Shea, 1975) is an effective technique for increasing and maintaining parent-teacher communication and cooperation.

The passport is an ordinary spiral notebook that the child carries daily to and from home and to and from the classrooms in which the child is instructed. The passport is a medium for communications among parents, special teachers, regular teachers, paraprofessionals, bus drivers, and others concerned with the child's behavior change or academic remediation program. All concerned adults are encouraged to make notations in the notebook.

Before the actual initiation of a behavior change program, the passport procedures are explained to the child, who is told that he or she will be rewarded for carrying the notebook and presenting it to the appropriate adults.

The child is rewarded with points for carrying the passport and for appropriate efforts, accomplishments, and behavior in the home, in the classroom, on the bus, in the gym, and so on. Points may be awarded at home for appropriate behavior and home-study activities. If the child forgets or refuses to carry the passport, he or she cannot earn points. At the appropriate time, the accumulated points are exchanged for tangible as well as social rewards.

Most elementary school students respond enthusiastically to carrying the passport, receiving points and awards, and reading the comments written about their behavior and achievement by adults.

Parents are introduced to the passport concept and procedures at an evening meeting. At this meeting, the method is explained and discussed. Parents' questions and concerns must be appropriately responded to by the teacher. At this session, instructions for making notations in the passport are given. Similar meetings or informal discussions should be held with other adults who will be using the passport, such as classroom teachers, special teachers, administrators, bus drivers, and so on.

The guidelines for writing comments in the passport are as follows:

1. Be brief. (Parents are busy, too.)
2. Be positive. (Parents know their child has problems. They do not need to be reinforced.)
3. Be honest. (Do not say a child is doing fine if he is not. However, rather than writing negative notes, write neutral ones or request a parent visit.)
4. Be responsive. (If a parent asks for help, respond immediately.)
5. Be informal. (You are a professional, but parents are still your equal.)

6. Be consistent. (If you use the passport, do so consistently and expect the same from the parents.)

7. Avoid jargon. (Parents do not understand educators' jargon. For that matter, do we?)

8. Be careful. (If you are having a bad day, personally, do not project your feelings onto the child or his parents.)*

Points are awarded to the child on the basis of a mutually agreed-on reinforcement schedule and rate. The procedures applied in the passport are similar to those presented in the section on the token economy in Chapter 5. Points are recorded on a point card similar to those presented in that section. The card is usually affixed to the inside of the front or back cover of the notebook.

Examples of the types of notations to be made in the passport are presented in Figures 9.2 and 9.3. The first set of examples involves an exchange of information among an elementary school teacher, a bus driver, a physical education teacher, and the child's parents. The second set of examples involves an exchange between an elementary school teacher and parents.

Daily Report Cards

It is generally true that report cards or grades issued periodically by elementary and secondary schools (and universities) have positive effects on student performance. It is also true that this positive effect is of short duration. During our years as secondary school and university teachers, it became obvious that students study more and behave better in the few weeks immediately before and after report cards or grades are issued. Unfortunately, this high level of student performance does not persist during those times when report card issuance is not imminent (Kroth & Otteni, 1985).

It would appear that acceptable levels of student performance, both academic and behavioral, can be maintained if feedback on performance is provided frequently to the student and parents. This proposition has led to several efforts to explore the use of *daily report cards* with nondisabled children and children with disabilities at various grade levels (Dickerson, Spellman, Larsen, & Tyler; 1973; Fairchild, 1987; Powell, 1980).

Edlund (1969) designed and implemented a daily reporting system that uses rewards available in the home to improve children's school performance. The system focuses on both academic performance and social-personal behavior.

Edlund's daily report card system is introduced to the parents during individual and small-group sessions. In these sessions, parents are introduced to the principles and procedures of behavior modification as applied in the reporting system. Specific attention is given to the daily checklist, principles of reinforcement, selecting rewards, and the application of the Premack principle. This initial education is followed up throughout the program by means of weekly parent-professional conferences or telephone communication.

---

* From "A Passport to Positive Parent-Teacher Communications" by A. Runge, J. Walker, & T. M. Shea, 1975. *Teaching Exceptional Children, 7*(3), pp. 91–92. Copyright 1975 by The Council for Exceptional Children, 1920 Association Drive, Reston, VA 22091. Reprinted by permission.

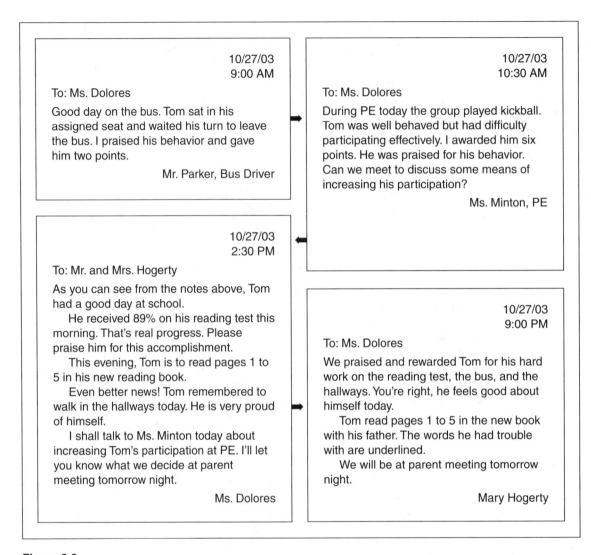

Figure 9.2
Sample passport notations between school staff and parents

Before the daily reporting system is implemented, baseline data are gathered by the educator and/or parents on the child's academic performance and social-personal behaviors. Using the baseline data, the reporting system is individualized for the child as a response to his or her particular learning or behavior problems.

Children earn points for completing academic assignments and for acceptable school behavior. Points are recorded on a checklist. Although not presented here, Edlund designed three checklists: (a) a report for academic performance only, (b) a report of personal-social behavior only, and (c) a composite report such as that presented in Figure 9.4.

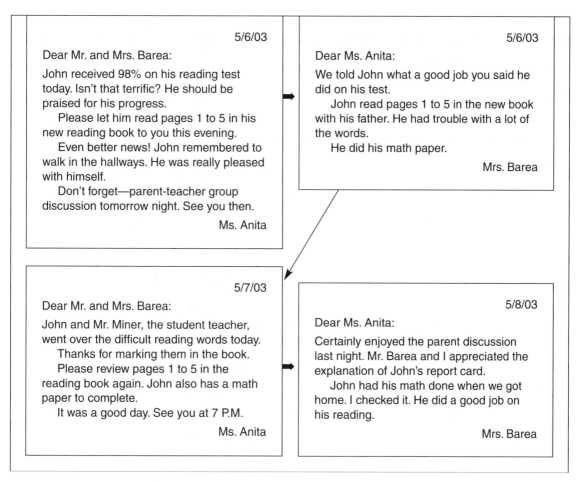

Figure 9.3
Sample passport notations between parents and teachers

The teacher awards points in the form of check marks at the end of predetermined periods of time or activities throughout the day. At the end of the day, the teacher reviews the child's checklist and initials it. The checklist is taken home by the child and reviewed by the parents, who initial it. The child returns the checklist to the teacher the following day. If a child fails to take the checklist home, he or she cannot be rewarded.

Rewards for school performance are given to the child at home during the afternoon and evening hours. The rewards are individualized. Care is taken to ensure that the child receives only those rewards that are earned and that are meaningful to him or her. A child who fails to earn rewards is assigned undesirable tasks at home, such as housekeeping chores, yard work, homework, and so on. Special rewards are given to a child for a "perfect day" or several perfect days.

Composite Academic Performance and Personal-Social Behavior Report

DAILY REPORT CHECKLIST

Child's Name _____

	Reading		Spelling		Arithmetic		Health		Social Studies		PE		Initials	
	Acad	Beh	Acad	Beh	Acad	Beh	Acad	Beh	Acad	Beh	Acad	Beh	Parent	Teacher
M														
T														
W														
Th														
F														
M														
T														
W														
Th														
F														
M														
T														
W														
Th														
F														

Figure 9.4
Composite behavior checklist

After several weeks of acceptable academic performance and/or behavior, the reward system is phased out over a period of days or weeks.

Edlund concluded that his daily report card system did improve the children's academic performance and acceptable social-personal behavior. He noted that the desirable behavior continued after the rewards were discontinued. The children learned to respond to the verbal praise and social recognition provided by parents and teachers, which naturally occurred as a result of their high level of performance.

The Edlund daily report card system has been applied successfully with children from kindergarten to high school. It has been used successfully with children classified as emotionally disturbed, mentally retarded, disruptive, school phobic, truant, economically deprived, and culturally different.

The *Teacher-Parent Communication Program (TPCP),* a daily report card system, was developed by Dickerson et al. (1973). This cooperative parent-teacher communication system is designed to help children improve their in-school academic performance and social behavior in exchange for rewards at home.

During a 4-year period, the TPCP was used with more than 1,000 children, ages 5 to 15 years, in regular and special education settings. Although Dickerson and others do not view the program as a "cure-all," it was reported by teachers who used it as effective in modifying social behavior and academic performance.

The TPCP centers around report cards issued by the teacher to the child periodically throughout the school day. The completed cards are taken home at the end of the school day. On the basis of the information on the cards, the parents either reward or do not reward the child's performance. Example report cards are presented in Figures 9.5 and 9.6.

The cards have a space for the teacher's evaluation of the child's academic performance and social behavior. The teacher may make notations on the back of the card if desired. Dickerson et al. recommend that the teacher's notations be neutral and positive. The cards are dated and signed by the teacher.

Although not included on the TPCP card, it may be helpful if the card provided space for the parent's signature and notations. The card could be returned to the

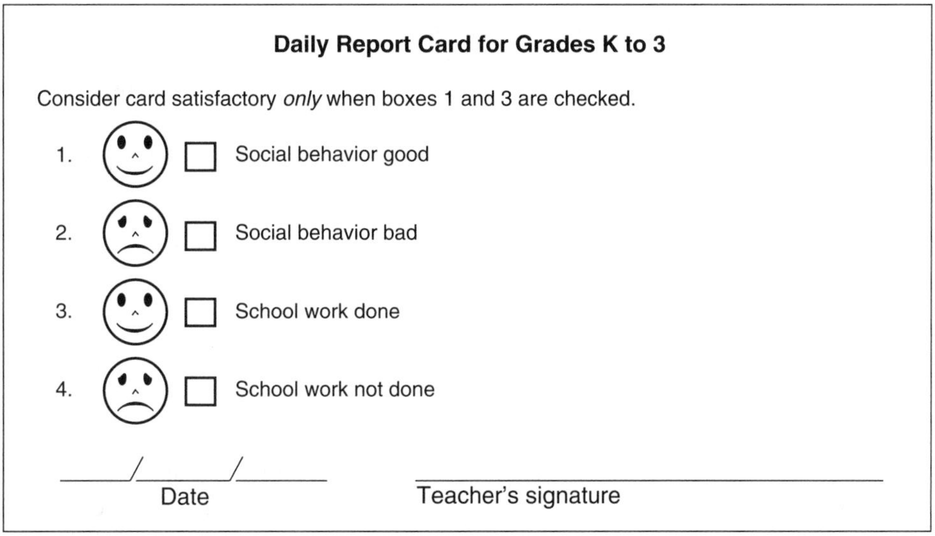

Daily Report Card for Grades K to 3

Consider card satisfactory *only* when boxes 1 and 3 are checked.

1. ☐ Social behavior good
2. ☐ Social behavior bad
3. ☐ School work done
4. ☐ School work not done

_____/_____/_____   _____
Date   Teacher's signature

Figure 9.5
Daily report card

Source. From "Let the cards do the talking-a teacher-parent communication program" by D. Dickerson, C. R. Spellman, S. Larsen, & L. Tyler. *Teaching Exceptional Children,* 4(4), 1973, pp. 170–178. Copyright 1973 by The Council for Exceptional Children. Reprinted with permission.

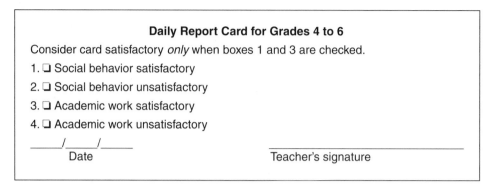

Figure 9.6
Daily report card

Source. From "Let the cards do the talking-a teacher-parent communication program" by D. Dickerson, C. R. Spellman, S. Larsen, & L. Tyler. *Teaching Exceptional Children,* 4(4), 1973, pp. 170–178. Copyright 1973 by The Council for Exceptional Children. Reprinted with permission.

teacher on the following school day by the child. Such a procedure would ensure that the parents received the card, that the child was rewarded, and that both parents and teacher were attending to the appropriate objectives.

The cards are issued to the child approximately every 40 minutes throughout the school day. At the end of the day, the child usually has 10 completed cards to take home.

Although not included in the Dickerson program, it may be desirable to provide space on the card for identification of the activity in which the child participated during the various time periods. This procedure would help the parents identify more precisely the child's problem subjects and situations. It may also be helpful to both parents and teacher if a master card were developed that presented "at a glance" the totals of the child's 10 daily cards.

With few exceptions, the TPCP cards are not acceptable for rewards unless both social behavior and academic performance are checked as acceptable by the teacher. Thus, a child who behaves appropriately but fails to do his work acceptably is not rewarded. The reverse of this is also true; that is, a child who completes his work but behaves inappropriately is not rewarded.

The presentation of rewards at home is based on the number of acceptable cards the child earns during the school day. The number of cards needed for a reward is initiated at the child's present level of functioning. This performance level is mutually agreed on by parent and teacher. As the child's overall level of performance improves, the number of acceptable cards needed for rewards is systematically increased.

If an acceptable number of cards is earned, the child is praised and encouraged by the parent. The child is permitted to engage in rewarding activities, for example, a later bedtime hour, television viewing, and the like. Special rewards are available for exceptional performance. If the child fails to earn the acceptable number of daily report cards, after-school and evening activities are restricted, or the child is assigned undesirable tasks, such as yard work, housekeeping tasks, homework, and the like.

TPCP Conference Checklist

CHECKLIST OF MAJOR POINTS COVERED IN PARENT ORIENTATION CONFERENCE

1. Ten cards will be sent home each day whether academic work is done or not.
2. One bad check makes a card unacceptable.
3. Cards must be signed by the teacher and free of erasures and extra marks.
4. The minimum number of good cards necessary to earn privileges should be explained.
5. The number of acceptable cards will be increased sometime in the future.
6. The program will at first emphasize the quantity of work and later the quality of work.
7. The backs of the cards should always be examined for notations.
8. Weekend bonuses may be earned for each week the specified number of good cards has been earned.
9. After-school and evening activities should be a direct result of performance in school.
10. Cards not received at home should be counted as unacceptable.
11. Cards should be reviewed with the child as soon as he or she arrives home.
12. The cards should be counted each day.
13. Praise and encourage the child for earning the acceptable number of good cards.
14. *Let the cards do the talking.*

Figure 9.7
Parent orientation for daily report cards

The TPCP is initiated by the teacher, who solicits the parents' cooperation and participation. During an orientation conference, the teacher explains the program to the parents. The purpose and benefits of the TPCP for the child are discussed. The teacher outlines the duties and responsibilities of the child, parent, and teacher. Dickerson et al. prepared the checklist in Figure 9.7 to facilitate parent orientation. The checklist ensures that all elements of the daily reporting system are reviewed.

After the parents and teacher agree to implement the TPCP, the teacher informs the child and makes him or her aware of the parents' participation. The child is given instructions concerning the purpose, objectives, and functioning of the system. The child is encouraged to participate in the process of determining his or her initial acceptable performance level and rewards.

The designers of the TPCP recommend that the daily report card system remain in force as long as the child needs it. However, after several weeks of acceptable performance by the child, the teacher, in cooperation with the parents, should begin to phase out the TPCP. Presumably, the rewards for a high level of academic performance and social behavior that naturally occur in the child's school behavior and home environments will maintain the acceptable performance levels without the TPCP.

In *It's Absolutely Groovy* (Kaplan & Hoffman, 1990), and *It's Positively Fun* (Kaplan, Kohfeldt, & Sturla, 1974), a variety of certificates, award forms, and other unique forms are presented. Many of these forms can be used in daily report card programs. The authors provide a brief outline for planning and implementing a daily home-school communication program. These texts are excellent references for professionals wishing to implement a daily report card system.

Kroth, Whelan, and Stables (1970) presented a parent-teacher communication system that included a daily reporting program as an integral part of a behavior modification intervention. This system provides several specific guidelines for professionals desiring a daily reporting system to focus primarily on student behavior.

The purpose of the daily report card system is to improve parent-professional communication for the benefit of the child. Attention is focused on both social-personal behavior and academic performance.

Teachers wishing to implement a daily report card program should consider several characteristics of the systems presented and individualize these characteristics in response to the needs of the children and parents with whom they work.

The mechanism used for reporting (communicating) should be specific and easy to complete. Complex mechanisms requiring extensive time and energy inhibit the conduct and effectiveness of the program.

The daily report card program should accentuate the child's positive social-personal behavior and/or academic performance. The child should be rewarded for attaining the mutually agreed-on objectives of the program and ignored if the objectives are not attained. Punishment should be avoided.

Both parents and teachers must remain cognizant of the fact that the conduct of a daily report card program is a shared responsibility. If either teacher or parents fail to meet their responsibilities, the program's effectiveness is inhibited.

Everton and Heshusius (1985) developed a weekly reporting system that they found to be effective in application with mainstreamed secondary school students. The system was recommended for communication among resource teachers, regular teachers, and parents. An additional benefit of this system was that it provided frequent feedback to the students on their performance.

◆ SUMMARY

In this chapter, a method that may be applied by the educator interested in educating parents in behavior modification procedures and principles is presented. The program is designed primarily to increase parental knowledge and skill in the application of behavior modification techniques. The education program also has the potential to increase parent-teacher collaboration. Although not a primary objective of the program, parents are provided a setting in which they may receive emotional support as they struggle with their child's problem.

◆ PROJECTS

1. Write a 300-word essay on the topic "Parent Education and Education: A Significant Component of the School Service Program."

2. List 25 home reinforcers not presented in this chapter. Classify these as social or tangible.

3. Conduct a psychosituational assessment interview in which a classmate plays the role of a parent. Record and analyze the interview.

4. Obtain, study, and write a report for verbal presentation to your class on one of the checklists and inventories listed in the chapter. As part of the verbal presentation, demonstrate to the group the administration of the instrument.

♦ REFERENCES

Bauer, A. M., & Shea, T. M. (2003). Parents and Schools: Creating a successful partnership for students with special needs. Upper Saddle River, NJ: Merrill/Prentice Hall.

Beale, A., & Beers, C. S. (1982). What do you say to parents after you say hello? *Teaching Exceptional Children, 15*(1), 34–38.

Bersoff, D. N., & Grieger, R. M., II. (1971). An interview model for the psychosituational assessment of children's behavior. *American Journal of Orthopsychiatry, 41*(3), 483–493.

Blackham, G. J., & Silberman, A. (1980). *Modification of child and adolescent behavior* (3rd ed.). Belmont, CA: Wadsworth.

Bronfenbrenner, U. (1977). Toward an experimental ecology of human development. *American Psychologist, 32,* 513–531.

Clements, J. E., & Alexander, R. N. (1975). Parent training: Bringing it all back home. *Focus on Exceptional Children, 7*(5), 1–12.

Courson, F. H., & Hay, G. H. (1996). Parents as partners. *Beyond Behavior, 7*(3), 19–23.

Croft, D. J. (1979). *Parents and teachers: A resource book for home, school, and community relations.* Belmont, CA: Wadsworth.

Dickerson, D., Spellman, C. R., Larsen, S., & Tyler, L. (1973). Let the cards do the talking—a teacher-parent communication program. *Teaching Exceptional Children, 4*(4), 170–178.

Dunst, C. J., Trivette, C. M., & Deal, A. G. (1988). *Enabling and empowering families: Principles and guidelines for practice.* Cambridge, MA: Brookline Books.

Edlund, C. V. (1969). Rewards at home to promote desirable school behavior. *Teaching Exceptional Children, 1*(4), 121–127.

Ehly, S. W., Conoley, J. C., & Rosenthal, D. (1985). *Working with parents of exceptional children.* St. Louis: Mosby.

Everton, J., & Heshusius, L. (1985). Feedback on secondary mainstreaming. *Teaching Exceptional Children, 17*(3), 223–224.

Fairchild, T. N. (1987). The daily report card. *Teaching Exceptional Children, 19*(2), 72–73.

Gardner, W. I. (1974). *Children with learning and behavior problems: A behavior management approach.* Boston: Allyn & Bacon.

Gordon, S. (1976). A parent's concerns. *The Exceptional Parent, 6*(3), 19–22.

Graziano, A. M., & Diament, D. M. (1992). Parent behavioral training: An examination of the paradigm. *Behavior Modification, 16*(1), 3–38.

Jogis, J. L. (1975). To be spoken sadly. In L. Buscaglia (Ed.), *The disabled and their parents: A counseling challenge.* Thorofare, NJ: Charles B. Stack.

Kaplan, P. G., & Hoffman, A. G. (1990). *It's absolutely groovy.* Denver: Love Publishing.

Kaplan, P., Kohfeldt, J., & Sturla, K. (1974). *It's positively fun: Techniques for managing learning environments.* Denver: Love Publishing.

Karnes, M. B., & Zehrbach, R. R. (1972). Flexibility in getting parents involved in the school. *Teaching Exceptional Children, 5*(1), 6–19.

Kratoville, B. L. (1975a). What parents feel. In L. Buscaglia (Ed.), *The disabled and their parents: A counseling challenge.* Thorofare, NJ: Charles B. Stack.

Kratoville, B. L. (1975b). What parents need to hear. In L. Buscaglia (Ed.), *The disabled and their parents: A counseling challenge.* Thorofare, NJ: Charles B. Stack.

Kroth, R. L., & Otteni, H. (1985). *Communicating with parents of exceptional children: Improving parent-teacher relationships* (2nd ed.). Denver: Love Publishing.

Kroth, R. L., Whelan, R. J., & Stables, J. M. (1970). Teacher application of behavior principles in home and classroom environments. *Focus on Exceptional Children, 1*(3), 1–10.

McDowell, R. L. (1976). Parent counseling: The state of the art. *Journal of Learning Disabilities, 9*(10), 614–619.

Powell, T. H. (1980). Improving home-school communication: Sharing daily reports. *The Exceptional Parent, 10*(5), 824–826.

Ross, A. O. (1964). *The exceptional child in the family: Helping parents of exceptional children.* New York: Grune & Stratton.

Runge, A., Walker, J., & Shea, T. M. (1975). A passport to positive parent-teacher communications. *Teaching Exceptional Children, 7*(3), 91–92.

Schmalz, N. (1987). Home-school notebook: How to find out what your child did all day. *The Exceptional Parent, 17*(6), 18–19, 21–22.

Seligman, M. (1979). *Strategies for helping parents of exceptional children: A guide for teachers.* New York: The Free Press.

Shea, T. M., & Bauer, A. M. (1985). *Parents and teachers of exceptional students: A handbook for involvement.* Boston: Allyn & Bacon.

Shea, T. M., & Bauer, A. M. (1987). *Teaching children and youth with behavior disorders* (2nd ed.). Upper Saddle River, NJ: Prentice Hall.

Shea, T. M., & Bauer, A. M. (1991). *Parents and teachers of children with exceptionalities: A handbook for collaboration* (2nd ed.). Boston: Allyn & Bacon.

Shea, T. M., Whiteside, W. R., Beetner, E. G., & Lindsey, D. L. (1974). *Microteaching module: Psychosituational interview.* Edwardsville: Southern Illinois University Press.

Stigen, G. (1976). *Heartaches and handicaps: An irreverent survival manual for parents.* Palo Alto, CA: Science & Behavior Books.

Susser, P. (1974). Parents and partners. *The Exceptional Parent, 4*(3), 41–47.

Winton, P. (1986). Effective strategies for involving families in intervention efforts. *Focus on Exceptional Children, 19*(2), 1–12.

Issues and Concerns in Behavior Management

◆ CHAPTER OBJECTIVES

After completing this chapter, you will be able to do the following:

1. Describe recent practices in school service delivery systems.

2. Discuss the potential impact of students from diverse ethnic, cultural, and linguistic groups on behavior management.

3. Discuss the potential impact of students at risk for behavior problems.

4. Describe continua of behavior management interventions.

5. Explain behavior management as prevention.

◆ ◆ ◆

Mr. Ledger is the teacher of 26 inner-city, streetwise 10th-grade adolescents. He is having little success teaching the subjects (consumer education and practical mathematics) outlined on the city curriculum guide for the 10th grade. In his opinion, very little, if any, formal learning takes place in his classroom. Each school day is filled with verbal and physical aggression among the students. Mr. Ledger is in constant fear for his physical safety. He is anxious throughout the day and emotionally fatigued when he arrives home in the evening.

Although he dislikes his present work assignment, he enjoys teaching. However, he has contemplated leaving the profession for employment in business. Mr. Ledger is desperate for some way to manage his classroom.

As usual on Friday after school, Mr. Ledger joins a group of other teachers for a little relaxation and libation at Archie's Place before going home. The conversation turns to behavior problems and behavior management. Several of Mr. Ledger's colleagues, who are more effective classroom managers than he, offer a variety of interventions they apply with success.

Ms. Weeping relates; "I scream at them. I can outshout them. If all else fails, I cry."

Mr. Scrooge comments; "Why bother? You can't teach them anything anyway. I'm just sitting on the lid of the dumpster."

Ms. Dupuis suggested; "Just use the discipline code. They're out of my room and in the principal's office."

Ms. Fox states; "I don't fool with them. It's in the door—shut up—get to work—and out the door. No discussion, no questions, no group work, and no jokes—no nothing."

As Mr. Ledger sat in the subway on his way home, he reviewed his colleagues' suggestions. Which, if any, should he use with his students? How to decide?

Ms. Jan was employed as a teacher in a private facility of elementary school-aged children with severe emotional/behavioral disorders. Although she enjoyed her work and believed she was an effective teacher, she was concerned about one of the interventions her supervisors ordered her to implement. Although they had discussed the intervention and Ms. Jan's professional reasons for viewing it as inappropriate and unethical, the supervisor remained adamant about its use.

The intervention was "extinction"—ignoring the head-slapping behavior of Tyrone. Tyrone slapped the sides of his head on an average of 61 times an hour during the school day. He slapped himself with such force that the hair on the side of his head had been pulled out and his temples were swollen and severely bruised.

Ms. Jan recognized that she must do something. But what? She needed her job, and she needed a positive recommendation from her supervisor if she were to be considered for her annual pay raise.

Prior to implementing the interventions presented in this text, the educator is encouraged to carefully study the issues and concerns discussed in this chapter. In the first section of the chapter, the practitioner is urged to apply an integrative framework or perspective of behavior management rather than strategies based in a single theoretical perspective. Next, the chapter reviews educational issues that impact on behavior management. These include inclusion, prereferral interventions, homework, and positive behavioral support. In addition, dealing with aggressive and resistant students is discussed.

Next, two groups of children who may become involved in behavior problems in school are discussed. The first group are children from diverse ethnic, cultural, and linguistic groups, that is, African American, Asian American, Native American, Hispanic, and Appalachian. The practitioner is urged to become familiar with the cultural background and experiences of these children. The second group of children who are prone to behavior problems are children of divorce, children of poverty, children who are maltreated, children suffering from prenatal exposure to drugs and alcohol, and children in substitute care. The chapter concludes with discussions of continua of behavior management interventions and behavior management as prevention.

INTEGRATIVE FRAMEWORK AND BEHAVIOR MANAGEMENT

The *integrative framework*, introduced in Chapter 2, offers the teacher a way to organize existing perspectives of human behavior, its etiology, and its management for implementation in the classroom and school. The integrative perspective is an ecological model that stresses that the understanding of human development and behavior requires examination of the ecological contexts (see Figure 2.6) in which the individual is functioning and is an inseparable part.

According to Jones (1986), the use of behavior management interventions tends to be recursive. In the 1940s and 1950s, classroom management interventions from the biophysical perspective were dominant. Intervention emphasized the reduction of extraneous environmental stimuli, routine, drill, and the careful sequencing of instruction. In the 1960s, the psychoeducational perspective dominated behavior management. Emphasis was on counseling, individualized interventions, inferring the reasons for behavior, and positive and productive interpersonal relations. This period was followed by a behavior management perspective that emphasized behavioral and learning theory. During this period, emphasis was placed on precise behavioral and instructional objectives and persistent and consistent intervention in students' observable behaviors. Organization and management skills and individual and group reinforcement of appropriate behavior were emphasized.

With the application of the ecological framework, there is a movement from the traditional emphasis on a single approach to the management of behavior to an integration of the biophysical, psychoeducational, and behavioral perspectives. In the ecological perspective, learning principles are applied (behavioral), with consideration of interpersonal relationships (psychoeducational) and with recognition of the impact of neurological and physical factors (biophysical) on children's behavior (Shea & Bauer, 1994).

According to Bauer and Sapona (1991), the role of the teacher in behavior management is to facilitate the development of each student rather than simply to intervene in inappropriate behavior.

Pinnell and Galloway (1987) outline the following in their discussion of behavior management from an ecological perspective:

- Teachers must recognize that students make a significant contribution to the educational process.
- Learning occurs when students feel a need to change or learn.
- Learning is holistic rather than a series of individual pieces of information or skills.
- Teachers must recognize the power of the social context of the classroom on learning.
- Teachers must develop a personal understanding of learning and development.
- Teachers must care about what takes place in their classrooms.

To effectively use the ecological perspective of behavior management suggested in this text, "teachers, then, must relate to students as capable persons, able to make choices and manage their own behavior. More specifically, they must trust in their students' abilities" (Shea & Bauer, 1994, p. 45).

EDUCATIONAL ISSUES THAT IMPACT ON BEHAVIOR MANAGEMENT

In the following section, issues that impact on behavior management are discussed. The discussion begins with inclusion, prereferral interventions, and positive behavioral support. The section continues with discussions of homework (a perennial issue for parents, students, and teachers) and working with students who are aggressive or resistant.

Inclusion

Inclusion is the philosophy that all students, regardless of disability, are a vital and integral part of the general education system. For these learners, special education services may be delivered inside or outside of general education classes but within the general education system. *Integration* refers to the placement of learners with disabilities in educational programs serving their peers.

According to Shea and Bauer (1994), the basic components of inclusion are as follows:

1. All students attend the school to which they would be assigned if they had no disability.
2. There are no more or no fewer learners with disabilities in a single school than would be found districtwide.
3. A zero-reject philosophy would be in place (that is, no student could be excluded from receiving educational services, regardless of disability).

4. Placements would be age and grade appropriate, with no self-contained special education classes.

5. Cooperative learning and peer instruction would be used in general instruction.

6. Special education supports would be provided in the integrated environment. (p. 448)

Lipsky and Gartner (1992) suggest that full implementation of the philosophy of inclusion requires the development of a "new" school or a reconceptualization of the construct "school" as it is presently understood.

In the inclusive school, students with mild disabilities would be served in general education classes. The general education teacher, however, may not be trained to instruct and manage the behavior of these learners without support. The general education teacher may be assisted through (a) peer collaboration and (b) consultation. In peer collaboration, teacher and peers engage in problem-solving activities on a case-by-case basis (Johnson & Pugach, 1991). As a team, they focus on the practical behavior management and academic problems of students. In the consultation process, the consultant works with the general education teacher through the processes of problem identification, intervention development and implementation, and evaluation (Johnson & Bauer, 1992).

Prereferral Interventions

Prereferral interventions (Graden, 1989; Graden, Casey, & Christenson, 1985, Shea & Bauer, 1994) are designed to assist general educators with the academic and behavior problems of specific students. The purpose of prereferral intervention is to assist the student in the regular classroom and to avoid identification as at risk for disabilities and referral to special education. According to Carter and Sugai (1989), 34 states recommend the implementation of prereferral interventions prior to referral for special education services.

Prereferral interventions are generally developed by a teacher assistance team through the process of collaborative consultation. The teacher assistance team is composed of school personnel (general and special education teachers, school nurse, psychologist, social worker, administrator) who assist each other in planning interventions to be implemented by the general education teacher. Teacher assistance teams are an excellent example of peer cooperation and collaborative problem solving.

There are several assumptions underlying the use of prereferral interventions (Pugach & Johnson, 1989). Prereferral activities are a function of general education, not special education. Collaborative consultation is a multidirectional activity in which all educational professionals within the school at various times serve as consultants to each other. General education teachers, given time and structure, are capable of solving classroom problems without the direct assistance of specialists. All problems do not require the same group of professionals to develop interventions, and that fluid membership in the prereferral team increases schoolwide commitment and involvement.

Positive Behavioral Support

The 1997 reauthorization of the Individuals with Disabilities Education Act (IDEA) mandates that the individualized education program team consider applying positive behavioral support (PBS) to address behaviors that impede a child's learning or the learning of others. Reauthorization requires that a functional behavioral assessment be conducted for the student, ensuring that the intervention plan is responsive to the student's individual needs (Bradley, 2001; Warger, 1999).

According to Fox, Dunlap, and Benito (2001), PBS is longitudinal and team based, involving school and family. Positive behavioral supports are continually adjusted to meet the student's changing needs and can become an essential factor in successfully including students in general education.

Unlike traditional management interventions that view the individual as the problem and strive to eliminate behaviors, PBS and functional behavioral assessment view systems, settings, and the lack of skills as part of the problem and work to modify these factors to support the student. From this perspective, long-term strategies are implemented to decrease inappropriate and unacceptable behavior, teach more appropriate behavior, and offer the contextual supports needed by the student for effective outcomes (Warger, 1999). Positive behavioral supports have several advantages, including the following:

- Being widely applicable to individuals with disabilities
- Contributing to the knowledge of how to use assessment as a basis for intervention and correct problems in the educational setting
- Being effective in reducing problem behaviors

Effective teachers often use many of the elements of PBS in their daily routines and management strategies. Effective teachers respond to the individual needs of students, alter environments to benefit their students, teach new skills, and respond to positive behaviors exhibited by students.

Effective behavioral support (EBS) is a systems approach to the application of PBS schoolwide (Lewis & Sugai, 1999). A team works systematically to solve problems and plan. The members of this team receive professional development in the areas of systems change and management principles and practices and the application of research-validated instructional and management practices throughout the school setting. The team works to secure a commitment to the EBS model, review the behavioral supports and practices in the school, and help develop plans to respond to unique student and staff needs.

There are three components to implementing EBS: schoolwide supports, non-classroom supports, and classroom supports. At the school level, components are consistent with best practices for schools. For example, there is a common approach to discipline, with the emphasis on teaching all students behavioral expectations and routines. Each school has (a) a mission, (b) schoolwide rules and expectations, (c) strategies for teaching and encouraging expected behaviors, (d) strategies for discouraging inappropriate behaviors, and (e) record-keeping practices. Scott and

Hunter (2001) state that administrator support and active involvement is essential to the success of a schoolwide support system.

Nonclassroom supports are an extension of the schoolwide system. In addition to responding to the needs of students outside the classroom (i.e., hallways, gym, cafeteria, library, office, bus), instruction is implemented to teach students the expectations for behavior in each setting. The team analyzes the specific settings and activities to assess the routines and physical characteristics of the settings and activities and to design appropriate supports.

The classroom system is also an extension of the schoolwide system. The systems overlap in order to (a) facilitate communication among students, staff, and parents; (b) increase the consistency with which behavior is handled in various school settings; and (c) ease transitions as students move from setting to setting. In order to support students, teachers use the following:

- Advance organizers
- Productive and authentic activities
- Consistent enforcement of school and classroom rules
- Consistent correction of rule violations and social interaction problems
- Planning and teaching of transition behavior

Because of the explicit nature of the management in these classrooms, the classroom support system is helpful to students at risk for behavior problems.

Individual support systems are used to offer immediate, relevant, effective, and efficient responses to students with significant behavior problems. This system is needed by a very small number of students (3% to 6%). Students who are in need of individual behavioral support are identified, and an easy procedure for teachers to request and receive assistance is in place. A functional behavioral assessment is conducted, and an individualized behavior support plan is implemented and monitored.

The greatest issue in implementing EBS is school and classroom climate. A significant shift from responding to negative behaviors to supporting positive behaviors must be made.

Homework

Homework is a shared activity of students, parents, and teachers. It is one of the traditional ways in which parents work with their children (Shea & Bauer, 1991). Both parents and teachers become discouraged when homework assignments are not completed or are misunderstood by the student and the parent. Horner (1987) suggested several reasons for this parent discouragement about homework. Children may experience failure at home similar to the failure experienced at school, frustrating parents, child, and teacher when the assignment is incorrect or not completed. In addition, parents may not have the required teaching skills or may be unable to apply them consistently. This may result in tension between parent and child. Parents may have personal time constraints, and the child may be deprived of time needed for leisure and relaxation. Finally, parents may feel guilty if they are unable to help their child.

Teachers may involve parents in four steps to make home assignments more successful. Thurston (1989) suggested that parents first be involved in the selection of materials, recognizing that parents are more comfortable practicing skills that the children have already learned rather than new materials. Next, the parents should be provided basic instruction in tutoring. Third, parents should be provided instruction in correcting errors with their children. Finally, parents should be instructed in record keeping.

In a nationwide survey of general education teachers, Epstein et al. (1997) affirmed earlier research that teachers perceive communication problems among teachers and parents as a serious impediment to the effective use of homework with students with disabilities. The authors reported little consensus among general education teachers regarding who has primary responsibility for planning, coordinating, and communicating to parents about homework. Data analysis suggested that general education teachers thought that serious homework communication problems exist in both the frequency and the quality of communication with parents about homework, parental attitudes about homework, the role of the special education teachers, the availability of teachers to communicate with parents about homework, and general education teacher knowledge of learning disabilities and homework strategies. These problems varied with school level, teacher experience, and teacher preparation in working with parents.

Homework in middle school has also been examined. Nelson, Epstein, Bursuck, Jayanthi, and Sawyer (1998) studied middle school students' preferences for various homework adaptations. Students were presented with 17 specific homework strategies in order to determine the reasons for their expressed preferences. Results of the study suggested that student preferences were not related to their learning or behavior disabilities or by their achievement. Rather, their reasons for adaptations they liked the most included their perceptions that particular adaptations would allow more time for other (e.g., extracurricular) activities or would make completion of homework easier. Students' reasons for adaptations they liked least included their belief that adaptations were unfair or would negatively affect their self-concept. Of the 17 suggested adaptations, the three most liked were the following:

- Assignments that are finished at school
- Opportunities for extra-credit assignments
- Grading assignments according to effort

The three least-liked adaptations were the following:

- Giving shorter assignments to students with learning disabilities than to other students
- Grading students with learning disabilities more leniently than other students
- Giving different assignments to students with learning disabilities

In three related studies conducted collaboratively with general and special education elementary teachers, Bryan and Sullivan-Burstein (1998) structured systematic strategies to improve spelling and mathematics homework completion and weekly quiz performance. Three strategies resulted in significant increases in homework completion: (a) giving students real-life assignments (i.e., assignments that connected homework to events or activities in the home) plus reinforcements, (b) using homework planners, and (c) graphing homework completion. The strategies benefited students with learning disabilities and average-achieving students with homework problems more than average-achieving students with no homework problems.

Students identified as having attention deficit disorders may struggle with completing their homework. Stormont-Spurgin (1997) offered several strategies for these students, with a particular emphasis on organization. These strategies include the following:

* Organize cooperative homework teams
* Implement contracts and positive reinforcement strategies
* Develop and implement routines and checklists with regard to homework
* Use assignment folders and daily planners
* Collaborate on homework assignments

Aggression and Resistance in School

During the past few years, student aggression, resistance, and antisocial behavior have increased significantly in classrooms and school (Myles & Simpson, 1998). Such behavior has come to the attention of the national media and as a result has become of great concern to many parents, teachers, administrators, and students. It is common to have security personnel in schools and on the school grounds. Students, their possessions, and their lockers are searched for various kinds of contraband. Here we explore these problems as they confront the general education and special education teacher.

Aggression is learned and maintained in a manner similar to other behaviors (Fitzsimmons, 1998). Fitzsimmons suggests that there are three essential elements in the development and modification of aggression: modeling, positive reinforcement, and negative reinforcement (these concepts are presented in Chapter 5). The aggressive student may be modeling the inappropriate and unacceptable behavior of others, including peers, teachers, administrators, parents, and siblings. In addition, others may reinforce the aggressive behavior of the student in the environment either wittingly or unwittingly. Finally, allowing the student to escape may negatively reinforce the student's aggression

Melloy (2000) described four types of aggressive and violent behavior: situational violence, relationship violence, predatory violence, and psychopathological violence. Situations and relationship violence are the most frequently found in school. Melloy suggests that the manifestation of acting-out aggressive behavior follows a prescribed cycle, namely, calm, trigger, agitation, acceleration, peak, deescalation, and recovery. Interventions imposed to change these behaviors may include social skills and self-management instruction.

The characteristics of the aggressive student include deficits in social information processing, poor impulse control, low frustration tolerance, limited ability to generate alternative responses to stress, and limited insight into the feelings of self and others. Aggressive students frequently lack the skills needed to respond effectively to frustration (Fitzsimmons, 1998). Among the variables that may have a negative impact are (a) disorganized or inconsistent teachers, (b) failure, (c) boredom, (d) lack of positive reinforcement, (e) irrelevant curriculum, (f) overexposure to punishment, and (g) feelings of powerlessness (Abrams & Segal, 1998).

Aggressive behavior is frequently the consequence of frustration. The stages of frustration and the appropriate teacher responses are as follows: (Abrams & Segal, 1998; Fitzsimmons, 1998; Myles & Simpson, 1998):

1. Anxiety: Student signs or uses other nonverbal cues to demonstrate his or her anxiety. At this stage, student behavioral changes are minor and may or may not be linked to an impending aggressive or violent act. The teacher must be alert to minor changes in the student's behavior. The appropriate response by the teacher includes active listening, nonjudgmental talk, and surface behavior management strategies (review these concepts in Chapter 7).

2. Stress: The student may exhibit a minor change in behavior. The surface management techniques of proximity control, interest boosting, and hurdle helping are recommended.

3. Defensiveness: At this stage, the student may complain or argue with the teacher. Inappropriate behaviors include verbally or physically lashing out or threatening the teacher or other students or withdrawing physically or emotionally. Among the interventions the teacher may implement are (a) reminding the student of the rules and routines of the classroom, (b) applying conflict resolution strategies, (c) acknowledging the student's difficulties and encouraging him or her to request assistance, and (d) redirecting the student to another activity.

4. Physical aggression: The student loses control and may engage in a variety of behaviors, including hitting, biting, kicking, and throwing objects. The target of these behaviors may be other students, the teacher, or the setting. When physical aggression occurs, teachers should move other students to a safe place and physically escort the aggressive student from the classroom. If this is not possible, the teacher should ask for assistance.

5. Tension reduction and regaining self-control: The student generally releases his or her anger by verbally venting or crying. The student will become sullen and withdrawn. At this stage, the teacher must decide whether punishment or supportive intervention is appropriate. Regardless, the student must be helped to gain insight into his or her feelings and behaviors. This final stage is an essential teaching and learning time.

The most effective response to the potential for aggressive behavior in the classroom and school is prevention. School personnel should plan and have in place primary, secondary, and tertiary preventive strategies (Walker, 1998). Primary prevention is designed to prevent the problem from occurring and includes a nurturing, caring environment and curriculum to help students learn effective problem-solving, conflict resolution, and social skills. Secondary prevention strategies are available to respond to students who are at risk for violence and aggression and include, among other strategies, counseling and individualized behavior management planning and implementation. Tertiary prevention involves "wraparound services" that include the classroom, school, family, social agencies, and community services. Wraparound services are implemented to assist students who are at high risk for violence and aggression.

The therapeutic teacher is the best preventive measure for student aggressive and violent behavior (Abrams & Segal, 1998). Abrams and Segal suggest that the therapeutic teacher can manage the stress of working with students and create an environment that meets students' needs on several levels, reducing the frustration experiences by students in the classroom. The therapeutic teacher has good mental health and communicates respect, caring, and confidence in self and others, especially students. He or she displays enthusiasm for learning and positive expectations for students and creates a positive environment. The therapeutic teacher establishes trust and develops and maintains rapport with students. The teacher is nonthreatening and respects students' dignity. The teacher is a model of self-control. He or she is aware of and understands the stages of anxiety and frustration and is able to deescalate tension in the classroom.

Student noncompliance (i.e., refusal and resistance) is one of the most frustrating and time-consuming problems confronting teachers daily (Walker & Sylwester, 1998). Maag (2000) suggests that noncompliance is a "gateway" that leads to more serious forms of deviation. Guidelines for reducing noncompliance and consequently increase compliance are the following:

- Create a nurturing and caring environment that is characterized by cooperation and responsiveness to the needs of students.

- Focus on initiating action (i.e., completing activities) rather than on terminating action (i.e., not completing activities).

- Disengage if there is noncompliance and the difficulty is escalating. Reengage when the situation becomes calm.

- Review your own behavior. If the student's behavior is similar to yours, you may be aggravating the problem.

ETHNIC, CULTURAL, AND LINGUISTIC DIVERSITY

The general population of the United States is 80% Caucasian, 12% African American, 9% Hispanic, 3% Asian American, and less than 1% Native American. (The total exceeds 100% because Hispanic peoples may be of more than one race.) It is projected that during the first decade of the 21st century, one in three Americans will be members of a minority group (African American, Hispanic, or Asian American) (Yates, 1987). By 2020, if present trends continue, Hispanics will outnumber African Americans, and the Asian American population will quintuple, rising from 8 million to 41 million. Educators and schools are obligated to address the characteristics and needs of children representing minority groups through appropriate programming. Society, including its schools, must move toward a pluralism that represents *ethnic, cultural, and linguistic diversity* and permits members of such groups to continue to participate in their traditional customs while participating and contributing to society as a whole (Kochman, 1991).

There are five significant minority and ethnic groups in the United States. These are African American, Asian American, Native American, Hispanic, and Appalachian. Children from these groups bring to school unique characteristics and needs that impact on how they learn and behave. Teachers must be aware of these differences and respond to them appropriately.

Hispanics are learners of all races whose culture is tied to the Spanish language and the Latino culture (Fradd, Figueroa, & Correa, 1989). Hodgkinson (1985) projected that the Hispanic population would represent 47 million of the 265 million Americans by the year 2000. The Hispanic population is composed of several subgroups: Mexican American, Chicano, Puerto Rican, Cuban, and Central and South Americans. The customs of each group differ in some degree. Hispanic Americans tend to concentrate in urban areas and in isolated housing and schooling areas. According to Hyland (1989), Hispanic children are significantly behind the general population in achievement. Language represents a significant problem for some Hispanic children. Hispanic culture places emphasis on social cohesiveness, group or collective problem solving, and intellectual exchange rather than individual problem solving and competition.

Lockwood and Sacada (2000) report that nearly one of every three Hispanic students leave high school, in that they fail to believe that remaining in school will improve their lives. They contend that teachers should present content in ways that interest and challenge Hispanic students. The roles of language, race, culture, and gender should be recognized. Lockwood and Sacada recommend that schools use Hispanic parents as partners in their children's education, working together to envision a future for their students.

The African American population in the United States has remained between 10% and 12% since 1900. It is projected that there will be 35 million African Americans in the United States during the first decade of the 21st century (Allen & Majidi-Ahi, 1989). The lifestyles of African Americans vary greatly, but all confront the problems of racism, which impact motivation, self-confidence, and self-esteem (Peters, 1981). In the area of achievement, Hanna (1988) found that African American inner-city children considered academic book learning to be "white." In addition, she found that African American children who operated in a dual system of standard English dialect and black English vernacular carried a more demanding cognitive burden than individuals operating in a single language system in which fewer translations are necessary.

The Native American population, once estimated to be 10 million, is now between 1.5 and 1.8 million because of "cultural genocide" (LaFrambroise & Low, 1989). The Native American population of the United States is extremely diverse and includes 517 federally recognized entities or nations (196 in Alaska) and 36 state-recognized tribes.

SixKiller Clarke (2002) reports that many Native American youth confront frequent opportunities to participate in self-described illegal behaviors. Illicit drug use is far more common than among non-Indian peers. He reports a pattern of "reckless living" among Native American youth living in "Indian Country," demonstrated by the rate of death from motor vehicle accidents almost three times higher than that among their majority-culture peers. Suicide is the second leading cause of death, with a rate 2.5 times higher than that of all other races combined. For many families, the interruption of the transgenerational transmission of culture imposed by boarding school continues to have effects. In addition, some families feel alienated from mainstream education systems. "Assimilationist schooling" caused the weakening of native cultures and languages, marginalized the students' identities, alienated them from the goals of schooling, and produced high rates of leaving school while failing to produce good outcomes for the students who persisted (Lipka, 2002). The result is described as "subtractive bilingualism" (Lipka, 2002, p. 2), with many students failing to attain academic competence in English while losing knowledge of their native languages and culture (Deyhle & Swisher, 1997).

There are a relatively small number of schools that enroll large numbers of native students (Pavel, 1999). When working with native populations, teachers must empower students and prepare them to move comfortably among cultures while valuing their home, community, and heritage (Jacobs & Reyhner, 2002). Spirituality and reciprocity are essential parts of Native American learning. Most teachers, however, are not Native American and need to become acquainted with the spiritual traditions of the local families. Though they are unable to help students develop their native identity, they are able to honor the role and contribution of family members and tribal elders.

The Asian American population is composed primarily of Chinese Americans, Japanese Americans, and Southeast Asians. Chinese Americans were excluded from the United States through the Chinese Exclusion Act of 1882, which was the first legislation designed to exclude a particular minority group. This was followed by the Oriental Exclusion Act, which was passed by Congress 60 years later. From 1890 to 1945, more Chinese left the United States than entered. In the early 1900s, most states had laws that prevented Japanese Americans from marrying Caucasians. Until 1952, Japanese persons were not allowed to apply for American citizenship. During World War II, all persons of Japanese ancestry were removed from their homes, businesses, and communities on the west coast of the United States and placed in internment camps in the interior of the country.

The majority of the Southeast Asians in the United States today lived amid the extreme violence of war in their native land. They have experienced great personal loss, anxiety, and discontinuous education and health care. They have been torn from their native cultures and extended families, which were the center of life in their native land. The vast differences between American culture and the Asian Americans' native culture is frequently a barrier to learning. In addition, language is a barrier to learning for many Asian Americans.

Unlike many students from minority cultures, Asian Americans are usually stereotyped as successful and high achieving (Feng, 1994). Feng argues that this stereotype masks students' individualities and conceals real problems. The American emphasis on independence, individualism, and competition may be a considerable challenge to the traditional self-effacement of Asian culture.

Appalachians are a distinct but not easily recognized cultural group. They are individuals who were born, or whose ancestors were born, in a federally defined region of 397 counties and five independent cities in portions of 13 states, including New York, Pennsylvania, Maryland, Ohio, Virginia, West Virginia, Kentucky, Tennessee, North Carolina, South Carolina, Georgia, Alabama, and Mississippi (McCoy & Watkins, 1980).

Appalachian children appear not to understand the subtleties of language, such as indirect questions and commands. They tend to interrupt and speak out when the teacher is speaking (Heath, 1983).

This brief overview of the characteristics of the five largest minority groups in the United States is inadequate to prepare the educator to respond to all the academic and behavior problems that children from diverse cultures may present in the classroom and school. It is presented here to stimulate interest and further study.

STUDENTS AT RISK FOR BEHAVIOR PROBLEMS

There is a significant population of children and youth enrolled in the schools who are at risk for behavior problems. Among this group, in addition to students with disabilities, are children of divorce, children of poverty, children who have been maltreated, children suffering the effects of prenatal drug and alcohol exposure, and children living in substitute care.

It is essential that special and general education teachers be aware of the potential impact of these conditions on the behavior of students (Shea & Bauer, 1994). In this section, we briefly discuss the characteristics of *students at risk for behavior problems.*

In the United States, the frequency of divorce has increased to one in every two marriages. There is general agreement that divorce creates stress in children (Guidubaldi & Perry, 1985). In studies comparing divorce to other life crises, such as death, illness, and unemployment, Wallerstein and Blakeslee (1989) found that divorce more often involves anger. Parents seeking a divorce often give priority to their adult problems, which reduces their capacity to parent. The support system usually available to parents and children is less available during divorce because friends and relatives attempt to avoid the conflict within the child's immediate family. In a study of children experiencing and not experiencing divorce, Wiehe (1984) found that the children of divorce had poorer social and academic skills and lower self-esteem. In addition, these children viewed personal events as occurring outside their control and had more negative attitudes toward both their parents. The effects of divorce endure over time and are more evident in boys than girls. Boys exhibited externalizing behavior problems, such as fighting and inappropriate language, whereas girls demonstrated internalizing behavior problems, such as withdrawal and depression (Guidubaldi & Perry, 1985). Girls experienced more disruption than boys when the parents remarried (Hetherington, Cox, & Cox, 1985).

Guttman, Geva, and Gefen (1988) found that the knowledge that a child's parents are divorced has an adverse effect on evaluations of the child's academic, social, and emotional functioning. The stereotype "child of divorce" is present in the perceptions of both teachers and peers.

In 1985, according to the American Humane Association (1987), there were 2 million official reports of child maltreatment in the United States. In 1996, the National Committee to Prevent Child Abuse recorded 3.1 million calls with regard to child abuse in the United States. *Child maltreatment* is a generic term used to describe both child abuse and child neglect and refers to physical or mental injury, sexual abuse, or neglect of a child under the age of 18. In an extensive review of the literature, Youngblade and Belsky (1989) concluded that maltreatment is associated with dysfunctional parent-child relations, as evidenced by the likelihood that, during infancy, the child will form an insecure attachment for the maltreating parent. This insecure relationship may result in the child seeing him- or herself as unacceptable and unlovable. The child may be preoccupied with attachment concerns that interfere with the ability to adapt to the environment (Cicchetti, Toth, & Hennessy, 1989). Cicchetti et al. found that maltreated preschool children use proportionately fewer words to describe internal psychological states than their nonmaltreated peers and have a negative self-image that leaves them feeling less competent and less academically motivated. Maltreated children demonstrate more avoidance and aggressive behavior toward others than their peers. They demonstrate limited social skills and a greater frequency of withdrawal. In comparison to nonmaltreated peers, children who have been maltreated are more anxious, inattentive, and apathetic and depend more on their teachers for encouragement and approval. Crittenden (1989) found that maltreated children were more disruptive, defiant, and aggressive in interpersonal confrontations with peers and teachers. Conversely, children who have been maltreated may be so compliant and overly concerned with meeting the standards of others that they rarely experience joy of discovery or the satisfaction of achievement.

According to Crittenden (1989), the needs of children who have been maltreated are the following:

- To predict events in their environment to facilitate the organization of behavior

- To achieve desired objectives in socially acceptable ways

- To communicate openly with others and use developmentally appropriate language and cognitive skills

- To develop trust through carefully regulated, unambiguous, and consistent affective experiences

- To develop the self-confidence, self-motivation, and self-control needed to enjoy and benefit from the intellectual stimulation of educational programs

Children are said to be in *substitute care* when their primary caregivers are persons other than their biological parents. Substitute caregivers may be relatives, informal foster parents, licensed foster parents, adoptive families, or group home personnel (Shea & Bauer, 1994). Ideally, foster care is a planned, temporary service, and the child and biological family are reunited. Frequently, however, children remain in foster care for a long period of time and are moved from placement to placement until they reach majority.

According to Schor (1988), since 1983 the foster care population in the United States has grown in absolute size and contains a higher proportion of older children and children with disabilities. Today, foster children exhibit more serious physical and emotional problems than in the past.

The foster care population is composed of equal numbers of males and females, with 40% being from minority cultures. In addition, 25% of the population is disabled, and 75% is in foster care because of maltreatment. Children in foster care exhibit more frequent and serious health care problems than children living with their biological parents. These problems include chronic medical disorders, dental needs, prenatal exposure to drugs and alcohol, and congenital infections.

Baumeister, Kupstas, and Klindworth (1990) suggest that unless a significant effort is forthcoming, a "biological underclass" of children will emerge in America whose problems are related to poverty, lack of adequate and timely prenatal care, the prevalence of human immunodeficiency virus (HIV), and other chronic illnesses.

Parker, Greer, and Zuckerman (1988) state that the impact of poverty on children's development is "double jeopardy" because the factors of biologic vulnerability—secondary to prematurity, maternal depression, temperamental passivity, and inadequate environmental stimulation—and the insufficient social support available to the poor interact with each other.

According to Shea and Bauer (1994), when families become involved in substance abuse (drugs or alcohol), two things happen to children. The normal interactions that usually occur between parent and child do not occur because the parent is preoccupied with obtaining the substance of abuse. In addition, parents involved in substance abuse do not have the same priorities as other parents. They are concerned with getting and using their drugs of choice, not caring for children. Usually, the children are neglected and live in an unstable, dangerous environment. According to Weston, Ivins, Zuckerman, and Lopez (1989), maternal behavior associated with drug-induced mental disorders are seizures, paranoid and suicidal ideations, violent or aggressive behavior, harming self and others as a consequence of delusions, and impaired motor coordination.

There are two groups of children discussed in the remainder of this section. The first group is children exposed to cocaine, usually in the form of crack. The second group is children prenatally exposed to alcohol.

According to Frank et al. (1988), cocaine is reported to be associated with a greater risk of sexually transmitted diseases; the increased use of alcohol, tobacco, marijuana, and opiates; and the increased use of drugs during pregnancy. Cocaine used 1 or 2 days prior to delivery can be detected in the urine of the newborn child for as long as 96 hours after birth. Among the frequently reported characteristics of cocaine-exposed babies (*crack babies*) are low birth weight and growth retardation, which are related to delayed cognitive, motor, and perceptual performance (Harvey, Prince, Burton, Parkinson, & Campbell, 1982). Neurobehavioral abnormalities exhibited by cocaine-exposed babies include unexplained jitteriness, depression in interactive behaviors, and poor organizational responses to environmental stimuli. These children also exhibit physical abnormalities, such as small head size and malformed limbs. In addition, they are in the low average range on developmental scales (Howard, Beckwith, Rodning, & Kropenske, 1989). According to Dixon and Bejar (1989), there is great concern for cocaine-exposed children regarding abnormal neurologic, cognitive, and behavioral development as they approach school age.

There are two syndromes that are related to the effects on the child, in utero, of alcohol consumption by the mother: fetal alcohol syndrome and possible fetal alcohol effect. According to the Fetal Alcohol Study Group of the Research Society on Alcoholism, the symptoms of *fetal alcohol syndrome* are as follows (Rossett & Weiner, 1984):

1. Prenatal and/or postnatal growth retardations: weight, length, and/or head circumference below the 10th percentile when corrected for gestational age
2. Central nervous system involvement: signs of neurologic abnormality, developmental delay, or intellectual impairment
3. Common facial characteristics with at least two of these three symptoms: microcephaly, widely spaced eyes, poorly developed median groove between upper lip and nose, thin upper lip, or flattening of the jaw

It is suggested that if only one or two of the symptoms are evident and if the mother is suspected of alcohol use during pregnancy, then the diagnosis of *possible fetal alcohol effect* may be made (Abel, 1984).

According to Streissguth, Herman, and Smith (1978), among children prenatally exposed to alcohol, a significant relationship exists between physical symptoms and intellectual functioning. Spohr and Steinhausen (1987) found persistent distractibility and hyperactivity among these children.

Cooper (1987) noted a variety of school problems that are characteristic of central nervous system impairment. Children are characterized by a poor attention span, longer reaction times, and deficits in memory, problem solving, focusing and maintaining attention, and regulating impulsivity (Sampson, Streissguth, Barr, & Bookstein, 1989).

As part of a 4-year longitudinal study (Project SUCCESS) and to develop prevention strategies for application in the general education setting with at-risk elementary school students, Montague, Bergeron, and Lago-Delello (1997) studied a population of 103 students at moderate to high risk for behavior problems. The purpose of their research was to (a) identify students at risk for developing serious behavioral/emotional problems who had not been referred for special education services, (b) develop comprehensive interventions for identified students, and (c) evaluate students annually to ascertain their problems. During the study of classroom dynamics, they found that general education teachers behave differently toward the at-risk students than the not-at-risk students. The at-risk students experienced more teacher rejection, low teacher expectations, more negative and nonacademic teacher feedback, less academically engaged time, and fewer instructional accommodations in response to their learning and behavioral needs.

Montague et al. suggested several principles for teachers implementing prevention strategies in the general education classroom for at-risk students. They should do the following:

• Accommodate to the differences presented by the children assigned to the classroom

- Assess student strengths and weaknesses using functional assessment strategies
- Apply a positive approach in the classroom and provide positive feedback to the students
- Select the most appropriate and effective strategies for teaching the specific students assigned to the classroom
- Apply individual, small-group, and whole-group strategies appropriate for the students in the classroom
- Monitor the effectiveness of the strategies applied

Montague et al. suggested several prevention strategies, including behavior management strategies (smooth transitions, effective time-out procedures), academic enhancement procedures (self-monitoring, peer tutoring), and social development strategies (personal and social skills instruction).

CONTINUA OF BEHAVIOR MANAGEMENT INTERVENTIONS

Prior to studying this section, the reader is urged to review the section on the ethics of behavior management in Chapter 1.

It is unethical for practitioners to impose behavior management interventions that are unnecessary or more restrictive than necessary to change the child's behavior. For example, it would be unacceptable to impose seclusion time-out on a child if observational or exclusion time-out would effectively change the target behavior. Likewise, it would be unacceptable to use a verbal counseling or extinction technique with a child who is physically assaulting other persons or is self-injurious when a more restrictive intervention is needed.

In the first example, seclusion time-out is considered unacceptable because it restricts the child's freedom more than is necessary. In this situation, seclusion would be imposed only after the less restrictive time-out procedures—observational and exclusion time-out—have been systematically applied over a period of time without success.

In the second example, extinction and counseling are inappropriate because they are too benign to change the target behavior and thus protect the child and others from harm. Of necessity, the practitioner must impose a more restrictive intervention (e.g., time-out).

Each classroom, school, and local education agency should conduct a periodic inventory among school and cooperating community agency personnel to determine the behavior management interventions available and to ensure that professionals are trained and competent to change the behavior of children. These interventions may include many of the interventions discussed in Chapters 5 through 8 and many others not reviewed in this text.

The behavior management interventions included on the inventory are ordered on a *continuum*. The interventions are placed on the continuum to range from the *least* restrictive to the *most* restrictive with regard to the child's freedom to function in comparison with the average child.

Example of Continuum of Interventions

1. *Stimulus change:* The existing environmental conditions are altered to ensure that the target behavior is temporarily suppressed.

2. *Reinforcement of behavior other than the target behavior:* A reinforcer is given at the end of a specified period of time provided that a prespecified misbehavior has not occurred during the specified time interval.

3. *Reinforcement of an appropriate target behavior:* A reinforcer is given following the performance of a prespecified appropriate target behavior.

4. *Reinforcement of incompatible behaviors:* A reinforcer is given following the performance of a prespecified behavior that is physically and functionally incompatible with the target behavior.

5. *Extinction:* The reinforcer that has been sustaining or increasing an undesirable behavior is withheld.

6. *Nonexclusionary time-out:*

   a. Head down on desk or table in work area in which target behavior occurred

   b. Restriction to chair in a separate area of the classroom but able to observe classroom activities

   c. Removal of materials (work, play)

   d. Reduction or elimination of room illumination

7. *Satiation:* The target behavior is eliminated by continued and increased reinforcement of that behavior.

8. *Overcorrection:* The repeated practice of an appropriate behavior in response to the exhibition of an inappropriate target behavior.

9. *Exclusionary time-out:*

   a. In-school suspension

   b. Quiet room

10. *Physical restraint.*

Figure 10.1
Sample continuum of behavior modification interventions

An example continuum using selected behavior modification interventions is presented in Figure 10.1. It is obvious that no *continuum of interventions* is perfect. The exact location of an intervention on the continuum should be accomplished through discussion and consensus among those responsible for the behavior of children in the school and community, including parents and administrators.

Morris (1985) and Morris and Brown (1983) developed the continuum of aversive interventions presented in Figure 10.2. This continuum varies on the dimensions of (a) restrictiveness and intrusiveness and (b) aversiveness. Level I includes interventions judged to be the least restrictive/intrusive and aversive, with Level III interventions judged to be the most restrictive/intrusive and aversive.

Level I Procedures

Reinforcement (including differential reinforcement techniques)

Group reinforcement

Shaping

Behavioral chaining

Modeling

Token economy system

Contingency contracting

Self-control

Reinforcement of incompatible behaviors

Relaxation training

Extinction

Situation control

Level II Procedures

Contingent observation

Exclusion time-out

Response cost system

Contact desensitization

Level III Procedures

Overcorrection

Seclusion time-out

Physical punishment

Figure 10.2
Levels system of aversive interventions

To promote a climate for learning in the classroom, Smith and Rivera (1995) suggest matching disciplinary infractions with interventions. To accomplish this task, they offer an "intervention ladder." From the least to the most intrusive, their continuum includes prevention, specific praise, ignoring, rules, contingency instruction, contingent observation, criterion-specific rewards, fines, group contingencies, peer management, self-management, parent action, overcorrection, time-out, punishment, and exclusion. They offer a detailed definition and example of each of these strategies.

Educational agencies should develop procedures to ensure the ethical and effective use of behavior management interventions. Among the items to be considered when planning the procedures to be used in behavior management are the following:

1. The behaviors to be targeted for change must be noted in the child's individualized education program (IEP).

2. The behavior management interventions to be implemented are to be described in the child's IEP. The purpose for which the intervention is imposed must be stated. The procedures to be applied to evaluate the consistency of application and effectiveness of the intervention are stated.

3. Initially, the least restrictive intervention feasible is to be applied unless, in the judgment of the IEP team, to do so would be ineffective. The intervention is to be selected or designed through the process of consensus among the team members, including the student's parent(s) or parent surrogate(s). During the meeting, the team may list subsequent and more restrictive interventions to be imposed if the initial intervention is demonstrated to be ineffective.

4. Data collection procedures are to be developed before the implementation of the intervention. These procedures are applied by the practitioner throughout the time during which the intervention is imposed. A written record of the data collected is to be enclosed in the student's file.

5. Initial techniques and all subsequent techniques are to be imposed for a specified number of school days before being changed or discontinued.

6. Documents on the student's behavior management plan and its application are to be available in the student's IEP file for periodic review by appropriate persons.

In addition, practitioners should be knowledgeable about national, state, provincial, and local statutes and policies governing behavior management practices in schools. Practitioners should be trained in a broad range of behavior management interventions from various theoretical perspectives. Finally, a human rights committee should be established in each school or district to supervise the practice of behavior management with children and youth.

Procedures such as those just mentioned safeguard the child from potential mistreatment and the practitioner from potential charges of wrongdoing.

BEHAVIOR MANAGEMENT AS PREVENTION

Most of the behavior management literature is concerned with the remediation of academic and behavior problems in the home, school, institution, and clinic. Efforts have generally been directed toward the increase of acceptable behaviors and the decrease of unacceptable behaviors. Very few research reports and position statements have focused on the maintenance of the acceptable behaviors of normally functioning children.

There are many opportunities in the classroom to prevent the development of inappropriate behavior by systematically maintaining the existing acceptable behavior. If teachers understand and apply the principles of behavior management (presented in Chapter 3) as part of their normal teaching methodology, many potential problems and conflicts can be avoided.

Concerned teachers monitor and evaluate their personal teaching behaviors and the learning behaviors of the students in their classrooms. They do this by systematically evaluating the teaching-learning process. They recognize that children need positive reinforcement (rewards) and that only the child being rewarded can indicate with certitude what is rewarding.

Experienced practitioners understand that they can and do reinforce inappropriate behavior on occasion. Consequently, they attempt to reward only appropriate behaviors. They realize that the younger, less experienced child needs to be immediately reinforced for exhibiting appropriate behavior. They also recognize that delayed rewards are more desirable, from a societal point of view, than immediate rewards and that social rewards are more desirable than tangible rewards. They always give the child social reinforcement in conjunction with tangible rewards.

Prevention-minded practitioners recognize that new behaviors must be rewarded more frequently and more consistently than established behaviors and that although continuous reinforcement is necessary when a new behavior is being established, intermittent reinforcement is ultimately desired and will effectively maintain established behaviors.

Prevention-conscious practitioners systematically use high-frequency behaviors to facilitate the development of low-frequency behaviors.

By using the principles of behavior management as a standard part of the teaching-learning process, practitioners need not anxiously wait for problems to arise in the classroom but can prevent them and use the time saved to teach children those things they must know to live productively in society.

◆ SUMMARY

In this final chapter, several important issues and concerns in behavior management, general education, and special education are briefly discussed. The authors reinforced their belief that the integrative perspective of behavior management is most appropriate and effective for the organization of interventions for application with students with behavior problems. The integrative perspective encourages educators to apply interventions that are compatible with student needs and teacher training and expertise. Using the integrative perspective, the teacher may select from interventions associated with the biophysical, environmental, psychoeducational, and behavioral theories.

In the past decade, services provided by the schools have changed significantly. The number of students with disabilities and at risk for disabilities entering general education increases annually. Students from many ethnic, cultural, and linguistic backgrounds are entering the schools. All educators must become familiar with and sensitive to the cultures of these students and respond appropriately to their needs. Students from diverse cultures, because of their lack of familiarity with the majority American culture, function at a disadvantage in school and are at risk for behavior problems.

A group of children who often arrive in the classroom operating at a deficit with regard to behavior are those labeled "at risk" in this chapter. They are the children of divorce, children of poverty, children who are maltreated, children suffering the effects of prenatal alcohol and drug exposure, and children in substitute care. Educators must be familiar with the problems and characteristics of these children and strategies for helping them.

Schools are encouraged to develop a continuum of behavior management interventions for application, as needed, by the professionals available in the school and community. It is suggested that the emphasis in behavior management be placed on prevention.

Throughout the text, behavior management is presented as a complex, dynamic problem demanding significant professional knowledge and expertise in its conduct. It is stressed that for the effective management of behavior there are no simple formulae—no gimmicks—that can be applied to solve the behavior problems that exist in today's schools and in society.

♦ PROJECTS

1. After reviewing the pertinent information in Chapter 1 and this chapter, write a 300-word paper citing the advantages and disadvantages of the integrative perspective.

2. Interview the following public school educators to discuss changes in the school's service delivery system during the past decade:

   (a) Principal

   (b) Special education administrator responsible for students with disabilities

   (c) One or two general education teachers

   (d) One or two special education teachers

3. Research and write a 300-word paper on cultural diversity in special education.

4. Give a 10-minute presentation to the class on one of the following: (a) children of divorce, (b) children of poverty, (c) children who are maltreated, (d) children prenatally exposed to alcohol, (e) children prenatally exposed to drugs, or (f) children in substitute care. All topics should be presented.

5. As a group, conduct an inventory of the behavior management interventions available for use in a school. Organize the results of the inventory into a continuum. Attempt to reach consensus on the location of each intervention on the continuum.

♦ REFERENCES

Abel, E. L. (1984). Prenatal effects of alcohol. *Drug and Alcohol Dependence, 14,* 1–10.

Abrams, B. J. & Segal, A. (1998). How to prevent aggressive behavior. *Teaching Exceptional Children, 30*(4), 10–15.

Allen, L., & Majidi-Ahi, S. (1989). Black American children. In J. Gibbs & L. Huang (Eds.), *Children of color* (pp. 148–178). San Francisco: Jossey-Bass.

American Humane Association. (1987). *Highlights of official child neglect and abuse reporting*. Denver: Author.

Bauer, A. M., & Sapona, R. H. (1991). *Managing classrooms to facilitate learning*. Upper Saddle River, NJ: Prentice Hall.

Baumeister, A. A., Kupstas, F., & Klindworth, L. M. (1990). New morbidity: Implications for prevention of children's disabilities. *Exceptionality, 1,* 1–16.

Bradley, M. R. (2001). Preface: Positive behavior support research to practice. *Beyond Behavior, 11*(1), 3–4.

Bryan, T., & Sullivan-Burstein, K. (1998). Teacher-selected strategies for improving homework completion. *Remedial and Special Education, 19*(5) 263–275.

Carter, J., & Sugai, G. (1989). Survey of prereferral practices: Responses from state departments of education. *Exceptional Children, 55,* 298–302.

Cicchetti, D., Toth, S., & Hennessy, K. (1989). Research on the consequences of child maltreatment and its application to educational settings. *Topics in Early Childhood and Special Education, 9*(2), 33–55.

Cooper, S. (1987). The fetal alcohol syndrome. *Journal of Child Psychology and Psychiatry and Allied Professionals, 28,* 233–237.

Crittenden, P. M. (1989). Teaching maltreated children in the preschool. *Topics in Early Childhood Special Education, 9*(2), 16–32.

Clark, A. S. (2002). *Social and emotional distress among American Indian and Alaska Native Students* (ERIC Digest Special Edition No. EDO RC 01 11) *www.indian research.net.*

Deyhle, D., & Swisher, K. (1997). Research in American Indian and Alaska Native education: From assimilation to self-determination. In M. W. Apple (Ed.), *Review of research in education* (vol. 22, pp. 113–194). Washington, DC: American Educational Research Association

Dixon, S. D., & Bejar, R. (1989). Echoencephalographic findings in neonates associated with maternal cocaine and methamphetamine use: Incidence and clinical correlates. *Journal of Pediatrics, 115,* 770–778.

Epstein, M. H., Polloway, E. A., Busk, G. H., Bursuck, W. D., Wissinger, L. M., Whitehouse, F., & Jayanthi, M. (1997). Homework-related communication problems: Perspectives of general education teachers. *Learning Disabilities Research and Practice, 12*(4), 221–227.

Feng, J. (1994). *Asian-American children: What teachers should know*. Urbana, IL: ERIC Clearinghouse on Elementary and Early Childhood Education (ERIC Document Reproduction Service No. ED 369 577).

Fitzsimmons, M. K. (1998). *Violence and aggression in children and youth*. ERIC/OSEP Digest E572 (ERIC Document Reproduction Service No. ED 429 419).

Fox, L., Dunlap, G., & Benito, N. (2001). Vincent's story: From Head Start to fourth grade. *Beyond Behavior, 11*(1), 5–6.

Fradd, S., Figueroa, R. A., & Correa, V. I. (1989). Meeting the multicultural needs of Hispanic students in special education. *Exceptional Children, 56,* 102–104.

Frank, D. A., Zuckerman, B. S., Amaro, H., Aboagye, K., Baucher, H., Cabral, H., Fried, L., Hingson, R., Kayne, H., Levenson, S., Parker, S., Reece, H., & Vinci, R. (1988). Cocaine use during pregnancy: Prevalence and correlates. *Pediatrics, 82,* 888–895.

Graden, J. L. (1989). Redefining "prereferral" intervention as intervention assistance: Collaboration between general and special education. *Exceptional Children, 56,* 227–331.

Graden, J. L., Casey, A., & Christenson, S. L. (1985). Implementing a prereferral system: Part I: The model. *Exceptional Children, 51,* 377–384.

Guidubaldi, J., & Perry, J. D. (1985). Divorce and mental illness sequelae for children: A two-year follow up of a nationwide sample. *Journal of the American Academy of Child Psychiatry, 24,* 531–537.

Guttman, J., Geva, N., & Gefen, S. (1988). Teachers' and school children's stereotypic perception of "the child of divorce." *American Educational Researcher Journal, 25,* 555–571.

Hanna, J. (1988). *Disruptive school behavior: Class, race, and culture.* New York: Holmes and Meyer.

Harvey, D., Prince, J., Burton, J., Parkinson, D., & Campbell, S. (1982). Abilities of children who were small for gestational age babies. *Pediatrics, 69,* 296–300.

Heath, S. B. (1983). *Ways with words.* New York: Cambridge University Press.

Hetherington, E. M., Cox, M., & Cox, R. (1985). Long-term effects of divorce and remarriage on the adjustment of children. *Journal of the American Academy of Child Psychiatry, 25,* 518–530.

Hodgkinson, H. (1985). *All one system.* Washington, DC: Institute for Educational Leadership.

Horner, C. M. (1987). Homework: A way to teach problem solving. *Academic Therapy, 22,* 239–244.

Howard, J., Beckwith, L., Rodning, C., & Kropenske, V. (1989). The development of children of substance abusing parents: Insights from seven years of intervention and research. *Zero to Three, 9*(5), 8–12.

Hyland, C. R. (1989). What we know about the fastest growing minority population: Hispanic Americans. *Educational Horizons, 67*(4), 124–130.

Jacobs, D. T. & Rehner, J. (2002). Preparing teachers to support American Indian and Alaska Native student success and cultural heritage. ERIC Digest (Special Edition), EDO-RC-01-13, January 2002.

Johnson, L. J., & Bauer, A. M. (1992). *Meeting the needs of special students: Legal, ethical, and practical ramifications.* Newberry Park, CA: Corwyn.

Johnson, L. J., & Pugach, M. C. (1991). Peer collaboration: Accommodating students with mild learning and behavior problems. *Exceptional Children, 58,* 454–461.

Jones, V. (1986). Classroom management in the United States: Trends and critical issues. In D. P. Tattum (Ed.), *Management of disruptive pupil behavior in schools* (pp. 69–90). Chichester: Wiley.

Kochman, T. (1991, March). *Culturally based patterns of difference.* Paper presented at the University of Cincinnati.

LaFrambroise, T. D., & Low, K. G. (1989). American Indian children and adolescents. In J. Gibbs & L. Huang (Eds.), *Children of color* (pp. 114–147). San Francisco: Jossey-Bass.

Lewis, T. J. & Sugai, G. (1999). Effective behavior support: A systems approach to proactive schoolwide management. *Focus on Exceptional Children, 31*(6), 1–24.

Lipka, J. (2002). Schooling for self-determination: Research on the effects of including native language and culture in the schools. ERIC Digest (Special Edition), EDO-RC-01-12, January 2002.

Lipsky, D. K., & Gartner, A. (1992). Achieving full inclusion: Placing the student at the center of educational reform. In W. Stainback & S. Stainback (Eds.), *Controversial issues confronting special education: Divergent perspectives* (pp. 3–12). Boston: Allyn & Bacon.

Lockwood, A. T., & Secada, W. C. (2000). *School practices to promote the achievement of Hispanic studens.* New York: Clearinghouse on Urban Education. (ERIC Document Reproduction Service No. ED 439 186).

Maag, J. W. (2000). Managing resistance. *Intervention in School and Clinic, 35*(3), 131–140.

McCoy, C. B., & Watkins, V. M. (1980). Drug use among urban ethnic youth. *Youth and Society, 11,* 83–106.

Melloy, K. (2000) Development of aggression replacement behaviors in adolescents with emotional disorders. *Beyond Behavior, 10*(2), 8–13.

Montague, M., Bergeron, J., & Lago-Delello, E. (1997). Using prevention strategies in general education. *Focus on Exceptional Children, 29*(8), 1–12.

Morris, R. J. (1985). *Behavior modification with exceptional children: Principles and practices.* Glenview, IL: Scott, Foresman.

Morris, R. J., & Brown, D. K. (1983). Legal and ethical issues in behavior modification with mentally retarded persons. In J. Matson & F. Andrasik (Eds.), *Treatment issues and innovations in mental retardation.* New York: Plenum.

Myles, B. S., & Simpson, R. L. (1998). Aggression and violence by school-aged children and youth: Understanding the aggression cycle and prevention/intervention strategies. *Intervention in School and Clinic, 33*(5), 259–264.

Nelson, J. S., Epstein, M. H., Bursuck, W. D., Jayanthi, M., & Sawyer, V. (1998). The preferences of middle school students for homework adaptations made by general education teachers. *Learning Disabilities Research and Practice, 13*(2), 109–117.

Parker, S., Greer, S., & Zuckerman, B. (1988). Double jeopardy: The impact of poverty on early child development. *Pediatric Clinics of North America, 35,* 1227–1240.

Pavel, D. M. (1999). Schools, principals, and teachers serving American Indian and Alaska Native students. ERIC Digest, EDO-RC-98-9, January 1999.

Peters, M. (1981). Parenting in Black families with young children. In H. McAdoo (Ed.), *Black families.* Newberry Park, CA: Sage.

Pinnell, G. S., & Galloway, C. M. (1987). Human development, language, and communication: Then and now. *Theory Into Practice, 26*(Special Issue), 353–357.

Pugach, M., & Johnson, L. J. (1989). Prereferral interventions: Progress, problems, and challenges. *Exceptional Children, 56,* 217–226.

Rossett, H. L., & Weiner, L. (1984). *Alcohol and the fetus.* New York: Oxford University Press.

Sampson, P. D., Streissguth, A. P., Barr, H. M., & Bookstein, F. L. (1989). Neurobehavioral effects of prenatal alcohol: Part II: Partial least squares analysis. *Neurotoxicology and Teratology, 11,* 477–491.

Schor, E. L. (1988). Foster care. *Pediatric Clinics of North America, 36,* 1241–1252.

Scott, T. M., & Hunter, J. (2001). Initiating schoolwide support systems: An administrator's guide to the process. *Beyond Behavior, 11*(1), 13–15.

Shea, T. M., & Bauer, A. M. (1994). *Learners with disabilities: A social systems perspective of special education.* Madison, WI: Brown & Benchmark.

Shea, T. M., & Bauer, A. M. (1991). Parents and teachers of children with exceptionalities: A handbook for collaboration (2nd ed.). Boston: Allyn & Bacon.

Smith, D. D., & Rivera, D. P. (1995). Discipline in special education and general education settings. *Focus on Exceptional Children, 27*(5), 1–14.

Spohr, H. L., & Steinhausen, H. C. (1987). Follow-up studies of children with fetal alcohol syndrome. *Neuropediatrics, 18,* 13–17.

Stormont-Spurgin, M. (1997). I list my homework: Strategies for improving organization of students with ADHD. *Intervention in School and Clinic, 32*(5), 270–274.

Streissguth, A. P., Herman, C. S., & Smith, D. W. (1978). Intelligence, behavior, and dysmorphogenesis in the fetal alcohol syndrome. A report on 20 patients. *Journal of Pediatrics, 92,* 262–267.

Thurston, L. P. (1989). Helping parents tutor their children: A success story. *Academic Therapy, 24*(5), 579–587.

Truesdell, L. A., & Abramson, T. (1992). Academic behavior and grades of mainstreamed students with mild disabilities. *Exceptional Children, 58*(5), 392–398.

Walker, H. M. (1998). First steps to prevent antisocial behavior. *Teaching Exceptional Children, 30*(4), 16–19.

Walker, H. M., & Sylwester, R. (1998). Reducing students' refusal and resistance. *Teaching Exceptional Children, 30*(6), 52–58.

Wallerstein, J., & Blakeslee, S. (1989). *Second changes: Men, women, and children a decade after divorce.* New York: Ticknor & Fields.

Warger, C. (1999). Positive behavior support and functional assessment. ERIC/OSEP Digest E580. (ERIC Document Reproduction Service No. ED 434–437).

Weston, D. R., Ivins, B., Zuckerman, B., & Lopez, R. (1989). Drug-exposed babies: Research and clinical issues. *Zero to Three, 9*(5), 1–7.

Wiehe, V. R. (1984). Self-esteem, attitude towards parents, and locus of control in children of divorced and nondivorced families. *Journal of Social Service Research, 8*(1), 17–28.

Yates, J. R. (1987). Current and emerging forces. *Counterpoint, 7*(4), 4–5.

Youngblade, L. M., & Belsky, J. (1989). Child maltreatment, infant-parent attachment security, and dysfunctional peer relationships in toddlerhood. *Topics in Early Childhood Special Education, 9*(2), 1–15.

GLOSSARY

Abscissa points   Points on a graph on the horizontal axis representing hours, days, sessions, or observations.

Americans with Disabilities Act   Civil rights law enacted in 1990 to provide accessibility and deter discrimination against individuals with disabilities.

Antecedents of effective management   A broad range of factors manipulated prior to instruction to enhance the probability that learning will occur.

Antianxiety and antipsychotic drugs   Medication prescribed for calming effects.

Anticonvulsants   Medication prescribed for seizures.

Antihistamines   Medication to counteract the effects of various allergies.

Attitudes (in psychosituational interview)   The beliefs and feelings of the referring agent, that is, the parent or parents, about the child, behavior, and environment.

Aversives   Noxious and sometimes painful consequences of behavior; undesirable results of behavior the individual would normally wish to avoid.

Baseline data   Quantitative data collected on the target behavior before a behavior change intervention is implemented.

Behavior (in psychosituational interview)   The actual behavior for which the child was referred, including antecedents and consequences.

Behavioral psychology   The study of psychology from the perspective of behavior.

Behavioral theory   Theories that see the cause of behavior as existing outside the individual in the immediate setting.

Behavior influence techniques   Management techniques, based in psychodynamic theory, that are designed to be immediately responsive to ongoing unacceptable behavior.

Behavior management interventions   All those actions (and conscious inactions) teachers and parents engage in to enhance the probability that children, individually and in groups, will develop effective behaviors that are personally fulfilling, productive, and socially acceptable.

Biophysical interventions   Preventive and curative techniques to maintain or enhance the individual's well-being.

Biophysical theory   Theories that place emphasis on the organic origins of human behavior; postulates a relationship between physical defects, malfunctions, and illnesses and individual behavior.

Central nervous system stimulants   Medication prescribed for its calming effect on prepubertal boys and girls.

Child maltreatment   Generic term that includes child abuse and neglect and refers to physical and mental injury, sexual abuse, and neglect of a child under 18 years of age.

Comprehensive intervention   Interventions carried on throughout the day that are aimed at rapid, lasting, and generalized behavior change and increase the student's success.

Consequence   (see Reinforcer).

Contingency contracting   The process of contracting so that the child gets to do something he or she wants to do following completing something the parent or teacher wants the child to do.

Continuous schedule   The presentation of the reinforcer immediately after each occurrence of the target behavior.

Continuum of interventions   The inventory of behavior management interventions, ranging from the least restrictive to the most restrictive of a child's freedom to function in comparison with the average child, available for application in a school.

Contract   An agreement, written or verbal, between two or more parties, individuals, or groups that stipulates the responsibilities of the parties concerning a specific item or activity.

Counting behavior   Enumerating the number of times a behavior occurs in a given period of time.

Crack babies   Children exposed, in utero, to cocaine in the form of crack.

Cuing   The process of using symbols to communicate essential messages between individuals.

Daily report cards   A daily home-school reporting system designed to facilitate communication on child performance.

Desensitization   The process of systematically lessening a specific, learned fear or phobic reaction in an individual.

Diet   The regulation of the intake by the individual of specific food solids and liquids.

Differential reinforcement   The process of reinforcing an appropriate behavior in the presence of one stimulus and, simultaneously, not reinforcing an appropriate behavior in the presence of another stimulus.

Discrimination   Learning to act in one way in one situation and another way in a different situation.

Ecological theory   Theories that place emphasis on the interrelationships between an organism and its environment.

Ecology   The study of behavior in regard to an organism adjustment or adaptation to the environment and the interactions between the organism and the environment.

Environmental interventions   Interventions that focus attention on the manipulation of groups and the environment in which the individual or group is functioning.

Environmental theory   Theories that emphasize the impact of the environment on individuals and groups.

Environments/situations (in psychosituational interview)   The specific places and circumstances in which the behavior occurs, including the presence of significant others.

Ethics   The rules that guide moral (right, good, or correct) behavior.

Ethnic, cultural, and linguistic diversity   Groups of people who differ from the majority population (in this text, African American, Asian American, Native American, Hispanic, and Appalachian).

Expectations (in psychosituational interview)   The specific performance that the adult would like the child to achieve (short-term objectives); the long-range aspirations or goals the adult has for the child.

Expressive media   Interventions that encourage and permit individuals to express personal feelings and emotions in creative activities.

Expulsion   Removal of a student from school for more than 10 days.

Extinction   The discontinuation or withholding of a reinforcer that has previously been reinforcing a behavior.

Fading   The systematic and gradual elimination of prompts.

Fairness   (see Principle of fairness).

Fetal alcohol syndrome   Children exposed to alcohol, in utero (symptoms include growth retardation, central nervous system involvement, and specific facial characteristics).

Fixed schedule   Reinforcement is presented on completion of a specific number of tasks or definite periods of time.

Formalism   All individuals are born with rights and needs that are superordinate to the interests of society.

Functional behavioral assessment   The identification of antecedent and consequent events, temporarily contiguous to the behavior, that occasion and maintain the behavior.

Generalization   A learned process whereby behavior reinforced in the presence of one stimulus will be exhibited in the presence of another (also known as the transfer of learning).

Graphing (charting) behavior   Preparing a visual display of enumerated behavior.

Home reinforcers   The consequences of behaviors exhibited in the home; may be tangible or social, positive or negative.

IDEA 97   Individuals with Disabilities Education Act, reauthorized in 1997 and strengthening general education emphasis

IEP   Individualized education program.

IFSP   Individualized family service plan.

Inclusion   The philosophy that all students, regardless of disability, are a vital and integral part of the general education system.

In-school suspension   Removal of a student from regular or special education class but not from the school.

Instructional objectives   The specific learning tasks the learner must master to meet his or her long term goals.

Integrative framework   An ecological model that stresses that the understanding of human development and behavior requires examination of the ecological contexts in which the individual is functioning and is an inseparable part.

Interobserver reliability   Mathematical formula designed to determine the reliability of the behavior modifier's observations during the behavior change intervention.

Interval schedule   Reinforcement is dependent on the exhibition of behavior after a definite period of time.

Intervention data   Quantitative data collected on the target behavior during intervention.

ITP   Individualized transition plan.

Keystone behaviors   Behaviors that have the potential to make the greatest positive effect on a child's behavior.

Levels system   An organizational framework designed to shape students' social, emotional, and academic behaviors.

Life-space interview   Here-and-now interviewing intervention built around an individual's direct life experience to enable the individual to solve the problems confronting him or her.

Loss of privileges The taking away of an individual's present or future reinforcers (also known as response cost and deprivation of privileges).

Measurability Quantifying observed behavior.

Milieu therapy An intervention strategy that considers, during the therapeutic process, the total environment a child lives in—the whole culture that surrounds the child —or, in other words, everything that is done to, with, for, or by a child in the place where that child finds him-or herself.

Modeling The provision of an individual or group behavior to be imitated or not imitated by the individual.

Negative reinforcement The strengthening of a behavior as a consequence of the removal of an already operating aversive stimulus.

Normalization (see Principle of normalization).

Observability The capacity of behavior to be observed in the environment, that is, seen, heard, and so forth.

Ordinate points Points on a graph on the vertical axis representing frequency, duration, and percent of occurrence.

Parent education Instruction in the behavior management techniques and their implementation.

Passport A home-school notebook for daily parent-teacher communication concerning the child's performance.

Phasing out Systematic reduction in the presentation of reinforcers during the behavior change process.

Positive reinforcement Presentation of a desirable reinforcer after the behavior has been exhibited; process of reinforcing a target behavior in order to increase the probability that the behavior will recur.

Possible fetal alcohol effect Possibly exposed to alcohol, in utero; one or two of the symptoms of fetal alcohol syndrome are present; diagnosed when mother is suspected of alcohol use during pregnancy.

Preference list List of potential reinforcers used to assist the student and teacher or parent in the selection of potential reinforcers.

Preference scales Scales designed to assist student and teacher or parent in the selection of potential reinforcers.

Prereferral interventions Interventions implemented in the general education classroom by the general education teacher to assist individual students exhibiting academic or behavior problems to avoid referral for special education services.

Principle of fairness Fundamental fairness—due process of law—that requires that in decision making affecting one's life, liberty, or vital interests, the elements of due process will be observed, including the right to notice, to

a fair hearing, to representation by counsel, to present evidence, and to appeal an adverse decision.

Principle of normalization To let the handicapped person obtain an existence as close to the normal as is possible.

Principle of respect The right to be treated as a human being and not as an animal or a statistic.

Principles of reinforcement A set of rules to be applied in the behavior change process; the rules for learning.

Prompting The process of providing verbal, visual, aural, or manual assistance to a student during the behavior change process to facilitate the completion of a task.

Psychodynamic model A group of theories that have in common a belief in the existence of an intrapsychic life.

Psychoeducational approach A broad perspective for education and management associated with the psycho-analytic-psychodynamic approach.

Psychology The study of human behavior.

Psychosituational assessment interview An information-gathering interview technique used to obtain from the parents (or others) descriptive data about the child's behavior and the circumstances surrounding it.

Public Law 99-457 Education for the Handicapped Act Amendments of 1986.

Public Law 101-336 Americans With Disabilities Act of 1990.

Punishment The addition of an aversive stimulus or the subtraction of a pleasurable stimulus as a consequence of behavior.

Ratio schedule The presentation of the reinforcer on completion of specific tasks.

Reality therapy An interviewing intervention designed to help an individual in need of psychiatric assistance to grapple successfully with the tangible and intangible aspects of the real world and as a result be able to fulfill personal needs.

Reinforcer The consequence of a behavior (may be tangible or social, positive or negative).

Reprimand To be scolded, "yelled at," "bawled out," or otherwise verbally chastised for exhibiting an inappropriate behavior.

Respect (see Principle of respect).

Rules The specification of a relation between two events (may take the form of instruction, direction, or principle).

Schedule A list of activities or events in a program.

Schedule of reinforcement The pattern with which the reinforcer is presented in response to the exhibit of the behavior.

Section 504 Section of the Rehabilitation Act of 1973 designed to deter discrimination against individuals with disabilities.

Self-discipline   The process of attaining control over one's personal behavior in a variety of circumstances in association with many individuals and groups.

Self-management   The process of structuring one's own behavior.

Shaping   The systematic, immediate reinforcement of successive approximations of a target behavior until the behavior is established.

Social skills curriculum   Curriculum designed to help students focus on increasing their awareness and understanding of personal emotions, values, and attitudes through educational activities.

Sociological theory   The study of the development, structure, and behavior of organized groups of humans.

Sociology   The study of behavior from the perspective of social organization and group functioning.

Students at risk for behavior problems   Children of divorce, children of poverty, children who are maltreated, children in substitute care, and children suffering the effects of prenatal drug or alcohol exposure.

Substitute care   Child's primary caregivers are other than the child's biological parents.

Suspension   Removal of a student from school for fewer than 10 days.

Target behavior   The specific behavior to be changed as a result of intervention.

Teacher-Parent Communication Program (TPCP)   A daily report card system.

Time-out   The removal of an individual from an apparently reinforcing setting to a presumably nonreinforcing setting for a specific and limited period of time.

Time sampling   Selecting periods of time that can be devoted to observing a target behavior; assumes that selected times are representative of the total time the behavior could be observed.

Token economy   A system of exchange in which the individual earns tokens, as reinforcers, and exchanges them for tangible and social reinforcers.

Transition service   The movement from one activity or event to another.

Transition plan   A plan written for learners with disabilities who are 16 years of age (or younger, when appropriate) that includes interagency responsibilities or linkage (see also Transition service).

Utilitarianism   The interests of society precede the interests of the individual; rights are given by society and individuals are valued for their actual, or potential, contributions to (or the degree of burden placed on) the society.

Variable schedule   Reinforcement is presented around the response mean or average of the exhibition of the behavior.

WORK SHEETS AND FORMS

Work sheets and forms used in this text may be copied from this section as needed.

Target Behavior Selection Checklist

1. What is the target behavior to be modified? _____

   _____

   _____

   _____

2. Each characteristic of the behavior that should be considered in the target behavior selective process is listed below. An X should be marked by each characteristic as it is considered. The pertinency of these characteristics varies with the specific target behavior under consideration.

(X)	Characteristic	Comment
( )	Frequency	
( )	Duration	
( )	Intensity	
( )	Type	
( )	Direction	
( )	Observability	
( )	Measurability	

3. Restate the target behavior in precise and specific terminology. _____

   _____

   _____

   _____

   _____

Behavior Chart

Child _____

Observer _____ Date _____

Target behavior _____

DIRECTIONS: Indicate rate, frequency, etc., for vertical axis; hours, days, etc., for horizontal axis. Enter ordinate and abscissa points.

Ordinate points (rate, frequency, duration, percent, etc.)

0

Abscissa points (hours, days, sessions, treatment, etc.)

Student _____ Date Initiated _____

Objective _____

FREQUENCY OF BEHAVIOR

15	15	15	15	15	15	15	15	15	15	15	15	15	15	15	15
14	14	14	14	14	14	14	14	14	14	14	14	14	14	14	14
13	13	13	13	13	13	13	13	13	13	13	13	13	13	13	13
12	12	12	12	12	12	12	12	12	12	12	12	12	12	12	12
11	11	11	11	11	11	11	11	11	11	11	11	11	11	11	11
10	10	10	10	10	10	10	10	10	10	10	10	10	10	10	10
9	9	9	9	9	9	9	9	9	9	9	9	9	9	9	9
8	8	8	8	8	8	8	8	8	8	8	8	8	8	8	8
7	7	7	7	7	7	7	7	7	7	7	7	7	7	7	7
6	6	6	6	6	6	6	6	6	6	6	6	6	6	6	6
5	5	5	5	5	5	5	5	5	5	5	5	5	5	5	5
4	4	4	4	4	4	4	4	4	4	4	4	4	4	4	4
3	3	3	3	3	3	3	3	3	3	3	3	3	3	3	3
2	2	2	2	2	2	2	2	2	2	2	2	2	2	2	2
1	1	1	1	1	1	1	1	1	1	1	1	1	1	1	1

←————————————————————————————— *criteria* →

| 0 | 0 | 0 | 0 | 0 | 0 | 0 | 0 | 0 | 0 | 0 | 0 | 0 | 0 | 0 | 0 |

DATES
_____

Directions:
- Indicate behavior counted.
- Enter criteria line.
- Cross out one number each time the behavior occurs.
- Circle number of times the behavior occurs each date.
- Connect the circles to form graph.

Student _____ Date Initiated _____

Objective _____

TRIAL RESPONSES   DATES

A	15	15	15	15	15	15	15	15	15	15
B	14	14	14	14	14	14	14	14	14	14
C	13	13	13	13	13	13	13	13	13	13
D	12	12	12	12	12	12	12	12	12	12
E	11	11	11	11	11	11	11	11	11	11
F	10	10	10	10	10	10	10	10	10	10
G	9	9	9	9	9	9	9	9	9	9
H	8	8	8	8	8	8	8	8	8	8
I	7	7	7	7	7	7	7	7	7	7
J	6	6	6	6	6	6	6	6	6	6
K	5	5	5	5	5	5	5	5	5	5
L	4	4	4	4	4	4	4	4	4	4
M	3	3	3	3	3	3	3	3	3	3
N	2	2	2	2	2	2	2	2	2	2
O	1	1	1	1	1	1	1	1	1	1
P	0	0	0	0	0	0	0	0	0	0

Directions:

- Enter objective.
- Place a slash (/) over the number in the dated column for a correct response.
- At the end of the lesson, circle the number in the column that corresponds to the total correct responses (slashes) for the lesson.
- Connect the daily circles to make a graph.

Date _____

Contract

This is an agreement between _____
                                                Child's name

and _____.The contract begins on
                    Teacher's name

_____ and ends on _____. It will be reviewed
        Date   Date

on _____.
            Date

   The terms of the agreement are:

Child will _____

_____

_____

_____

Teacher will _____

_____

_____

_____

   If the child fulfills his or her part of the contract, the child will receive the agreed-on reward from the teacher. However, if the child fails to fulfill his or her part of the contract, the reward will be withheld.

Child's signature _____

Teacher's signature _____

Contract Work Sheet

Child _____

Teacher _____ Date _____

(X)	Tasks	Comments
( )	1. Establish and maintain rapport.	
( )	2. Explain the purpose of the meeting.	
( )	3. Explain a contract.	
( )	4. Give an example of a contract.	
( )	5. Ask the child to give an example of a contract; if there is no response, give another example.	
( )	6. Discuss possible tasks.	
( )	7. List child-suggested tasks:	
	_____	
	_____	
	_____	
( )	8. List teacher-suggested tasks:	
	_____	
	_____	
	_____	
( )	9. Agree on the task.	
( )	10. Ask the child what activities he or she enjoys and what items he or she wishes to possess.	
( )	11. Record child-suggested reinforcers.	
( )	12. Negotiate the task-to-reinforcer ratio.	
( )	13. Identify the time allotted for the task.	
( )	14. Identify the criterion or achievement level.	
( )	15. Discuss methods of evaluation.	
( )	16. Agree on the method of evaluation.	
( )	17. Restate and clarify the method of evaluation.	
( )	18. Negotiate the delivery of the reinforcer.	
( )	19. Set the date for renegotiation.	
( )	20. Write two copies of the contract.	
( )	21. Read the contract with the child.	
( )	22. Elicit the child's verbal affirmation and give your own affirmation.	
( )	23. Sign the contract and have the child sign it.	
( )	24. Congratulate the child (and yourself).	

Point Card*

Child's name _____   Date _____

1	2	3	4	5	6	7	8	9	10
11	12	13	14	15	16	17	18	19	20
21	22	23	24	25	26	27	28	29	30
31	32	33	34	35	36	37	38	39	40
41	42	43	44	45	46	47	48	49	50
51	52	53	54	55	56	57	58	59	60
61	62	63	64	65	66	67	68	69	70
71	72	73	74	75	76	77	78	79	80
81	82	83	84	85	86	87	88	89	90
91	92	93	94	95	96	97	98	99	100

*Teacher circles the cumulative total.

Point Card for Multipurpose Token Economy

Child _____ Day _____ Date _____

Work Period	Readiness	Social behavior	Work effort *	Work success *	Teacher comments
9:00–9:15					
9:15–10:00					
10:00–10:30					
10:30–10:45			*	*	
10:45–11:30					
11:30–12:00					
12:00–1:00			*	*	
1:00–1:30					
1:30–2:45					
2:45–3:00			*	*	

* Points for work effort and work success are not available during these periods due to the nature of the activity: opening exercises, recess, lunch, and closing exercises.

Point Tally Form

Child _____ Date _____

Monday													
Tuesday													
Wednesday													
Thursday													
Friday													

TOTAL	
Monday	
Tuesday	
Wednesday	
Thursday	
Friday	
Week	

Time-Out Log

Child _____

Supervisor _____

Date _____

Time		Behavior before time-out	Behavior during time-out	Behavior after time-out
Enters	Leaves			

Behavior Log Form

Target behavior _____

Child _____

Observer _____

| Date | Time | | Antecedents | Consequences | Applied Interventions | Comments |
	Begins	Ends				

Composite Academic Performance and Personal-Social Behavior Report

DAILY REPORT CHECKLIST

Child's Name _____

	Reading		Spelling		Arithmetic		Health		Social Studies		PE		Initials	
	Acad	Beh	Acad	Beh	Acad	Beh	Acad	Beh	Acad	Beh	Acad	Beh	Parent	Teacher
M														
T														
W														
Th														
F														
M														
T														
W														
Th														
F														
M														
T														
W														
Th														
F														

Daily Report Card for Grades K to 3

Consider card satisfactory *only* when boxes 1 and 3 are checked.

1. ☺ ☐ Social behavior satisfactory

2. ☹ ☐ Social behavior unsatisfactory

3. ☺ ☐ Academic work satisfactory

4. ☹ ☐ Academic work unsatisfactory

_____ / _____ / _____   _____
      Date   Teacher's signature

Daily Report Card for Grades 4 to 6

Consider card satisfactory *only* when boxes 1 and 3 are checked.

1. ☐ Social behavior satisfactory
2. ☐ Social behavior unsatisfactory
3. ☐ Academic work satisfactory
4. ☐ Academic work unsatisfactory

_____ / _____ / _____   _____
      Date   Teacher's signature

NAME INDEX

362

SUBJECT INDEX